Australians Speak Out

Australians Speak Out

Persuasive Language Styles

Rodney G. Miller

Parula Press

Australians Speak Out: Persuasive Language Styles
Text of review, criticism, and comment copyright © Rodney G. Miller 2022
For copyright of speech and writing texts, see permission acknowledgements.
All rights reserved. No portion of this book may be reproduced, distributed, or transmitted in any form by any means without the prior written permission of the publisher, except brief quotations within reviews and specified noncommercial uses permitted by copyright law. For permission requests, write to 'Attention: Permissions' at: Parula Press, 1971 Western Avenue #147, Albany, NY 12203, United States of America

Second printing 2022

Notice: Every effort was made to trace the holders of copyright material. If you have any information concerning copyright material in this book, please contact the publishers at the address above.

Cover: Image from the book *Dot and the Kangaroo*, date 1899 or earlier, https://commons.wikimedia.org/wiki/Template:{PD-US-expired}

Note: Throughout the book, Australian spelling, punctuation, and grammar are used. Quoted speeches and writing are as in the original texts, except for the correction of apparent misprints.

Cataloging-in-Publication Data
Name: Miller, Rodney G., author
Title: *Australians Speak Out: Persuasive Language Styles*
Description: Albany, NY: Parula Press, [2022] Includes language studies of Sir Samuel Griffith, Louisa Lawson, Alfred Deakin, Dame Nellie Melba, John Curtin, Dame Enid Lyons, Sir Robert Menzies, Oodgeroo Noonuccal [Kath Walker], Kevin Gilbert, Gough Whitlam, Germaine Greer, Bob Hawke, Michael Kirby, Sallyanne Atkinson, Paul Keating, John Howard, Kevin Rudd, Julia Gillard, Noel Pearson, Scott Morrison, and more / Rodney G. Miller; speech and writing texts, bibliography, index
Subjects: LCSH: 1. English Language – Style 2. Rhetoric – Political aspects – Australia 3. Communication – Speech and Writing

ISBN: 978-1-7374895-1-1 (hardback)
ISBN: 978-1-7374895-0-4 (paperback)

Warning: This book contains the names of First Nations people now deceased.

Library of Congress Control Number: 2021913509

For my brother Bruce,

who speaks out

Contents

Acknowledgements viii
1: How to Use This Book 1
2: Language for Persuasion 14
3: Democratic Talk of John Curtin and Sir Robert Menzies 29
4: Polemic and Propaganda 37
5: Rhetorical Humour 55
6: Political Words and Gough Whitlam 63
7: Choices for Public Talk 73
8: The Quiet Rhetoric of Sir Samuel Griffith 94
9: Louisa Lawson on Womanhood Suffrage 108
10: Alfred Deakin's Language Strategy 116
11: Sir Robert Menzies's Measured Style 127
12: Action Calls of Kevin Gilbert and Oodgeroo Noonuccal 138
13: 'Revolution' Rhetoric of Germaine Greer 151
14: Winning on Television–Bob Hawke 166
15: Reform Advocacy of Michael Kirby 180
16: Continuing to Speak Out–Paul Keating, John Howard, Kevin Rudd, Julia Gillard, Noel Pearson, and Scott Morrison 192
17: Conclusion 208

18: NOTABLE SPEECHES AND WRITING ... 213

Sir Samuel Griffith–The Certainty of Australian Federation ... 214

Louisa Lawson–Womanhood Suffrage ... 217

Sir John Forrest–Trans-Australia Railway ... 221

Dame Nellie Melba–Goodbye ... 225

John Curtin–Speech to America ... 226

Sir Robert Menzies–Eulogy for Churchill ... 230

Kevin Gilbert–Needs of First Nations ... 233

Gough Whitlam–Partnership in the Pacific after Vietnam ... 240

Michael Kirby–The Australian Community and Anti-heroes ... 246

Robert J. Hawke–National Economic Summit ... 257

Sallyanne Atkinson–Expo '88 Welcome Speech ... 265

Paul Keating–Redfern Park Speech ... 267

John Howard–Gun Rally ... 273

Julia Gillard–Misogyny Speech ... 278

Scott Morrison–Amid the Coronavirus Pandemic ... 284

APPENDICES ... 286

Appendix 1: Glossary of Terms ... 287

Appendix 2: Tables of Counted Language Features ... 292

SOURCE NOTES ... 296

BIBLIOGRAPHY ... 325

PERMISSION ACKNOWLEDGEMENTS ... 351

ABOUT THE AUTHOR ... 353

INDEX ... 354

Acknowledgements

For encouraging my review, criticism, and comment concerning public communication, I thank former communication colleagues and students at Queensland University of Technology (QUT) in Brisbane, Australia. I also appreciate insights on speeches that the late Graham Freudenberg AM generously shared in discussion. My thanks go to The Hon Michael Kirby AC CMG for astute comments and for insights on his public communication. For glimpses into their speechmaking, I acknowledge the late Hon Gough Whitlam AC QC, Sallyanne Atkinson AO, and Germaine Greer.

I am grateful to Roslyn Petelin for enjoyable years teaching with her and for insights and referral of some cited works. Thanks go to Tom Dixon AM, Bruce Molloy, Marguerite Meredith, the late Roger Joyce, and Joan Mulholland for early insights, and to Eleanor Gilbert as well as Halina Duce and Malcolm Duce OBE for suggestions that improved the book. Some ideas here were developed from my contributions to The Royal Society of Queensland, Australian and New Zealand Communication Association, The Australian and New Zealand Association for the Advancement of Science, *Australian Journal of Communication*, *Australian Journalism Review*, and Applied Linguistics Association of Australia.

My appreciation for the efforts of library staff spans decades, particularly Kay Bodman and Elizabeth Jordan then at the Queensland University of Technology Library, as well as librarians at The University of Queensland, the Mitchell and Dixson Libraries, The University of Sydney, The University of New South Wales, the National Library of Australia, and the State Library of Queensland. Thanks also go to Jebby Phillips, who alerted me to several speeches reviewed here. I appreciate all who took the trouble to reply to my enquiries, whether or not they were able to help. I remain grateful to former faculty of the English department at The University of Queensland–particularly Marguerite Meredith and in memory of David Lake, Richard Wilson, and Stanley Gerson–who enabled my initial understandings of rhetorical stylistics. None of these acknowledgements should imply that anyone else shares in deficiencies that remain; for these I take full responsibility.

With special appreciation in memory of my parents, as well as many thanks to family and friends. And finally, to Christine, thank you for all we have and hold dear since meeting under a Mediterranean moon so many years ago.

1: How to Use This Book

For a great many Australian children for more than a century, one of their earliest encounters with persuasive language was in the popular story, *Dot and the Kangaroo*,[1] written by Ethel C. Pendley and published in 1899. This is a story about a little girl lost in the Australian outback, whom a kangaroo and several other marsupials befriend. The kangaroo gives Dot some berries that let her understand the language of the animals.

The story contains much criticism of human mistreatment of the environment. When Dot met the 'knowledgeable Platypus' illustrated on this book's front cover, the diminutive Platypus stood firmly on hind legs to sing a lament that bemoaned the loss of earlier species. Perhaps this unusual and passionate mammal, which so strongly asserted its name as 'Ornithorhynchus Paradoxus', might today bemoan the limited awareness concerning the many Australians who have spoken powerfully in the country's modern history, to advocate a variety of causes that initiated social and political change.

Recently and earlier in its history, Australia has benefited from a very large number of powerful speakers. This book assesses the persuasive language of more than 20 Australians who have spoken out to argue imaginatively for change. It reviews how each chooses words, sentence shape, and passage development to argue successfully to change opinions or actions.

Persuasive Power

These were individuals who helped to mould public decision-making and life in Australia. Their language carried persuasive power, helping to transform the colonies of Britain into a multicultural nation on the world stage. These informed, literate, articulate leaders, as concerned citizens, helped to shape Australia by advocating practical expressions of truth, law, and justice.

As in their time, speaking up and speaking out remain the best assurances for Australia or any nation to sustain a lifestyle based on such values, which are nonetheless so often taken for granted.

Democratic Values

No nation is immune from attempts to destroy the very system that assures the rights and freedoms we enjoy. As witnessed on 6 January 2021 at the Capitol in the United States, it was the hasty barricading of internal doors leading to the legislative chambers, where Congressional lawmakers were in session to certify the presidential election result, the greatly outnumbered police, and some 'dumb luck' that stopped a riotous mob, who were reportedly incited to kill democratically elected lawmakers and overthrow the will of the voters.

As the former Australian prime minister Gough Whitlam said about another difficult time in American politics, if that 'democracy had been less free it could scarcely have survived so traumatic an encounter'.[2] Inarguably, as Albert Camus astutely observes, 'the best case for democracy is what it prevents'.[3] A concern in this book is to better understand the ways that notable Australians have spoken out to effect change, and thereby strengthen representative democracy.

Some earlier generations of Australians acquired in the educational system only limited guidance about the way words were used for public communication. Perhaps ask yourself who among the accomplished public figures mentioned in this book's table of contents you have heard or read in their complete text, or whether you know what changes they helped bring to life in Australia. This book is a window into both.

You can read it right through from beginning to end. This will take you through some arts of language and communication. Alternatively, you can first look to specific areas outlined in the table of contents, or at the conclusion of this chapter, or to any of the public figures who particularly interest you. In each case, you will progressively add to understandings of how these Australians were effective spokespersons for their causes.

Familiar and Unfamiliar

Some will be familiar, others less so. Unfamiliar to many of us are speeches of the nation's founders, like Alfred Deakin,[4] or Sir Samuel Griffith.[5] Along with other 'founding fathers', each performed leading roles in many conventions and conversations to help make the federation of the Australian colonies a reality. Likewise unfamiliar are many celebrations of national growth, such as former Western Australia premier Sir John Forrest welcoming the construction of the Trans-Australia railway.[6] Important to recall also is the spirit that the nation's artists bring to us, represented here in the refined farewell from our first international diva, Dame Nellie Melba.[7]

As each year passes, fewer people remain with us who listened to the impassioned address in 1942 of prime minister John Curtin,[8] as he appealed directly on the radio to the people of the United States, for a stronger alliance to fight a joint enemy in the Pacific. This further advanced a change to Australia's foreign policy forever, away from a subordinate dependence on the motherland of Great Britain. Only occasionally recalled too is the persuasive language in the speeches of Sir Robert Menzies and Gough Whitlam, who respectively committed and removed Australian troops in support of the United States in Vietnam. Through almost two decades as Australia's longest serving prime minister, Menzies reached 'the hearts and minds of [his] …immediate audience', in the 'essence' of his speeches.[9] Whitlam, with a speaking ability that 'rather awed his opponents',[10] during just a few years in the early 1970s as prime minister, propelled a remarkable reform agenda.

The provocative address by Germaine Greer in 1971 to the Washington Press Club[11] on women's rights, while promoting the publication of *The Female Eunuch*, is now a more distant memory. Greer's book reached a wide readership, taking her advocacy of women's rights to an international stage, and urging women to experience joy in the struggle for 'revolution'. Surprising to some might be the powerful language of Louisa Lawson's social activism[12] that helped secure women's right to vote on the same terms as men in 1902, among the first women in the world to do so.

Yet people of the First Nations were unable to vote until 1962. Unknown to many is the advocacy for land rights by Oodgeroo Noonuccal [Kath Walker][13] and Kevin Gilbert.[14] For decades, Oodgeroo persistently enlisted supporters in the churches, education, and the community, pressuring largely resistant national leaders to help enable some recognitions, including voting rights. Gilbert's ability to visualise the reality of the lives of people made clear the case to recognise land rights for First Nations. Better known are the more recent prime ministers Paul Keating on reconciliation[15] and Kevin Rudd on the Apology.[16]

To empower a life-long commitment to law reform, Michael Kirby drew upon his tremendous communication ability to work tirelessly for laws that respect human rights. Bob Hawke's intelligent negotiation of a consultative but assertive 'ocker' approach in person and on television helped enable his leadership as Labor's longest-serving prime minister. Highly regarded locally, nationally, and internationally is the first and, for now, only woman to lead Australia's largest city council, Lord Mayor of Brisbane, Sallyanne Atkinson. During two terms in office, she helped facilitate much change in how the City's residents viewed their way of life, here expressed in her welcome to Her Majesty The Queen and His Royal Highness The Duke of Edinburgh to open Expo '88.[17]

More recent speeches assessed are from other prime ministers, John Howard speaking to transform gun ownership,[18] soon after the Port Arthur massacre in 1996, and Julia Gillard delivering to parliament in 2012 a powerful objection to sexism[19] that resonated around the world. Reviewed also are Noel Pearson's moving eulogy[20] in 2014 for prime minister Whitlam, and prime minister Scott Morrison's address on the coronavirus pandemic in 2020.

These notable Australians, and many more, engaged other Australians to help bring change to the nation. Some brought sea change. This is a rich legacy of individuals using language persuasively to advance benefits for the nation. I hope the illustrations of language use in this sampling of the nation's concerns will help stimulate future generations to explore persuasive language styles—enabling the detailed understanding that such speech and writing deserve—and further encourage public talk that sustains commitment to democratic decision-making.

Effective Communication

People respond to talk about consequential concerns in everyday words. How well public speech or writing motivates an audience will determine its success. A rhetorical flourish or poetic turn of phrase often helps motivation, emphasis, or memory. However, most audiences will include individuals favourable to a proposition, others interested but not decided, others apathetic, and still others opposed.

As it is believed Shakespeare did, the best speakers and writers consider a variety of audience segments when choosing topics and language. An effective communicator navigates differences among different individuals within an audience to gain attention, define a problem, explore a solution or not, or visualise a solution, or seek action.[21] The effective speaker or writer is ever alert that communication happens in the minds of listeners or readers when they interpret the words. Anticipating these interpretations is the best guide to sequencing topics through to choices in language and delivery. These choices enable a speaker or writer to relate with an audience, be seen as authentic, and move hearts and minds.

Approaching Style

Extraordinary speakers and writers project personality that empowers ideas by engaging the emotions of an audience with a cogency that resonates. For anyone with interest in words, the notable Australians reviewed in this book embrace a range of national concerns and are people with diverse causes, interests, and ideologies, whose communication abilities empowered their success. To speak out, each developed a variety of ways to use language for specific occasions and integrated personal qualities with subtleties in language use to creatively stimulate and sharpen interesting ways to think about matters. I hope you will enjoy and learn from their experience.

Drawing upon the background of a variety of approaches to language style reviewed in Chapter Two, the approach to language style used for the assessments in this book was to describe particular language choices and to consider their effect on communication with an audience in a particular context. Brought together here is much that I have learned about the ways that extraordinary Australians used ordinary words to move people. Understanding their successful application of principles and practices provided a foundation for my teaching and research of communication, speech, and writing at Queensland University of Technology (QUT) in Brisbane, Australia for more than a decade, as well as for a wide range of consulting with corporate, government, and nonprofit organisations on communication, speech, and writing, and for leading change in universities and other organisations in Australia and internationally. Understanding the language strategies of notable Australians who argued successfully for change can enable anyone to find common ground with audiences.

Public Rhetoric

While studies in government and politics address the why of rhetoric and its impact, this book focuses on both how and why speakers and writers used language in individual ways. Any serious discussion and study of politics should include systematic and deeper understandings of political talk. This is one means by which social power is obtained or shared.

Some analyses and critiques of political and government leaders by a variety of political scientists connect leaders' decisions with their public talk. Particularly in Australia, New Zealand, Britain, and Europe, there is resurgent interest to teach politics by using rhetoric as a framework for discussing political leaders and political actions, which is especially welcome. These teacher-researchers show in specific cases why, in a 24/7 news world, the authenticity of leaders' public comments impact political outcomes. Commenting on an insight from Mark Rolfe, John Kane observes that later Australian prime ministers like John Howard mastered Australian ordinariness, with flat accents and 'low-key tones', implicitly declaring 'no essential distance between leader and led'.[22]

With some focus on the Westminster system, a rapidly expanding variety of writing is now available that refers to four of the five canons of rhetoric, touching on aspects of invention, arrangement, style, and delivery. Importantly in 2004, a perspective setting article from Rolfe reviewed some premises in the discussions of leadership and language, when commenting on a book by James Curran.[23] More recent was Dennis Grube's examination of the public talk of leaders of the public service,[24] in what he calls the 'Wash-minster' (that is, Washington and Westminster) systems of government, speaking truth to power.[25] In addition to his other work in Australia, Paul Corcoran (1994,[26] 1998[27]) provides content and thematic analysis of references to *democracy* in the concession speeches of United States presidential candidates.

Further studies include publications by Finlayson (2004,[28] 2007,[29] 2015[30]), Atkins *et.al.* (2013),[31] Bennister (2012),[32] Charteris-Black (2011,[33] 2014[34]), Kane and Patapan (2010),[35] Martin (2014,[36] 2015[37]), Rolfe (2016),[38] Uhr and Walter (2014),[39] Uhr (2015),[40] Young (2007a,[41] 2007b[42]) Dryzek (2010),[43] and Fairclough (2013).[44] With some using approaches within Critical Discourse Analysis (CDA), these analysts mainly expanded on the method of American scholars, who so well brought into focus 'the rhetorical presidency and presidential rhetoric', such as Tulis (1987,[45] 2007[46]) and Medhust (1996a,[47] 1996b[48]), Ellis (1998),[49] Stuckey (2010),[50] and Friedman (2012).[51]

Communication Goals

Public figures, including politicians, seek limited goals in a particular speech, especially in the complex context of planned campaigns. Any speech must be integrated with publicity, other speeches, personal appearances, advertising, and digital efforts within the total framework of campaigns for a cause or an election. Although especially memorable speeches will be much quoted and often effective in highlighting an issue through to recommending the leadership competence of a speaker, the path to effect social or political change is often long, usually requiring many negotiations through many communications.

Even a simple rally speech might be designed only to draw attention to certain issues, and then only for the faithful; or a TV speech might be concerned wholly with national issues or be intended simply to give an appearance of the speaker's competence in an official context.[52] As Dan Nimmo notes, the total impact of any politician's campaign, as for any speech within it, can be as simple as obtaining publicity for the politician.[53] Some business and professional people enter the election stakes merely to seek publicity for their real business or cause.

A speech can be for very specific goals, such as to secure airtime on broadcast media with small segments of seven to 30 seconds or so, that are complete in themselves;[54] ideal for extraction to be inserted into a short timeslot within a news report, or more often nowadays YouTube or Twitter. When any of these are unstated goals, an analyst faces a more complicated task in assessing the effectiveness or otherwise of a speech.

Not only the why but how individuals use language for rhetorical literacy have increased significance in the context of digital communications. As the perceived importance of digital media continuously grows, concurrently, social media companies generally find ways to minimise their responsibility for their editorial content. There has never been a greater need to assess communication quality and be rhetorically literate.

Persuasive Language

Surprisingly little criticism or review was published over the years about how Australian public figures use language to persuade audiences. Description of the early prime minister Deakin's speaking[55] and some studies of the communications of others that are published are listed later in the source notes and bibliography. At least until relatively recently, public figures in Australia seem to have outstripped most scholars in developing detailed understanding of persuasive language within public communications processes. More deserve close assessment.

Whether reading public communications to speak out more effectively, or to assess persuasive language, or to pursue interest in the documented history of the nation, the resources are now available as never before. The increased availability of speeches includes such anthologies as *Well May We Say* (2004, 2014), *Men and Women of Australia!* (2005, 2014), *Great Australian Speeches* (2009), *Stirring Australian Speeches* (2004), *Speaking for Australia* (2004), and *Australia Speaks* (1969),[56] among others, with audio and video versions increasingly available on YouTube, Speakola.com, and elsewhere online. Outstanding speeches of women and people in First Nations thankfully are now more often recorded. Sustained efforts are needed to uncover more of these speeches from earlier times.

Especially in recent decades, just the greater interest of Australians in ways to speak out warrants better understanding of such speeches. Likewise, the communication studies courses and service subjects throughout Australian higher education that require study and proficiency in oral communication, the focus on rhetoric among teachers and students of politics, and the continuous teaching of public speaking and speech analysis within speaking and service clubs, including *Rostrum,* as well as high school curricula, suggest a continuously growing interest of Australians to speak up and speak out. To do so effectively requires ever better understanding of principles and practice in using persuasive language.

At a seminar for graduates of a *Professional Speech Writing* course that I developed and taught at QUT, the late, great Australian speechwriter, Graham Freudenberg provided valuable practical insights. Responding to a question from a recent graduate who asked how to groom an aspiring manager for leadership, he sensed that the graduate was really seeking advice for himself.

Freudenberg simply advised the graduate to join a suburban speaking club to develop speaking skills and secure speaking engagements in front of community groups in his specialty, and then, as confidence and ability increased, he suggested moving speaking efforts into the city's business centre.[57] The questioner's strategic talents and communication savvy propelled his career within a few years to become the national public affairs director for a major mining company.

Of course, it takes time, understanding, and practice either to speak out more effectively on matters you care about or to appreciate better the principles and techniques public figures use to highlight or subordinate matters. A purpose of this book is to share with you the practices that some of Australia's most persuasive public figures found effective.

Ideas into Action

Yet you might ask, given the apparently casual character of the messages that dominate public communications today, what is the value of energy spent to examine communications from an earlier time? In a thoughtful podcast discussing his book on the art of political speeches from Pericles to modern times, the former prime ministerial speechwriter in Britain, Philip Collins, confirms the sentiment that speeches are still the main way that public figures communicate what they think. He points out that deciding what to say in speech writing is the way to 'clear away really bad ideas.'[58]

Amid the continuous change of a 24/7 news cycle and constant social media, notable Australians still choose to speak out directly or through Zoom at a special event, seminar, or conference, or on the broadcast media, to propose significant ideas or to advocate change, with YouTube and social media delivering reach to further audiences.

Despite new risks in a digital age, the more extended public communications in forms such as the speech, book, article, podcast, or blog do look set to persist as core methods of communication for public discourse. They remain primary venues for directly sharing and shaping ideas for action. In addition, they are resources that set the agenda for many of the soundbites scavenged and disseminated digitally, making the language choice for the original speech or other public communication additionally important.

Whenever public figures have transitioned their public talk, from just gathering a few people around them, to jumping onto a tree stump or another *ad hoc* platform to make a stump speech,[59] through the addition of newspaper reports, to having a megaphone, to using a loudspeaker system, to radio, to television, to YouTube, to other digital offerings, many adjustments and tradeoffs were made. For each transition in mode of delivery, the opportunity to be heard by more people often brought increased risks of distortion or depersonalisation.

When broadcast media first provided access to mass audiences, public figures soon understood the importance, ironically, of a more intimate conversational voice on these media. The broadcaster's guidance was that the mass audience comprised the multiplication of many groups of two to three people or of small groups listening.

With digital media came further opportunities for public figures. Some of these opportunities brought risks for both the public figure and the audience. Most obviously, the risks of interference and distortion are high in the digital age and the already substantial sophistication of audience analysis and socio-psychological targeting continues to grow, which should concern audiences.

Changes

Looking back to the late 1800s through the late 1900s in Australia, it is tempting to describe this period of public talk as a silver age of Australian rhetoric. Not a golden age, to be sure. There were instances of flourish and reaching for the heights of Mount Kosciuszko, if not Olympus. Germaine Greer once described with characteristic candour, after she read the verbatim text of her *Address to the National Press Club* in Washington DC, that it struck her as silver-tongued oratory. Delivered as all her addresses are without notes, she felt the syntax followed the uneven progress of the working mind.[60] Greer was also intimating how speakers thoughtfully shape their words.

In recent times, pseudo-populist talk in modern politics has shunted into squawks and squeals of outrage, which deliver a cacophony, like the noise of pigs and chickens assembled, a kind of 'por-cken' quality of speech. Of course, there was also plenty of argot in earlier times. Richard Denis Meagher described the Sydney newspaper owner John Norton as a 'scaly scurvy contemptible viper'. Or, there was the couplet about prime minister 'Billy' Hughes in 1916 that claimed his talk was like opening a bottle of beer, such that 'only froth comes out'.[61] A wag might say that not much fizz from speakers is so artistic now.

Thinking to Talk

For a public figure or anyone composing any communication, the problem is to think through issues of fact, opinion, or ideas, in relation to a particular audience, in a specific context. Roslyn Petelin aptly describes this task as 'an essential key to unlocking thinking and learning'.[62]

To address the issues that are often swirling around or implicit to any speech or writing occasion, a problem-solving approach prompts questions to enable the necessary choices to solve the communication problem.[63] What is the goal of the communication? What effect is sought? What are the issues to be addressed, side-stepped, or ignored? What are the concerns of listeners/readers and their current understandings? How are any opponents likely to respond? Sometimes, what specific points or turns of phrase might be included?

Such questions are the guide to find direction, either to communicate or to assess others' communications. Addressing these concerns helps a speaker or writer to sort out the best ideas to share with an audience. The search for key issues that most concern people about a subject propels a process to persuade ourselves and others about what merits attention. When engaged in this process, people draw on reason, feelings, and imagination, to invent and arrange ideas by finding a style for delivery that might bring the best sense of the ideas to the forefront of others' thinking.

Rhetorical Choices

By taking account of the audience's knowledge and sophistication, a speaker or writer decides what ideas to share, as well as what are the appeals, conventional modes of expression, topics, words, and form of delivery that will accentuate attention and recommend the value of the ideas. Rhetorical choices that are available to advance a case within any given subject area were described in classical times by Aristotle, with application and refinement of the rhetorical system occurring ever since. Isocrates, Francis Bacon, Wayne C. Booth, and many others have enlarged rhetorical knowledge through the ages, progressively enabling the integration of aspects of rhetoric, stylistics, and linguistics to understand persuasive style.[64] The rhetorical canon describes invention, arrangement, style, memory, and delivery as the available means for using the persuasive techniques and language that are needed to understand and share truth in the expression of ideas.

Rhetorical principles advocate making an appeal to an audience through the speaker/writer's personality and stance *(ethos)*, arousal of the audience's emotion *(pathos)*, and reasoning *(logos)*.[65] The conventional modes of expression that an audience might expect, or genre, for fitting talk to a purpose and occasion were described as *deliberative* discourse for persuading action or a change of mind, *judicial* discourse to argue the justice of charges or claims, and *epideictic* discourse as appropriate to ceremonial praise or blame.

Although these divisions of genre might be useful to help align a purpose to an occasion and listeners, in practice the public figures reviewed here were fluid in their use of the genres or hybrid genres to achieve specific goals. Examples of the use of hybrid genres include Louisa Lawson's call for womanhood suffrage, Sir Robert Menzies's eulogy for Churchill, and the then vice chancellor Sir Zelman Cowen's ceremonial welcome to new university students.

Likewise, public figures flexibly used other features of the rhetorical toolbox, including *Argumentative Figures, The Tropes, Stance Figures,* or other figures.[66] Whether to speak out or to evaluate language, an understanding of these features is valuable. Many are commonly used, and often have descriptors in everyday language to help identify, describe, or assess the pertinent rhetorical stylistic features that point to the persuasive process at work. A brief glossary of the language features, rhetorical, and grammatical terms used for the language assessments in this book are noted in Appendix One.

For the individuals reviewed throughout the book, understandings inevitably gained from underpinnings of western education and culture likely helped each intuitively or consciously to frame many language choices. To put thoughts into words, an individual's ideology will certainly influence the choice of words to frame the ideas. Stylistic analysis is an observation of these choices.

The following chapters review a variety of rhetorical stylistic choices to describe the language dynamics of public figures in a representative democracy, with reference to some notable Australians. Some share similarities in persuasive language use, although each has distinct abilities worthy of individual understanding. Some of the commonalities and differences in the choice of language features are summarised in Chapter Seven.

Australians Speaking Out

The book contains detailed language studies of: Sir Samuel Griffith, 1845-1919 (Chief Justice 1903-19); Louisa Lawson, 1848-1920 (poet, writer, publisher, activist for women's suffrage); Alfred Deakin, 1856-1919 (Prime Minister, 1903-05, 1905-08, and 1909-10); Sir Robert Menzies, 1894-1978 (Prime Minister 1939-41 and 1949-66); John Curtin, 1885-1945 (wartime Prime Minister 1941-5); Gough Whitlam, 1916-2014 (Prime Minister 1972-5); Oodgeroo Noonuccal [Kath Walker], 1920-93 (poet, artist, author, and activist for First Nations); Bob Hawke, 1929-2019 (union leader, then Prime Minister 1983-91); Kevin Gilbert, 1933-93 (author, artist, poet, and activist for First Nations); Germaine Greer, born 1939- (author, academic, and activist for women's rights); and Michael Kirby, born 1939- (law reforming jurist and High Court Justice 1996-2009).

The language of many other Australian public figures is also explored or touched upon, including Sallyanne Atkinson (Lord Mayor of Brisbane 1985-91), Sir Macfarlane Burnet (Nobel-awarded immunology researcher), Sir Roderick Carnegie (Chairman of the mining company Conzinc Riotinto of Australia), Sir Zelman Cowen (university Vice Chancellor, then Governor-General of Australia 1977-82), Fred Daly (federal politician 1943-75, Leader of the House of Representatives, and cabinet minister), Sir John Forrest (explorer, first Premier of Western Australia, and cabinet minister in the first Australian parliament), William M. ('Billy') Hughes (wartime Prime Minister 1915-23), Sir James Killen (federal politician 1955-83 and cabinet minister), Dame Enid Lyons (federal politician 1943-51, cabinet minister, and first woman elected to the Australian House of Representatives), Sir Ian McLennan (Chairman of the conglomerate Broken Hill Proprietary Company), Dame Nellie Melba (opera singer), Sir Mark Oliphant (co-discoverer of nuclear fusion, then Governor of South Australia 1971-76), Linden Prowse (workplace reform advocate), and Thomas Joseph Ryan (Premier of Queensland 1915-9 and federal politician 1919-21).

In more recent times, powerful speeches examined are from prime ministers Paul Keating on reconciliation in 1992, John Howard on arms recall after Port Arthur in 1996, Kevin Rudd on the Apology in 2008, and Julia Gillard on sexism in 2012, together with a powerful eulogy by Noel Pearson in 2014 and an address to the nation by prime minister Scott Morrison, amid the coronavirus pandemic in 2020.[67]

Plan of the Book

As a plan of approach to assess public communications, the book has three sections. In the first section, this initial chapter and five chapters following review approaches for describing rhetorical style in language, touching on some historical context. In the second section, the next eleven chapters detail more specifically the language styles of some notable Australians. In the third section, a selection of speech and writing of notable Australians is available.

This **first section** explores the use of language for persuasion in public talk, along with the roles of polemic, propaganda, humour, and some types of special political vocabulary. Chapter Two reviews rhetorical stylistic approaches to persuasive language that identify conspicuous language features with stylistic relevance—such as the higher frequency or absence in the occurrence of certain types of words, sentence structures, or other significances. Chapter Three describes the use of democracy in public talk to engage listeners, with a close look at the language of John Curtin and Sir Robert Menzies.

Chapter Four examines some polemic and propaganda processes and how three types of polemical strategy are used to attract attention, frame context, and sustain persuasion. Chapter Five explores how speakers use humour to make their presence felt. Types of humour are outlined, including how speakers use this feature to set both the agenda and their relationship with listeners. In Chapter Six, the use of political vocabulary in persuasion is described, focusing on symbols, slogans, jargon, and slang. How Gough Whitlam used such political words for persuasion is examined, with detailed review of his motion of no confidence in the government, delivered in parliament.

The **second section** provides close study of the persuasive language of ten notable speakers and writers, as well as commenting on the language of many more. Chapter Seven examines rhetorical and stylistic choices of notable Australians whose efforts helped transform the nation from the late 1800s onwards. The effects of individual language choices are described, and considerations to use language persuasively are listed. Chapter Eight details how the early politician and later so-called 'radical chief justice'[68] Sir Samuel Griffith developed a quiet rhetoric, including ways that his language anticipated the emotionalism of his audience. Chapter Nine examines the rhetorical power of Louisa Lawson's speech for womanhood suffrage, describing the range of her logical and emotional appeals that touched daily life. Chapter Ten explores the confident negotiation with listeners of the early prime minister Alfred Deakin, who artfully redefined circumstances to find common goals and construct new accommodations and alliances.

The language of mid-to-later twentieth century and more recent public figures is reviewed from Chapter Eleven, which examines Sir Robert Menzies's measured language style. This includes an assessment of his eulogy for Sir

Winston Churchill,⁶⁹ in which he simulated the language of Churchill's wartime speeches as a precursor to his expanding Australia's commitment to the Vietnam War. Chapter Twelve outlines the persuasive approaches of Kevin Gilbert and Oodgeroo Noonuccal [Kath Walker] to advocate recognition of land rights for First Nations in Australia. Their contrasting styles of speech in a shared purpose and with some similarity in stances are discussed. Chapter Thirteen looks at how Germaine Greer reached readers in her book *The Female Eunuch*. Detailed analysis of her book's final chapter, titled 'Revolution', identifies Greer's rhetorical literacy to set a tone that engaged readers.

The campaign speeches and television appearances of national leaders in the 1983 Federal election campaign are examined in Chapter Fourteen. The politician Bob Hawke's 'tele-speech' enabled him to win campaigns and retain the role of prime minister. Both language and nonverbal practices of Hawke and his first opponent, the then prime minister Malcolm Fraser, are noted. For the 1984 Federal Election, Australia's first televised leadership debate performances of Hawke as prime minister and his Liberal challenger, Andrew Peacock, are compared. Chapter Fifteen explores the variety and power of Michael Kirby's speeches and writing to advocate ongoing law reform initiatives to honour human values.

Chapter Sixteen discusses persuasive language in speeches of more recent former prime ministers Paul Keating on reconciliation, John Howard on arms recall after Port Arthur, Kevin Rudd on the Apology, and Julia Gillard on sexism, as well as Noel Pearson's eulogy for Whitlam and prime minister Scott Morrison on the coronavirus pandemic. The book's Conclusion comments on the ongoing evolution of public communication and the pertinence of understanding persuasive language principles and practices for the digital age.⁷⁰

The **third section** of the book, in Chapter Eighteen, contains 15 speeches and writing of Griffith, Lawson, Forrest, Melba, Curtin, Menzies, Gilbert, Whitlam, Kirby, Hawke, Atkinson, Keating, Howard, Gillard, and Morrison. These texts speak to Federation, womanhood suffrage, trans-Australia communication, artistic appreciation, allied support in war, recognition of Churchill, land rights, national partnership in the Pacific, law reform, economic cooperation, a city's transformation, national reconciliation, gun control, non-sexist behaviour, and the coronavirus pandemic.

Finally, the **appendices** provide: (1) a glossary, with brief descriptions or examples of stylistic/grammatical terms; (2) tables of counted language features in 600-word samples, comparing ten speeches of notable Australians, as well as the social commentary style of Greer, compared with other reformist writers, Kate Millett, George Orwell, and Ronald Segal.

2: Language for Persuasion

...persuasion ...the creation in the mind of the listener...[71]

— Sir Robert Menzies

In 1854 near Ballarat in the Colony of Victoria, in what some see as the start of democracy in Australia, gold miners revolted against the police and military, who were imposing an unfair system of licensing. The miners constructed a stockade and beneath a flag bearing the Southern Cross, their leader Peter Lalor declared:

> We swear by the Southern Cross to stand truly by each other and fight to defend our rights and liberties.[72]

This was solemn rhetoric, a prayer for the common bond of the dissenters.

Lalor's brief words, together with his delivery, the context, and the imagery of the flag surely intensified feelings of responsibility in his fellows. The verbs 'swear... stand... fight... defend...' in his oath set a path to finding freedom, echoed in references to the 'Southern Cross... rights and liberties'. Lalor's choices of word, image, vernacular, and context apparently combined well to shape understanding and commitment in the miners' minds.

Although these rebels were defeated in the ensuing battle and suffered severe casualties, they eventually brought about the changes that they sought. Perhaps rhetoric and democracy truly were reborn in Australia through this event, as they had been born together 'in the same moment, in the winter of 431 BC in Athens',[73] as Collins astutely notes. Certainly, the indications of Australians drawing on rhetorical principles appear early among Australian public figures.

Tough or Sweet?

Whether appealing to an audience through personal credibility, audience emotions, logic, or some combination of these, a speaker or writer will generally be both assertive and responsive to make emotional connection with an audience. A powerful example of this is the refined conciseness of Dame Nellie Melba's farewell remarks, after her 'final performance' at His Majesty's Theatre in Melbourne in 1924. Audiences worldwide regularly flocked to hear her soprano voice, described by Sarah Bernhardt as 'pure crystal' effortlessly floating on the air. At the time of this farewell, Melba was highly regarded with substantial international accomplishment, and was back on stage in the City from which she had drawn her pseudonym. Her gala performance that evening helped raise what was a considerable sum at the time, to benefit 'limbless soldiers'–all combining to place her at a peak of great esteem. Additionally, this was believed to be the last opportunity to hear her sing in person, likely causing elation and gratitude touched with loss, and a full array of feelings such an occasion brings.

Melba's performance and the spectacular character of the evening, so vividly described in *The Argus* newspaper the next day,[74] provided an exceptionally charged setting. Her apparently simple remarks following the performance outshone the experienced national and local public figures speaking that night to honour her. With full command of words and occasion, Melba began:

> Tonight the curtain falls on my last operatic appearance in Australia, and I have to say to you the most difficult word in life–Good-bye. I shall try to say it with a smile, not only on my lips, but with my heart, a smile that comes not from the memory of achievement, but from the knowledge that I have done my best and that I have tried to keep faith with my art.

Her beginning with figurative and literal reference to what was thought to be her final curtain call immediately focused everyone's deepest concerns on the one word, 'Good-bye'. This single word gathered strong feelings, as a bridge to the give-and-take that followed. After sharing that her heart was breaking but smiling with gratitude for all her country had provided, Melba framed her own feelings in a logical request that the audience help her to keep composure and refrain from tears. With all clearly feeling for her departure from performance, she said:

> But you cannot expect me to say too much–you do not want me to break down. (Cheers). You want me to go away with a smiling face, and I am determined to do that. (Prolonged Cheers).[75]

Sensitive to the occasion and her public, Melba appealed through *ethos* and *pathos*, framed in the playful logic of her few words. These she focused through repetition and parallelism, to share and accentuate her unity with the audience–simply and strongly.

Appealing to the Ear

From the beginning of a speech or written piece, to enjoy the benefit of rhetorical understandings, an effective speaker or writer attracts the attention of the audience and moves directly to introduce a topic. Strikingly, on the steps of parliament house in 1975, the sacking of Gough Whitlam as prime minister, by Governor-General Sir John Kerr, provoked the history-catching response:

> Well might he say 'God save the Queen'; because nothing will save the Governor General. The proclamation you have just heard was counter-signed 'Malcolm Fraser'—who will go down in history as 'Kerr's Cur'.[76]

During a press conference later that day, Whitlam reportedly also referred disparagingly to a note in the vice-regal proclamation that named Fraser as caretaker prime minister, saying that it was the first time the burglar had been appointed as caretaker.[77] Ever ready with an apt and imaginative pun, literary or historical allusion, Whitlam could better an opponent verbally, inside or outside parliament, to attract attention, set the scene, and introduce his case.

Australian public figures have illustrated diverse ways to rivet attention and focus their topic through introductory remarks. In colonial 1895, the plain-speaking Sir Samuel Griffith began an article that condensed an address he had made in 1891 to the Royal Geographical Society. He distilled geographical features of the country, which he later asserted made federation 'inevitable':

> The physical conditions of Australia are unique in the world. It is surrounded by ocean. It contains no large ranges of mountains, no wide and deep rivers dividing one region from another.[78]

In 1912, the well-known explorer and public figure, Sir John Forrest, accentuated the significance of the long-worked-for rail-link to the west, at a ceremony to mark the commencement of the Trans-Australia Railway:

> As a representative of Western Australia, I feel grateful for the honour His Majesty The King has done to this historic occasion by sending the gracious message which the Governor-General has received and just read to us. [*Cheers.*] I thank His Excellency the Governor-General and His Excellency the Governor of South Australia and others for the kind references which they have been good enough to make to myself. I have been a constant advocate of this railway on public grounds for many years, and I am naturally proud that the long-looked-for event has come at last.[79]

Dame Enid Lyons in 1943 focused the historical significance of her maiden speech in parliament:

> It would be strange indeed were I not tonight deeply conscious of the fact, if not a little awed by the knowledge, that on my shoulders rests a great weight

of responsibility; because this is the first occasion upon which a woman has addressed this House.[80]

Almost half a century later in 1992, former senator Susan Ryan adapted the well-known feminist expression 'a woman needs a man like a fish needs a bicycle', to open her speech questioning whether women in parliament were still 'as unnatural and unlikely as fishes on bicycles'.[81]

Sir Roderick Carnegie, as chairman of Conzinc Riotinto of Australia, opened his address to a legal audience in 1975 by inviting them to hold in their hands and consider the loss in value of 'a dollar note, or a ten dollar note if you wish',[82] due to inflation. He then asserted that he was not making a political speech, yet he reflected the controversies surrounding Federal politics at the time. He advocated the importance of individual responsibility and initiative in a 'free enterprise' community. With language that was crisp and to the point, his visualisation of an otherwise abstract concept of inflation, together with further relevant examples in the speech, made his argument tangible.

In 2002, prime minister John Howard contrasted the idyllic quality of Bali with the mourning for Australians among the lives just lost there to terrorism:

> As the sun sets over this beautiful island, we gather here in sorrow, in anguish, in disbelief and in pain. There are no words that I can summon to solve in any way the hurt and the suffering and the pain being felt by so many of my fellow countrymen and women and by so many of the citizens of other nations.[83]

Showing a further range of options for imaginative introductions that established an emotional link with an audience, to introduce comments on industrial democracy techniques, Linden Prowse focused attention on a single word, followed by a rhetorical question, 'Work–isn't that a beautiful word?'[84] More subtly, Robert Manne opened with a confessional approach to discuss his own identity in a multicultural nation.[85] The Nobel-awarded immunologist, Sir Macfarlane Burnet began a Boyer lecture on ABC Radio by reflecting on the need to appreciate life and the impact of research on it. He noted the dream of human beings to be free of 'war and cruelty, poverty, hunger and disease, and death itself',[86] putting perspective on human beings in a long view of history.

Beginnings to Ends

Engaging an audience takes talent. Whether comedian, TV anchor, journalist, or speaker or writer for any purpose, how one starts sets the stage for all that follows. Especially in a snappy world so influenced by social media, the choice of first words, the context, and visual support matter greatly. With distraction just a click away, listeners and readers seek to answer early why a communication matters personally.[87] Conventional wisdom rightly calls for an introduction, a body, and conclusion. It is even better wisdom to begin with and sustain a focus on what matters to the audience. The best introduction attracts attention to this focus on the topic along with the speaker or writer, while directly developing a theme and direction. Audiences connect with anyone who does this well.

From the introduction, the shape for the development of a topic emerges. As will be discussed later, the simplest organisation of ideas, especially for a speech, is usually advisable. What is generally true is that the introductions that are longer and, where possible humorous, serve best to engage an audience. Sometimes, developing a story, literally or figuratively, and/or choosing visual media to illustrate or underscore specifics will advance a case strongly. Effective speakers or writers know that what they choose to mention among facts, opinions, and ideas that might interest audience members, along with the choice of words, the shaping of sentences, and the development of passages, all impact how an audience hears or sees, and then relates to them.

The talent to make choices well grows from thinking to do, from thoughtful 'listening', and from practice. In an opening passage, as with any first meeting, a listener or reader intuitively looks for shared interests, along with signs of who the speaker or writer is in the words chosen, which combine to signal tone, role, stance, and personality. Words and the subtleties of delivery,[88] with sometimes expected or other times surprising adjustments in tone, pace, pause, volume, inflection, gesture, facial expression, or other nonverbal qualities working together, help develop ideas and secure changes in feeling, belief, or action. Analyses of nonverbal and language style provide insights about such choices.

Style as Choice

In each of the cases just outlined, the speaker or writer invested personal perspective in the initial words. Each chose an individual way to attract attention to the speaker or writer and a topic, thereby beginning to shape a personality of the speaker that an audience might recognise. Personal style comes from the combined effect of choices of fact, opinion, and idea, nonverbal opportunity, along with the use of specific words or types of words and language structure. These choices that project persona, that is the role chosen, and personal style convey the authenticity and trustworthiness of a speaker or writer and engage an audience. People consciously and unconsciously make many such choices 'independently of the topics communicated'.[89]

A first step in analysing style is to read a text, or listen to, or view a presentation with attention to its setting of time, place, contemporary issues, culture, and the language-context of the text itself. This first 'reading' is to look for the conspicuous features that might hold promise of stylistic relevance to both context and purpose. This is followed by further analysis and evaluation.

Individual Personality

Marked differences in individual style and stance surface in the following excerpts. The first was the final address by a prisoner in court, showing a mix of bravado and self-proclaimed humility, verging on what is perhaps understandable self-pity:

> Well it is rather too late for me to speak now. I thought of speaking this morning and all day, but there was little use, and there is little use blaming any one now. Nobody knew about my case except myself and I wish I had insisted on being allowed to examine the witnesses myself... I do not blame anybody—neither Mr Bindon [defence lawyer] nor Mr Garrison [the Crown Prosecutor]; but Mr Bindon knew nothing about my case. I lay blame on myself that I did not get up yesterday and examine the witnesses, but I thought that if I did so it would look like bravado and flashness.[90]

This was the Australian bushranger Ned Kelly at his trial, after he was convicted. His apparent concession to the processes of the court in this excerpt was at odds with the report of his continuous interruptions throughout the trial. Consistent with Kelly's legacy, he here inferred his being wronged, including by proffering his own unwillingness to be perceived as too assertive.

Less widely known are the comments of the trial judge, who replied to Kelly:

> You are self-accused. The statement was made voluntarily by yourself. Then you and your companions committed attacks on two banks, and appropriated therefrom large sums of money, amounting to several thousands of pounds. Further, I cannot conceal from myself the fact that an expenditure of 50,000 pounds has been rendered necessary in consequence of the acts with which you and your party have been connected... to be deplored. When such examples as these are so often repeated society must be reorganised, or it must soon be seriously affected. Your unfortunate and miserable companions have died a death which probably you might rather envy, but you are not afforded the opportunity...[91]

Here, the judge Sir Redmond Barry used language that, in the context of Kelly's reported continuous interjections and contradictions of court proceedings, was especially precise. Barry's strong use of verb forms, such as 'self-accused', 'was made voluntarily', 'appropriated', 'cannot conceal from myself', and 'to be deplored', succinctly and firmly held to administering principles of established law and to keeping some perspective in the courtroom. Kelly's accumulated references to himself, of 14 first-person singular pronouns compared to Barry's one use of 'I', accentuated Kelly's self-portrayal as the victim.

Even when reading the news report of this interchange, what is remarkable is Barry's careful discussion of the harm Kelly caused, while also politely phrasing his comments in a way that might avoid additional angst to Kelly. This sense of Barry did not make its way into Australian popular culture, as the largely positive folklore about Kelly has.

Finding Balance

Following the withdrawal in 1973 of United States troops from Vietnam, and just nine months after the president Richard Nixon resigned due to the Watergate scandal, in June 1975 a notable Australian addressed the *National Press Club* in Washington DC. He sought a new perspective on Australia, in the mediating role of a neutral middle power in the Pacific:

> In the two years since I last spoke to you, America has undergone a vast domestic, as well as a vast international, catharsis. *With* those profound traumas behind you, *with* their bitterness and misery being purged away, what better time to profit by experience and build on the true strengths of American democracy and Australian idealism? Here is an opportunity—not just for America but for all of us—to end *our* long preoccupation with military alignments in Asia, *our* ideological confrontations, *our* cold war hangups, and open a new chapter in Western co-operation. Let the deeper issues of poverty, overpopulation and mal-distribution of the world's wealth assume their proper importance in our hearts and minds. *These are the real problems* of Asia. *These are the real problems* of the world. *These*, I trust, will be the real concerns of the United States. *With your* great tradition of moral leadership, *your* unexampled generosity, *your* vision, *your* energy, *your* sheer zest for accomplishment, *you* will find new inspiration in this task—a task in which Australia will be a ready and a willing partner.[92] *[my italics]*

Even without reading these words aloud in the heavy-breath accent so characteristic of the speaker, the rhythm and cadence of prime minister Whitlam come through. Alternating between diplomacy and bluntness, while forthrightly asserting a new role for Australia, Whitlam used a characteristic range of rhetorical features to soften the bluntness and strengthen his emphases. This included *anaphora*, that is, repetition of the same word at the beginning of successive phrases, clauses, or sentences, as well as other parallelism, historical reference, and analogy.

Creative Engagement

With individual style at the formal occasion of the opening of Expo '88, The Right Honourable Lord Mayor of Brisbane, Sallyanne Atkinson, drew differently on these and additional language features to invite celebration of Brisbane as an 'international city'. From the platform of the officials' stage positioned on the riverbank, and with a background of the city skyline of tall buildings that testified to the scale of the City's growth, Atkinson presented her remarks in a moderated voice tone befitting the opening of this major international event. Blending everyday words of celebration into the occasion, she commenced by expressing her pride in Brisbane, and invited Her Majesty The Queen and His Royal Highness The Duke of Edinburgh to join in the celebration of the City's growth— as guests of honour with assembled visitors and residents. Her tone of voice and other nonverbal nods to the formality of the occasion were balanced by exuberant personal touches characteristic of conversation, and she injected vitality into her expression of pride and confidence in the City's future:

> I am very proud this morning to be Lord Mayor of Brisbane.
>
> Expo 88 is something like a coming of age celebration for our City. We are honoured and delighted that Your Majesty and Your Royal Highness are the guests of honour at our party.
>
> Today is the opening of a six month event to which we have invited the rest of the world. Today we formally and officially become an international city.
>
> Your Majesty and Your Royal Highness have been part of the growing-up process. When you first came here more than 30 years ago we were still a city finding its feet.
>
> Back in 1954, we felt we were living in a large country town, friendly and relaxed. City Hall was our tallest building, the railway tracks (and the train) still held up traffic as they crossed the road at the 'Gabba, and Southerners called Brisbane a cultural desert.[93]

This was a theme consistent with Atkinson's first mayoral address to Council three years earlier. During two terms as Lord Mayor, she opened up river frontages for public use, as well as facilitating outdoor dining and an Arts hub of performance venues, art gallery, and museum as part of the later redevelopment of the Expo site.[94] Well-regarded for her gracious and down-to-earth personal touch, intelligence, and wit, Atkinson here engaged listeners as do friends talking, refreshingly welcoming Expo as the City's 'coming of age' party.

By focusing attention on tangible examples of growth, people, places, and lifestyle, she traced the 'growing up' of the City since the royal couple's first visit, while emphasising the constancy of Brisbane as a 'friendly and relaxed' place. Atkinson's use of everyday language, such as 'finding its feet', 'country town', 'Gabba', 'Southerners', 'cultural desert', 'friendly and relaxed', and 'can-do', mixed understatement and exuberance to express colourful informality.

Conversational qualities included sentence fragments, short breath groups, simple sentences, series, and a higher-than-average number of compound clauses. The direct address of using 'you' and 'your', other personal pronouns, and the specific naming of people and places kept this 'conversation' tangible.

Mainly concrete nouns and strong transitions, such as the repeated use of 'today' and 'now', add to the liveliness in her frequent infinite verbs, 'to be' verbs, and present tense. In closing, she directly invited the Royals to share in our life:

> Now as the capital of Australia's *fastest growing* state on the edge of the Pacific Rim, the *fastest growing* region in the world, *we* feel not only proud of *our* past, but confident of the future.
>
> Expo is *our* opportunity *to show off* to the world, *to invite* other nations *to witness, share* and *enjoy* the exciting and dynamic city that is Brisbane.
>
> But most of all it is an opportunity for the people of Brisbane to say to *Your* Majesty and to *Your* Royal Highness, that *we* are glad *that you* have been with *us* along the way, and *that you* are most especially welcome today.
>
> *We* hope *you enjoy* our party.[95] *[my italics]*

This was a remarkably engaging speech. In correspondence, Atkinson provides a 'bit of background' that all speakers at the opening ceremony were asked to keep to two to three minutes and she indicates that in her 'usual way, still, of writing speeches' she thought 'about the topic for a few days but... actually put it down close to delivery'. She adds that she does not 'usually write a speech, except where there is a time requirement, as in this case'.[96]

Prior to Expo, Her Majesty was reported as understanding that Brisbane had an interesting Lord Mayor. This recorded a sentiment concerning Sallyanne Atkinson's leadership shared widely among the residents of Brisbane, others throughout Australia, and a variety of world leaders.

Describing Style

Such perception of the style of a speaker or writer derives from the combination of prior reputation, what facts, ideas, opinions, or beliefs are chosen for focus in public talk, as well as how matters are thought about and dealt with as these are interwoven with language and nonverbal choices. Language style is developed through the distinct patterns in word choice, structures of phrases, clauses, or sentences, and deviations from the rules of language, or the style expected in a particular text type or context.

Style can be viewed broadly as the motivated choices that stimulate an audience. Stylistics or the study of language style, as Peter Verdonk suggests, looks at the foregrounded elements in texts.[97] Important also is to look at the subordinated elements in texts and to evaluate how such choices impact communication. As Jeanne Fahnestock notes of rhetorical style, 'rhetorical stylistics provides a point for making choices, or observations of others' choices'.[98] Most common among various approaches to identifying style in persuasive language is to note the language features in texts that point to how or why a communication might be effective, or not.

At the basic levels of language, identifying the choices that a speaker/writer makes requires understanding of the rhetorical toolbox and other branches of language study, including word sounds (phonology/phonetics), patterns of written language (graphology), how words are constructed (morphology), how words combine with other words to form phrases and sentences (syntax/grammar), the vocabulary of words used (lexical analysis/lexicology), the meaning of words and sentences (semantics), and the use of words and sentences in everyday situations (pragmatics/discourse analysis).[99] Useful in stylistic analysis are checklists that overview categories of linguistic features, such as what Geoffrey Leech and Mick Short developed[100] to study style in fiction, identifying potential style markers on lexical categories, grammatical categories, figures of speech, context, and cohesion. Based partly on this is Maarten van Leeuwen's checklist of word use, grammatical phenomena, classical rhetorical figures and tropes, and cohesion and coherence.[101]

Thoughtful Integration

Among the many stylistics publications describing analytic methods[102] are studies of linguistic and non-linguistic context,[103] as well as intersections with cognitive linguistics,[104] to better understand how communication occurs in the minds of audience members. When rhetorical, stylistic, and linguistic methods and insights are integrated to explore persuasive language, the resources from these fields are mutually strengthening. The common rhetorical resources of alliteration, allusion, analogy, anaphora, antithesis, hyperbole, metaphor, oxymoron, parallelism, simile, and understatement are used for different effects, along with lesser-known devices used to emphasise or subordinate facts, opinions, or ideas for communication impact.

One approach within the eclectic field of stylistics, critical discourse analysis (CDA), primarily addresses more ideological concerns than some other fields of language study, seeking to identify the ideology of a speaker/writer from language.[105] Researchers in discourse studies are concerned with 'all linguistic features and processes of that discourse…in that they serve to express that single ideology'.[106] These researchers argue that '*all* linguistic features of the text are congruent', whereas more widely in stylistics 'it is not assumed that all linguistic features in a text are semantically congruent'. Teun van Dijk reviews various approaches and issues of this approach, to describe a form of multidisciplinary CDA.[107] Within the CDA field and more generally, some researchers explore the persuasive role of metaphor in political language to build trust[108] and to frame the discourse.

Purpose and Evidence

Within such studies concerns persist, as represented in Craig Hamilton's concern of 'how to strive for analytical objectivity without falling into the trap of producing analyses that confirm one's opinions about certain political leaders'.[109] This caution is relevant to conducting critical analysis in a variety of fields, since analysis will always require personal choices on smaller or larger matters. Salient questions for text analyses are whether the analyst's choices elucidate the way a communicator's apparent purpose is advanced and how well the evidence from the text supports the critical interpretation.

Neither quantitative nor more qualitative methods avoid subjectivity, at the very least in making decisions concerning features to examine and classifications of these features. Quantitative methods used in stylistics include descriptions of syntax,[110] personal style,[111] or authorship attribution,[112] including an asserted use for fraud detection.[113] Many approaches set inventories and descriptions of stylistic stimuli, using linguistic concepts prior to close interpretation.[114] One approach to syntax was first to parse the text, then to count the proportions of word-classes, as well as the 'distance' between locations in a text.[115]

Some studies in this book make limited use of quantitative analyses of word and syntax choices to consider or compare with intuitive analyses of language. These counts also cast a wider net to capture what might not be evident using only qualitative methods. Put another way, it was hoped that this 'bottom up' approach might deliver further understandings about how the speaker/writer's choices advance a purpose while projecting some sense of language style.

Roles of Metaphor

Notable among better-known rhetorical features is metaphor, or 'understanding and experiencing one thing in terms of another',[116] which was used in a variety of the public communications that were examined. George Lakoff and Mark Johnson observe the general conceptual importance of metaphors to set 'how we perceive, how we think, and what we do'.[117]

Szilvia Csábi, for example, amid her survey of stylistic approaches to metaphor, provides a description of Thomas Paine's explanation for America's separation from Britain as that 'specific time in every family's life when the child, America, has to start going its own way and has to separate from the parents, Britain', in order to start an individual life.[118] She outlines a range of examples, highlighting how some metaphors explain occurrences in terms of understanding the world in relation to experiences of our own human bodies, such as life events being represented as a journey, or a voyage in space, or a journey through time.[119] The versatility of the speakers and writers studied was evident in their use of metaphor for various purposes.

National Identity or Direction

Among the notable Australians reviewed, one use of metaphor was to help define a direction or identity for the nation. Menzies, for example, metaphorically asserted a self-image for Australians when he spoke with foreground or background affinity for all things British. Rhetoric acknowledging the British Crown for formal occasions has continued beyond the twentieth century in Australia,[120] although emphases have moderated in nuanced ways.

Emerging through the twentieth century into more recent prime ministerial rhetoric, with some individualised adjustments and shifts in emphasis, are what Brooke Gizzi-Stewart calls 'new visions and vintage values'.[121] Curtin, Menzies, Whitlam, Hawke, and others used earlier versions of 'narratives' that Gizzi-Stewart describes in twenty-first century Australian prime ministers' speeches. Among these are 'keeping Australians in safe hands', 'appealing to the Australian spirit', 'the right leadership', 'the opportunity society' or the time for opportunity, 'party values as Australian values', 'a new way', 'fighting on', and 'family values as the building blocks'.[122]

Other Framing of a Topic

Speakers also variously used metaphor to frame the communication topic. Lawson identified the suffragette cause as a fight to protect home values, strikingly asking 'If a viper coils by your sleeping child, / Is the gentlest too weak for a blow?'[123] Griffith built the principle of almost his entire argument for federation on a logic that geography dictated the boundaries of a nation.[124] Hawke neatly compiled a memory of Albert Monk[125] as a builder of the union movement. Oodgeroo profoundly framed the land rights claim of First Nations in the powerful metaphor, 'the land is our mother'.[126] Forrest equated the effort to construct the railway link to West Australia as a battle.[127]

Gilbert portrayed 'whites' as 'bastards' to introduce the centrality of indoctrination for emphasis in his case and then as 'sharks',[128] to highlight the predation of 'whites' on people in First Nations. Kirby built the metaphor of a mob of Australians, who violated authorised laws, as anti-heroes.[129] Burnet identified his training as a doctor for treatment of the human body as equivalent to treatments for human ethical issues.[130] In Lyons's first speech to parliament, she extended her metaphor of being the new broom with 'sound views', who expected to be potentially 'very unpopular in the broom cupboard',[131] thereby lightly preparing her fellow parliamentarians for the changes to policy that she was to advocate later on during this maiden speech. The corporate leader, McLennan equated the growth needed in management education to the growth of industry.[132]

Framing Events, Facts, Opinions, or Ideas

On other occasions public figures framed events, facts, opinions, or ideas through a metaphor that was core to their case. Hughes framed military training to defend one's country as an obligatory personal duty equivalent to feeding and caring for one's own children,[133] which was not to be delegated. Interestingly, this concept of duty was later also a basis for successfully establishing compulsory voting in Australia. Carnegie visualised inflation tangibly as cash lost from one's hand.[134] Curtin used the visually powerful 'from the skies of the Pacific pours down a deadly hail',[135] identifying bombing attacks as a deadly storm and framing a focus on the severity of the enemy's air attacks.

Direct Emphasis

Elsewhere, in conjunction with these purposes or for a singular purpose, some used metaphor for more specific and direct emphasis. Menzies equated liberty to a 'precious metal'.[136] Whitlam used metaphor readily to condemn others or their ideas, such as in the historically referenced name-calling, 'Bourbons',[137] or the clichéd 'stab in the back theory'.[138] Cowen identified the government computer as *Tyrannosaurus Rex*,[139] to characterise the government's insatiable demand for detail. Greer used pun and ambiguity to raise a laugh that underscored her mockery of sexism in the news, by pointing out 'a story about Miss Vaughan in the jogacratic sports section, who is apparently a Razors mascot of extraordinary dimensions'.[140] Oliphant asserted the purpose of someone in a university as an explorer searching 'for knowledge'.[141] In contrast, Prowse referenced the lost wandering of the early Australian explorers Burke and Wills, to emphasise how approaches to work were changing and to contrast that younger Australians 'do not want to be just sleepwalkers'[142] in exploring their futures.

Content and Context

To interpret metaphor as well as other features, such as vocabulary, grammar, and syntax, the studies here focus on the persuasive aspects of language style. To do so, individual choices that public figures made are noted. Although the effectiveness of persuasive language and its assessment depend greatly on the context, it is important to acknowledge that, when looking after the fact at a speech or written piece, only some sense of the time, place, and situation is accessible. Similarly, the public figure, in preparations prior to delivering any words of course, might have only a partial sense of what is most pertinent in the full range of contextual issues.

Although now removed in time from many of the specific concerns of the audiences with whom these public figures interacted, some broad features of

Australia's cultural transformation from the late 1800s should be kept in mind. Following the arrival of the First Fleet from Britain in 1788, Australia long sustained a metaphor of the nation as Britain transported. In a society so dominated by British cultural heritage through social, educational, business, and union influences, including the governments, newspapers, and broadcast systems that were largely modeled on Britain, this was hardly surprising.

Even well into the twentieth century, growing up in Australia involved substantial exposure to British media for example, with uniquely Australian media emerging in fits and starts, and mostly in the later decades of the twentieth century. United States' mass media also became increasingly influential during the twentieth century, especially after the Hollywood studios virtually annihilated the early vibrant Australian film industry by buying up Australian cinemas and flooding Australia with American movies.[143] But the increasingly strong influences of America, Asia, and Europe were most evident relatively recently.

Until then, the common acceptance of Australia's identity as a British nation framed many public communications. Key policy issues like multiculturalism or the dispossession of First Nations remained unresolved in societal understandings. Despite the federation of colonies in 1901 and Britain's legislation to realign Australia as a dominion of the British Commonwealth in 1931, Australia progressed through a gradual repositioning of national identity.[144]

Events such as the Eureka Stockade or the efforts of Australian soldiers at Gallipoli are seen as significant in redefining Australian identity. Historical interpretations attribute variously to diggers on the goldfields, the bush worker, the larrikin, the immigrant worker, the digger-soldier, and the suburban homeowner some role in shaping Australian commitment to independence, egalitarianism, and anti-authoritarianism. A variety of communications of media, government, education, business, and neighbourhoods doubtless played a part in shaping Australian distinctiveness. Propelling change were people in all these places, as well as social action and special interest groups providing avenues for sharing, discussing, and evolving assumptions about identity.

Anglo-Celtic

During the century or so of modern history in which many of the notable Australians reviewed here spoke or wrote, it was often a tussle between and with Anglo and Celtic legacies that was evident in public communication. Menzies was devoted very much to an Anglo-Celtic heritage, even though he seemed not to allow this to get in the way of the reality of needing to build strategic alliances beyond the Commonwealth nations, such as with the United States. During election campaigns in the 1950s, my father and Irish grandfather in the evening would attend Menzies's election rallies locally at Brisbane's Festival Hall. They returned home enjoyably sharing stories of his deftly but imperiously handling interjectors in a mode akin to someone from the ruling class in Britain.

As late as the 1960s in public talk, Menzies still referred to this land in the southern hemisphere as a British nation. When Her Majesty The Queen visited in 1963, he proudly asserted an apparent incongruity, that Australia was the 'most democratic monarchy in the whole, wide world'.[145] Yet, Australians also held regard for anti-heroes like Peter Lalor and the outlaw Ned Kelly, who had Irish heritage. Often conveniently disregarded was the reality that the Australian population also consisted of people in the First Nations who were largely ignored or abused, as well as immigrant Germans, Greeks, Italians, Turks, Chinese, West Indians, Americans, and a multitude of races from a variety of national origins.

Multicultural Reality

In the decades toward the end of the twentieth century, Australian government policies progressively caught up with the centuries long reality that Australia was a multicultural society. It gradually became much less acceptable for adherents to one culture to dominate other cultures. Public figures build relationships with a variety of audience members by anticipating what different segments of an audience are listening for and by showing understanding of diverse characteristics, including cultural sensitivities. Increasingly considered necessary for effective communication was respect for individual diversity, implicitly with mutual cultural understanding.[146]

In a country so outwardly committed to egalitarianism and 'mateship', perhaps it should be straightforward to align Australians through this egalitarianism, enveloping mutual regard for principles of democracy. Compared with the *rhetors* in ancient Greece, for whom it was claimed there was a 'common cultural heritage',[147] Australia's policies toward First Nations and migrants through the twentieth century presented complexities in finding a cultural heritage that might be truly considered commonly shared.

Australia has progressively become more publicly alert to its nature as a modern pluralistic society.[148] To communicate persuasively, a speaker or writer needs to evolve a complex of mutual understandings with audiences. The extent to which the perspectives of the public figure and an audience align or at least find mutual accommodations might be the main influence on how true the communication will be. Principled, effective public communication requires sincere advocacy for contemporary concerns of the community, with sensitivity to valued beliefs and social realities.

3: Democratic Talk of John Curtin and Sir Robert Menzies

A public who listens and speaks out

— a root of democracy[149]

One very clear social assumption in modern Australia, inherited through the combined influences from western thought and British settlement was the evolution of a representative government based on Westminster. This system of parliamentary democracy not only framed government systems in Australia but has also infused a commitment to free and open debate, still epitomised in the display of 'no-holds-barred' debates in the British House of Commons.

Australia has claimed freedom from great inequalities, espousing 'mateship' and egalitarianism as integral to its national ethos. Unsurprisingly, many notable Australians underpin public talk with direct references or inferences of commitment to democracy. Most have aligned themselves directly or impliedly with widely accepted democratic ideals. Public figures often appeal to democratic ideals, presuming this as common ground with listeners.

Australian prime ministers show a tradition of referring to the nation's democratic framework for government. Just some who appealed to the democratic ideal, its freedoms, or higher democratic aims were Howard speaking on gun control, Hawke at an economic summit, and Hughes's argument to compel military training. Likewise, in John Curtin's radio broadcast to the people of the United States in 1942, he framed his impassioned appeal on behalf of the Australian Government for the Australian people, by stating that he looked to '...America as the paramount factor on the democracies' side.'[150] Addressing the National Press Club in Washington DC in 1955, Robert Menzies spelled out that prime ministers of a democratic country were unable to wander the world to offer '...new policies off their own hook'.[151] At the same venue in 1975, Gough Whitlam said:

> So in accepting your invitation for a second time, I again pay tribute to the manifest and enduring strength of the democracy of the United States, of which the press is so fundamental a part.[152]

Former BBC broadcaster Brian Groombridge has noted that 'democracy provided the official ideology and rhetoric of our society'.[153] Media freedom is likewise considered a central lifeforce for a democratic system of government to continue.

Keys to Democracy

The concept of democracy has a long association with communication. Aristotle prescribes that for democracy to exist a state's citizens must be informed, curious, and capable speakers.[154] In Montesquieu's view, the durability of free government depends on a nation's capacity for self-correction,[155] with persuasive communication as a principal way for democracies to make orderly self-correction. As in earlier times, an improved understanding of what makes public talk effective will empower future public communication, as the best assurance that democracy thrives.

Within representative democracies such as Australia, Canada, New Zealand, the United Kingdom, and the United States, public figures often project their integration of practical real-world savvy with an intention to sustain freedoms and individual rights. On some occasions, features of democracy are simply mentioned as the touchstone for commentary. At other times, the word itself will be repeated to assert a public figure's support for democratic ideals. On ceremonial occasions or to reflect incumbent authority, allusions to democracy, such as 'Westminster', 'Parliament', 'the Constitution', 'Old Glory', 'the Rule of Law', or other references are made. Also reflecting democratic values, figurative references as various as 'freedom', 'justice', or 'the Anzac breed' can pack emotional punch for these purposes, embellishing a shared experience of democratic values.

Nods to Democracy

Comparing speeches of two prime ministers, John Curtin and Sir Robert Menzies, illustrates how these notable Australians nodded to democratic principles for differing occasions. In an especially powerful and historically significant speech directed to secure democracies against a foreign invader during World War II, in March 1942 Curtin addressed the people of the United

States by reaching across the Pacific via radio. The appeal to democratic values in his *Speech to America* at a time of great threat to Australia drew on a shared desire of America and Australia to defeat foreign aggression and preserve democracy. Curtin made a rallying call for the United States to join in full partnership with Australia in the fight against the aggressive actions of Japan in the Pacific. By looking to America rather than Britain, he also furthered a new direction for Australian foreign policy.

Even though the surprise attack on Pearl Harbor had occurred three months before Curtin's speech, some United States listeners might have been interested but undecided, and some apathetic, or some opposed to Curtin's proposition for a stronger partnership that required commitment of American resources. Curtin surely knew he needed to motivate different segments of his audience, and he put a spotlight on the need to obtain 'first-hand contact with America'.

Finding Alignment

Disseminated in all newspapers and press services as well as on American radio, Curtin's speech strongly emphasised the warning that, if Australia fell, the west coast of the United States would be Japan's next invasion target. Although directed overtly to the American audience, the speech in Australia appeared to enjoy public support, capturing front page headlines. The full text of the speech was printed in Australian newspapers, in the *New York Times*, and widely otherwise.[156] Curtin began:

> Men and women of the United States: I speak to you from Australia. I speak from a united people to a united people, and my speech is aimed to serve all the people of the nations united in the struggle to save mankind. On the great waters of the Pacific Ocean war now breathes its bloody steam. From the skies of the Pacific pours down a deadly hail. In the countless islands of the Pacific the tide of war flows badly for you in America. For us in Australia it is flowing badly.[157]

Curtin presented startlingly simple and vivid illustrations of common interest and united purpose. He directed attention to the basic elements of the problem facing the two nations and sought to overcome any inertia, to secure common ground. Curtin moved quickly through the causes of the problem with powerful imagery, mounting evidence by sharing common experiences and seeking agreement on general principles. He then applied these principles to show how his plan for a substantial commitment from the United States was the best solution going forward.

Curtin later reminded of the credentials and preparedness of Australians, when he requested the 'materials and machines' needed, for 'the Anzac breed …hallmarked as pure metal' to do the job of Australia's defence. In closing, he visualised his own optimism, seeing allied flags flying in the name of freedom—as a vivid image of the outcome that he asked listeners to work for. This was a powerful speech, touching every pertinent stage of the motivating process.

'Speaking to You'

Curtin initially used variations of the phrase 'I speak… to you…' to gain attention and give a setting for the speech, then later used this framing to intensify both his warnings of danger and his pledge of Australian support. Churchill had used a similarly personalised framework, namely '*I/We/They/Us Against Them*' in his post-Pearl Harbor address to the United States Congress less than three months earlier.[158] Curtin highly concentrated personal pronouns, underscoring that he was talking directly with the American people, moving among stances of orator, fellow sufferer, sage, and Pacific friend. He kept attention on the personal quality of the appeal, with his repeating the mode of address, 'I speak to you'. In the first five paragraphs, he used the following forms:

> I speak to you
>
> I speak from a united people to a united people
>
> Let me …address you
>
> [Let me] …tell you
>
> I am not speaking to your government
>
> [but] …to the people of America, I am now speaking
>
> …to you who are …fighting
>
> …to you who are …sweating
>
> …to all of you who are making sacrifices
>
> I speak to you

This powerful emphasis of relationship with listeners helped to underscore the similarity of difficulties faced by the American and Australian peoples.

Within these first passages of the speech, Curtin initially used 'we' to denote only Australians, then shifted the use to include his American listeners. He pivoted in the third paragraph to 'But facts are stern things. We, the allied nations, were unready'. From this point, 'we' then denoted Americans and Australians together, whom Curtin stated were united against democracy's joint enemy, using as a counterpoint the then too familiar racial slur, 'the yellow aggressor'. His varied use of 'we' seems targeted to intensify the allies' emotional affinity, by strengthening the speaker's relationship with listeners and helping to focus the urgency for a personal, human, and emotional response at a time of international threat.

Curtin's words painted a dramatically dangerous picture vividly, using both fresh and well used metaphors to emphasise the status of the joint effort of the two countries in the fight against the enemy in the Pacific. From the high ground of a 'struggle to save mankind', Curtin accentuated the partnership of two peoples who were aligned in this common interest. He used the powerful metaphor of a storm-force deadly deluge of munitions, to alert his geographically distant listeners in the United States of the seriousness of the threat.

Sharing Similarities

To highlight similarities between America and Australia, while promoting American uneasiness about the progress of the war in the Pacific, Curtin said firmly and clearly:

> It is to the people of America I am now speaking; to you who are or will be fighting; to you who are sweating in the factories and workshops to turn out the vital munitions of war; to all of you who are making sacrifices in one way or another to provide the enormous resources required for our great task. I speak to you at a time when the loss of Java and the splendid resistance of the gallant Dutch together give us a feeling of both sadness and pride.[159]

He implied here and stated later in the speech that America needed a strong partner in the Pacific. With a swift recognition of the daily exhausting work that the American people were already devoting to this 'great task', he also set the platform for later incorporating symbolic language that sustained his elevation of their efforts in service of a noble cause.

Fight to Sustain Democracy

By highlighting the similarity of the two countries' egalitarian commitment to democratic principles, Curtin sought a strengthened relationship between the United States and Australia. The metaphoric early opening sentences of the speech had made the war visually real, as a shared problem that the two countries faced. The very evident parallelism of phrases from his opening, progressing from 'I' to 'united people' to 'all the people' to 'mankind', underscored his assumption and projection of a united purpose. This was rapid movement to common ground.

Later in the speech, Curtin identified respect for the United States president 'Mr Roosevelt' and for General Douglas MacArthur, and emphasised attractive features of Australian soldiers, Australian institutions, Australia's new foreign affairs representative, H.V. Evatt who married an American, and the Australian people. Australia was neither a great economic nor military power internationally. It was largely by Curtin's own vitality and forcefulness pointing to shared qualities that Americans would note or act on an appeal from their ally. He sustained an uncommon mix of personal touch with projections of a future reality as a highly symbolic appeal, to conclude:

> I may be looking down a vista of weary months; of soul-shaking reverses; of grim struggle; of back-breaking work. But as surely as I sit here talking to you across the war-tossed Pacific Ocean I see our flag; I see Old Glory; I see the proud banner of the heroic Chinese; I see the standard of the valiant Dutch.
>
> And I see them flying high in the wind of liberty over a Pacific from which aggression has been wiped out; over peoples restored to freedom; and flying triumphant as the glorified symbols of united nations strong in will and in power to achieve decency and dignity, unyielding to evil in any form.[160]

Curtin thus concluded with realities mixed in optimism for accomplishing peace, to enjoy deeply appreciated freedoms and values of humanity shared by the two nations. He focused on the values of democracy and civilisation in the two nations as the cause that united two peoples, addressed in everyday words, to build a powerful call to action. The only measure of the success of this speech would be the level of commitment of the United States people's support to keep intensifying involvement in the Pacific war.

Constructing and emphasising Curtin's stance as the plain-talking person appealing person-to-person were his language choices. Compared with other speakers noted in Appendix Two, Curtin's language combined many everyday concrete words, with substantially higher-than-average use of proper nouns, and a slightly greater-than-average number of action verbs to make more tangible and immediate the serious scene he portrayed. With careful use of the collective first-person pronouns, 'we, us, our', he negotiated a feeling of common purpose and established common ground, aided by his forthright everyday vocabulary and sentence structure. He made higher-than-average use of interpolation, helping to provide a sense of conversation, albeit through the radio.

As with much public talk, in this case, any concern about whether Curtin's recommendation was the only or best way to defeat the enemy in the circumstances of the time, or any other equivocation was sidelined. Instead, attention was focused on graphic presentation of the speaker's recommended actions, with judgments of worth likely based on his apparent trustworthiness, coherence, and competence, or the authenticity of his concern for his listeners.

Curtin exuded many characteristic features of the straightforward, independent, resolute Australian, and was at his credible best in this speech. His clarity of expression impressed that he spoke bluntly and truthfully, giving the impression that what was revealed of his thinking was truthfully revealed.[161] He could stand credibly as an aggressive defender of democracy.

Allusive Appeal

In a distinctly different way, Menzies often framed his statements within echoes of democratic processes through his dissection of events, without ever mentioning the word democracy. During a long political career, Menzies modulated his stance within a system of constitutional monarchy, democratic government, and the rule of law.[162] By stating his own interpretations of these concepts across a variety of situations, he made *ad populum* and *ad hominem* appeals and adjusted or refined such terms of reference when considering people, actions, and events. He was able to incline on different occasions to be closer to listeners in apparently shared values across a range of listening voters, from those favourable to those opposed.

In the time and context of 20 November 1961, during an election campaign broadcast on national television as a 'Talk to the Nation', Menzies foregrounded the parliamentary process and his own role within it. He thereby made parliamentary democracy, as a form of representative democracy, his touchstone, without mentioning it by name. He advocated that Australians would be 'freer' with his continued leadership, because a unified approach in governing was required to ensure a better future. He projected himself as that protector of national unity. By focusing attention on what he asserted as an inability of his opponents to agree with one another, he sought support for the greater certainty of his unified Government. Quite specifically, he stoked fears of disunited government, which has remained a continuous thread in Australian political rhetoric. Menzies said:

> Because if the truth is–and I think it is–that we have enjoyed in Australia 12 years of remarkable growth and remarkable prosperity, with a remarkably high level of employment, notwithstanding small occasions; if these things have happened, and the nation is stronger, and the people themselves are better off, happier, freer, then I doubt very much whether you would want to change the government, and hand it over–to whom? Hand it over to a collection of people–and about those people I want to say this, with great respect–a collection of people who haven't been able to live together, politically, haven't been able to govern themselves, politically? And now they're asking you to put us out, and to let them govern this country for you. That seems to me to be the very great issue in this election.[163]

This claim for the stability of his own Government was starkly contrasted with Menzies describing the opposition as an 'unstable collection of people'. He emphasised the contrast by repeating positive aspects of his Government, with variants of 'remarkable' for emphasis. He asserted the country's 'remarkable growth… prosperity' and that people were 'stronger', 'better off', 'happier', and 'freer'. Menzies soon afterwards portrayed his opponents as 'wrangling and disputing', as a ramshackle group unable to govern themselves. He depicted them as the *antithesis* of what voters expect of government, whereas, he said of his Government 'We don't wrangle, and dispute. We argue, we agree, we act'.

In this speech, he also used the metaphor of 'good housekeeping' or synonyms for personal well-being and liberty to align himself with listeners. Menzies's approach provided common ground with listeners, while enhancing his credibility as someone in touch with the Australian way of life. As will be described in Chapter Eleven, in furtherance of a sense of having a common touch, Menzies often constructed simulated dialogue with his listeners, to suggest direct conversation in which the supposedly real conversations implied that his views aligned with what real people thought.

Opponents of Curtin, Menzies, or another public figure, and perhaps even some of their supporters, might describe more emotionally charged claims within such speeches as propaganda. During many years of public service, both leaders participated in public debate, analysing issues while demonstrating or urging free and open discussion of the benefits or challenges in initiatives to serve the public good, unlike their contemporaries in autocratic states. While Curtin and Menzies were not strangers to using propaganda processes, the norms and checks of parliamentary democracy in their time tended to moderate the language and actions of politicians to respect individual freedoms. History would likely judge that both leaders not only spoke well, but with commitment to free enquiry and debate while respecting the advancement of truth, law, and justice for the common good.

4: Polemic and Propaganda

...shall we because the way is rough and the sun hot be content to sit

beneath our own vine and fig tree, to be pleasing to the eyes of men,

to pander to their tastes[164]

– Louisa Lawson

Australian public figures have commonly used polemic as a tool to aggressively attack or refute the opinions or principles of another, producing controversy.[165] As the leaders of public causes or nations weave public talk among issues, opinions, or conflicts, they themselves can become controversial or invent controversy. Often, they will also partner humour with polemic, building on hyperbole or overstatement to advance serious persuasive efforts. Essential skills for public communication include navigating potential shocks to listeners' economic, religious, moral, or other norms, as well as standing up to an opponent's polemic. Australia has produced plenty of public figures adept in these areas in its brief, modern history.

William Morris Hughes's fiery, effective polemic became well-known, provoking both admiration and dislike. He was very controversial, and his advocacy is credited in securing Australia's representation separate from Britain at the League of Nations, following World War I. Just one sampling of his sharp tongue was during the 1929 federal election campaign, when he described his conservative opponent S.M. Bruce as sounding the 'bugle for shameful retreat.'[166] Others with earned reputations for effective debate have included Sir Samuel Griffith, Louisa Lawson, Alfred Deakin, Sir Robert Menzies, Oodgeroo, Germaine Greer, Gough Whitlam, Sallyanne Atkinson, Bob Hawke, Sir James Killen, Fred Daly, and Julia Gillard. Many public figures who are accomplished in debate will adeptly use polemic for a variety of purposes, including to decry an opponent, highlight an issue, or produce diversion.

Opposing Views

Controversial statements centre on basic disputes of fact, value, or policy.[167] A proposition framed in any one of these areas requires its own basis of proof. As much as some opinion pollsters might imply otherwise, quantifiable concepts or statistics, including opinion polls themselves, will often have inbuilt controversy.[168] Few numerical or other statements contain their own evidence for truth.

To stimulate controversy is simply intuitive to many public figures. The perception of the speaker or writer also influences the nature of controversy. It is a triad of propositions—fact and value and policy—that coordinate with three main modes by which controversy arises. When in a statement (1) meaning is vague, (2) a value statement is implicit, or (3) polar viewpoints are raised, the potential for controversy is increased.

Polemic, through its effects on the emotions, including the listener's admiration of the verbal acrobatics involved in the construction and delivery of polemic, can be powerful in persuading an audience. On the flipside, when the audience considers polemic excessive, its use can alienate, because of its bitterness or being perceived as overdone. Polemic is also a key tool of the propagandist, and this use will be examined later in the chapter.

Despite the potential for negative effects and despite generally bad connotations often attached to the word 'polemic' in everyday understanding, polemic also has a long and honourable history in public communication, such as through artful applications in parody and satire. With such a range of applications possible, polemic on different occasions might be used to decry opponents, to increase a speaker's apparent dynamism, to capture the attention of listeners or the media, to sustain polarised political debate, or to attract new followers to a cause.

The long association of the polemical mode with public talk is known to be at least since earliest recorded Graeco-Roman history, fueled by people's inclination to think in terms of opposites. And every polemical exchange involves 'opposed views'.[169] The nature of debate on any issue presumes there are at least two sides to be considered. Classical writers felt that pairs of opposites were at work in most situations. A general law had its origins in the ancient argument that opposites come to be out of opposites, so that just as less grows into greater, less comes from greater, or waking follows from sleeping, and so on.[170] Plato recommends dialectic as giving coherence to a person's knowledge,[171] and it has become a commonplace that people use statement of thesis and antithesis to give coherence to argument.

Sensation or Nuance

Frequently, public figures will contrast ideas by using polar propositions. They might also incorporate the conflict of ideas within a metaphor when representing a proposition or to frame a perspective and debate.[172] Obviously, debate presumes the consideration of opposed ideas to 'weigh up' the forces operating and decide on a course of action. In the adversarial context of political communication, polar thinking is institutionalised in various ways, including through the existence of relatively few or just two major political parties in representative democracies. Political campaigns also, by their nature, institutionalise the process of resolving opposite views. In an election, voters choose one view or its supposed opposite.

Hugh Dalziel Duncan wrote that:

> ...a model of rhetoric as used in a democratic society must be a conflict model. Conflict of all kinds, ranging from government by opposition under parliamentary rules, to war, must be accepted as normal to rhetoric. We must accept the fact that as we perfect rhetoric we increase our chances for hate and doubt, as well as love and certainty. Democratic rhetoric involves risk to superiors, inferiors, and equals alike.[173]

Although many issues have more nuances than just two opposing positions, political argument and urgings are often set up to frame reality as a bi-polar competition. Mass media routinely emphasise the polarity of 'two-sides to a case' or two available courses of action, whether or not this is truly so. The news media's attraction to sensationalism results in a preponderance of stories that focus on an extreme, with each extreme implying its own opposite, as well as offering a change from the everyday humdrum for many in the media's audience. Typically, extremes become formulae for what is considered newsworthy, with focus on stories that concern disaster, celebrity, crime, sex, and violence.[174] Long before the Twitter-sphere was added to the village gossip chain, people were prone to such over-simplification and extreme thinking. The prominence of polemic might never become less, with mass media constantly targeting ratings, advertising sales results, and followers, continuously attracted to the extreme case, the catchy phrase, and the controversial quotable quote.

With controversy so megaphoned by mainstream and social media, it is important to recognise the causes and effects of polemic in public talk. More recent polemic that is shaped from nihilist or anarchic conspiracies has produced a stream of manufactured outrage to capture media attention and attract public gaze. To sustain democracy, it is imperative to push back against what are often unanswered monologues that set the public agenda on exaggerations and lies. It is important to hone interpersonal skills to effectively call out inappropriate language and arguments, whether used by public figures or other citizens.

In classical times, a key advocate for democracy was the *rhetor* or responsible citizen, who had interiorised what was best in the culture and applied this knowledge in public forums, influencing fellow citizens to act in accord with their cultural heritage.[175] In Isocrates's view, the *rhetor* pursued the ideals of freedom, self-control, and virtue.[176] The *rhetor* today is the person who is so prepared to speak out and strengthen democracy as civil society.

Within any speech or writing are indicators of the intent, belief, and capability that signal whether someone is a true *rhetor*. How someone represents actions, events, or other citizens will indicate the extent of a person's alignment with values of democracy, one handy expression of which is within the *Universal Declaration of Human Rights* as life, liberty, and security of person.[177] An intent to sustain or strengthen freedoms, including individual freedoms that respect and protect others, might be stipulated as a key distinguishing quality of the modern *rhetor*.

Determining the intent of a speaker or writer though can sometimes be at least as challenging as proving intent in court proceedings. Accordingly, the effects of a communication on individual rights and well-being, along with apparent sincerity in observing truth, law, and justice, are often the better guides to whether someone is committed to democracy. Ethical debates about 'rhetoric' and 'democracy' and their relationship might at least agree that 'virtue must be the care for every city',[178] and for every leader or responsible citizen within it.

Considering the power of polemic, especially in amplifying the effectiveness of propaganda, a wider understanding of and response to the different types of polemic are important—not only to advance proposals responsibly for the common good, but likewise for actively advancing the system of democracy.

Types of Polemic

The pragmatics philosopher, Marcelo Dascal, notes that a polemical exchange involved the employment of language as 'a confrontation of attitudes, opinions, arguments, theories, and so forth'. Aristotle had described types of reasoning as demonstrative, dialectical, and contentious,[179] distinguishing reasoning from opinions that were generally accepted, premises true and primary, or opinions seeming to be generally accepted. Dascal more fully describes three ideal types of polemic as *discussion*, *dispute*, and *controversy*, and urges their detailed evaluation in practice. The concern of *discussion* polemic is truth, with its mode as problem-solving, allowing for solutions by acknowledging mistakes about concepts or procedures. *Dispute* polemic is concerned with winning, with its mode rooted in differences of attitude, feelings, or preferences. It has no mutually accepted procedures for deciding solution. The remedies are punishment, therapy, or disregard.

As a third type of polemic, Dascal viewed *controversy* polemic as an intermediary state between discussion and dispute. Its concern is persuasion, and the mode is deliberative. *Controversy* can begin with specific problems and spread to other problems, leading to profound divergences that are neither solved nor dissolved, and are at best resolved. During *controversy*, which might extend over a considerable time, factors like the weight of evidence and emergence of modified positions might prove acceptable or be clarified as potential resolutions.[180]

Polemical Positions

In both formal and informal talk, speakers can transition among these types, even within a single occasion. When Sir Roderick Carnegie spoke of *Euthanasia by the Independent Australian* in 1975, it was a time when Australian business and conservative groups were feeling buffeted by the pace and reach of legislative and regulatory change driven by Whitlam's reform government. Carnegie was addressing a Law Society event in Sydney when many members of his audience were likely favourably disposed to his position.

Carnegie's key tasks to engage listeners were to intensify interest and vividly illustrate new aspects of the situation, to energise personal responsibility as the call to action. He did not state a solution, did not argue against specific opposing arguments but, with mild exaggeration,[181] requested listeners to take initiative. Using predominantly *discussion* polemic, he began his address by challenging any suggestion that as the head of a company he should refrain from political comment and asserted his right to speak out as 'a vital part of our democracy'.[182] Soon afterwards, he provided a deliberative framework for the controversy that concerned him, by proposing the duality of discipline and freedom of choice, stating that both were required for civilisation.[183]

The activist for First Nation land rights, Kevin Gilbert similarly began his outline of *The Needs of First Nations* (1974) in the mode of *discussion* polemic. He addressed the protection-segregation practices, which caused both bodily and mental harm to First Nations.[184] Doubtless used to addressing audiences who were largely apathetic or opposed to the cause of land rights for First Nations, early in his remarks Gilbert sought to overcome inertia with startling statements, such as stating that some spokespersons of First Nations thought '...all white people are bastards'.[185]

Gilbert hit vital spots with vivid illustrations to find common ground in some attitudes, beliefs, and experiences.[186] He positioned his speech to tell his truth to an audience of mainly European heritage. Soon afterwards, he outlined a core principle from which to shape and sustain his deliberative approach, with the strong statement that 'Europeans ...are taught to be sharks'[187] for their own advancement. He then disputed head-on a series of misunderstandings and mistakes by 'whites', along with highlighting their stereotypes of First Nations peoples, periodically returning to the *discussion* mode.

When women's rights activist, Germaine Greer spoke at the Washington DC Press Club (1971), within her audience were likely some who had limited understanding of her position and beliefs. Doubtless there were also some who were favourable to the thrust of her argument through to others who saw her, as she described herself later, as a 'media freak'.

Greer positioned for *dispute* polemic from her first words to listeners, by sharing her own internal debate about whether to address the assembled group of media representatives as 'Ladies and Gentlemen' or 'Men and Women'–which she said reversed the order. By the end of the second sentence, she carried this question to conclusion, with acknowledgement for '...the elitism of this group by simply calling ourselves "Ladies and Gentlemen."'[188]

Greer then sought common ground. She shared observations about that day's news media, highlighting facts from the day's news stories to illustrate points or to draw conclusions which challenged conventional thinking among her listeners. She made startling statements with potential to stimulate the apathetic in her detailed analysis of the day's news. This exploration of specifics was well suited to engaging the interested but undecided, as well as enabling her to include vivid illustrations that might help engage anyone who was already in favour of her proposition.[189]

Shifts in Polemic

Shifts between the three ideal types of polemic abound among the speakers reviewed. Sir Zelman Cowen (1970)[190] moved readily between polemic of *discussion* and *controversy*. He even-handedly paid tribute to the lasting impact of the 1950s Murray Commission of Inquiry into Australian universities, then directed humour at the Commonwealth Government with a mocking observation. In contrast to the respected Murray Inquiry, Cowen sharply and amusingly differentiated the government reviews in his time:

> The great growth and development of our universities owes much to the political initiatives which established a Commission of Inquiry (known as the Murray Commission for its distinguished British Chairman) which reported in the latter 1950s and had shattering things to say about the state and standards of Australian Universities... It is not that hope springs eternal in the human breast; it is that a rigorous job has been done on us, rather like

Pavlov's dogs, and we go on mechanically doing the job. The difference is that Mr Pavlov was kind to his dogs.[191]

Dame Enid Lyons (1943) moved between what might be *controversy* in the thinking of some of her listeners, 'the weak shall not go to the wall',[192] and *discussion* modes of polemic, addressing 'human values and human hearts and human feelings'.[193] Sir Ian McLennan (1969), as chairman of BHP, mainly adopted a *discussion* mode to outline problems and his solutions within the framework that 'Much has been done… but… there is much to do'. He also subordinated his more controversial suggestions by introducing them with indirect wording, such as 'In terms of numbers, this country also lags far behind USA', or only calling on his industry-audience for '…a substantial degree of financial support'[194] for management education in the last words of the speech.

Varied Approaches

In some speeches, one type of polemic will dominate for much of the speech, such as in Louisa Lawson's case for women's rights, with the mainly passive voice of verbs softening the *dispute* polemic:

> Since the time when equal suffrage was first agitated the subject has been grossly misrepresented and basely caricatured. From the beginning the women who have been its public adherents have been held up by the press and the people as unwomanly creatures, seeking to stir up strife and dissatisfaction, or at least obtain personal notoriety. (1891)[195]

Linden Prowse (1975), arguing for worker's rights, was contentious and taciturn, using *dispute* polemic throughout his remarks. He jumbled metaphors at times to make a point, urging parties '…to get off their individual hobby horses… and pull as a national team'.[196]

Others tended to advance discussion with touches of polemic, framing their contention as a well-circumscribed topic or problem.[197] In a formal eulogy by then union leader Bob Hawke (1975) honouring his predecessor Albert Monk, Hawke sustained a *discussion* mode. While retaining the solemnity of the occasion, any opponents of Monk were reminded of the man's core positive attributes and accomplishments. Using *antithesis* to highlight the breadth of Monk's vision, Hawke sidelined controversy by framing Monk's actions in life within wider principles, recording for posterity that he was committed to justice.[198]

When Sir Samuel Griffith (1895) proposed actions not widely accepted by his audience, he often sustained a *discussion* mode to frame a proposition within general principles. When making his case for federation, Griffith sought to establish a natural law which dictated that only geographical boundaries should separate peoples.[199]

Moves, Tactics, and Appeals

Within the three types of the polemical mode, Dascal also describes tactics employed as three moves, namely *proof, stratagem,* and *argument*.[200] In what he considers to be neither an exhaustive nor exclusive list, he details *proofs* as being inference, induction, reserving retraction rights, or presumptive; *stratagems* that include fallacy, feint, extension, diversion, irritation, confidence building, or compensation; and *arguments* that carry invalid logic in the forms of appeals of *ad hominem* or 'slippery slope', 'causal disaster', 'domino effects', or uselessness of a move.[201]

Just as speakers transition among polemical modes, Dascal outlines how they make transitions among such moves and tactics, with intermingling of these at times. Following are examples mainly framed in the polemical move indicated.

PROOF – to establish truth beyond a reasonable doubt:[202] A speaker uses this mode by stating propositions, using inference and induction. The aim is to develop further propositions or conclusions that support a position–thereby moving listeners toward a presumed truth, such as when Griffith asserted:

> But between one nation and another there was always some physical obstacle of land or water which prevented convenient and rapid communication. It is impossible to point to a single instance where a people, speaking the same language and occupying a territory over which communication was easy and unimpeded, has remained permanently divided for political purposes by artificial boundaries.[203] (Griffith, *The Certainty of Australian Federation*, 1895)

Likewise, Gilbert developed the proposition that being able to vote was worthless, by inferring from the actions of elected politicians that they 'couldn't give a damn' about the lives of First Nations families:

> You showed in the 1967 referendum on Aboriginal rights that you were sincere. But what has it availed the people? Nothing. It's allowed them to go into the pubs. It has allowed them to vote for politicians who couldn't give a damn about their kids dying.[204] (Gilbert, *The Needs of First Nations*, 1974)

Burnet explained why scientists cannot reach final answers, by sharing the inductive process by which scientists reach conclusions. He proposed that this process obligates considering what has 'not yet proved to be wrong'.[205] In these excerpts, Griffith and Burnet were formal in their word choice, sentence length, and sentence structure, putting attention on concepts. In contrast, Gilbert drove home his argument by rapidly listing a series of tangible events in the lives of families, using parallelism and repetition in short phrases to strongly visualise how politicians neglect and abuse the families in First Nations.

STRATAGEM – to cause the audience to (re)act in a certain way, by inducing audience members to believe a proposition to be true:[206]

> Men tell us we are responsible for the home and education of children, that the morals of society are in our keeping; they have bound our hands and placed us in the front rank of the battle raging against intemperance, gambling and impurity, they hold us responsible, and yet take away the only weapon with which to fight. Once in America a body of women presented a petition a quarter of a mile long, bearing the signatures of 200,000 women, with the result that it was rejected as valueless, women having no vote.[207] (Lawson, *Womanhood Suffrage*, 1891)

After stating the responsibility that men had set upon women, Lawson deftly illustrated the fallacy of this circumstance, and highlighted the lack of sincerity in the expectation made by men.

During her maiden speech in parliament, Lyons eloquently yearned to be living at the time when Australia's 'great social and political movements were born' she said, so that she could have experienced the Australian ethos taking shape:

> I should like to have been alive in the days when bushrangers flourished, when life was hard and even raw, when gold was discovered, when colonies became states, and when all of the great social and political movements were born which so coloured the fabric of Australian life; because, during all those years very much of what we now know as the Australian character was formed.[208] (Lyons, *Address-in-Reply*, 1943)

This also anticipated her own bold advocacy of social welfare reforms later in the speech.

Speaking against efforts to conscript Australians as soldiers to fight for the Empire in World War I, the Queensland Premier Thomas Joseph (T.J.) Ryan was a formidable opponent. He mustered substantial support and explained that sufficient troops were already enlisted but not yet deployed. Here Ryan addressed the Commonwealth's efforts to censor the record of this public debate:

> ...the censorship during this campaign is being used for the purpose of suppressing the views of those who are opposed to the conscription proposals of the Commonwealth. [Hear, hear!] The issue that is before the country is of the very gravest importance; it is a proposal to take the power over the life and liberties of the people, and it is imperative that there should be the greatest freedom both in speech, and to the Press...[209] (Ryan, *Government Gazette Extraordinary*, 1917)

In a fluid exchange in 1972, prime minister William McMahon sought to dismiss the visiting American consumer advocate, Ralph Nader, by claiming America would not have received an Australian who was the 'professional pot stirrer' that McMahon had accused him to be. Nader coolly and quickly countered by pointing out that Germaine Greer had been 'very well received'[210] in the United States.

Each of these speakers used polemical tactics with the common purpose of rendering the listeners unable to react with a satisfactory countermove.[211] Lawson took to its logical extension a common deflection used by men, thereby demonstrating its fallacy. Lyons built patriotically charged reasons for wanting to have lived at an earlier romanticised and vibrant time of Australia's development, as a precursor to advocating bold reforms herself. To safeguard 'life and liberties', Ryan opposed conscription and offered context for the censorship by the Commonwealth, asserting that prime minister Hughes was duping voters. McMahon used a variety of schemes to seek an advantage over Nader, who nonetheless called him out.

Inferences of the type used in *stratagems* commonly employ fallacy, feint, extension, diversion, confidence building, compensation, and a host of variants to obtain advantage. The excerpts noted included extension and irritation (Lawson), *ad populum* and confidence building (Lyons), extension and confidence building (Ryan), as well as name-calling, irritation, feint, and diversion (McMahon).

ARGUMENT – to persuade the addressee to believe that a proposition is true. Urging belief in a claim, a speaker provides 'recognisable reasons' presumed to be accepted by an audience.[212] *Argument* might focus on facts but alternatively addresses presumptions figuratively, drawing on the power of analogy, allusion, or inuendo.

Hughes drew on these modes both to propose that military training be compulsory and later to pillory an opponent in parliament.[213] In 1907, speaking to a British audience, he opened a speech at Westminster on the topic of military training by aligning the needs of Australia and Britain, and then appealed to his British listeners by recognising what he called the motherland's greater needs. He likened a duty of compulsory military training successively to nursing children or vaccination against diseases, claiming that by analogy such duties were not to be delegated. He dismissed as positions wrong or unpatriotic the arguments that avoided what he considered to be some primary responsibilities of a citizen. More vigorously, he used exaggeration and colourful language during a famous exchange in the Australian parliament in 1909, to mount a comparison of recent actions of Alfred Deakin with those of Judas. He finally dismissed any drawing of similarity between Deakin and Judas, because, unlike Deakin, Judas did the 'decent' thing by hanging himself.

In her National Press Club speech, Greer used the tangible example of a news story from that day's news to encourage her journalism-focused audience to consider a contentious view of their own roles. She made a quick content analysis of the day's news reports to point out that journalists also 'make' the news. She contrasted the greater coverage given to herself, whom she referred to as a 'complete media freak', compared with the 'more important' Child Care Bill which rated 'five column inches and no graphics or pictorials and not even much of a heading'.[214] This and her other examples proposed a much broader principle that journalists created news, then a proposition not without controversy.

Yet another illustration of using Argument as a mode of polemic was Gilbert's highlighting the ongoing debasement efforts of 'European Australians' that continuously denied the identity of First Nations, which is discussed further in Chapter Twelve. Gilbert repeated with variation the powerfully negative verbs 'debase' and 'kick' to visualise the abuse and neglect that caused shame and resulted in efforts of some members of First Nations to try to pass themselves off as white.[215] Each speaker focused on the emotional implications of a claim to assert it as true.[216]

Tactics

Dascal further points out that speakers seeking to have a proposition believed as true using Argument will draw on a variety of tactics to demonstrate the uselessness of an opponent's proposition or secure an obligation from listeners to adhere to social norms. These include slippery slope, causal disaster, and domino effects–for example, during the Cold War era, the threat of communist invasion of successive countries.

Even in the early stages of election campaigns, such polemic is common enough in just about any campaign talk. During the communist scaremongering in Australia at the time of the Petrov Affair, Menzies opened his election campaign in 1954 with a policy speech plainly focused in this way.[217] He asked a series of loaded questions about where Labor leaders stood in relation to communism. His questions defied simple answers and could only leave negative inferences hanging heavily in the air. He modeled explicitly for listeners that they should conclude that Labor leaders were 'trimming their sails to the prevailing winds of public opinion'.

Akin to this approach, John Curtin in a 1940 campaign pamphlet directly addressed the 'enemies' of his party. He declared:

> To the irresponsibles, the propagandists and the controversialists, I say: Devote your energies to something more useful in the national interest ... Labor has pledged its all. It is giving its all. We will win through by the strong arm of the working men and women; not by the idle chatter of disruptionists.[218]

The inference that the worker is the salt of the earth has not decreased in potency or breadth of appeal; nor has the potency of exorcising propagandists.

Both Menzies and Curtin, from opposing political parties, recognised the value of controversy for persuasion. Each chose issues that were local in application and stimulated wider passions. Their comments furthered controversy, to affirm the support of believers and potentially to persuade people to change from one side to another, while assisting with the recruitment of new adherents from the uncommitted.[219]

Election Polemic

The Election Policy Speech by Australian Labor leader John Curtin in 1937 provided some representative examples of the integration of polemical modes and tactics within a party platform speech. The speech also has some historical interest, since, although Curtin lost this election to the incumbent United Australia Party, he reunited his party and saw its vote rise by a remarkable 16.3 percent to 43.1 percent. This was the party's best performance since 1929. Curtin opened the speech at the Town Hall in Freemantle, Western Australia on 20 October 1937 with the statement:

> The real decision which the people of Australia are called upon to make at this election is one of values. The Labor Party declares that the immediate task of statesmanship is to overcome the forces which are undermining the moral, social and economic foundations of civilisation.[220]

Well in evidence was the characteristic Curtin style, with forceful, clear, unequivocal statements—the predominantly plain speaker—the instructor—the straightforward person concerned with the nation's future.

The speech very soon made use of four polemical approaches common in Australian politics. The first was to blame opposing individuals for particular social ills. Curtin made the comment about his opponent, Joseph Lyons:

> In his policy speech three years ago the Prime Minister said that the government would engage in a number of sound major employment works... He also promised to assign a Commonwealth Minister to definite responsibilities for Commonwealth action in relation to employment, but no such Minister was appointed... As against this record of unfulfilled promises: the government has embarked upon frequent Ministerial visits to other countries.[221]

Alleged failure to address unemployment and the portrayal of ministerial travels overseas as tourist jaunts occur frequently in Australian political campaigns.

The second approach was to play on traditional fears and distrust of elitist groups, or communists, or other minorities. After a long tirade against favoured groups in the community, Curtin pivoted to address the concerns of neglected constituents:

> I ask the workers if they are enjoying a prosperity unexampled in our history? I put the same question to the farmers and the primary producers generally. I put it to many in the middle class? And in each instance the answer must be an emphatic negative.[222]

Curtin continued then to show the opulence of 'powerful financial groups'. Such statements have occurred frequently in speeches of Labor Party leaders.

Thirdly, Curtin made loud his party drumbeating. He said:

> From its very inception the Labor movement has stood for Australian national defence. It provided the first Australian Government which transformed words into facts. It gave Australia a Navy—a well-trained Navy—a national small arms factory, a national woollen mills [sic], a national clothing factory, a national munition works and behind all these essentials to the defence of the nation it gave Australia the national note issue and the Commonwealth Bank.[223]

Such revival of past glories to challenge an opponent's record again is common in the rhetoric of Australia's political parties and carries emotional loading.

Finally, Curtin made explicit an aspect of his social philosophy in an assertive manner. He said:

> The best way in which a widow with dependent children can do her greatest work in Australia is not by competing for wages, but by carrying on to the best of her ability in her home the work of mothercraft so that her children may be given the best maternal guidance to become the future citizens of a great Commonwealth.[224]

Of note here were the not too subtle puffery for Australian greatness and that home fires were warmest for a widow, in 1937.

Controversy and Values

In these sample excerpts, Curtin's tone was argumentative and the subject, to varying degrees, controversial for the circumstances of the times. In each case, he made an evaluative statement or value judgment laden with emotional overtones and presented these as if he were making mere statements of fact. Curtin pushed the envelope on Australians' general preference for understatement by including words with varying levels of emotional loading, such as 'unfulfilled promises', 'Ministerial visits to other countries', 'powerful financial groups', 'national defence', 'mothercraft', and 'a great Commonwealth'. Throughout the speech, he sustained his argument with a sincere tone and an impassioned overtone, showing concern for the welfare of a broad sweep of people and the country. In his closing comments, he drew together the ideas of policy and associated these with the name of the Labor Party—the party that he advocated would safeguard the 'peace and happiness' of the people.

The extent to which this speech or any policy speech was successful is of course an individual interpretation within the time of its delivery, with some insight on impact potentially glimpsed in press reports. Curtin's policy speech three years later seemed somewhat modelled on this 1937 version and might be considered a far more powerful speech. The extent of media coverage the morning after each speech delivery suggested that at least journalists and editors found the 1940 speech better press. With the onset of war by 1940, Curtin's slogan 'We must win the peace as well as the war' was given prominence.[225] The more open-ended slogan of 1937, 'For a happy and self-reliant Australia' received little press attention. Concrete aspects of Curtin's 1937 speech, such as 'unemployed insurance' during the recovery from the Great Depression, naturally, were given prominence. So too, was a statement from Joseph Lyons as prime minister taking issue with Curtin's remarks on communism.[226] How the world changes in some ways but changes so little in the type of concerns that attract media attention.

Curtin, in the eyes of diverse political groups, was widely regarded as one of the most sincere and forthright politicians in Australian history. Menzies paid Curtin about as generous a compliment as offered to an opponent in politics when the Labor Government replaced his, by saying that although Curtin had rendered him 'many wounds... none of them have been in the back'.[227] Throughout Curtin's public life, on many occasions he made use of polemic that supported his overall purpose of recommending the value of his party's ideals. In this, listeners appeared to relate well to his continuous seriousness as projection of authenticity.

Humour with Polemic

Added impact occurs when polemic and humour combine well in public talk, with listeners welcoming the added dexterity of a speaker to handle a situation and words for humorous effect. In political speech, this is particularly so when the abuse of an interjector is turned back on that opponent. In the 1975 federal election campaign, responding to an interjector who demanded to hear Whitlam's policy on abortion, Whitlam said that in the case of the interjector 'it ought to be retrospective'.[228] This swiftness of reply projected Whitlam's dynamism.

Polemic, which so effectively targets an opponent, highlights for listeners the awareness, intelligence, and liveliness of the speaker. On another occasion, a question to Whitlam in parliament, from a Liberal opponent, drew attention to Whitlam's own comments on the subject under consideration. This stimulated Whitlam's comeback that he appreciated having his opponent's speech drawn to his attention, remarking that it was a 'splendid speech... mostly comprised... [of] ...quotations'[229] from Whitlam's own speeches. The prime minister Paul Keating was also very artful in this to-and-fro of debate, such as in his reworking a gibe, which had variants in Britain and Australia back to at least 1966, to describe his opponent John Hewson in 1989 as '...simply a shiver looking for a spine to run up'.[230]

It was Menzies though, perhaps more than any other Australian political figure, who showed consistently the value of using verbal projectiles to target an opponent, often mixing *dispute* polemic in a simulated *discussion* mode. Menzies displayed a cutting wit and is remembered for his ability to join in a verbal brawl and win, perhaps almost as much as for his long tenure as prime minister. Election meetings with Menzies as the star were not to be missed, as he took on even the most denigrating interjectors, treated them with humorous contempt and came out on top. One famous incident widely reported from an election meeting at Williamstown, Victoria typified his art. During his speech, a woman interjected from the side of the hall that she would not vote for him if he was the Archangel Gabriel. To which Menzies imperiously replied, 'If I were the Archangel Gabriel, madam, I'm afraid you wouldn't be in my electorate'.[231]

Lively Words

A relatively small group of Australian politicians are remembered as the lively figures able to place politics on a light-hearted plane, while using *dispute* polemic unambiguously in their efforts to contest opponents and seek support. Fred Daly, in the intense aftermath of Whitlam's dismissal in 1975, indulged in mockery, claiming at a public rally in Brisbane that the Treasurer who was appointed two days previously 'Phil the Plumber...[Lynch]...he can't even read'.[232] This received a rousing response in support from attendees at the rally. Lynch's recent role in destabilising the Whitlam cabinet provided fuel for this polemic and Daly added to his own reputation as a colourful figure, as someone interesting to listen to.

Foremost among Daly's sparring opponents was the Member for Moreton in Queensland, Sir James Killen. The conventions of ornate invective established between these opponents could sustain extended, scathing exchange, during which each seemed to enjoy as much as listeners the verbal acrobatics and one upmanship occurring. During an exchange between Killen and the Labor firebrand Eddie Ward, even the strongest personal attack could appear to reach a satisfying détente with Killen's gibe '...you wouldn't be respectable crow bait'.[233] With one-upmanship as the goal, *dispute* polemic will often accept no resolution or remedy other than submission or continued contest.

Coherent or Not?

One of the most effective politicians to use polemic to advance his own position was the Queensland premier, Sir Joh Bjelke-Petersen, who polarised the community and consolidated supporters in tribe-like loyalty behind him. Even conferences with the media that he held late most afternoons, he openly disparaged as 'feeding the chooks' [chickens].

In his incoherence or incongruity of statements, Bjelke-Petersen often appeared unintentionally humorous, such as the banality for the context of the time, of thanking 'men and women… who have been working together with their husbands'. Despite almost 20 years as premier (1968-87), Bjelke-Petersen's attempt to become prime minister failed, but delivered yet more confusing polemic. He challenged someone's claim that the 'wheels were coming off' his campaign for prime minister, by asserting 'the wheels are still on'[234] and threatening to run over anyone who was in his way. Bjelke-Petersen's apparently disconnected ramblings were assiduously tracked and reported by journalists—to be pilloried by opponents and applauded by supporters.

Bjelke-Petersen characteristically used *non sequiturs* in *ad populum* and *ad hominem* appeals to unite some listeners with him, sharing laughter at the discomfort of a victim. One of his more outrageous and widely reported comments was directed at Helen Bonner, an anti-uranium campaigner and former Miss Australia. She took exception to being labelled by Bjelke-Petersen as a communist by association, after she had expressed sympathy for the rights of street-marching protesters. Bjelke-Petersen rejoined with a triad that anyone flying, squawking, and looking like a crow '…can't yell out if you get shot at'.[235]

Performance

A public figure who crafts polemic 'as a menace which threatens the total personality'[236] of another travels the propagandist's path. Even when the abuse or threat of the individual is said to be intended as humour, display, or theatrics, it is short distance to the erosion of individual freedoms.

Such demagogue-like performance conforms to the ritual of public theatre, in which 'the political prisoner (the so-called cause of the conflict) is caught within the ritual and becomes a sacrificial victim whose suffering and "death" absolves the speaker and the community of sin and guilt'.[237] According to this interpretation, the frame of public theatrics absolves citizens of any obligation or opportunity to be involved. This explanation contends that the public argument is represented as between the sacred and the profane, with conflict as a burden comparable to a sin. By watching the defeat of the individual who 'caused the conflict', vicariously, citizens become purified.

Whether such a speculative interpretation adequately explains the often-subdued response of citizens to the public pillory of another citizen by a government leader of higher social power is debatable. Certainly, an analogous situation would be our finding humour in complicity against a victim in slapstick. Polemic directed against people in this way constitutes abuse that is no longer tolerated elsewhere in the community, such as in the home or workplace.

When public debate becomes just a ritual of polarisation and distraction, its predictability can outpace any initial sparks of interest, ultimately resulting in audience boredom and/or apathy. The failure to moderate this dynamic delivers conditions suitable for a demagogue to dismantle the democratic system without objection. Public communications become meaningless or ineffective, other than as distraction and catharsis of sorts for the lead participants. Such behaviours invite barbarism, dressed up as theatrical display.

Effects of Polemic

When concentrated polemic is continuously used for such attention-getting, a climate of outrage can all too quickly dominate. Unless moderated, this behaviour feeds into some media belief that it will be able to sustain an audience through continuously updated reports of the outlandish. In this circumstance, political speech becomes oversimplistic and moribund. Perhaps these effects are most enabled by the conventions that govern the media, often preoccupied with the story or programming that exhibits little that is truly innovative or remarkable. In the sometimes-glittery process of polemic, wherein the rules are largely known, and the players are safe within certain bounds of the law and some mercurial norms of propriety, what takes shape is formulaic polarity that seems to appeal to the media.

With public figures yearning so much for access to the megaphone the media offers, it will be increasingly important to moderate manufactured outrage effectively. It will also be important to increase the strength of a free media, for it to play its pivotal role in helping to sustain democracy. In this context, the government itself has a duty to sustain true freedom of information. Peter Robinson, a former editor of the Australian *Financial Review*, remarked as long ago as 1976 that '…it is … grossly wrong for government–as it does–to hold out the threat, for any reason, of cutting off basic news sources to the media'.[238]

Adept use of startling or controversial statements is bait by which public figures influence and seek to dominate the content of the media, to control attention in an important sphere of public discourse. Polemic is a powerful tool for public figures to set the agenda of the public's attention, and to substantially impact how the media and public figures interact. Regrettably, as witnessed in Australia, the United States, and elsewhere more recently, some public figures are very skilled in using polemic to take command of mainstream and social media. They seem prepared to say whatever ensures media coverage, good or bad, in their belief that all media coverage is good. Such talk will often be so outrageous that it distracts from ulterior motives or actions of bad actors.

Moreover, in Australia voters are compelled by unique laws to vote at all elections. Yet the law cannot likewise legislate political awareness. Many years ago, one serious commentator remarked:

> Australians are subject to almost continuous electioneering and it may be no wonder that a large number of them remain immune to most of it, take little or no interest in policies and when forced to the polls thankfully accept one party's 'How to Vote' card, take it into the booth (which is contrary to the law) and copy it. It would take a great deal of political interest for a citizen to keep abreast of the candidates, campaigns and issues.[239]

Voters in a modern democratic society clearly deserve better ways to evaluate and improve political speech, to enhance the effectiveness of democracy.

At the simplest level for individual action, to defeat bad actors in the image of earlier infamous propagandists, some practical steps are:

1. Ignore any verbal refuse designed to distract, deny, or delay the initiatives or actions that advance truth, law, and justice—by all means, counter with the truth, but stop repeating the words of the propagandist—you are just being a megaphone for what you oppose.
2. Friends in the media need to be told apparently that there is not much that a bad actor fears more than being ignored—at the very least, media commentators and journalists should stop using or repeating a bad actor's name, stop repeating direct quotes in the lower thirds of the television screen, and stop showing 'B-Roll' of a bad actor, instead of doing the job of a media journalist or anchor-person, which is to paraphrase (at most) the bad actor's comments, if needed at all.
3. Encourage leaks of sensitive information that expose lies and fraud.
4. Reverse any serious lie right back onto the liar, using words much like the graffiti artist sprays a beard, moustache, or horns on a propaganda poster.
5. Exponentially grow networks of person-to-person communications, especially through personal emails and personalised tweets.[240]

When what is outrageous is given play without mediation, whether to satisfy the 24/7 news cycle's thirst for audience ratings or for any purpose, this puts democracy at risk. We all share responsibility to call out public figures who use polemic to skew message accuracy or threaten individual freedoms. Democracy only thrives when people speak out to sustain informed and conscious dialogue about realities. Finally, if enough citizens believe in winning by communicating, and commit the effort to do so vigorously and well, democracy will win.

5: Rhetorical Humour

When the ears of an audience are tickled

the approaches to its intelligence and sympathy become easier [241]

– Sir George Reid

A most potent way to make serious advocacy is through humour–to make one's presence felt and set an agenda and relationship with an audience. The Australian poet Les Murray suggests 'the ability to laugh at venerated things, and at awesome and deadly things may…be one of Australia's great gifts'[242] but this is not unique to Australia. Alfred Deakin displayed an elegant and acerbic wit, commenting that Sir Henry Parkes always had to adjust himself '…in his mind's eye… [to] …his own portrait as that of a great man'.[243] Such personal mockery of vanity or the 'tall-poppy' is just one way that notable Australians have influenced an audience's view of the target of the humour and the competence of the speaker, while on occasion attracting the attention of the news reporter.

Quite a few of the public figures considered here used humour in public communications. Sir Robert Menzies frequently used impromptu and prepared humour to build rapport with an audience, further enhancing belief in his competence and promoting his ideas. These multiple purposes were in play when, on the Fourth of July 1963, he commenced the Jefferson Oration at Charlotteville, Virginia by noting the 'rare privilege for the Prime Minister of a nation of something under eleven millions of people to be invited' to deliver the address, as the only non-American at that time ever asked to do so. He further commented in the speech that:

> When people in England make jesting remarks to me about these lowly origins of our now thriving and law-abiding Commonwealth, I make the good-natured retort that, though many thousands of convicted persons were sent to America and many thousands to Australia—the records show—that the great majority of persons convicted in England during the transportation era remained in England![244]

Personal Humour

Bob Hawke was adept at using humour to build a personal relationship. He often used a mix of humour directed at both listeners and against himself. In an address to the Australasian Society of Accountants, not always an easy audience for a union leader as he then was, Hawke related an unflattering description of the auditor, before moving to conclude the speech by acknowledging that his audience might think similarly of his own role as a union leader.[245] Such careful avoidance of making a slight or insult of anyone listening is recommended unless, as Hawke frequently ensured, the speaker is at least as severely a butt for the humour. This advice is often ignored by politicians, especially during interjections or in 'roasts', where the speaker feels there is opportunity to bring the crowd onside at the cost of another as the 'victim'.

Gough Whitlam frequently used humour for effect and seemed especially fond of pointing to historical significances or parallel events in history to strengthen his case. When the Liberal-Country Party Coalition Government announced the date of the election for 1972, which Whitlam would go on to win, he responded to the notification of the date:

> So now we have the date, and I must say that I think it is jolly decent of the Prime Minister to let us know officially.
>
> The second of December is a memorable day; it is the anniversary of Austerlitz. Far be it from me to wish, or to appear to wish, to assume the mantle of Napoleon, but I cannot forget that 2nd December was the date on which a crushing defeat was administered to a coalition—a ramshackle, reactionary coalition.[246]

Whitlam drew attention to what is ordinarily a routine reply to an announcement of election day by offering a fresh way to view the event. This was more than mere display on his part[247] for, although his wide knowledge was exceptional, his choices of humorous historical or literary allusion were invariably apt to reinforce his case.

Previously, Whitlam had identified the Liberal-Country Party Government of the time as being like the Bourbons.[248] In doing so, he seemed to moderate his language carefully, perhaps in an attempt to diminish his listeners charging him with intellectualism, as will be discussed later, in Chapter Six. This aspect of

Whitlam's humour appeared to be prompted by a deep understanding of parallels in actions or events and, in some cases, a concern that others should recognise that history need not be repeated.

Getting Attention

With a different tenor, but the comparable purpose of gaining attention, Greer's humour often relies on shock value to reinforce her message. In her address to the United States National Press Club, she reinforced a point within her remarks that the news media, in cooperation with business created artificial wants in women as a type of exploitation. She highlighted what she called 'the great vaginal odour story', indicating that pharmaceutical companies had 'discovered... what is called in marketing manuals "spare capacity"'.[249] Her tackling a taboo topic, with a combination of intelligent subtlety and play on words, seemed to be well received by this audience that was so committed to words in their profession.

In addition, this is both hostile and sexual, according to Freud's classification of types of humour,[250] having particular 'edge' at that time when spoken by a woman, since people seemed wrongly to stereotype women as timid and submissive.[251] Not only did this story elicit her first laughter from the gathered group, but the story, of all the contents of the speech, was picked up by newspapers and covered widely—an important consideration, since her speech was also to promote her then recently published book, *The Female Eunuch*. Using the wordplay or pun gave added impact, and this is a common form of humour in Greer's communication.

Exploring Humour

Victor Raskin's theory of humour for short verbal jokes suggests two distinct and opposite 'scripts' are juxtaposed and Michael Phillips-Anderson notes three major approaches to political humour, namely superiority, relief, and incongruity.[252] Through these approaches, effective humour locates a speaker or writer's stance on the topic and toward an audience. Yet no formula guarantees guidance for creating or assuring humour. Certainly, the effective, humorous speech needs to be more than formulaic strings of jokes that too often weave a web of mediocrity. When humour is used well, it identifies, integrates, and reinforces elements of the communication or the entire theme.

The better explorations of humour distinguish between what creates humour and its effects. To stimulate humour, Walter Nash noted the need to build into the language of humour some cultural precedent common to the speaker/writer and the audience. He observes that material facts set an expectation and likely direction, and some word or phrase then serves as the *language trigger* cum centre of energy. Nash suggests that the humorous effect dances on an ambiguity, allusion, hyperbole, parody, or over/understatement etc., as well as setting anticipation of a punchline through a surprise outcome. This is delivered by the *language trigger*[253] through a pun, insult, or other quip.

Henri Bergson maintains that we find humour in what is strictly human and that we admire the intelligence required to create humour. He suggests that at the point of laughing an audience is emotionless toward people who suffer insult and, in slapstick, injury.[254] In these cases, the effect is that members of an audience can share a group feeling of complicity against the victim.[255] Stephen Leacock facetiously distinguishes his own humour as but a rather ingenious mixture of hyperbole and *meiosis*.[256]

Political Effects

In relation to the political effects of humour, Phillips-Anderson provides a review of theories of humour in these contexts.[257] He suggests that the strategies commonly used in political communication demonstrate cleverness, deflect personal criticism, and attack an opponent personally, while maintaining the esteem of the audience. He observes that some combination of these might be accomplished with a single humorous quip or narrative.[258]

A common approach to suggesting cleverness that he notes was to influence the audience's feelings about the speaker and situation. In this mode, the early prime minister, Sir George Reid likely connected well with listeners through his quick comeback to being hit by an old egg that a heckler threw, 'Another of my opponent's arguments—rotten, of course'.[259] Likewise, at a banquet in 1974, Whitlam recommended to the Lord Mayor of London their shared interest in rowing, rather than cricket, as an especially suitable sport in public life, 'because you can face one way while going the other'.[260] Not to be bettered by an interjection during an address at the All Nations Club on Australians' racial origins, Menzies pivoted on the interjector to advance the theme of his speech:

> When I married my wife, I thought she was of practically pure Scots derivation. I discovered too late that she is practically Irish to the back teeth. [*Laughter.*] Well, there we are, you see. These things are all a mixture. And when you talk about an Englishman (*Interjection:* 'That's the best of the part'.) Would yer mind saying that with a bit of a brogue? [*Laughter*][261]

The second identified strategy of deflecting attention enables a speaker to otherwise divert the audience's attention away from an inconvenient matter. This will be done by making light of a matter, to set a personal distance from it, and making it easier to introduce a new topic. Especially in press conferences, Menzies was the master of diversion. During a visit to Indonesia, when a journalist put a question concerning the shared border of the two nations, '…will

Australia remain passive if Indonesia uses armed forces to release West Irian?',
Menzies mockingly replied:

> You know that is rather like the old question: 'If you had a brother would he like cheese.' [*Laughter.*] I am much too old, though, in this business to be answering hypothetical questions. [*Laughter.*]262

On another occasion, Menzies quickly redirected focus to the self-serving character of an opponent's compliment, to deflect attention:

> QUESTIONER: The Leader of the Labour Party in the Queensland Parliament Mr Duggan, has described you as one of the outstanding public men Australia has ever had... PRIME MINISTER: I bet there's a catch coming [*Laughter.*] QUESTIONER: ...but he says that you are politically lazy, he said: 'Mr Menzies had done great disservice to Australia because every international Mission with which he had been associated had been a colossal failure'. Would you reply to his statement? PRIME MINISTER: Oh, I wouldn't dream of sitting in judgment on Mr Duggan; I doubt whether I'm equal to that task.263

Likewise, in the spirit of avoidance, was Whitlam's exchange with the British television interviewer, David Frost, which had commenced with a question of how many Russian spies there were in Australia. After a follow-up series of questions and responses about the number of spies in Australia from China, Britain, and America, Frost asked 'Do you have spies in Britain?', to which Whitlam responded, 'That's a secret'.264

The third strategy Phillips-Anderson notes is to maintain or create with an audience an image of the public figure or of an opponent. The prime minister Alfred Deakin used humour in this way to completely shift perspective about a dilemma he faced in 1904. Following the first two federal elections, none of the three political parties could rule workably. When addressing this serious situation at a luncheon of the Australian Natives' Association, Deakin said:

> What a game of cricket you would have if there were three elevens in the field instead of two, and one of those elevens sometimes playing on one side, sometimes on the other, and sometimes for itself. [*Laughter.*] I think that homely illustration best describes the difficulty. That is the difficulty which the new parliament has to face, and it is a task the difficulty of which has been exceeded. [*A voice.*–It is simply 'cut throat euchre'.] [*Laughter.*] Mr Deakin.–If the interjector has found that a simple game it is not my experience. [*Laughter.*] It is a game in which the "joker" plays' too large a part. [*Laughter.*]265

Multiple Values

When used well, humour is a potent means by which an individual expresses dynamism, intelligence, and sensitivity to an audience, since laughter is a cognitive, emotional, and physical response to both the ideas expressed and to personality. When analysing conversational style, Deborah Tannen comments on the distinctiveness of humour to set a 'person's style' and make 'one's presence felt'.[266] Other analyses of humour suggest that laughter in conversation is used for a variety of communicative functions, from 'covering delicate passages… to demonstrating understanding'.[267]

In a review of the hurly-burly of parliamentary and electoral politics in Australia, Mark Rolfe sketches some continuous patterns of Australians both laughing *with* and *at* politicians.[268] He neatly points to three tactics concerning the 'snout-in-the-trough' stereotype of personal greed often ascribed to politicians. He shares various examples that have been used to *connect* greed and corruption to an opponent; *damn* an opponent as representative of the political class, committed to gorging themselves; or *make contrast* with the binary of the crooked politician, in the form of a newcomer to politics, who is able to be the untainted saviour of democracy. Rolfe notes representations of what are 'today dismissed as the politics of envy'.[269] Both worker representatives and conservatives have made use of such humour to characterise opponents, by using a turn of phrase to deliver the humorous *language trigger* and produce the sting.

For a great many years, the humour in Australian politics reflected the humour of men, with focus on blatant abuse, insult, or obscenities. The relatively few women in the Australian Parliament predominantly faced patronising sexism. Dame Enid Lyons in 1943 used 'homely metaphors', comparing herself to a new broom, as an amusing signal to her male counterparts of the reforms she would advocate.

Ken Inglis notes that Kathy Martin Sullivan in 1993 testified to her experience after twelve years in the Senate and the House that when a woman spoke in parliament, most of the men 'close their ears believing that they are about to hear fringe-feminist rhetoric which is to be automatically rejected'. The Democrat Senator Vicki Bourne recalls that, unable to get a word in, she eventually began shouting back. 'They shut up. I started off with the conciliatory approach and was treated with utter contempt. When I reverted to the aggressive male style, I was treated with respect.'[270]

Metaphor and Beyond

Of all the speakers considered in the public sphere, Michael Kirby is perhaps the most adept at incorporating humour for a variety of purposes, as will be described further in Chapter Fifteen. He readily sustained a story against himself and his profession and used word play ('Kellymania'[271]) or irony of situation to make an apparently easy and full integration of the humour to express a theme or major point of a speech. As with other speakers, Kirby used much more humour than the prepared or recorded manuscript of a speech captured. Speakers will often add in some appropriate quips during delivery.

Delivery qualities are especially important for the effective use of humour. Kirby comments more broadly on the value of nonverbal qualities beyond the printed words. He notes the importance of the 'physical appearance of the speaker; the tone and attractiveness of the voice; and the pauses, interruptions and eyebrow raising that can make the whole thing work', remarking that 'Churchill was an absolute master of the pause'—with much being lost when oral humour is reduced to print.[272] The following excerpt though shows Kirby's incorporation of humour to encourage consideration of a serious subject:

> My task is to 'define' the Media Peace Prize. I am under instructions to do so briefly. Of course, a lawyer (and a judge) is almost professionally incapable of brevity. One famous English judge never hesitated to speak for hours on occasions such as this. He once confided to a colleague that he never troubled when the audience looked at its watch. How do you know when to stop, he was asked, 'It's when they look at their watch and shake it, that I know'.
>
> Another judge on one occasion droned on for an hour and a half. He finished what he had to say with the following pearls:
>
> 'Mr Chairman. I fear I have gone on far too long. I have to apologise to everyone. You see, the trouble is I have no watch with me. And there is no clock in the hall'.
>
> From the back of the hall came a laconic comment:
>
> 'There is a calendar on the wall behind you'.
>
> I shall be brief. There *is* a calendar in front of us all. It reminds us of the transiency and fragile quality of human existence. As we meet, war, catastrophe, crisis and confrontation exist in the four corners of the world. The Media Peace Prize is a practical Australian initiative to reward the most constructive efforts of those who, in the year past, have used the modern media of communication to promote the non-violent resolution of conflicts.[273]

Here Kirby used instructions given to him concerning the preferred duration of his speech to link his humorous quips. He then converted the literal meaning of 'calendar' to a metaphorical sense, as a method to introduce a second meaning of 'time', now in the sense of 'timeliness'. He thereby introduced the theme of his speech, which might be paraphrased as the timeliness, importance, and worthiness of an award for responsible journalism. Such shifting of a frame of reference for humorous effect is common enough,[274] but even though humour lends itself to use in this way, in public talk much sophistication in speaking ability is needed to do so. Beyond this, a further level in the use of humour is as the framework to organise an entire speech. A speaker then weaves humour throughout the speech around a central theme to highlight a sequence of issues. Relatively few speakers and some humourists or comedians manage such performances on a regular basis.

Among Australian humourists, Phillip Adams is especially notable for astute political satire of this quality since the 1960s. His social and political commentary in his satirical columns for many newspapers, and continuously in *The Australian*, offers inspiration for individuals to find new approaches and methods. Comedians like Paul Hogan and, from New Zealand, John Clarke[275] have also shown how to sustain routines or satire for extended comic commentary on current events or culture.

These talents are somewhat akin to the celebrated hayseed humourist, Will Rogers, in the early twentieth century in the United States, whose apparent bumbling through complicated non-sentences included interspersed punchlines or 'zingers' that often triggered from a single word, to echo authenticity and a sense of wisdom. Sophisticated speakers and writers might look to these exemplars of artfulness to use humour in sustained ways, for serious purposes. Sir Winston Churchill captures the spirit of such rhetorical humour, commenting, 'During my life I have often had to eat my own words and I have found them a wholesome diet'.[276] It is the rare speaker or writer who is able to live up to this boast.

6: Political Words and Gough Whitlam

'...to restore faith in this Parliament... it should have the courage to submit itself

and the actions of a minority to the judgment of the people...[277]

– Gough Whitlam

In a variety of communications, public figures persuasively use the political vocabulary of symbol,[278] slogan,[279] jargon, and political slang. Slogans will often be most noted, because of their frequent use in high profile election campaigns. Campaign slogans serve to focus debate and unify, even though a slogan's persuasive value in an election matters less than often thought. In speeches or writing, public figures less frequently use slogans, which tend to be found in a principal party policy speech or in emotive speeches at other rallies.

Slogan

A *slogan* is a short and striking or memorable phrase associated with a political party, movement, or other group, or a word or phrase used to express a characteristic position, or stand, or a goal to be achieved.[280] Slogans encapsulate such rallying cries as *Black lives matter, Scotland forever,* and *No taxation without representation,* or campaign slogans like *It's time, I like Ike,* and *Had enough?* Many slogans though have potency for only a limited time.

An opponent's mockery or attack of a slogan can also influence its emotional impact when the opponent's response resonates, such as when the 1957 British Conservatives' slogan, *Never had it so good* was rebuffed with the Labour Party's response, *Never been had so good.* Some slogans endure through continuous refreshment, such as Australia's annual commemoration of the nation's loss of life in wars, with *Lest We Forget*, or the commemorative slogan in the United States in reference to the 11 September 2001 terrorist attacks, *Never Forget*.

In the context of Australian elections, Sally Young has noted the changing character of election slogans with different uses in different times, especially with the greater personalisation of politics, the focus on party leaders, and a downplaying or de-emphasis of political parties.[281] A well-remembered slogan in Australian electioneering is the *'It's time'* campaign that marked the Labor Party's sweep to power in the December 1972 federal election. This campaign made Whitlam the first Labor prime minister in 23 years and *It's time* became one of the best-known slogans in Australia. Less recognised is that the New Zealand Labour Party had earlier used this slogan successfully, in its 1972 campaign.

Political words that notable Australians more commonly use in their speech and writing are symbols, jargon, and political slang. This chapter explores how such words are used to inform and persuade, by reviewing Whitlam's use of political vocabulary for powerful effect in a speech to parliament. This Motion of Want of Confidence in the Government was delivered on 15 March 1971, when Whitlam was Leader of the Opposition.[282] It offers a range of examples in the use of political vocabulary, from an especially adept parliamentary speaker[283] who was well steeped in the significance of symbolism and specialist political language.

Symbol

In this review, the *symbol* is stipulated as a simple, suggestive, repetitive element which has an immediate impact, creating a favourable environment for the acceptance of a psychological theme.[284] Symbols are basic to the political myth, providing some common experience for people in a state. Harold Lasswell's claim that a nation holds key symbols permanently in its consciousness[285] is difficult to substantiate, but it can be acknowledged that some well-established norms and beliefs do endure for long periods of time.

Symbols include widely used, very old words with complex meaning, such as *democracy*,[286] *rights*, and *freedom*,[287] or four virtues of western civilisation, namely *wisdom, courage, temperance*, and *justice*.[288] There is usually only gradual change in the experience that such words provide, although there may be differing experiences of symbols by people, especially in different nation states.

The varied uses of *democracy*, including the word's use to name as democratic apparently different political systems, can result in various interpretations of the word. The frequent questioning of what is *democracy*, along with debates about whether the word appropriately describes a particular state or actions within it, can confuse as much as clarify understanding of just what *democracy* denotes.

Some generic qualifications have included *representative democracy* or, in the Westminster system, *parliamentary democracy*.

Jargon

Jargon is defined here as the terminology or characteristic idiom of a special activity or a group; sometimes, jargon is potentially obscure and pretentious language marked by circumlocutions and long words.[289] Mostly in politics jargon is terse; and it is also basic to the political myth. Political jargon is not necessarily based on experience shared uniformly throughout the community.

Whitlam's use of *collective responsibility* though is well understood in Westminster systems to denote the convention of government members being bound by decisions of the cabinet.[290] The duty of any member seriously dissenting from the collectively approved opinion is to resign.[291] A strong connotation of 'good' attaches to this practice, with the recorded technical meaning of the term contributing some consistency to its use.

A connotation of 'good' also attaches to the jargon *proper civilian authority*. This lacks a clear referent though, and the term is predominantly evaluative when Whitlam uses it as a passing reference to some arbiter of what is 'good'. Whether or not denotative meaning is clear, jargon will frequently carry a loaded connotation of 'good' or 'bad', in addition to what it may denote. Whitlam's uses of *collective responsibility* and *proper civilian authority* were largely for evaluation[292] of the Government's actions. With the technical meaning of *collective responsibility* also defined and potentially well-understood, he could spotlight expectations of responsibility through honourable action as a core thrust in developing his case.

Political Slang

Additionally, *political slang* is offered as a grouping of words commonly occurring in public discourse. These are terse expressions that are neither basic to the political myth, nor form the characteristic idiom of the special activity of people engaged with politics. These words aid political discussion by providing short description, such as for political institutions, principles, elements, individuals, groups, or processes.

Political slang includes neologisms or words transferred to use in new ways, generally for critical or evaluative impact. This includes simple name-calling, such as Churchill variously describing Hitler as 'the Austrian corporal', 'the repository of evil', 'this wicked man', and 'this bloodthirsty guttersnipe'. Somewhat more subtle was some slang in Whitlam's speech, including the neologism *Gortonism* and his repurposed use of *Bourbons*, as well as in quite different ways the more fluid term *people's aspirations*.

Transitions and Variations

Over time and usually gradually, political words might be recategorised, especially between symbol and slogan for example. People might also subjectively categorise some words differently. The famous and enduring national motto, the unifying moral purpose for France, with its origins in the French Revolution, *Liberté, égalité, fraternité* (Liberty, Equality, Fraternity) is classified by some as a slogan–perhaps due to its concise inference to act in protection of these values. Is this a motto or slogan, or is it both in the minds of some people?

Within a living language, as the linguist David Crystal notes, a linguistic expression might refer to different sorts of things through a transfer in meaning, including through various kinds of figurative language, such as metaphor.[293] Raymond Williams notes that the word *jargon* itself has become easy to use as slang in a loose way, because of its earlier, much broader senses.[294]

The common vocabulary of politics consists of both the words from the many provinces related to the policy or legislative concerns of a community[295] and the specialist words that people involved in politics will mostly use. Some words used in government can have different nuances of meaning in everyday use in the community, including *democracy* and *collective responsibility*, or from provinces such as the armed forces, *morale, authority*, and *security*. Other words will have little use outside government, such as *the Honourable* and its variants. Some of these variants are used in quite specific ways in Whitlam's No Confidence Motion in the Government.

Parliamentary Motion

Whitlam's motion would not succeed in its formal objective of removing the government while the prime minister maintained majority support within the senior party of the governing coalition. But Whitlam moved this motion in the House at a time of instability in the governing senior political party. As he highlighted within the speech, three days beforehand the majority governing party, the Liberals, changed leadership. Thirty-three members of this ruling party, 'barely one-sixth of the members of this Parliament', as Whitlam noted[296] in a flourish, voted in the party room against the prior prime minister, John Gorton, to remove him from the Office.

Whitlam's speech could be considered emotional groundwork for the case he would successfully prosecute in his election campaign the following year. Both this speech and the subsequent election campaign were directed at overcoming inertia and apathy among voters, to interest the undecided, and to intensify the interest and commitment of a variety of groups in the community. The emotive power in Whitlam's appeal was that it was time for the voice of the voting population to rule, rather than the self-interest of an elite few. From early in a speech chock-filled with symbol, jargon, and slang, he drew on symbolically powerful connotations in *democracy* and *parliamentary democracy* to frame this appeal. Whitlam urged that his motion proposed the best solution to address what he called 'ramshackle' government behaviours. He began with a colourful call for the elected members to act in the interest of voters:

> The aim of the motion is not just to let the people pass judgment on the extraordinary events of the last week but to give them a voice on who should govern them. The clean air of public opinion should be allowed to flow through Canberra's musty corridors of power.[297]

Calling out the Government's alleged failure to represent the public interest while pursuing private ambitions, Whitlam tapped a symbolic bulwark of Westminster government, namely that elected members should perform their duties with *honour*. He used the invented slang *Gortonism* to unsubtly refresh memory of disagreements within both the Gorton and McMahon Governments. Whitlam used short interrogatives to attract attention to the doubts he raised. He demanded a prompt reply, which he then supplied:

> Was the so called unfitness of the former Prime Minister the only issue raised last week? Was he the only person *responsible* for the deficiencies of the Gorton Government? *Gortonism* is not just an aberration of *Liberalism*; ...Is that what these men born to rule were reduced to? There were important, crucial issues involved. There was the issue of *Cabinet responsibility*; responsibility by the *Cabinet* to the *Parliament* and by every member of the *Cabinet* to every other member of the *Cabinet*, the Gorton *Cabinet*, the McMahon *Cabinet*. This is the question of *responsibility*; *collective responsibility*.[298] *[my italics]*

'Born to Rule'

In fewer than 100-words, Whitlam accumulated the emotive power of symbol, jargon, and slang to question repeatedly and pointedly the Government's 'fitness' to govern. Through swift contrast of *Gortonism* with the ruling government party's commitment to *Liberalism*, he modeled what to think of the Liberals. He emphasised a claim that 'these men' considered themselves 'born to rule', rather than having concern for the will of the people.

As with much slang, the neologism *Gortonism* is largely evaluative. With or without context or clear denotation, slang often highlights shades of 'good' or 'bad', such as with Whitlam's use of *people's aspirations* and *public opinion*. He also drew on the positive connotations in the role of *parliament* to enable *democracy* and *freedom*, symbolically and actually, to advocate that an election be scheduled to allow the people to express their will. He began a long paragraph with short electric sentences that outlined events of the previous week, and then interpreted these events to highlight his advocacy for holding an election:

> When I gave notice last Tuesday there was a Gorton Government. Now there is a McMahon Government. That is all that has changed. The Liberal leader and deputy leader have changed places and the former Prime Minister supplants his destroyer as Minister for Defence. All the essential elements of Gorton Government remain, with all their contradictions, tensions, dissensions, selfishness and rivalries exposed but utterly unresolved. They can be resolved only by an election.[299]

Whitlam critiqued the previous and the new Government as shuffling Cabinet members' positions without making any real change. With the accumulation of evaluative words, 'changed places', 'supplants', and 'destroyer', he surrounded the Government with words carrying negative connotations. 'They' were linked to the evaluative words 'contradictions' and 'tensions…[to]…rivalries'. In contrast, he emphasises the positive connotation of holding an 'election', locating this word at the emphatic end of a short sentence.

Honour

Then Whitlam associated the 'honourable members' of Government with an echo of Shakespeare's famous Mark Antony oration over the body of the betrayed Caesar. He spotlights the Cabinet's violation of the *honour* required for Cabinet's *collective responsibility*, impugning the Government members as 'chief participants in a conspiracy'. He asserts they were concerned with secrecy of 'rewards' and 'punishments', rather than behaving honourably:

> He does not want the Parliament to know the composition of the new Ministry, to know whether the honourable member for Wannon (**Mr Malcolm Fraser**) has been rewarded, whether the Minister for Defence (**Mr Gorton**) will serve with the honourable member for Wannon, or what rewards and punishments are to be meted out to the chief participants in last week's conspiracy. He does not want the honourable member for Wannon to be answerable as a Minister for his extraordinary allegation of last Tuesday.[300]

Associating the Government members as dishonourable conspirators underscored Whitlam's assertion that 'dishonour' was endemic in the ruling Liberal Party. He portrayed the characters of the Liberal Party as lacking the positive values and *honourable* action expected within *Parliament*. He called on the Government to follow *proper procedures* by declaring an election, thereby respecting *parliamentary democracy*.

Through this adept use of emotionally laden political words, Whitlam elevated his procedural motion to an advocacy for the restoration of a fundamental principle of parliamentary government. His narration of events impugned the Government's actions, when compared with good procedures respectful of Parliament. The Government leaders' actions were presented in stark contrast to the requirement that elected representatives in the House address each other during proceedings as 'the honourable member'. Whitlam's continuous focus is on the 'honour' expected in the Westminster system. Against this, he placed the 'dishonour' that he impugned in *Gortonism*.

Purposes

The instabilities in the Liberal Party leadership at this time in 1971 conjured a slight possibility that one or more Government members might break convention, to record at least some oral protest to the leadership jockeying within the Party. Not all that long before in 1969, Edward St. John's vote against Gorton's Liberal Party Government in which he was a member, albeit on a different matter, had stemmed from a conviction about dishonourable actions that were attributed to Gorton and his supporters. Whitlam's consistently using words that connote 'dishonour' or 'bad' behaviour when speaking of the Government, its members, and their actions seemed to frame conditions for a response such as St. John had made.

Whitlam's effort to shame the Government though was likely aimed through the media for the attention of the voting public. He powerfully outlined a contention that the Government leaders' dishonour derived from their own perception of being 'born to rule'. By aligning the Liberals with the *Bourbons*, referencing a European dynasty that for a very long period ruled French and other countries' thrones, Whitlam contrasted the expectation that within a democracy it was voters who should decide who ruled. He called on the name, *Bourbons*, as slang to associate the Liberals with a legacy of what was 'bad', relative to democratic ideals:

> The very malaise that was at the heart of last week's convulsion—the bypassing of Parliament and its proper procedures—continues unabated. The Bourbons have learned nothing. They never will learn. The sickness is too far advanced.[301]

Whitlam risked different audience members' potentially different responses to the word *Bourbons,* perhaps ranging in reaction from considering the reference insightful to feeling it was overly intellectual. Few in the audience might be as familiar as Whitlam with the word's connotations, including the association with the powerful family that had controlled Europe's thrones, much less the word's transfer into the political lexicon of the United States as the nickname for a

Democrat who was behind the age and unteachable.[302] In correspondence with the author, Whitlam clarified his purpose, 'I should mention that my reference to the Bourbons was spurred by Dumouriez' and Talleyrand's statements after the Revolution that the Bourbons and their courtiers in exile had "learnt nothing and forgotten nothing"'.[303]

The negative connotation of the word in context though would be sufficient to make the point.[304] From the linguistic context in the speech itself, there is a sense that *Bourbons* connotes 'badness', being syntactically related to 'learned nothing', and semantically related to 'never will learn' and 'sickness…too far advanced'. Whitlam used short simple sentences to make this inference and set up a minor climax in the speech. The suggestion that the Government politicians were not learning from their mistakes, while continuing to 'rule', accentuated Whitlam's further strike at the alleged dishonour of the Government.

Audience Connection

Whitlam's sophisticated use of special political words with emotional loading permitted his impugning the behaviours of fellow House members, who were members of the Government, while abiding by the courtesies for debate within parliamentary conventions. Throughout a long public career, Whitlam respected the forms of parliament and parliamentary practice while connecting with audiences through his great versatility in language use.

Whitlam inclined to formality, often using historical allusions along with the formalities of written language when speaking, which made him an interestingly formal leader of a worker's political party. He was well-known for using formal language within passages of long complex sentences. He balanced this tendency with features more common in spoken than written discourse, such as a mix of short sentences and interrogatives. Predominantly, Whitlam adhered to a conventional order in sentences of Subject (S), Predicator (P), Adjunct (A) and sometimes Complement (C) elements. He used very little slang, and not occurring at all in this speech was the sentence fragment, which is one of the most unique identifiers of conversation identified by the researcher E.H. Flint.[305]

Commonly though Whitlam integrated within longer, complex passages some lighter touches more characteristic of spoken discourse,[306] including:

- Sequences of semantically related interrogatives
- Short, simple sentences near the beginning or end of paragraphs
- Brief quotes of relevant newspaper reports
- Specialist political words common in everyday language (*security, loyalty*).

Both in this speech and elsewhere, he used short simple sentences to attract attention or to emphasise important conclusions.

Meanings to Audiences

Whitlam used both formal and conversational language, with a mix of familiar and less familiar political language to emphasise his main points. For example, in the use of *Bourbons*, he shifted from the formal long paragraph ('When I gave…'), with the hint of Shakespeare's Mark Antony oration, into a short paragraph. After the long, complex first sentence to this short paragraph ('The very malaise…'), he followed with three extremely short, five-word average, simple sentences, potentially sweeping the audience past the allusion to *Bourbons*. He frequently used a burst of short sentences in this way to offset any distancing effects, which would be helpful to engage a general audience.

Among the challenges of using a specialist political vocabulary is that these words can be over-used. Frequent repetition over an extended time can diffuse impact or cause political words to become clichéd. Attempts to redefine meanings in new contexts sometimes also result in omnibus phrases, like *parliamentary representative democracy*. With political talk mostly intended for the public, omnibus phrases in politics are usually too unwieldy to permit effective communication. In the future, as perhaps increasing numbers of nation-states claim to be democratic, for example, there might be increased use of a nation's name paired with *democracy* to strengthen a shared experience of this symbol within a nation.

Sentence Shape/Passage Development

For the time of his speech though, Whitlam could use the symbolic power of *democracy* in his final paragraph with confidence that listeners were familiar with its connotations in relation to Australia. He articulated his assessment of how *parliamentary democracy* would be best served in the context of the Government's actions:

> *(i)* Parliamentary democracy has been discredited by the conduct of the Gorton Government and by the events of last week. *(ii)* One of the things most undermining faith in parliamentary democracy in this country is the growing feeling that the electoral processes cannot change anything–that the people's aspirations cannot be met by those processes. *(iii)* Last week was a classic instance of Government changes. *(iv)* The people were impotent and irrelevant. *(v)* Nothing can do more to restore faith in this Parliament than that it should have the courage to submit itself and the actions of a minority to the judgment of the people. *(vi)* If this Parliament fails to do this it will be *not only* the Prime Minister who is discredited, *not only* the Liberal Party, *not only* the Government, *but the whole* of this institution.[307] *[my italics, with lower-case italic Roman numerals, such as 'i', used to identify sentence numbers within the passage]*

Parliamentary democracy as the first words were repeated in the second sentence, emphasising the topic of the paragraph. Whitlam used parallel phrases and similar breath groups for emphasis (in sentences *iii* and *iv*). He also varied from the normal SPC sentence structure (*vi*), making the 'if' clause within the sentence more emphatic.[308] This enhanced his assertion of the consequences from a failure to vote for his motion. Whitlam emphasised these consequences by an accumulation of:

- Progression from one man (prime minister) to all (institution)
- Three parallel 'not only' phrases
- Concentration of short breath groups
- Breaking the pattern of the 'not only' phrases with a 'but' phrase
- At the emphatic end point of the sentence.

Although the word 'discredit' occurred twice in the final paragraph, these occurrences were widely separated. Whitlam put focus on the 'discredit' that he asserted would accrue to the 'whole of this institution' near both the emphatic beginning and end points of the paragraph.

Conclusion

By incorporating special political words that not only condensed information but carried emotional loading, Whitlam was able to powerfully advocate that an election be held, for the people to have a voice in their government. He urged that failure to set an election would bring discredit to the members in Parliament, diminishing the stature of Parliament itself in the eyes of voters. In the end then, much of the strength of Whitlam's speech came from his elevating the emotional significance of the Government's leadership change as an alleged violation of the ideals of Parliament and democracy. He used special political words imaginatively, recalling and evaluating actions of the Government to help advance his argument. While observing the formalities required for parliamentary debate, he called on the connotations of special political words to inject immediacy, and to spotlight what was the responsible personal decision that he requested of his colleagues in the House.

On a variety of occasions, public figures will integrate emotion-laden political vocabulary in their language. These words compress concepts, or diminish or strengthen the formality of speech, or grip a listener's attention with dramatic or emphatic effect. Speeches within the legislature might sometimes be clearly emotional, but much political talk incorporates the use of political words with denotative, evaluative, and emotional effectiveness analogous to what Whitlam accomplished with his use in this parliamentary 'Motion of Want of Confidence in the Government'.

7: Choices for Public Talk

We regard speaking well to be

the clearest sign of a good mind...[309]

— Isocrates

How speakers and writers choose to foreground or subordinate matters to engage an audience's emotional commitment is individual to a circumstance and each person's approach. Whitlam for a motion of no confidence, or Menzies for an election broadcast, or Atkinson welcoming attendees to Expo '88, or Greer speaking at a press luncheon to advance women's rights, or a speaker for each different subject, audience, and occasion, will consider different specifics to engage an audience.

Key Considerations

What is common for effective speech and writing is the need to consider carefully (1) what might the audience know and want to know about a subject? (2) what the speaker/writer believes are important facts, ideas, opinions, and nuances on the subject to highlight or subordinate? and (3) what is the aim of the speech or writing: to inform or stimulate some change to belief or actions? Speeches and writing require such forethought particularly because, unlike conversation, there are relatively few or no cues to what an audience feels and thinks about a subject or the speaker/writer.

For what is essentially a monologue, this puts focus on anticipating and navigating ways that different segments of an audience might differently interpret public speech or writing. The challenge is to identify what will engage an audience, by clarifying for oneself what choices of topics and language will initiate, accentuate, or moderate the motivation of audience members' attention, awareness, interest, attitude, or action.

Public talk that motivates an audience makes appeals through *ethos*/credibility, or *pathos*/audience emotions, or *logos*/logic. While *ethos* and *pathos* are much discussed for their emotive power, *logos* with its rational basis is conventionally considered contrary to the emotions. Yet logic can emotionally engage an audience in many contexts. Public talk often incorporates a rational framework. This was so for example in Whitlam's advocacy to honour the principle of parliamentary democracy, or earlier in Melba's use of logic to visibly engage her admiring audience at her farewell. For anyone committed to pursuing a proof, logic can carry extraordinary emotional power. The recognised 'potent, pervasive, predictable'[310] role of emotions as drivers of decision makes it important to consider as many features as possible that contribute to the emotional strength of a communication.

Speaker Samples

This chapter illustrates language features used to motivate audiences, in the speech samples of ten notable Australians. At different times from 1891 to 1980, these speakers addressed a variety of audiences, subjects, and occasions. They advocated federation (Sir Samuel Griffith, 1891), women's right to vote (Louisa Lawson, 1891), support in war (John Curtin, 1942), honouring of Sir Winston Churchill's life (Sir Robert Menzies, 1965), national partnership in the Pacific (Gough Whitlam, 1975), rights for First Nations (Oodgeroo Noonuccal, 1970), honouring of Albert Monk's life (Bob Hawke, 1975), rights for First Nations (Kevin Gilbert, 1974), women's rights (Germaine Greer, 1971), and law reform (Michael Kirby, 1980).[311] They illustrate a range of rhetorical styles to engage audiences through truthful, lawful, and just speech.

Reviewed firstly are ways the speakers framed their speeches, by drawing on genres, metaphor, controversy, or humour. Considered here also is how each shaped passages, with individual choices in types of sentences and clauses to sequence thoughts and develop topics. Detailed secondly are ways that the speakers appealed to audiences by reflecting conversational effects and by sustaining liveliness through choice of language structure and word types. This includes their use of interpolation, pairs, ellipsis, lists or series, sentence fragments, pronouns, proper nouns, and everyday vocabulary to reflect conversation. Also detailed are some ways the speakers sustained lively language, by using special political words, neologisms, verb functions, or through their choice of verbs and nouns. Thirdly, some rhetorical qualities used to help secure audience attention or commitment are described, including the speakers' use of rhetorical figures for emphasis. Concluding the chapter is a summary of considerations for framing public communication based on this review.

In the 600-word introductions to the speeches, I manually counted more than 40 language features,[312] with the resulting counts and working assumptions noted in Appendix Two. The speakers used such language features intuitively or consciously to moderate tone and speaker-listener relations, to emphasise or subordinate facts, ideas, and opinions, and to motivate an audience from attention through to action. Additional studies could explore further aspects of communication style and effects, including types of vocabulary (concrete v abstract nouns, mono-/bi-/polysyllabic words, and Romance or Germanic language derivations), or additional aspects of sentence structure, or types of passage formation.

Speaker Advocacy

From their first words, the speakers explicitly or implicitly set specifics for an occasion:

> The next item on the program before me is the President's anniversary address... (Griffith)

> It is said that 'the greatest discovery of the nineteenth century is the discovery of women'... (Lawson)

> I speak to you from Australia. I speak from a united people to a united people... (Curtin)

> As this historic procession goes through the streets of London to the Tower Pier, I have the honour of speaking to you from the crypt of St. Paul's Cathedral... (Menzies)

> It is not quite two years since I had the honour of addressing this national Press Club... (Whitlam)

> In my speech tonight, I will attempt to pinpoint how well off Aborigines are in modern-day Australia... (Oodgeroo)

> It is in the nature of our affairs as human beings gathered together in a particular community that some individuals emerge as conspicuous leaders... (Hawke)

> I would like to try and communicate some of the needs of the Aboriginal community... (Gilbert)

> I was debating with myself how to address you... (Greer)

> Foreign observers and newcomers to Australia must find some of our objects of national pride and celebration curious, to say the least... (Kirby)

Each set the frame for what was to follow by referring to the agenda, topic, location, speaker, connection, or purpose.

Choice of Genre

In a straightforward way these statements focused on the speaker, topic, and theme, while establishing the platform for speaking in a genre appropriate to the subject and occasion. When considered broadly, genres function to help constitute a culture, embedding histories, ideologies, and contradictions that become social recognitions.[313] The *deliberative, judicial,* and *epideictic* genres in the rhetorical tradition provide expected or typical response to a rhetorical situation and have wide application. An appropriate rhetorical genre accommodates an audience's expectations concerning the tone, content, and purpose of the speech. Public figures both speak to and extend audience expectations in the use of genre and do not necessarily adhere strictly to one rhetorical genre, with the use of a hybrid of genres common. For some circumstances, speakers tend to use one genre. For example, election speeches are mostly deliberative, with a well understood purpose of persuading voters, but often include appeals for justice or other benefits portrayed as accruing from one candidate's election.

With the continued proliferation of varieties of genre in different modes of communication and substantial shifts in social norms, the future classifications of many conventional situations for public talk are likely to keep adjusting. With social norms influencing language, along with language influencing social norms, the expected tone in public talk is progressively transitioning from formal to informal, to consultative, to colloquial or casual, and even to a sense of the intimate. This trend aligns with a noticeable national trait of Australians to think and speak informally—not only with the use of analogy, rhyming slang, imaginative omission, and colloquial substitutions, but also generally.

Framing of Speech

From early in their remarks, each of the ten speakers variously used metaphor, allusion, or other figurative language to structure how the audience perceived, thought about, or might act on points within the speech[314]—as reviewed earlier, speakers might choose metaphors that help to frame the overall organisation and tone of a speech or for other specific purposes.

Curtin, Menzies, and Gilbert led the ten speakers with most frequent incorporation of well-used figurative language, such as:

> comrades in this war / freedom-loving people / Old Glory (Curtin)
>
> streets of London / Churchill's time / we thank God for him (Menzies)
>
> the handout system / competitive spirit / down the drain (Gilbert)

For use of fresh figurative language, Lawson stood out, at more than three-times the average frequency of others' use, such as:

> the sailor boy / Alpha and Omega of his infantile dreams / tottering mass of rottenness (Lawson)

All speakers used metaphor, to define a direction or identity, frame a communication topic or events, facts, or opinions, and/or make direct emphasis of a point.

Potential of Controversy

Conscious use of polemic, or unexpected controversy, can substantially impact an audience's interpretation of a speech. All moderated some form of polemic in the samples, to attract and hold attention, or make impact, or strengthen relationship with an audience, while enhancing the liveliness and effectiveness of speech.

The three types of polemic described by Dascal occurred in the samples.[315] *Discussion* polemic used persuasion through deliberative argument—to seek truth in problem-solution:

> But facts are stern things. We, the allied nations were unready… We have all made mistakes, we have all been too slow; we have all shown weakness—all the allied nations. This is not time to wrangle about who has been most to blame. Now our eyes are wide open. (Curtin)

Dispute polemic contested attitudes, feelings, or preferences—to win:

> Can we wonder that a woman in defence of self and children smashed the mirrors and decanters in a drinking den where her husband spent his time and money to the neglect of his home and family? Is it to be wondered at that this woman took the law into her own hands, seeing how worse than useless was the outlook…? (Lawson)

Controversy polemic discussed matters in a truth-telling mode—to resolve problems:

> Many commentators have said that but for the chance of time, the Kelly Gang would have been at Gallipoli, showing the courage in the field of war which is still the chief object of our military pride. Yet Gallipoli must seem to outsiders a strange battle for a country to commemorate. (Kirby)

Beyond the ten speakers reviewed, many others including Deakin, Hughes, Lyons, Carnegie, Prowse, Cowen, Keating, and Gillard were observed to use polemic.

Value of Humour

Though not an option in all situations, personable public figures often incorporate humour. The ten samples overwhelmingly dealt with serious subjects in serious ways. Humour was foregrounded only in the Greer sample, such as with her opening challenge about how she would address her audience. A touch of amusement was also implicit in the Kirby sample, such as 'the suggestion that Ned be made a saint... [or] ...settle for what was apparently thought the next best thing: a posthumous knighthood!'–which Kirby quoted to reassess what had been proposed as serious suggestions.

On other occasions, Menzies, Whitlam, Hawke, Greer, and Kirby used humour. Hawke frequently sought rapport through quips against himself. He repeated some of these on different occasions,[316] which tends to be the fate of effective anecdotes. What people find humorous varies widely, with pun and wordplay commonly occurring in speeches. Compared with the informal humour of Twitter and YouTube, at times Australia's earlier speakers might seem stuffy, but the principles and techniques of humour are little changed, serving then as now for potent personalising, point-scoring, emphasis, or credibility-building effects.

Sequencing Thoughts

The sampled speakers used various approaches to organise thoughts about a subject through topic sequencing, both to shape passages and structure sentences. A simple and versatile approach to organisation that Menzies used, both in his eulogy for Churchill and often elsewhere, was to structure a speech using doublets and compound clauses. Typically, an entire speech grew from a simple opening remark to the effect:

> I have two things to say: A and B.
>
> A is P and Q, which leads to X and Y,
>
> and about Y, I just want to say this...
>
> ... The second point concerns B...

He then treated B similarly, and in concluding this approach in the eulogy for Churchill, he commented:

> There are two other things I want to say to you on a day which neither you nor I will ever willingly forget.[317]

This provided a compelling and simple way to structure ideas for a general audience, while allowing extended discussion of additional points to whatever extent he chose, sustained by further doublets and compound clauses.

Some speakers first focused on a principle and then drew together related matters to elaborate the application of the principle and build a case. Griffith proposed a geographical principle as a natural law early, then pointed out the changes that people should make to 'obey' this 'law'. Lawson introduced an aphoristic principle that touched daily life, and followed with a sequence of tangible narratives, metaphors, similes, or allusions that illustrated the value of cooperative action in support of women's rights. Whitlam highlighted 'the strength of democracy' as a principle, to sensitively outline perspectives that debunked America's past foreign policy and then suggested a path forward in partnership with Australia after Vietnam. Hawke initially outlined a principle for how a leader emerged from a community, and then recounted how the growth of Monk and the trade union movement benefited the audience.

Other speakers inductively built a case. Initially, Kirby explored some 'curious' features of Australia history and 'national pride' to suggest fresh perspectives on the need for continuous reform of the law, so that the law could meet the emerging needs of society. Curtin moved from his graphic figurative descriptions highlighting the severity and state of the war, to narrate shared wartime experiences, encouraging the joint commitment needed to win the war in the Pacific. More overtly adopting reporting roles, Oodgeroo, Gilbert, and Greer made observations about pertinent realities, then advocated remedies for what they had described.

Shaping Passages

Audience members likely engaged well with these sequenced narratives, descriptions, analyses, evaluations, and recommendations—as the speakers shaped and sustained interest through their choices in sentence length and structure, clauses, interpolations, pairs, lists or series. Later in this chapter, some of the rhetorical features used to shape passages are also described.

Sentences: Important as short sentences are for emphasis or liveliness, the average sentence length in the samples was 24.6-words. This is slightly longer than the less than 20-words more typically considered an appropriate average sentence length.[318] Curtin and Kirby led all others in using brief sentences, piling up a rapid sequence of images or observations, with sentences sometimes just a relatively few words in length:

> I am not speaking to your Government. (Curtin)

> They broke the law. They refused to pay taxes. (Kirby)

Griffith and Greer had the longest average sentence length, with others slightly above or below the average. For comparison, Hawke's sentence lengths were 26-words in his eulogy for Monk, and 29-words in the prepared policy speech that will be reviewed in Chapter Fourteen—about half as long again as Kirby at 18-words. More extreme was Griffith's 42-word average sentence length. Whitlam, at 22-words average, periodically incorporated parallel components, which required sensitivity in delivery to avoid a chaotic effect.

While the length of a sentence was once considered important for clarity,[319] it is the sentence structure that is more significant than the weight given to sentence length in most readability formulae.[320] Relative and subordinate clauses and, in a different way, compound clauses tend to increase sentence length and sometimes sentence complexity.

Clauses–relative and subordinate: Griffith, Gilbert, and Greer led others in the occurrence of relative and subordinate clauses. These speakers nonetheless managed the greater complexity to sustain clarity, such as with parallel constructions:

> Mostly we find the tribal woman, or the person *who has been* de-tribalised, *who has been* on the fringe is the one to *make the effort* and *send the child* to school. *[my italics]* (Gilbert)

Other speakers used relative or subordinate clauses at about the average use in the samples, some also using parallelism to help with clarity and emphasis.

Although the deep embedding of clauses and phrases was not included in the counts, it was mainly Griffith and Whitlam who used elaborate sentences, sometimes mentioning a succession of items in extended commentary. Griffith used deep embedding of clauses to appear direct, but subordinated information potentially negative to his case.[321] Whitlam used relative and subordinate clauses frequently, which combined with his use of triads and parallelism to create complexities in his language structure.

Clauses–compound: Analogous to how Menzies simplified the structure of an entire speech on 'two points', then followed with a further 'two points', some speakers used the connectors 'and', 'but', and 'or' to simplify passage development. Louis Milic in his study of the style of Jonathan Swift[322] suggests that careful use of compound clauses projected a personalising effect, perhaps because people commonly 'string together' ideas in compound clauses in conversation. While sentences that begin with connectives do not come within traditional grammar's definition of compound clauses, these were included in counting, since they are characteristic of informal speech.

Menzies's preference for compound clauses was at almost double the average use in the samples, with Menzies and Lawson most often using compound clauses. Curtin, Oodgeroo, Gilbert, and Greer also showed more use of compound clauses than others:

> And some will be able to say, 'I knew him, and talked with him, and was his friend'. (Menzies)

> And even in broad day light keepers of gambling houses come out upon our footpaths and take half-crowns from little children who sell newspapers upon the streets, and where does the respectable boy clerk get the half sovereign which he stakes upon a horse in our King Street tobacconist shop? (Lawson)

In contrast, Kirby's consistency in using very simply structured sentences meant that he did not often exploit the value in using compound clauses in ways that others found effective for structural development and emphasis (Lawson 15/ Curtin 11 / Menzies 18 / Kirby 3). Likewise, this limited Kirby's opportunity to use compound clauses combined with both *anaphora* and other parallelism to emphasise ideas (Menzies 13 / Whitlam 8 / Gilbert 12 / Kirby 3).

Sustaining 'Conversation'

The language structures and word types used to create a conversational effect while shaping passages include interpolations, pairs, ellipsis, lists or series, compound clauses (as reviewed previously), sentence fragments, exclamations and questions, contractions, and dashes. Word types that ordinarily occur with higher frequency in much conversation include personal pronouns, proper nouns, everyday vocabulary, infinite verbs, clichés, and slang. Many of these features occurred in the samples.

Interpolations: During conversation people commonly self-interrupt, and interpolation in a speech provides the similarly useful opportunity to qualify or emphasise comments, or just to provide a pause. Many or long interpolations of course can confuse meaning. In the longer interpolations of Griffith and Menzies, each incorporated parallelism that helped retain clarity and impact:

> I think it will be found, if you refer to the history of other parts of the world, that the political geography—that is, the divisions of the world into nations, or into parts of the globe occupied by different peoples—corresponds to a very great extent with the physical divisions of nature. (Griffith)

> Many of you will not need to be reminded, but some, the younger among you, the inheritors of his master-strokes for freedom, may be glad to be told that your country, and mine, and all the free countries of the world, stood at the very gates of destiny in 1940 and 1941… (Menzies)

Greer, Hawke, Whitlam, and at times Menzies, used shorter interpolations, with Kirby the shortest of all. Griffith and Gilbert, though stylistically different in other ways, were similar in their high frequency of interpolation:

> So we have confusion as to the identity of the people: that you are the bastards because you will not recognise the conditions of the Aboriginal people, you will not live up to the ideals you profess—justice, humanity, decency. (Gilbert)

Use of interpolation by Lawson, Curtin, Menzies, and Hawke was at about the average level of use by the group, with least use by Whitlam, Oodgeroo, Greer, and Kirby. Interpolation is a rhetorical feature commonly used by many public figures, including Howard, Keating, and some others. Crystal notes that the Internet[323] has caused a blending of the properties of traditional written and spoken language in the use of interpolation.

Pairs: The immediate repetition of a word or word type interrupts language flow and will sometimes provide emphasis—especially when the same word is repeated. The pairs counted were recurrences of a word, separated at most by punctuation and/or an article, as well as conventional couplings of word types. These were *adjective plus noun*, or *noun plus modifier*, or words and word types repeated, namely *noun plus noun, adjective plus adjective,* or *verb plus verb.*

Oodgeroo, Hawke, and Kirby led all others in total use of pairs, which resulted mainly from use of the common *adjective plus noun* form that all speakers used. Less common was the *noun plus modifier*, which only Oodgeroo and Hawke used more than once, and others used minimally or not at all. Oodgeroo and Kirby used *noun pairs* most, with Gilbert's use greater than the average:

> anti-hero, Ned Kelly (Kirby)

> a European–a migrant / Austcare, Freedom from Hunger (Gilbert)

While the *noun pair* often occurs in lists, this form was also used for emphasis or contrast:

> ...past mistakes—mistakes in which both countries shared (Whitlam)

Griffith used the *noun pair* commonly in this way in his written communication. For *adjective pairs*, that is two adjectives occurring together, Menzies, Hawke, Greer, and Kirby used these most. The *adjective pair* was used for qualification and for precision but multiple- or over-qualification can confuse or distract.

Substantially leading others in the use of the *verb plus verb* pair were Menzies, Whitlam, and Gilbert, which accentuated the strength of their verb use:

> threatened to engulf / scorned to fall / want to say (Menzies)

> honoured to address / happen to lead / was defeated was not / bound to fail (Whitlam)

> taught to be / decided to start / needed to be applied / allowed to determine/ want to be (Gilbert)

These uses illustrated one way that speakers used verbs, particularly the infinite verb, to project an in-touch, vigorous style.

Ellipsis: Omission of words is common enough in conversation, especially the optional relative pronoun[324] or the subject of a second verb in a coordinate sentence. Ellipsis of sentence subject occurred most in Menzies and Gilbert, less often in Lawson, Curtin, and Oodgeroo, with few occurrences in the remainder:

> and therefore speak / and talked with him / but is gloriously remembered (Menzies)

> and pay his own rent, buy his own car / and will return (Gilbert)

Verb ellipsis occurred little in the samples, only in Menzies and Hawke. The total occurrence of ellipses was greatest in Menzies, then Lawson, Curtin, Oodgeroo, Hawke, and Gilbert. Using fewer ellipses were Griffith and Greer, with Whitlam and Kirby making least use. Although Crystal and Davy note that some ellipsis occurs in certain formal discourse, including the English Bible, they point out that its effect in these cases is to suggest the informality of conversation.[325]

Lists or series: Commonly in everyday conversation, people list items. Some lists omit the connectors 'or', 'and' or 'but', which simplifies a sometimes-complex sequence of thoughts, to put most emphasis on the items in the list. On occasion, Whitlam sequenced statements without a connector, in parallel short sentences, or in combination with *anaphora*. At the close of his speech to the Washington Press Club, Whitlam directly addressed listeners using the second-person pronoun 'you/your'–to stress what he urged were vital concerns for attention:

> *These are* the real problems of Asia. *These are* the real problems of the world. *These,* I trust, will be the real concerns of the United States. With *your* great tradition of moral leadership, *your* unexampled generosity, *your* vision, *your* energy, *your* sheer zest for accomplishment, *you* will find new inspiration in this task–a task in which Australia will be a ready and willing partner.[326] *[my italics]*

This simplified sequencing of items, combined with the parallelism and emphasis from the *anaphora* and language rhythm, put a spotlight on the final interpolation–especially stressing Australia's willingness for partnership, at this emphatic end of the passage and speech.[327]

Sentence fragments: A sentence type that is especially helpful in giving an audience a sense of being engaged in conversation is the sentence fragment.[328] With the sentence fragment occurring little or not at all in written language, its use in a speech can provide much impact as a conversational effect. Although no sentence fragments occurred in the ten samples, this sentence form was used elsewhere by the speakers. Also, it will often be omitted or otherwise edited in the written record of a speech.

Pronouns: The accumulation of personal pronouns can play a substantial role in suggesting conversational relationship, additionally offering ways to negotiate relationship. The first-person singular pronoun 'I' and, more strongly, 'myself' assert the speaker's presence. The direct address of Curtin and Menzies, in the mode 'I speak to you...', provided opportunity to strengthen engagement with an audience.

Overuse of the first-person singular pronoun, however, can give an impression of being dominating or too egotistical, and can attract criticism. Griffith, Menzies, Whitlam,[329] and Greer have sometimes been criticised for egotism or arrogance. Griffith, Curtin, Menzies, Whitlam, and Greer used 'I' most frequently, with lower occurrences or complete absence in the samples of Lawson, Hawke, Oodgeroo, Gilbert, and Kirby. Although Kirby used more self-reference in other speeches,[330] generally his use of 'I' was minimal, enabling sharp focus on the speech content.

An effective way to subtly engage an audience was by adjusting the use of personal pronouns. Whereas Kirby little used this opportunity, Griffith, Curtin, Menzies, Whitlam, Oodgeroo, Greer, and other speakers commonly shifted from discussion in terms of 'I' and 'you' early in a speech to 'we' later, thereby suggesting their inclusion with the audience, often near a climax in a speech.[331]

Noted previously, in Curtin's *Speech to America*, was how he advanced through his various uses of the first-person plural pronoun, so that 'we' came to include him with both his United States and Australian listeners. The significance of using pronouns to engage an audience is reported in an interesting statistical study of leaders' use of 'we-referencing' in 43 Australian Federal elections since the Federation of Australia in 1901. This study suggested that 'victors used more collective pronouns than their unsuccessful opponents in 80% of all elections'.[332]

In the speech samples reviewed here, Lawson, Curtin, Menzies, Whitlam, and Oodgeroo most used 'we-referencing', negotiating relations with listeners by this means. Curtin, Menzies, Gilbert, and Greer used second-person pronouns most frequently, to directly address listeners and strengthen personal connection. Lawson, Menzies, Hawke, and Gilbert used third-person pronouns most, sometimes to focus the 'otherness' of the people discussed—which is also a commonly used device to distance or be dismissive of ideas or suggestions.

Proper nouns/names: These most concrete nouns refer specifically to people, places, organisations, or other entities and items by name, and occur frequently in conversation. Particularly when the names that a speaker uses are familiar to an audience, proper nouns are useful to help find common ground, especially in introductory passages. Reflecting everyday talk, proper nouns keep speech tangible and help to set context. Curtin, Hawke, and Kirby made substantial use of proper nouns, partly because the speeches used for counting dealt with many historical details.

Although occurrences of proper nouns largely result from what subject is being addressed, variations in choice and usage are still possible. Curtin,

Whitlam, Hawke, Gilbert, and Kirby most referred to people and places, with Griffith, Lawson, Menzies, Oodgeroo, and Greer also doing so:

> Australia... Pacific Ocean... Mr Roosevelt... America... Dutch (Curtin)

> Australia... Britain's... America... Eureka Stockade... Ned Kelly (Kirby)

Everyday vocabulary: A higher proportion of mono- or bi-syllabic words and many words of Germanic origin, or other words with tangible referents are among the common word types in everyday talk. Kirby indicates his attraction to words of Germanic origin,[333] which tend to have concrete referents.

Especially suggestive of everyday talk are cliché and slang, which are reviewed here due to their strength for this purpose and since some speakers used these word types, while others avoided their use.

<u>Cliché</u>: Often reflecting colloquial discourse, cliché can range in effect from reassuring an audience by focus on the familiar through to suggesting that a speaker or writer is bland or lacking in originality. Cliché occurred only infrequently in the samples, with four occurrences in Lawson, few occurrences in Curtin, Menzies, Whitlam, Gilbert, and Greer, and no use by other speakers:

> gambling den / inhumanity to man (Lawson)

> gates of destiny / second front (Menzies)

> stab in the back (Whitlam)

<u>Slang</u>: As a striking marker of informality,[334] slang is sometimes used with a surprising or startling effect in a speech. With 11 occurrences of slang, Gilbert led all others in earthy everyday talk:

> goes on walkabout / lazy bastards / paper education (Gilbert)

> have no truck (Whitlam)

Lawson, Curtin, Whitlam, Oodgeroo, Hawke, and Greer made limited use of slang, while Griffith, Menzies, and Kirby did not use slang in the samples. Kirby notes this as conscious avoidance, '...I was relieved to see the high score I received from you for the absence of clichés and slang. There are some prices no-one should pay for better communication!'[335] It was rare for Menzies to use slang, other than in quoting others, and both Hawke and Whitlam used slang occasionally.

Whitlam's speechwriter, Freudenberg, indicates that they usually reserved the use of slang for shock affect,[336] as in 'cold war hangups'.[337] Greer seemed to feel no such constraint. As will be detailed in Chapter Thirteen, she made use of both slang and, to some extent, expletives for their personalising and polemical value. In conjunction with her use of other slang, Greer commonly talked directly with listeners using the direct address, 'you/your'. At times, she also seemed to seek a more personal relationship through her use of expletives, while she held the upper hand as controller of the conversation and occasion.

Because slang is one of the relatively few language features that changes more rapidly, a speaker can show currency and being in the 'in' group through its apt use but must manage the personal factors in what often makes the use of slang a more emotionally charged exchange.

Words that Engage

In addition, the speakers used a variety of other word types and words that reflected conversation to engage audiences. These ranged from the special 'political words' described more fully in the previous chapter through neologisms, verb functions, verbs relative to nouns, and function words, which in various combinations can provide a sense of liveliness or other vitality.

Special political words: Powerfully used in some of the ten samples were symbols, slogans, jargon, and political slang, which condensed information and/or incorporated emotional punch. Some of the versatility in the use of these words included symbols that set a favourable psychological frame:

> Old Country (Curtin)
>
> democracy (Curtin, Whitlam, Kirby)
>
> justice, humanity, decency (Gilbert)
>
> Eureka Stockade (Kirby)

or slogans and slogan-like statements that expressed a characteristic position, or stand, or a goal to be achieved:

> by Almighty God (Menzies)
>
> rising for better conditions, better opportunities for their children (Gilbert)
>
> from a united people to a united people (Curtin)

or jargon that condensed thoughts, and/or for evaluation:

> political geography (Griffith)
>
> a policy of foreign intervention (Whitlam)
>
> assimilated gunya (Oodgeroo)

or varieties of slang that suggested informality, and/or for evaluation:

> an assassin at Pearl Harbor (Curtin)
>
> so-called superior race (Oodgeroo)

'triple crown' (Hawke)

'Jacky' (Gilbert)

media freak (Greer).

Neologism: Creating new words or using words in new senses displays the creator's inventive control of language but relies on the audience's mutual interest in the novelty for its effectiveness. A colloquial neologism is useful to make language less formal or more conversational, with the effect of course depending on the case. Coinage of words is common in some communications, such as advertising language.[338]

The use of neologism in the samples was minimal, with Curtin and Menzies using none, although each used neologisms elsewhere. Inventively coining words rather than just using others' neologisms in the samples were Lawson, Oodgeroo, Gilbert, Greer, and Kirby, suggesting creativity and/or astuteness, as well as providing emphasis:

hellward (Lawson)

Kellymania (Kirby)

Verb functions: How speakers used verbs was significant both to simulate conversation as well as to suggest a lively or action-oriented personality. The higher counts for use of verb functions by Lawson and Gilbert contrasted markedly with the relatively low counts for Hawke and Kirby, and indeed on some counts of verbs, all others:

> … it *can be looked* upon as a miracle *should* a boy *reach* man's estate and *escape* the contaminations of vice which daily example *makes* him familiar with from boyhood. *To be able to smoke, swear, drink,* and *gamble*…(Lawson) *[my italics]*

> … are *taught to be* sharks, *to use* your initiative and competitive spirit in order *to advance*, and particularly *to advance*…(Gilbert) *[my italics]*

The aggregated counts of occurrences of the verb forms that particularly suggest liveliness, namely *action verbs, infinitives,* B *('to be') verbs,* and *present tense* were Griffith 106, Lawson 158, Curtin 98, Menzies 105, Whitlam 76, Oodgeroo 83, Hawke 31, Gilbert 148, Greer 113, and Kirby 77. As with total verbal functions, the higher use of these especially 'lively' verb forms was by Lawson and Gilbert, while the least use was by Whitlam, Hawke, and Kirby.

Action verbs: Defined as any verbs that denote or connote a definite identifiable action,[339] with cognitive verbs defined as all others. The proposition is that a higher proportion of action verbs suggests a more action-oriented individual[340] noticeably connecting to immediate or specific actions. Lawson, Curtin, and Gilbert led all others in this use. The use of action verbs by Kirby and Oodgeroo at a level slightly above average likely helped to project commitment to action concurrently with their thought-orientation.[341]

Most fond of cognitive verbs were Griffith, Menzies, Whitlam, Hawke, and Greer, suggesting a preoccupation with intellectual and abstract discussion. Lawson, Curtin, and Kirby showed least use of cognitive verbs.

Infinitives: Accumulated infinitives also suggest liveliness and conversational effect, especially the verb 'to be'. Lawson and Gilbert substantially led all others, using infinitives at about twice the average rate.

B verbs ('to be'): Adding directness and liveliness were different forms of the verb 'to be', with Greer's usage leading all others and only Hawke well below the average use.

Negative verbs: The positive form of the verb is the liveliest, most forcefully providing a spotlight on the topic and speaker. Hawke and Kirby were almost routinely positive. Negative verbs were most used by Gilbert, then Whitlam, Curtin, and Greer.

Imperative finite verbs: The imperative in some contexts will be powerful to engage attention or for emphasis. It occurs infrequently in speech though, with its use implying special knowledge, power, or control of the speaker over others. Also, excessive use of the imperative potentially suggests dogmatism or despotism that might alienate. Imperatives occurred twice in Lawson, once in Curtin, and not at all in the samples of others. Crystal and Davy note that even the language of daily conversation includes few imperatives. They suggested that when these verbs do occur, their forcefulness is usually softened through some device, such as an additional clause related to the informality of an occasion.[342]

Present tense: Strengthening the immediacy of their speech, Griffith, Lawson, Gilbert, and Greer made the greatest use of present tense, sometimes even when referring to matters in the past:

> …is obviously true. Islands standing by themselves and countries separated from one another by large mountains or great rivers are naturally at first separate peoples… (Griffith)

Other tenses: Verbs in other than present tense address matters in the past or conditionally and tend to distance events, actions, and relations. Likely because of their subjects, Menzies, Oodgeroo, and Kirby frequently used other tenses than the present tense (respectively 47, 60, and 50, versus an Average at 39.5). A positive effect in this use is to underscore speech as historical perspective–implying that a speaker has a sense of history, and perhaps suggest freedom from concern with ongoing stimuli or current events.[343]

Kirby's speeches often provided an informed historical context for current events:

> We commemorate the modern history of Australia, in the knowledge that it began very largely by accident and as a direct outgrowth of Britain's loss of the penal colonies in America following the American revolution. Our colonial history started with nothing more elevated that the establishment of a prison colony. (Kirby)

Perhaps basic to Kirby's activities as a law reformer, he focused on precedent and past events to consider future needs. His substantial use of *other tenses* touched closely on his ethos–both in relation to his personal stance and his responsibilities when delivering this speech, as Chairman of the Australian Law Reform Commission.

Passive voice was used more frequently by Oodgeroo and Kirby (respectively at 9 and 15, versus an Average at 5.6). Kirby might seem less personal than others at times, partly because of this high occurrence of passive voice. Lawson, Oodgeroo, and Gilbert were also above the average of all speakers for use of passive voice.

Most advice is to use active rather than passive voice as much as possible, to focus the immediacy of a speaker and topic. The eminent linguistic researcher, Geoffrey Pullum challenges views proscribing the use of passive voice and suggests widening attention to the significance of passive clauses. He outlines a variety of subtleties for identifying and using passive voice.[344] Certainly, there are situations in which a speaker might use passive voice, such as the obvious and frequently poor use to help evolve an ethos as an authority figure.

Verbs/Nouns: A greater use of verbs rather than nouns projects an impression of a more in-touch and lively speaker, partly since verbs imply a speaker's ability to correlate things, concepts, people, actions, or events–and, this high level of relational ability might correlate with emotional stability.[345] In addition to making connections, verbs are process-oriented and tense-situating.[346] Likely, the nominal style is judged less effective because nouns: (i) are static and generally less vivid than verbs; (ii) lead to longer and less vivid sentences; and (iii) do not provide a diversity of sentence patterns.[347] Nouns are objectlike, without tense, and without modality. The heavy use of nominals is thought to detract from effective communication, by the actor often being deleted, or distancing of the speech event,[348] or creating static classifications and categories.[349]

A complete comparison of verbal to noun functions would count all verb and noun related word types.[350] The speakers were generally similar though in their use of verb functions compared to nouns: Griffith .57; Lawson .58; Curtin .46; Menzies .63; Whitlam .58; Oodgeroo .53; Hawke .41; Gilbert .75; Greer .62; and Kirby .40. Only Gilbert stood clearly apart from others with 98 occurrences of verb functions, compared with the group average of 75. Gilbert, Menzies, and Greer led the group in the use of verb functions.

Recommendations to use verbs heavily, rather than nouns, have a long history and seem well founded. These public figures' relative usages comport with the recommendation to favour verbs where possible.

Rhetorical Passage Shaping

Of all the rhetorical features, *anaphora* occurred often in the samples as well as widely within other speeches reviewed in this book. Other *parallelism* and *rhetorical questions* also frequently occurred in the samples, with the simple and otherwise common rhetorical figure of *alliteration* occurring little.

Anaphora: This repeating of the same word at the beginning of successive phrases, clauses, or sentences is easy to create for frequent use in speeches. While its creation requires forethought, and therefore might suggest a formal or analytical mind at work, *anaphora* often actually sounds like more personal dialogue–perhaps partly due to its simulation of the less structured repetitions of words so common in conversation.351 Here it was distinguished from other parallelism of sentences, clauses, or phrases. *Anaphora* was most common in the samples of Curtin, Menzies, Whitlam, and Gilbert:

> ... the *one* occasion when *one* man, with *one* soaring imagination, with *one* fire burning in him, and with *one* unrivalled capacity... (Menzies) *[my italics]*

> ... *under which* they live and *under which* they are raised... (Gilbert) *[my italics]*

Hawke, and to some extent Greer and others, minimally made use of *anaphora* in the samples. At times, Curtin, Menzies, Whitlam, and Gilbert used *anaphora* in short bursts, injecting a break to longer or more complicated passages:

> *Some* day, *some* year... (Menzies) *[my italics]*

For a variety of speech contexts, Whitlam often managed a series to emphasise with *anaphora* the scale of a significance, such as:

> For *so great* a disaster, *so great* a mistake, *such great* suffering, cannot be easily dismissed or even forgotten'.352 (Whitlam) *[my italics]*

Parallelism (other than anaphora) of phrases, clauses, and sentences: More subtly than *anaphora*, parallelism is also used to organise thoughts and/or to provide emphasis. This requires the formal arrangement of material into equivalent syntactical constructions in a structured way. The incidence of parallelism was greatest in Gilbert, with Curtin and Menzies, then Lawson, Oodgeroo, and Hawke using parallelism less, followed by Whitlam, Kirby, and Greer–and occurring not at all in the Griffith sample.

Curtin used other parallelism as well as *anaphora* within clauses and phrases toward the end of his speech to the United States people. These parallelisms, as well as the incorporation of the iconic parallelism in the Lincoln quote, assisted Curtin's emphasis of similarities of the two nations–thereby seeking the attention and approval of both Americans and Australians, to urge joint commitment to a common cause:

> *We fight what we have*, and *what we have* is our all. *We fight* for the same free institutions that you enjoy. *We fight* so that in the words of Lincoln, 'Government *of the people, for the people, by the people*, shall not perish from the earth'. Our legislature is elected the same as is yours, and *we will fight for it* and *for the right* to have it, just as *you will fight* to keep the Capitol in Washington the meeting place of freely elected men and women, representatives of a free people.[353] (Curtin) *[my italics]*

Griffith, Curtin, Menzies, Whitlam, Hawke, and Gilbert were fond of parallelism in conjunction with repetition and interpolation, which provided a conversation-like pause–often indicated in a speech transcript by the em dash:

> If the employers have the choice, *they will hire* a European–a migrant or an Australian–before *they will hire*… (Gilbert) *[my italics]*

> Here is an opportunity–*not just* for America *but for* all of *us*–to end *our* long preoccupations with military alignments of Asia…[354] (Whitlam) *[my italics]*

Rhetorical Question: Such questions are asked other than to get an answer. The rhetorical question's use is frequently for dramatic effect, such as to attract attention, or to make a persuasive point. Often the answer will already be known or be obvious, but the question format is used to cause the listener to think or to direct attention to an important item. Although no answer is expected, sometimes a speaker will ask the question and quickly answer it. A speaker might also accumulate a sequence of rhetorical questions one after another, to infer or emphasise a key point or conclusion. Although commonly used by speakers elsewhere, only Griffith and Lawson used rhetorical questions in the samples:

> Why is one people different from another? (Griffith)

> …and dare you think a mother cares less for her child? (Lawson)

Alliteration: A common rhetorical feature little present in these samples was alliteration, whereby two or more nearby words or syllables begin with the same consonant. Although extended alliteration occurs in an ornate or more formal genre, even in daily speech it can be subtly used as a feature for emphasis. The few occurrences of alliteration were in Lawson and, perhaps coincidentally, in the speeches of the legally trained Menzies and Whitlam, but the occurrences were so few that generalisation was not possible.

> … the votaries of vice hold dominion (Lawson)

Accumulated Impressions

While the speakers reviewed here expressed complex thoughts in well-shaped passages to secure attention and advocate a case, effective communication is not always clear. Former Queensland state premier Bjelke-Petersen was often incomprehensible but persuasive to some listeners, who thought him 'country-smart'–also clear speech often fails 'to affect others, let alone persuade'.[355]

Powerful for effective persuasion are impressions that result from the accumulation of *function words,* which grammatically provide cohesion, coherence, connectivity, and continuity. These include personal or impersonal pronouns, negations, conjunctions, prepositions, articles, auxilliary verbs, factive verbs, and nonreferential adverbs. While *lexical or content words* identify referents, *function words* keep discourse together, but also reflect thought and attention patterns from which an audience infers personal qualities and relationships.

High rates of articles and prepositions are thought to suggest more analytical speech, with low rates suggesting more experiential and narrative ways of communicating ideas. Pronouns, adverbs, negations, auxilliary verbs, and conjunctions are thought to indicate a more informal, personable approach. Using statistical methods,[356] some research suggests function words infer people's relative status or influence/'clout' in a social hierarchy, with higher-status people tending to focus more on others, using 'you' and 'we' at higher rates.[357] Reflections from such ongoing research efforts offer potential for insight about the accumulated effects of some language choices.

Making Impact

It is the individual talents of speakers and writers that create individual impact. Based on the review of some commonly occurring features of language in earlier chapters and here, it is wise when thinking through the preparation or analysis of speech or writing to:

1. Determine the appropriate genre for a purpose and situation–matched to whether the **primary aim** is to persuade a change of opinion, attitude, or action, or to consider the justice of charges or claims, or to praise or blame ceremonially.

2. Assess whether **segments of the audience** are likely to be favourable to a proposition, interested but undecided, apathetic, or opposed, and consider application of the motivating process to accomplish the primary aim.[358]

3. Consider **appropriate appeals** through credibility, audience emotions, and reason.

4. Find **aligned interests** of the speaker/writer and listeners/readers.

5. Clarify 'tells' of **propaganda,** lies, or bad behaviours that might impact the speaker or subject, and identify approaches that dismantle propaganda, especially propaganda challenging a community's pre-existing attitudes or democracy itself.

6. Assess use of **metaphor** or other **figurative language** to frame thinking and make events, scenes, and feelings tangible, for emphasis or other purposes.

7. Determine approaches that deal with **controversy** of a topic, public figure, or circumstance, alert to polemic to seek truth, winning, or dispute resolution.

8. Explore uses of **humour** to strengthen relationship with an audience and to emphasise or deflect matters.

9. Consider how **symbols, slogans, jargon,** or **slang** provide economy to specify meaning or build emotional appeals.

10. Identify colloquialisms, clichés, slang, contractions, or infinite verbs **implying informality.**

11. Explore how uses of interpolations, pairs, ellipsis, lists or series, compound clauses, sentence fragments, personal pronouns, exclamations and questions, contractions, and dashes, as well as proper nouns, everyday vocabulary, infinite verbs, clichés, and slang **simulate conversation.**

12. Review habits or patterns of using **function words** that might project individual styles or levels of formality.

13. Examine how an action orientation is set with **verbs relative to nouns** and verbs inferring action, active voice, shorter sentences and phrases, especially the verb 'to be', positive verbs, finite verbs, or 'will' as an auxilliary verb.

14. Identify how **matters are made more tangible or immediate** with present tense, everyday concrete words, proper nouns, specifics of dates, time, and details of people, places or events, examples, sense-based descriptions, mono-/bi-syllabic words, or Germanic-derived words with concrete referents.

15. Determine how the **formality** or **distance** of a speaker/writer and/or specific subject is set through longer or complex sentences, embedded clauses, elaborate parallelism, passive voice, past tense, negative verbs, or cognitive verbs.

16. Explore uses of *anaphora*, other parallelism, imperative verbs, exclamation, interpolation, pairs of the same word or word form, or alliteration that **emphasise matters.**

17. Clarify how omission, ambiguity, passive voice, deep clause embedding, and past or conditional tense **subordinate matters.**

18. Review ways that irony, neologisms, coined words, polemic, or humour might infer **creativity** or **astuteness.**

Success in choosing among such ingredients ordinarily results from considering together the ideas to be expressed, an audience's interests, and the context, while sensing how best to engage an audience's emotional commitment. Each of the ten speakers chose individual ways to connect with listeners, drawing intuitively or consciously on rhetorical principles and practice. Each tells us more about the qualities needed for effective public communication. What was common to all was the ability to call on the power of words to move people.

8: The Quiet Rhetoric of Sir Samuel Griffith

...for pure English, for nicely balanced expression, for a true realisation

of the meaning of all he said, and a keen sense of proportion,

Sir Samuel Walker Griffith stands pre-eminent. Analytical and cold

at most times yet he could on occasion rise to flights of eloquence...[359]

– C.A. Bernays

During the late nineteenth and early twentieth centuries, when Sir Samuel Walker Griffith was at the peak of his public life, the State of Queensland within the Australian economy depended heavily on rural and mining industries for economic growth. The State's principal source of wealth was from rural industry, especially wool and sugar, and the local political events in the major centres of population of Ipswich and Brisbane were dominated by the concerns of rural dwellers. Perhaps for this reason, public discussion of political matters tended to address basic concerns.

A widely held view, which persisted in the remainder of Australia long after these times, portrayed Queensland as culturally, intellectually, and politically conservative[360] and provincial. The State had produced or attracted many poets, writers, artists, performers, and others who made many contributions to social and intellectual concerns. Yet, the public figures who tried to raise the level of political awareness and discussion in Queensland were largely met with public controversy. Within this historical context, this chapter examines the communications of Griffith as one of the most capable public figures in Queensland and Australia at that time. He stood out in the period as someone who could go to the core of any matter and speak lucidly about complex issues.

Emotional Audiences

Opinions of Griffith ranged from loud acclaim at some public meetings to abuse and vilification on other occasions and in the press. Thomas McIlwraith, a long-time political enemy but later a partner in their coalition Government, describes Griffith as 'one part fool and one part raving imposter',[361] and A.G. Stephens's book *Griffilwraith* describes:

> ...the sinuous career of Griffith ... etched in tell-tale outlines from the time 'before the coalition' to his present enthronement on the Supreme Court Bench–from the time when he competed with Mr Glasey for the leadership of the Labour Party till, in July 1880, the Labour leaders expressed their distrust of him, and he began to Judasise and *right* down to his crowning treasons against his party and his country.[362]

Griffith was bitterly challenged on occasion from various directions for allegedly holding what would have been concurrently contradictory positions; of being against the graziers, the workers, the 'kanakas',[363] and subsequently for being the 'black-man's friend' as well as a 'slave-dealer'.[364] Especially seriously perhaps, Griffith during his political campaigns faced antagonistic audiences, and a group from one meeting of some 7,300 people afterwards went:

> ... to the blacksmith's got an effigy of Sam, kicked [it] to pieces! Preparations were made to burn it–liberally sprinkled with kerosene but Constable Fairbrother intervened–[and they] had a game of football with it.[365]

Other meetings received Griffith with considerably less drama. Yet he often faced audiences who were toward either extreme of being opposed to or in favour of his positions. To address these emotionally charged groups, he sought common ground in attitudes, beliefs, and experiences, particularly by seeking agreement with a foundational principle pertaining to a matter. Throughout a long public career, he retained a calm, balanced approach to most matters.

Rational Approach

Griffith was someone with immense learning in the law, classics, and natural sciences, and yet he confidently sought informed conversation with average citizens. He showed himself to be an adept advocate of his ideals. In common with thinkers of the Enlightenment in the seventeenth and eighteenth centuries, he often favoured inductive reasoning and tried to identify laws of nature[366] to establish social order. When he concluded that people had organised society contrary to a law of nature, as a practical person, Griffith adopted rhetorical means to help society see its error, so that people felt impelled to 'return to the right way ... [however] ... long and painful'[367] that return might be. Griffith often drew conclusions that would require his audience to make adjustment to their own behaviours or actions.

He tried to remedy social ills and resolve political problems through a temperate persuasiveness in his speeches, journal articles, pamphlets, and other public communications. Griffith's exploration of foundational principles to advocate solutions for the advancement of the public good enabled him to shift attention away from confrontation. In an apparent attempt to contain the uncontrolled emotionalism of some audiences, he invested his public communication with the steady, persuasive voice of a quiet rhetorician.

A Quiet 'Voice'

Griffith frequently adopted a stance as the humble contributor of his thoughts. This is reminiscent of the classical *rhetor* or the trial lawyer, who appears only to state facts in a quiet voice. Regardless of whether he followed his own *dictum* of saying what he had to say without first reducing it to writing, Griffith's language reverberates with this sense of a measured voice. He spoke as a rational person who adapted himself to a variety of situations.

Newscuttings and personal reports from those who knew Griffith indicate that what he expected of himself, namely brevity and clarity in the use of language, he also sought from others. Throughout his public life, he demanded these qualities from counsel or colleagues in his dealings with them.[368] His great strength was to deal with complex matters simply and clearly, making intelligent use of language features that accentuated or subordinated matters for the attention of an audience.

From Report to Advocacy

Commonly exhibiting the stance of a disinterested reporter of facts, Griffith would present a subtly convincing brief. He neatly converted occasions of report into opportunities for presenting his own opinions. One of many instances of this was in his *Notes on the Draft Federal Constitution*[369] framed by the Adelaide Convention (1897). At the time, he was chief justice of Queensland. He placed on record that his invitation to attend the Convention was as President of the Queensland Federation League, to outline past proceedings towards Australian Federation. He indicated that, although circumstances debarred him from the advocacy of Federation, he '*will*' take part in the public discussion and fulfil the need for 'a plain exposition of the Convention Bill'.

By the second page of the reported discussions, Griffith was offering 'reasons why Australians should federate'. He also methodically outlined the differing temperaments of people who were considering federation, with descriptions of people who had extreme bias against or for the proposed change. He then condemned those he thought were prejudiced against change because they lacked commitment to the brotherly action needed to support federation. The clear message was that a reader should feel a sense of collegiality with those favouring change, rather than identify with the opponents of federation.

The Best Solution

On a wide range of occasions, Griffith would set out to show that his plan was the best solution.[370] Seemingly sensitised to the emotional climate of occasions, his advocacy of a proposal as if it had grown from fundamental principles was carefully crafted. In 'The Certainty of Australian Federation',[371] he initially focused attention on the uniqueness of Australia's geography, in its isolation from the world and its geographical unity. He then outlined the geographical features that he asserted 'universally' characterised the political organisation of peoples. It was not until the fourth paragraph that Australia was mentioned again. Griffith then implicitly associated Australia with the general notion of a country as 'fatherland' and stated that peoples gather into one nation when they are similar and not geographically separated. He concluded this was a 'common law of humanity' to which 'Australia must submit'.

The reader thus progressed from a brief statement of facts of Australian geography, through the formation of a general rule based on history, to the inevitable conclusion that Australia was bound by this rule–a progression that Griffith said was supported by the authority of the historical and geographical sciences, as these were then called.

In an article titled 'The Distribution of Wealth', he searched for rules of nature by which people should abide:

> The only underlying rule of natural right appears to be the fundamental truth already stated, that the products of a man's labour are his own.[372]

His opening sentence in this article was simple and restrained, while setting the stage for the assertion of a fundamental principle:

> It has been said that Political Economy is based upon the assumption that man is a moneygetting animal.[373]

In a more complicated statement within an electoral manifesto, Griffith was still straightforward in highlighting the principle for the argument that followed:

> In common with the rest of the community the Government have of late had their attention directed to the present condition of the sugar industry in Queensland, and especially to the difficulty of obtaining labour for carrying it on.[374]

The most eloquently ornate expression of this tendency to find a fundamental principle supporting his proposal for change was in 'The Social Problem', which is reviewed later in this chapter. By the time of this article in 1919, Griffith was retired from his role as Australia's first chief justice, and he questioned the very 'basis on which the actions of the community are founded'.[375]

Measured Emotions

Throughout his public life, Griffith seemed to anticipate that he would be accused of being a 'radical', 'socialist', or 'communist' because of his outspoken comments. To fend off this name-calling, he would cite eminent British figures as authority for his statements in support of his argument, such as the Archbishop of York and Lord Chief Justice Coleridge.

When Griffith attacked notions that might be warmly entertained by his audience, then he increased the degree of his qualification:

> It has been my constant experience to meet with well-meaning persons, professing the most liberal views and the warmest sympathy with the improvement of the condition of the people, who, as soon as they find out that their share of the future earnings of the community may be diminished by any change, at once withdraw their sympathy, and show themselves to be at heart Conservatives, and *perhaps unconsciously*, worshippers of the great god Mammon.[376] *[my italics]*

In this long sentence, some attention will inevitably focus on the qualifications and balanced parallelism that carefully frame his observation. With conversational ease, he clearly and simply dismissed the 'well-meaning persons' as driven by self-interest.

Griffith would anticipate opponents' nit-picking by framing propositions carefully and precisely–using such qualifications as 'not scientifically inaccurate'. In 'The Distribution of Wealth', he used the substantive 'something' and the adverb 'somehow' to attach vagueness to suggestions potentially challenging to his proposals. He was scrupulous in sequencing his thoughts and language.

Rhetorical Strategy

In 1891 he chose the occasion of his Anniversary Address as President of the Royal Geographical Society of Australia–Queensland Branch[377] to speak about Australia's federation movement. He was also the State's premier at the time and already a strong advocate for federation, but he incorporated a then expected deference to the ongoing discussions occurring at the meetings of the federation movement. He began with a lengthy personal request for indulgence from listeners, for presenting his Presidential annual address 'without first reducing it to writing' as was customary. This extemporaneous address was in the presence of the colony's governor and other leaders of Queensland and showed again Griffith's rationalising an occasion for report as an opportunity to advance his argument for federation.

Griffith initially proposed that features of geography and the common qualities among peoples established the basis for the formation of a nation. He then drew attention to the authority of geographical studies, and recommended the value of 'political geography' to consider the proposition that:

> The divisions of the world into nations, or into parts of the globe occupied by different peoples, corresponds to a very great extent with the physical divisions of nature.[378]

He argued that only geographical divisions, such as substantial mountain ranges, rivers, or deserts, would effectively divide a continent into independent states. Griffith used this principle to conclude:

> ...looking at the question from a merely geographical point of view... led me to the conclusion that the political unification of Australia is absolutely inevitable. Nothing can stop it, unless the operations of nature and the laws of common humanity should be changed in the case of Australia–which I think is a most unlikely event to happen. I hope that the unification will be accomplished before very long, because I believe it will be good for us all. I trust that I may again not be trespassing in the arena of politics, if I conclude with a hope that we may all live to see the natural result of the causes which I have endeavoured to indicate, and to see the union of Australia in one great Commonwealth under Her Majesty. [*Hear, hear.*][379]

He rested his case upon inevitability, derived from the features of geography and the common qualities among peoples, which he asserted set the basis for the establishment of a nation.

Throughout the address, Griffith used formal language suited to the situation and the time. He also used a generous number of cognitive rather than action verbs, appropriately matching his audience's commitment to intellectual enquiry. But he kept the discussion concrete with frequent use of proper nouns, mentioning some specific countries that he felt showed conformity to his 'natural law'.

Pragmatic Advocacy

Griffith later used this 'natural law' to model the structure of the short article, 'The Certainty of Australian Federation',[380] in which he led the reader more rapidly to the conclusion reached in the address to the Royal Geographical Society. Once again, he identified the natural law of geography and then applied the 'law' by specifically describing geographical features in Australia.

He addressed each of the existing lines on the map that marked the colonies, pointing out that these were unrecognisable by a traveller in the country, as 'imaginary', 'arbitrary', 'accidental', and 'not scientific frontiers'. Griffith used a metaphor of a travelling stranger crossing these lines of division but being unable to recognise them, to emphasise their illusory character:

> Nowhere is there such a difference in the character of the country that a stranger would ever guess on crossing the frontier that he had passed from one State to another.[381]

After reviewing the few natural divisions between the Australian states, he said that, apart from the desert separating Western Australia, these were meaningless. Griffith stated that the existing divisions into colonies were thus vacuous. In contrast to the illusion of these divisions, he immediately highlighted the single identifiable 'oneness' of the Australian '...people speaking *one* language, proud of *common* origin and enjoying *similar* institutions'. *[my italics]* His forceful questioning whether Australia could reverse the unhappy history of conflict between neighbouring states allowed him to conclude in a short emphatic paragraph that Australia's 'destiny ... is to be *one* people'. *[my italics]*

Finally, in the last paragraphs of the article, Griffith linguistically alienated those opposed to federation, while recommending his practical argument for accepting federation. Just as he had in the address to the Royal Geographical Society, he accumulated counterpoints of 'people/they', 'union/everyone', and 'province/Continent' to impel the reader finally to the conclusion that only good could come from federating and that:

> ...in a few years the opponents of union ... [will] ... be regarded as little better than curious survivals of a bygone era.[382]

The structure Griffith set in this article consisted of identification of the natural law, application of this to Australia, a dismissal of existing divisions as arbitrary, along with a concurrent building of the notion of 'oneness' into a climax—and finally, a denouement in which the futility of the opposition to the inevitable was emphasised.

Tackling Controversy

Griffith's close attention to handling the inflammatory character of specific circumstances was illustrated in the rhetorical strategies that he adopted in two documents relating to 'coloured labour'. In the late nineteenth century in Queensland, one of the most controversial legal-social-political issues was the importation of Pacific Islanders, who were employed very widely in the colony, especially to cut sugar cane on tropical farms.

At first, Griffith had sought to abolish this importation, which at its worst was exploitative and not noticeably different from a slave-trade. When he could not secure support to abolish the importation of Pacific Islanders, he made significant personal efforts over a long period of time to ensure that every recruitment was a genuinely contracted work arrangement with each individual native islander. Within government archives from the time are a very large number of handwritten notes he made on each native islander's case records, to regulate activities and assure medical and humane treatment.

His journal article 'The Coloured Labour Question in Australia'[383] and his open letter to the *Brisbane Courier* newspaper, headed 'Sir S.W. Griffith's Manifesto',[384] faced antagonism from many in his audience. This was both because the subject was controversial and because his arguments in favour of the temporary import of Islanders reversed his earlier public statements. These documents took account of the sensitive circumstances.

Unsurprisingly, Griffith used different language approaches to deal with controversial matters in these different publications. Likely expecting a careful reflective reader of the journal article, he couched his discourse with frequent doublets, such as 'extreme simplicity or great difficulty' and 'confident and exhaustive opinion' while pursuing a logically developed case. He showed a willingness to see at least two sides to issues, arguably modeling the consideration of more than one view of matters.

Although this use of doublets and balance in a closely-knit extended written argument might be suitable to help shape the thoughtfulness of an attentive reader of a journal article, Griffith seemed to anticipate a greater emotionalism of the reader of his open letter to the newspaper. Here he placed on record matters not helpful to his argument but subordinated these syntactically and rhetorically.

He used an elaborate sentence, for example, to subordinate the blame that people had attached to him because of the policies that both he and the Government had adopted concerning the use of Pacific Island labourers. His 'voice' was progressively 'lowered' as potentially more inconvenient facts were mentioned. Set out according to subordinations, this sentence would be read with each break below [/ and //] indicating a further level of subordination:

> But / while I am unable to attribute to this cause alone so much of the prevailing depression as some people are disposed to think, // many other causes being apparent / not only in Queensland / but throughout the rest of Australia, // I have arrived at the conclusion that it is the imperative duty of the Government, / and perhaps / more especially / of myself, // to whom, / rightly or wrongly / much of the blame or credit of the existing state of things has been attached, // to review the present position, / and to state plainly what we think is the right policy to be adopted by the country at this time.[385]

Here Griffith not only denied that the failure of the sugar industry was the sole cause of the depression in the colony but also claimed that he was not responsible. When he accepted that 'blame ... has been attached' to him, not only the passive voice and clinically detached connotation of the verb, but also a deep level of rhetorical subordination operated to distance Griffith's possible blameworthiness from the reader. Ostensibly, the main purpose of this sentence was to put on record his obligations in government. After the complication of this sentence, perhaps the reader would feel relieved to accept Griffith's brief deferral elsewhere in the piece, seeking indulgence for presenting his opinion in an open letter to the newspaper.

Repeatedly in the letter, he used this tactic of leading a reader into syntactic complexities when he discussed matters that might harm his argument unless they were disposed of. In a copy of the letter that Griffith sent to the former Governor's wife, Lady Musgrave,[386] of similar typeset and layout to what was published in the *Courier* newspaper and likely a galley proof, he had included 'urged in this letter' at the end of his final sentence: 'I should add, that while my colleagues concur in the conclusion I am alone responsible for the political retrospect, and for the arguments'.[387] What he was careful to make clear by disposing of a qualification was the range of arguments for which he took responsibility. Griffith was especially adept at rhetorically shrouding in subordinated breath groups matters harmful to his case. Ideally for Griffith, the reader would remember little of what was in subordinated passages, while accepting his detailed explanations as openness in presenting all matters.

Official Radicalism

When 74 years old, Griffith saw to the publication of the article 'The Social Problem' in the newspaper *The Daily Mail*.[388] The article crystallised his lifelong interest in the law as an instrument for ensuring social justice. He had long worked within a master-rule system, but, following ill health, retirement from the bench, and near the end of his life, he urged strongly that the injustices to which this system gave rise should be eradicated altogether. Perhaps Griffith no longer felt that what he perceived as injustices should be eroded only by ameliorating influences, such as he exercised in his public life.

Griffith argued that society should be restructured by replacing the principle of master-rule with one of fraternity. He outlined some of the far-reaching consequences of this change. To deal with such an important and controversial subject, he adopted an ornate style and incorporated aphorisms that potentially gave his proposition some official status. With Griffith's views on social matters regarded by some, including unsurprisingly some within the legal profession, as 'dangerous',[389] in this article he modulated the quietly persuasive voice. His language was quite formal and reflected an ornate expression of a voice of authority. The purpose seemed to be to reinforce his position as a respected and credible critic of the social system.

If Griffith had incorporated the views within this article in draft legislation, this would differ substantially from laws operating anywhere in Australia. Now later in life, he appeared to be at least radical in his perspective on this matter. Certainly, he could be included within the moderate definition of the Radical as someone who 'assumes that reform is worthwhile providing that there is not overwhelming consensus of opinion against it'.[390] In shaping this article, as with his other writing on society, Griffith sought the fundamental natural law to which he felt people must submit.

High Tone Authority

In the early part of the article, Griffith defined a civilised society as one in which people were bound by union to some common purpose or interest. He distilled this definition from illustrations in the natural environment, recounting observations on the seasons, bees, and the ant. He then moved inductively to identify derivative characteristics in human beings. He thus hinted at a conventional topic from the highly ceremonial classical funeral orations—the birth of a nation from the soil.

Griffith apparently intended that this deliberation on society should be regarded as having official authority. By commencing with such resounding phrases as 'all we like sheep have gone astray', he set a high tone that was reinforced by other trappings of an official voice, such as the accumulation of formal vocabulary as well as coordinate and balanced structures—as shown below, with formalisms *italicized,* and with each break [/ and //] indicating a further level of subordination:

> Every *sentient living creature* that comes into existence under *our present dispensation,* / whether it is called instinct or reason, / is *equally subject to* an *unformulated* and unknown law // which it is unconsciously *bound to obey* / but which in either case can be *disobeyed,* // as was said *long ago—* / *'All we like sheep*

have gone astray'— / subject of course to the *inevitable consequences of disobedience.*[391] [my italics]

These formalisms subdued the liveliness that his clearly reasoning voice frequently evoked. The article adumbrated with biblical and aphoristic echoes and gave the impression that he spoke as if he was a 'fountain-head of knowledge'. But Griffith shifted from this high formalism in the early part of the article to a suasive 'chattiness' later, when urging readers to take action.

His basic argument to return to the 'right' way was highly moral and the tone tended toward being sermonic. Yet he drew attention to everyday concerns by appealing to what people publicly said they wanted, namely, what is right. He made no subtle distinctions but divided his topics into 'fraternity/master-rule', 'conscious/unconscious', 'right/wrong', and so kept simple ideas constantly before readers.

Griffith appealed to wide interests by likening a community to a family. He distinguished obedience from mastery and drew on 'history and experience' additionally to support his claim that rules need to be obeyed. Finally, before explaining the genesis of his 'doctrines', Griffith returned to the article's central thread of concern with nature and its laws that he had said also govern a bee or ant. He strongly declared that there was 'not alternative … [to obedience] … but anarchy or jungle law'. His discussion had alternated between notions of 'bad' and 'good' up to this point but concluded by unambiguously identifying the 'evil' of anarchy by associating it with 'jungle law'.

Rules for Society

If accepted as outlined, Griffith's principles might have served as the basis for definitions in a Property Bill. As State Premier in 1890, he had drafted a Bill that was allowed to lapse, dealing with the rights of property and defining relations between capital and labour. But if a Bill incorporating the assumptions in this article were to become law, many people's actions would have to dramatically change for society to operate. The principles outlined in the article would hardly constrain a person determined to go against them, but perhaps Griffith astutely recognised the truth that laws operate most effectively when supporting the beliefs of society. 'The Social Problem' consolidated advocacy for a fundamental shift in beliefs, in an ornate piece that took shape as his aspiration for authoritative and enduring deliberation of what he believed nature would dictate must inevitably occur.

A first analytical reading of the article could allow an interpretation that Griffith was touched by some religious fervour in his later years. But the religious, not specifically Christian, overtone was likely a powerful framing for the time, to encourage respect for his views among then strongly religious and conservative citizens of Queensland. While the ornately formal tone of this article distinguished it from his other public writing, echoes of Griffith's compelling voice were still audible.

Informed Conversations

Throughout a long career, Griffith engaged confidently in informed 'conversation' with average citizens. He implicitly complimented the intelligence of his audiences by not 'dumbing-down' what he had to say. In many communications, his careful organisation of ideas and directness in language produced convincingly clear argument. To provide close linguistic support for his advocacy, his rhetorical language accentuated, pre-empted, or subordinated ideas in a variety of ways.

He integrated variations in the direction and intensity of both the ideas and the rhythm within his prose, which guided the intensity of his sequencing of topics and supported the thread of his argument. In the 'forethought' to his translation of Dante's *Inferno,* he had cited the saying, 'As a tune is to a song, and as its savour to a dish, so its rhythm to a poem'.[392] Especially in his writing, Griffith's commanding modulation of rhythm was helpful to keep the reader's attention. His moderation of sentence structure and breath groups slowed or increased the pace of his prose in a way that ensured his ideas might be more clearly stated, understood, and perhaps better accepted.

Comparing his address at the Royal Geographical Society with the samples of other speakers in Chapter Seven illustrated Griffith's extemporaneous language style. Even though this address focused on lessons from history, Griffith's language was enlivened by his speaking predominantly in the present tense. He did use longer sentences than others reviewed, at about double the average word-length, but was close to the average in the use of clauses that might have complicated his discourse, with some use of passive voice. He used no alliteration, *anaphora,* or neologism in the address, yet did so elsewhere. He used first-person singular pronouns at more than double the average of this group of notable Australians. His audience on that occasion might have largely forgiven so much self-reference, because of the esteem in which he was likely held by the invited group of dignitaries in his audience.

On occasion, Griffith would introduce colloquialisms or clichés, such as 'sweating system' and 'weakest goes to the wall'. He often inserted a cut and thrust of ideas in shorter sentences, sometimes with interrogatives:

> When the possessor of raw material has been strong enough, he has not always gone through the form of giving his labourers food in the form of wages, but has merely provided them with as much food, in the form of food, as he thought necessary. This was called 'slavery'. In what essential particulars

does the so called 'free' competition differ from slavery? So far from being free, it is the complete domination of the weak by the strong.[393]

About such an important issue of principle he was very clear. The compact argument of the piece from which this passage was drawn, *Wealth and Want*, was also salted with lighter touches, such as familiar analogy, direct paragraph, and sentence connectives ('Now...', 'The result...', and 'The preceding statement...'), a short simple sentence, uses of the copula 'is', rhetorical questions, and clichés ('goes to the wall').

In this and other apparently effective pieces, such as 'The Certainty of Australian Federation', 'The Coloured Labour Question in Australia', and 'The Social Problem', Griffith's rhetorical success rested in part on this modulation between rhythms of formal and colloquial discourse, to give clear expression to his ideas. In 'The Social Problem', he incorporated aphorism and other modes of an official voice to offer a highly decorative, aspirational, potentially definitive public statement. When, as in two other pieces 'A Plea for the Study of the Unconscious Vital Processes in the Life of Communities'[394] and 'Manifesto to the Electors of North Brisbane',[395] Griffith perhaps took for granted that he was the oracle to whom others would listen, or when he attempted an imaginatively enriched approach, he seemed less successful.

Griffith's prodigious contributions to the law and politics, as well as his commitment to such demanding personal relaxations as translating Dante's *Inferno* in evening light at the conclusion of full workdays, remain remarkable accomplishments. Some youthful verses in his Diaries, his private correspondence with his wife, and the translation of Dante are among the limited extant writing by which we might judge his facility in an imaginative mode. What few writings have survived of Griffith's efforts to create more imaginative communications were less exceptional. When in London as counsel in the Railways Case of 1881, he wrote to his wife:

> I always do feel tired when I have not the pillow of your dear heart to lay my head upon–I am looking forward to the time when I shall again clasp you in my arms and I am sure you are doing the same–I do not know how long the enquiry is likely to last but I think that everyone will try to get through with it as fast as possible... [he then outlines the prominent advocates opposing him; but] ...I am not afraid of them...[396]

Without doubt, Griffith's education in the classics and his experience as a lawyer, politician, and jurist honed a highly developed capacity for conceptual thinking. He made sophisticated use of language to temper the impact of his ideas. He seemed at his best and most effective in the role of an advocate/teacher, concerned to clarify matters, so that people might make the wisest choices for the future.

For Griffith's time and now, his public communications highlight an important issue concerning politics. He created contexts in which the public might consider seriously the merits of proposals to enhance society for the common good. A limited willingness of people in communities to engage in political and policy discussion then and now means that politically unsophisticated audiences apparently vote according to a projected image of a public figure, with limited consideration of the impact of causes, party platforms, or proposals for change.

Artfully, through his predominantly clear advocacy, Griffith presented proposals for change within a framework of higher policy set by fundamental principles. He illustrated how such principles directly touched people's daily lives. In this respect, Griffith was an especially powerful communicator.

9: Louisa Lawson on Womanhood Suffrage

Equality and Equity[397]

Louisa Lawson launched *The Dawn* on 15 May 1888 in Sydney, as a feminist journal published monthly. Through her writing, editorial, and business leadership, the publication was both influential and financially successful, read widely both in Australia and internationally. Writing initially under the pen name of Dora Falconer, she observes in the first issue that:

> There has hitherto been no trumpet through which the concentrated voice of womankind could publish their grievances and their opinions... Here then is Dawn, the Australian woman's journal and mouthpiece–phonograph to wind out audibly the whispers, pleadings and demands of the sisterhood.[398]

Production of *The Dawn* as well as the *Dawn Club* meetings occurred at the publication's premises from 1889. These premises then became a centre of the suffrage movement in Sydney. The Womanhood Suffrage League that evolved in 1891 developed with Lawson's support, and all these initiatives grew to be influential forces. Her efforts helped to reshape perceptions in the turbulent 1890s[399] and played a substantial role in securing the right for women to vote by 1902 in Australian federal elections, under the same conditions as applied for men.

Vision, Talent, and Perseverance

Soon after arriving in Sydney in 1882 from rural New South Wales, Lawson was motivated to remedy the dilapidated state of the grave of the poet, Henry Kendall. It was through her 'untiring efforts that a shabby little wooden cross on Kendall's grave in Waverley Cemetery was replaced by a worthy monument'.[400]

This was an early indication of the perseverance and talents that Lawson would bring to the womanhood suffrage movement. She was a poet, writer, publisher, suffragist, and feminist, who on her own as a parent and with little support raised her surviving children, including her son, the celebrated poet and author Henry Lawson. In her column for *The Dawn* in May 1889, she wrote:

> Though timorous at the outset we gained confidence as we journeyed. For have we not met scores of women whose aims and hope are like our own? Women whose thought proves like that of a mountain stream is of little effect alone but which when run into a general river of purpose can potently aid in turning the wheel of time and grind out a new era...As *The Dawn* is a proven paper of its kind in Australia, being edited, printed, and published by women in the interests of women. It has been looked upon by many as an uncertain venture, and we have frequently been asked by subscribers and advertisers the question 'Will it live' to all such we have but one reply. *The Dawn* has been a success.[401]

Through Lawson's private correspondences and conversations, she formed strong alliances with influential people. Among these were Lady Windeyer, who had long worked for women's rights, and Windeyer's daughter Margaret, who went on to advocate the League in the United States when she moved to Chicago.

Lawson was a strong advocate for the formation of the Womanhood Suffrage League. With the agreement of the *Dawn Club* members, she merged this *Club* into the new League, committing to activism to secure the vote:

> ...this is what we can do, stand together as mothers of men and demand our right to a voice in the making of the laws by which we and our children are governed.[402]

With the formation of the League on 4 June 1891, three years after the first issue of *The Dawn*, its members included experienced women who were actively involved in the cause of Womanhood Suffrage.

Challenge to Assumptions

Lawson was also widely appreciated as a rousing speaker, and she vigorously advocated for womanhood suffrage and equality in previously male-dominated domains, with confidence and effectiveness. She was well-regarded as a leading advocate of the cause when she spoke at the first public meeting of the new League, on 13 June 1891. In this speech, Lawson brought together a powerful case within the then socially dominant framework that defined women's role to care for the home. She urged that the home and children depended on the empowerment of new laws, which apparently only women were willing to argue for. Throughout the speech she put on full display the harmful actions of men. She called on women and men to recognise that, for justice and practicality, the vote for women was essential to ensure laws that would protect their children and the home.

A difference of Lawson's speech from many others was how she built a case by continuously piling up emotionally charged everyday scenes. She sketched vivid visual scenes that provided powerfully illustrative evidence in support of her reasoned and emotionally strong case. She often used language suggestive of a high tone, at times with biblical resonance. Her stream of appeals grew with the addition of each narrative, metaphor, simile, or allusion to boost the power of her case. Akin to her own metaphor noted earlier, it was as if the 'mountain stream' of her images, which might have 'little effect alone', when 'run into a general river of purpose can potently… grind out'[403] new impact.

The opening words to her speech contentiously challenged a claim that women were 'discovered' during the century in which they gathered. Lawson noted that if this were true, 'speeches to induce men to do justice to them' would not be needed. Beginning with this *dispute* polemic, she contested the disregard of women, and challenged the hypocrisy of assigning to women the duty of safeguarding the home without the resources needed to do so. She began:

> It is said that 'the greatest discovery of the nineteenth century is the discovery of women'. Would we were not compelled to make speeches to induce men to do justice to them. That great hearted worker for the 'world's women', Olive Schreiner, says:- 'If women were the inhabitants of Jupiter, of whom you had happened to hear something, you would pore over us and our conditions day and night, but because we are before your eyes you never look at us.'[404]

Lawson then tackled head-on the prevalent attitudes and misrepresentations of women and the women's movement. She put newspaper reporters on notice to report accurately the evening's speeches, and firmly stated that her main dispute was with attitudes, implying that, as the first remedy, justice required a change to attitudes. She asked:

> …how many newspapers will impartially or faithfully report a woman's rights meeting, or for that matter any other meeting of women. There will be the covert sneer, the attempt at witticism, the unkind comparison calculated to impress the public with women's weakness and inability, or to cast ridicule not only on the cause but upon the members themselves, and the pure heartfelt utterances of true generous women are omitted.[405]

Lawson surely understood that people in her audience and readers of the speech in the newspaper ranged widely in their attitude to the cause. From the strongly favourable, to the interested but undecided, to the apathetic, and to some who opposed the cause, she sought to engage this diverse group. Lawson sketched vividly the harm occurring to people and highlighted basic elements of the problem. She used startling statements to overcome inertia, relating points of agreement in attitude, beliefs, and experiences, while seemingly wary of exaggeration. She firmly stated a way forward for the cause by requesting specific actions,[406] indicating how each group within her audience could help.

She pointed out that women had long been told that their sphere and work was home, then quoted a moving verse that drew parallel with a bird's growing 'wild defending its nest'. Through graphic scenes she illustrated the iniquity of existing intrusions on daily home life:

> Useless indeed are women's tears and women's prayers while the votaries of vice hold dominion over our city, and single men may obtain licence to open any tottering mass of rottenness as a public-house for the purpose of giving the weak a push hellward... Can we wonder that a woman in defence of self and children smashed the decanters in a drinking den where her husband spent his time and money to the neglect of his home and family? Is it to be wondered at that this woman took the law into her own hands, seeing how worse than useless was the outlook for help from any other quarter.[407]

She questioned the circumstance whereby:

> ...according to present conditions it can be looked upon as a miracle that should a boy reach man's estate and escape the contaminations of vice which daily example makes him familiar with from boyhood. To be able to smoke, swear, drink, and gamble like a man is the Alpha and Omega of his infantile dreams.[408]

Tackling Contradictions

Most powerful when tackling contradictions, Lawson used metaphors combined with brief visual narratives to propel her appeal:

> ...see the traps laid for our sons and brothers—the sailor boy who has left home and mother for the first time...even in broad day light keepers of gambling houses come out upon the footpaths and take half-crowns from little children who sell newspapers upon the streets and where does the respectable boy clerk get the half-sovereign which he stakes upon a horse in our King Street tobacconist shop? What kind of hearts can the men have who take these boys' earnings from them? Darlinghurst gaol is full of their victims, and Gladesville Asylum is filled with the mothers of them.[409]

She swept the listener through the accumulation of visual images, each progressively more deeply touching, to reveal the forces that were shattering individual and family lives.

Lawson pointed out that men had cast women in the no-win role of protecting family without their having any legal standing. This was named by Caroline Chisholm, and later publicised in Australia by Anne Summers, as women being cast into the role of 'God's Police'.[410] Lawson's narratives vividly illustrated this contradiction and hypocrisy of expectation placed on women. To strengthen her highlighting of this contradiction, she piled up action verbs focused on the senses that progressed to one climax in her speech, of a wife smashing her husband's 'drinking den':

> says... hear... look... agitated... held up... report... cast... omitted... told... looked... reach... escape... smoke, swear, drink... gamble... walk... see... puts foot... tell... given... spend... transferred... come... take... sell... get... stakes... take... filled... hold dominion... obtain... open... giving... mourn... raise their voice... smashed... took the law into her own hands, seeing how worse than useless was the outlook...[411]

By holding up a mirror to the drunkenness of some groups in the nineteenth century colonial population, Lawson built her case to advocate that the remedy required was to enable women to vote, and thereby influence the laws. She asked, 'If man who is in power and makes the laws has not courage to put down these vices, how can the son be expected to avoid them handicapped as he will be by transmitted weakness?'[412]

Emotional Intensity

An outline of the main themes in the structure of Lawson's speech illustrates her progressively increasing the emotional intensity:
Introduction
Statement of historical position ('discovery of women')
Occasion ('since the time when equal suffrage was first agitated')
Speaker's authority ('public opinion is becoming greatly modified')
Introduce topic ('we have been told that women's sphere and work was
   home')

Body
(i) Current Realities
Mother defending her young ('the tiny bird grow wild defending its nest')
Society's threats ('miracle [to] ...escape the contaminations of vice')
Opposition ('took the law into her own hands')
Tragedy from inaction ('the cold iron of the railway line a fitting place to
   lay her distracted head upon... waiting for "Death" the only friend
   she wished for')
Failure to remedy ('man... has not courage to put down these vices')

Requires 'weak' to act ('Is the gentlest too weak for a blow') (CLIMAX)

(ii) Needed Steps
Responsibility ('they have bound our hands and placed us in the front line')
First business ('free ourselves before we can help any good cause')
Be responsible ('give us the power and sacredness of the ballot')
Reason for efforts ('for right and justice')
Relations ('of home to the equal suffrage work')
Dismiss comparisons ('need not follow in the footsteps of others')
Actions needed ('consecrate ourselves... press fearlessly onward')
Break needed ('dark ages gave to women eternal silence and servitude')
Outcome envisioned ('But I see a new heaven and a new earth') (CLIMAX)

Conclusion
Present ('women... coming to realise their responsibility')
New reality ('thousands and thousands of men... are coming... on... side')
Result ('for better laws... for better and purer homes') (CLIMAX)[413]

Resetting Expectations

In the lead-up to the first climax, in (i) above, Lawson:
- Stated as a principle that 'Here in Australia it is considered more a crime to steal a horse than ruin a girl'[414]
- Anticipated and dismissed the excuse often given that a girl at '14 years... is expected to understand the nature of advances made to her'[415]
- Pictured the girl in the local hospital 'with heart and limbs broken'
- Took listeners graphically through the suicidal action ('the cold iron of the railway line'),[416] and
- Placed the cause at the feet of the city who neglected the girl.

Following these scenes of pathos, she made an arresting call to action, quoting the verse, 'If a viper coils by your sleeping child / Is the gentlest too weak for a blow?'[417]

For Lawson's progression through 'Needed Steps' (ii) to the next climax, she related specific examples that spotlight the absence of logic and justice in blocking women's voices from being heard through the vote. While keeping a focus on women's responsibility and the 'sacredness of the ballot', Lawson's extended narratives illustrated the injustices and harm done to women through the role into which they were cast.

Stimulating Next Steps

These narratives were told in sentences that alternated between longer, complex or compound sentences and short declarations, some in the mode of aphorisms that reverberate with everyday wisdom. Lawson presented vibrant images of women, men, and children in specific circumstances, facing challenges in daily life. She sometimes used *anaphora* for emphasis, such as 'Selfishness is *easy to* teach and *easy to* learn, and they call it womanliness.' *[my italics]* She also invested her speech with personal language in her appeal to unite efforts for needed next steps.

The speech was lively and tangible, resulting from Lawson's use of emotive vocabulary, rhetorical questions, parallel phrases, verse, scripture, aphorism, alliteration, hyperbole, as well as proper nouns. Her descriptions reflected well both the extreme character and the proximity of the events and circumstances that she highlighted. She made powerful use of fresh and well-used metaphors, greater-than-average use of action verbs and present tense, in simple language. A close examination of the initial 600-words of the speech shows her use of a large proportion of words that were monosyllabic (70%) or bisyllabic (19%), many 'to be' verbs (36% or 25 of the 69 finite verbs), and many personal pronouns (32 in all).

Lawson rallied her audience using figurative language but moderated her 'voice tone', with each break [/ and //] indicating a further level of subordination:

> To take our ease / while gilded hells open on all sides / to lure our sons to gamble away their earnings, / while lives are blasted, // hearts broken and souls damned– // shall we / because the way is rough and the sun hot / be content to sit beneath our own vine and fig tree, // to be pleasing in the eyes of men, / to pander to their tastes and prejudices as a violet sweet, // and as a lute sounding fine harmonies, / and bury our hearts and our conscience alive?[418]

She here focused the figurative language in a way that reflected the language of a narrative or parable. Her swift answer to the final question rendered it only momentarily rhetorical in its effect. In the next sentence Lawson replied, 'No, selfishness is not loveliness...', intimating a sense of the wisdom of aphorism. After additional perspectives, she brought attention back to everyday human suffering, culminating in what might be news to her listeners that:

> ...as late as 1815 we find in one small district in England as many as 39 wives sold into servitude by their husbands, with the addition of sixpence for the rope with which they were led.[419]

With this brief item, she highlighted the apparent paltriness of women's lives in the view of husbands who subscribed to the cruel trade–in which even the rope, as another property, had a calculated price.

Empowering Action

Lawson then rapidly closed her advocacy for the practical rightness of women to be empowered to vote. She rested her case with a long (96-word) all-embracing sentence, preceded by the attention-getting ten-word vision, 'But I see a new heaven and a new earth'. This she followed with the even shorter declaration, 'Thank God the day is not far distant'.

Then, this final lengthy sentence underscored her emphatic conclusion:

> Not only are women in all sections of the country and every condition of life coming to realise their responsibility, but thousands and thousands of men, noble great-hearted lovers of humanity, are coming out on the side of home protection and not only bidding us Godspeed, but doing all in their power to bring about the day that shall see *brother and sister* standing *shoulder to shoulder* and *heart to heart* in the great fight for *right, truth and justice*, for better laws, *for better* protection to our sons and daughters, *for better and purer homes*.[420] *[my italics]*

With parallelism of pairs, a triad of virtues of western civilisation ('right, truth and justice'), the *anaphora* ('for better...'), and adumbrating aphorism, Lawson condensed and emphasised the high purpose and value of her listeners' collective efforts.

A principal focus for the movement was here restated as protection of 'our sons and daughters'. For final emphasis, Lawson neatly stated with powerful rhetorical effect the aim of Womanhood Suffrage in her closing visionary words, 'for better and purer homes'. She showed an inspirational pathway forward, to be built through the efforts of women and men jointly committed to a better future.

10: Alfred Deakin's Language Strategy

'...to speak to Australians simply as an Australian'.[421]

– Alfred Deakin

The early prime minister Alfred Deakin's accomplishment as an advocate, negotiator, and politician, who effected much long-lasting change to Australia, is beyond question. His anonymous observation in the (London) *Morning Post* on the new Commonwealth Constitution for the Federation of Australia showed how alert he was to the realities of political progress and the negotiations needed to be effective. He wrote that federation:

> ...will begin to take effect on the 1st of January, but everything which could make the union it establishes more than a mere piece of political carpentry will remain to be accomplished afterwards.[422]

Political carpentry is an apt metaphor to describe much in political life, and might describe Deakin's own political activities at times, along with something of how he sustained his variety of alliances and coalitions. When used in a positive sense of creative construction, political carpentry captures something of his public speaking strategy. He negotiated with listeners with a liveliness that built engagement, inviting listeners to join him in thinking about issues, people, and circumstances, thereby exploring common goals.

His flexibility in shifting among rhetorical approaches to build relations with the range of audience members before him was widely recognised. He appeared able to find connection with audience members from those favourable to his propositions through to those opposed. As appropriate, he drew on vivid illustration, startling disclosures, and arousal of personal responsibility to engage the favourable. To engage even those initially opposed to him, he found agreement on general principles applied to specific problems, to show his plan was the best solution. Although he did not always avoid exaggeration, he was judicious about where to use mild exaggeration, particularly to request definite action of supporters.[423]

Negotiated Relationship

With remarkable command of delivery and language, Deakin could confidently negotiate understandings with listeners, artfully defining circumstances to construct new accommodations and alliances. According to the biographer, John Alfred La Nauze:

> Deakin possessed most of the attributes of the traditional orator: a handsome presence, a manner that could range from passionate earnestness to light humour without loss of dignity, a rich musical voice best described as light baritone. His speaking was extraordinarily rapid ... but his articulation was always perfect; he never hesitated for a word...[424]

The biographer, Judith Brett also describes how he spoke:

> With rapid delivery, words, phrases, images, arguments, quotations and examples streamed from his mouth in complex, well-shaped sentences as he strode around the platform, gesturing for emphasis, his voice rising on crescendos of fervour and gliding down to quiet appeals.[425]

Purportedly 'at fever pitch he was capable of 200 words a minute',[426] compared with the average speaker's rate of around 120 to 150 words a minute. Both in Australia and overseas, there were many compliments for his speaking ability.

Deakin could deploy language required for speaking situations ranging from the ornate to the everyday. Early in the 1887 Colonial Conference in London, he established his speaking credentials with the participants there. In language long on flattery and conventional doffing to the Imperial hosts, he 'cordially agree[d] with the loyal sentiments which have been expressed with regard to the maintenance of Imperial interests'.[427] Soon after this, though, he foreshadowed his challenge to conventional assumptions:

> We know the great difficulties which must exist in communicating the wishes of a few millions of people, thousands of miles away, even to that Colonial Office which is specially charged with their interests, and we would be the last, from our own experience, to blame those officials, whether permanent or political, who would avoid difficult questions if it were possible to avoid them... we have by no means attained the full realisation of our hopes. Behind the Colonial Office there is the Foreign Office, which is still more difficult to reach; and behind the Foreign Office again lies that mysterious

entity, the Cabinet, which in this country [Britain] as in every other, owing to political exigencies is not only paved, but walled and roofed with good intentions unfulfilled.[428]

Respect with Challenge

Deakin's weaving of such respectful yet subtly challenging commentary understandably must have secured the regard of leading public figures in Britain. In this opening speech to the Conference, he later outlined shared interests to establish common ground:

> We cannot imagine any description of circumstances by which the Colonies should be *humiliated or weakened*, or their *power lessened*, under which the Empire would not itself be *humiliated, weakened and lessened*. And we are unable to conceive any circumstances under which the *wealth or status* of the Colonies could be *increased*, which would not increase in the same degree the *wealth and status* of the Empire.'[429] *[my italics]*

This sinuous exploration of the respective interests of the Empire and the Colonies was carried with parallelism, repetitions, and contrasts of individual words and doublets. A listener following the track of Deakin's thinking would likely recognise that the speech experience was to be a journey, encompassing accepted norms but exploring provocative concerns. He went on in this case to point out that 'indifference' in England's Colonial Office was damaging not only the Australian colonies but also England's interests. These he stated as 'views fairly, firmly, and fearlessly'.

Deakin's approach differed sharply from other colonial representatives—especially when compared with the very next speaker, who was the then Queensland premier Sir Samuel Griffith. Although Griffith also deferentially expressed appreciation to the English hosts, he was plain-spoken when pointing to a difference with the Imperial dignitaries. Addressing a different point than Deakin, concerning policy on New Guinea, he said:

> I believe there is no real difference between Her Majesty's Government and the Australian Governments upon the point; and that any difference that may have existed will prove to have been merely a difference or misunderstanding as to the meaning of the words, and the best way of expressing ideas. Difficulties of that kind can best be removed by verbal intercourse, and I trust upon that, as upon weightier matters you have referred to, we shall agree.[430]

Whereas Griffith reasoned with his listeners, stating commitment to plain, logical discussion, Deakin more often appealed to listeners' emotions to find alignment.

Toward Federation

Whether in addresses at conferences, dinners and lunches, or rallies for elections or other causes, Deakin negotiated his relationship with listeners within the norms of the society in his time. Yet wherever you start looking into the life story of Deakin, it will not be long before 'contradictions prevail which defy straightforward conclusions'.[431] Difficulty can be found in some of his views that were part of who he was,[432] such as his spiritualism and his 'unshakeable commitment to "race homogeneity" as the basis of a healthy national life'.[433] As the biographer Brett noted, Deakin's image of his society and nationhood was steeped in 'the nineteenth century Western political imagination: that a people united by territory, history, religion, race, and culture should be joined under a political rule to which they consent'.[434] He made direct *ad hominem* and *ad populum* appeals to some then dominant beliefs concerning Australian identity and nationalism.

Throughout his extensive public service, Deakin was committed to building capacities to advance Australia, Australians, and Australian industry—which he continuously advocated within a 'nation-building narrative'.[435] It was in his 'passion of nationality', as David Headon notes, that 'the closet creative writer was never far away in his most enlightened speeches'.[436] Framing this metaphorically when reflecting on federation, Deakin felt this passion would:

> …widen and deepen and strengthen its ties… [and that] as a wise seaman steers his ship to take advantage as far as possible of wind and tide, so should we shape our course so as to secure for this great movement every possible assistance, whether from the forces of sentiment or motives of self-interest, and thus to be enabled to reach the haven of Federation.[437]

History often details more the journey of the victors in social or political change, but the path to federation in Australia had many anti-federation forces, who delayed and sought to prevent the move. Even the negotiations among delegates to federation conventions over many years provided a potential threat of the whole effort coming to nothing. In one example in 1897, which related to a proposed power of the future Senate to amend rather than only reject money bills, Deakin himself showed that he was prepared to convey a threat of opposition to federation, to assert plainly the position of N.S.W. and Victoria in relation to the money powers of the Senate. To Queensland's Sir Samuel Griffith, he commented:

> …I thought it perhaps not untimely to offer you this private assurance that the statements then made were not mere bluff but correctly indicated a rock upon which the whole of our hopes and labours in the Federal cause may yet find shipwreck…[438]

Deakin's speech in the following year to the Australian Natives' Association Conference was made at one of the times when federation was far from certain.

Beyond Provincialism

On 15 March 1898 in Bendigo, Deakin concisely addressed the Australian Natives' Association Conference,[439] to urge an increased focus of efforts for federation. As Victorian leader of the federation movement, he advocated the value of federation to bring Australian unity. He distinguished his purpose from others speaking that night as politicians or Federal Convention delegates. Deakin sought 'to speak to Australians simply as an Australian'.[440] This avowed simplicity provided the context for him to reframe federation as a personal endeavour for members of the Association. When established in 1871 in Melbourne, the Association's membership was restricted to white men in Victoria born in Australia, with membership in 1872 extended to men born in other Australian colonies. This Association was active in providing much of the organisational and financial support for federation.

In his speech, Deakin chose to advocate a view beyond provincialism for that Association. He urged unity to defeat any resurgent threats or attacks against federation, as one report of the speech noted:

> Mr Deakin on that occasion said that the greatest achievement of the Australian Natives' Association was the Federal Convention itself, and he knew those who made the movement what it was would not desert it in its hour of danger... 'These are the times to try men's souls. Should the leaders cry "Retreat", obey not the order, but nail the colours to the mast and fight for victory. Never, during the past century, has the situation of the Mother Country been more grave, and we must have a Federal Constitution under which to face the future'. He trusted that the conference delegates would go back to their branches bearing the fiery cross, and stir up their districts to action, thus making Victoria move from end to end with the warm life-blood of Federation.[441]

Deakin portrayed the landscape of opposition as severe, and starkly stated the threat to all in not seizing the opportunity that federation offered. He showed artfulness in both setting the challenge as well as itemising the uncertainties. He invited his listeners to a united purpose and a collective effort that would advance higher goals through his generous use of the first-person plural pronouns 'we' and 'us'. He underscored the uncertainties, with the auxilliary verb 'may' partnered successively with the action verbs, 'resist... be inert... falter... sound the retreat'. He also grounded the appeal colloquially with the clichéd commonplaces of nailing a 'standard to the mast' and standing 'shoulder to shoulder'.[442]

Later in the speech, with his 'One word more...' he began a concluding peroration that became more than a quarter of the speech–in which he advocated the urgency of both individual and united patriotic effort.[443] Deakin portrayed this unified purpose for his audience as patriotism of a high order. Just prior to the close, he compounded inspirational pathos by quoting a recently deceased local young poet, who foresaw Australia to '...be one people–mighty, serving God!'[444] By stirringly outlining the efforts needed for federation, clarifying that the cause was by no means yet secure, but inspiring confidence in success through service to the Almighty, Deakin elevated the cause as a fervour. His call for united effort was in the inspirational terms of 'genius', 'duty', and 'souls', to 'rise' as 'one people'. Such rapid progression to an emotional close helped to seal his speech as a rallying cry going forward.

On the night before the Federation vote, Deakin addressed a final meeting in the Melbourne Town Hall in similarly powerful terms:

> When Australia raises its flag it would be a flag of a united nation and not even a Colonial Secretary in Her Majesty's Imperial Government would venture to pull it down... The swinging of this globe is bringing us nearer to tomorrow's dawn. When its sunlight silvers the vast panorama of this continent and the richly jewelled islands that lie within its seas, it shall shine upon a territory by which the act you will then perform and the solemn compact to which you will then enter will be bound once and forever in a united commonwealth, an indissoluble union, everlasting and strong–into an Australia–one and indivisible.[445]

Election Platform

Somewhat different from such highly figurative language, which Deakin could readily deploy, was his more deliberative approach in an election speech in 1903. This quite lengthy presentation in his home electorate of Ballarat dealt with much detail of political events and government policy in a more matter of fact manner, further illustrating Deakin's range as a speaker. Though more than 14,000 words (possibly around 80 minutes, by projecting timing at an average of 180 words a minute), this speech elicited continuously supportive interjections of 'hear, hear', 'cheers', and 'applause' throughout. He began urbanely, in setting the expectation that:

> The responsibilities of this occasion are such that I shall not be able to spare you as I would otherwise desire tonight, because it will be my duty however imperfectly, though at some length, to call attention to the number and magnitude of the interests over which you have control. [*Hear, hear.*][446]

This opening sentence, at some 50 words, with its interpolation and subordinate clauses, is two and a half times the length of what might be considered an appropriate average length of a sentence.[447] From these first words, Deakin was negotiating with listeners by mixing his alert concerning the expected duration of the speech with apparent humility. He placed on record that duty required his attending fairly to the listeners' concerns, at the risk of tiring their 'patience'. At the emphatic end focus of the sentence,[448] he stated that it was the listeners who 'have control'. Through this acknowledgement and disclosure, he secured their vocal approval, and their presumed agreement to the length of the speech.

Deakin then set the emotional climate with figurative language that appealed through a range of the senses, to advance his listeners' pride in the new Australian Commonwealth:

> From the perpetual summer of New Guinea to the spring in Ballarat, now in its blossom, and in Hobart, where the buds are scarcely beginning to break, from the place where I speak to you tonight to Perth, where the sun has yet to set, the Commonwealth flag flies over it all. [*Applause.*][449]

His powerful reminder of the sweep and scale of the new nation was the framework in which he emotively shared a survey of items that supported his characteristic narrative of 'character and citizenship' and 'nation-building'.[450] He called on his listeners to be better positioned for their role as 'citizens of the great Commonwealth', with needed energy and participation to do 'what is best for the people'.

This was a milestone speech that appealed to the character of his listeners to take action, alert to distinctions between states and Commonwealth. Deakin advocated '…an indestructible union of indestructible states. [*Applause.*]'[451] He then reviewed the recent events concerning the first Federal Ministry, quoting and recasting accusations of the Leader of the Opposition, who had claimed that Sir Edmund Barton was forced to resign as prime minister:

> I have to say in the clearest, calmest, and most emphatic manner that there is not one jot or tittle of truth in either of those accusations. [*Applause.*] In plain Saxon, they are absolutely false. Not one Member of the Ministry, not one Victorian representative in either House, desired the retirement of Sir Edmund Barton. We all most reluctantly consented to it. [*Hear, hear.*][452]

With short emphatic sentences and the reinforcing alliteration of 'tittle of truth', to help reinforce his trivialisation of the accusations, Deakin was reasserting his own credibility, since he was prime minister because of Barton's resignation. He kept attention, however, not on himself but on the collective intent of the Ministry and the Victorian House in this and the next passage.

National Development

For the remainder of the speech, he rapidly recounted extensive sketches of more than a score of government operations and initiatives, in passages briefly updating each. These included reports on The first Federal Parliament, The High Court, The electorate boundaries, New departments, Cost of federation, The trans-Australian railway, Patents, Status of Bills on Arbitration and Old-age pensions, White Australia, The tariff, Fiscal peace, Industrial arbitration, Murray waters, Iron bounty, The states and immigration, and so on. This was a sweeping set of reports, in which Deakin shared brief details of both actions and personalities, leading to his peroration on the 'Crux of the elections'.[453]

Here he again put emphasis on the individual character needed to sustain progress, 'Victoria will have to keep its solid phalanx if we are to guard against the dangers that beset us from want of discipline'.[454] Deakin called on combining qualities of personal effort, temperance, and self-control. He reminded of the need for unified effort against large forces, the classic of an underdog appeal, to strengthen unity needed against a stronger opponent:

> The struggle is upon us. Without the influences of wealth, without campaign funds, and with little organisation we can only succeed by the zeal and self-sacrificing exertions of those who share our principles.[455]

Woven into his final words is a reminder of the value of this self-sacrifice for nation-building. His speech was within the widely held perceptions in Australia at the time, of the nation being male and 'white', with peoples of the First Nations excluded from decision-making, and with women being able to vote for the first time on the same basis as men:

> I hope that the men of Australia out of their experience, and the women of Australia, who at this election are going to cast their virgin vote, will take up and repeat the Ballarat battle cry of National Trade—the cry of fiscal peace and preferential trade for a White Australia. [*Loud and continued cheering.*][456]

Tackling Turbulence

Three years later, in circumstances more challenging in some ways than this election, Deakin again faced his own electorate at Ballarat to assert a record of his acting honourably and morally, during the turbulent first years of Australia's federation. In December 1906, Deakin's incumbent Protectionist Party minority government, which he led as prime minister, was to face election. He was opposing the Anti-Socialist Party, recently renamed from the Free Trade Party, led by George Reid, as well as opposing the Labour Party, led by Chris Watson. In just half a decade since the 1901 Federation, this was the new nation's third federal election. There were also three changes of prime minister between the

1903 and 1906 elections, without a federal election occurring. The upcoming election was to be a test of whether any party could sustain stable government.[457]

On 17 October 1906,[458] Deakin tackled both the Free Traders and Labour. In the genre of deliberative rhetoric, Deakin defined his Party and his stance, centrally positioned between the extremes of the other two parties, and pragmatically accomplishing progress for Australia:

> I appear before you as a *Liberal Protectionist—a party* which has had an honourable record in this and other States, which is now establishing an Australian authority and influence; *a party* which has never lost *its* identity, although, during the recent Parliament, *it* has been subjected to a severe strain.
>
> When, owing to the existence of the three independent parties, a time for choice came, there were some who with me consented, under the faith of a written pledge, to assist Mr Reid; and when he deserted and betrayed *us* we joined with those who supported *us* in undertaking a task that was not of *our* seeking, and which cast upon *us* the most serious responsibility.
>
> Since then *we* have had the support, in a general sense, of the Labour Party, and that has enabled *us* to accomplish the work which I shall detail to you. *Our* arrangement with them lasted for the Parliament, and ends with the Parliament…[459] *[my italics]*

To build confidence in the party that he led, Deakin made clear the roles of the three competing parties. With initial words identifying him as a 'Liberal Protectionist', he asserted the party's 'honourable record', its 'Australian authority and influence', and its retention of identity—a clear contrast to his opponents, renamed as the Anti-Socialist Party. Soon afterwards he set about dismantling the credibility of this main rival and its leader, Mr Reid. He also pointed out that he maintained his own independence from the Labour Party.

This opening passage referred to Deakin's party 12 times by name or in pronouns, alongside his assertion of Reid's desertion and betrayal. In this way, he explained the cause and the terms of Deakin's having the support 'in a general sense' of the Labour Party, as an 'arrangement… [that] …lasted for the Parliament, and ends with the Parliament'. Within these first 160 words, Deakin had set the scene for listeners, and reinforced the good and independent standing of his own party in a temporary coalition with the independent Labour Party.

He used mainly simple words (just 15% with three syllables or more in the first 600 words) and described his opponent's actions in a conversational tone that sustained his monologue. Deakin's speech incorporated some complex sentences, with phrases and clauses in short breath groups that would need sensitive pacing in delivery. He used the repetitions in name and pronouns for his party, and other short declarations to set the context for emphasising that he had acted 'on faith to assist Mr Reid'.460

Highlighted Inconsistency

Deakin then recalled recent political events, mocking those who had named him as concurrently 'a great socialist' and 'the greatest enemy of socialism'; so named, he said, by 'eminent…gentlemen… hopelessly and absolutely in error…' He persistently placed before listeners that his opponent 'talked more and promised more and performed less than any man in Australia'. Contrasting his own record, Deakin said:

> …during the session just closed I have never missed a single sitting. It was my duty. In the session there were 84 divisions, and Mr Reid voted in four. He had the luck to get three in one day, and the fourth on the next. [*Laughter.*] He has perorated in Queensland, in New South Wales, and South Australia, and now he is perorating in Victoria; but work he did not and vote he did not.461

With rhetorical editorialising, Deakin colourfully elevated a moral choice, disparaging his opponent's performance. He rounded out this blistering attack with the contrast, 'Judge him by his works–judge us by ours.'462

Deakin asserted his own party to be between the extremes of '-isms', representing 'the practical section of this community.' He called out the use of 'catch-words', while mocking the 'substance' of his opponent and the opposing party. Describing his opponent's proposed programme as 'a mere vague, empty, illusory series of negatives, without proper advantage to the country', he argued that Reid had disclosed not a programme but 'a panic'. Deakin then wrapped this description in a strongly mocking visual metaphor, 'such a state of panic has he reached that if a cow chased him out of a paddock he would accuse her of socialism'.463

Doing the Work

As a background narrative, Deakin associated his party as doing the work in 'Parliament', named six times in the first 600 words, to protect the 'Commonwealth', 'Australia', and individual states (mentioned throughout the speech). Looming large in this speech was the over-arching nation-building narrative of economic progress through protectionism to 'place Australia and Australian industries first'. Deakin advocated that the initiatives of his party would 'accord with English and Australian laws', including 'fiscal peace', 'deportation of kanakas',464 favouring 'white settlement', 'labour and capital united', 'preferential trade proposals with New Zealand', and 'unconditional preference to the mother country'. He rejected Reid's plans as providing comfort for 'foreign invaders'. Deakin also pivoted off the anti-socialist stance of his opponent with a powerful repetition of the prefix 'anti-', directly questioning, 'Am I wrong when I say that their proper title is not *anti*-socialist, but *anti*-New Zealand, *anti*-British, and *anti*-Australian?'[465] *[my italics]*

After handling some interjectors without apparent interruption to the flow of his speech, Deakin stated what he regarded as the record for consideration:

> Tonight I deal with the record of work *by which* we ought to be *judged*, *by which* we shall be *judged* in the future, and *by which* we have the right to appeal to the electors to *judge* us now. Perorations I have nothing to do with to-night–only records... To the electors I say, analyse the programmes before you; ask what are the records of the men who put them forward, what have they *done*, what are they *doing*, and what are they going *to do*? On none of those questions will you, after full consideration in respect of the liberal protectionists, be in any doubt as to what the answer must be.[466] *[my italics]*

The repeated verbs 'judge' and 'do' and the *anaphora* beginning with 'by which' and 'what', set up crisply his final question for electors. When Deakin was then asked by an interjector what prevented his party making an alliance with the Labour Party, he took this opportunity to sharply differentiate his party's 'practical programme'. He used variants of 'practical' four times within 151 words and concluded his speech with an unambiguously emphatic statement of his view of Labour, 'They *fight* us, and we are bound to *fight* them when they *fight* us'.[467] *[my italics]* This was a strong close to the speech.

Converting Occasions

Deakin showed remarkable talent for engaging his listeners in a variety of settings, framing 'public conversations' in ornate or everyday language as appropriate to an occasion. Within the speeches reviewed here, Deakin was versatile in the use of genre, metaphor, controversy, or humour to frame, shape, and sequence his thoughts. He drew on a considerable understanding of rhetorical principles in practice.

His vision for national development and his creative capacity to use words to change beliefs and actions made a powerful combination. Deakin focused on pertinent concerns of listeners to make nuanced connection and build commitment. He had an uncanny ability to develop a shared exploration of a topic with listeners. Whether in a formal presentation as a convention delegate, or for a variety of addresses to community organisations, or during remarks and exchanges on the hustings, or in other settings, Deakin commanded an extraordinary range of communication abilities.

11: Sir Robert Menzies's Measured Style

'... in the hearts and minds of ordinary people'.[468]

– Sir Robert Menzies

Throughout a long public life, serving in total almost two decades as prime minister, Sir Robert Gordon Menzies highlighted dominance of things British as the common cultural heritage for Australia. He generally projected himself much like a patriarchal figure of transferred English aristocracy. As a political figure, Menzies also built a large popular base of support, often via radio broadcasts, with ordinary non-elite working citizens whom he called 'the Forgotten People'– especially those who were neither rich nor members of organised labour.[469]

In a landmark radio address delivered on 22 May 1942, Menzies appealed to this base in the homes of people who are 'nameless and unadvertised'.[470] For this broadcast and his wide range of speaking occasions, Menzies deployed a conversational everyday language, yet gave an impression as someone of some depth and substance. He identified issues of real concern to his listeners. This ability was likened to his pressing a 'magic button' of sorts in the Australian people before elections, at rallies and dinners, and through radio and television, even though he apparently gave televised addresses under sufferance.[471]

The Menzies 'voice' in the context of a digital world might not have resonated as strongly with today's listeners, but he was certainly widely accepted in post-war Australia. He was able to isolate and simplify issues that touched emotional chords in his listeners. His mixture of personal and formal qualities supported his responses to interjectors at public addresses, with a flexibility and showmanship that drew huge audiences to his public meetings. When an interjector on one occasion at Oakey, Victoria asked 'Watchagoin' to do about 'ousing?' he deftly responded, 'Put an 'H' in front of it'. On another occasion, he replied to an interjector, 'Madam, I have no objection to you speaking in this hall, providing you do so some other night or that you pay half the cost of it tonight'.472

Conversational Recollections

A favoured way for Menzies to connect with listeners on his own terms was to speak as if in conversation, including listeners in his recollections. This was quite common across his political and other public talk, ranging from eulogy to lecture to television broadcast. At times, he would sustain quite extended imaginary dialogues. In a 1961 television broadcast, Menzies said:

> If we had a poor record of performance, I could well imagine you saying: 'Well they've had their chance, they haven't done well. This is the time for an experiment, let's try somebody else'. But nobody really can honestly say that this country hasn't been prospering, that this country hasn't been going through a period of wonderful growth, that ordinary standards of living haven't been rising, that we haven't enjoyed the confidence and good will of the world. Nobody can honestly tell you that. And therefore, what you are really being invited to do by our opponents is to take a wild experiment, a sort of excitable act arising from the very prosperity of the country.473

The neat closure on this thought-process brings firmly home his point that the Menzies Government provided the security that his opponents sought to replace with uncertainty—in an 'excitable act' through a 'wild experiment' of supporting them. Here Menzies's broad vision and apparent concern about people's needs underpinned associating himself with the touted strengths and virtues of his Government, which he stated was responsible for 'wonderful growth' and unity. Deftly managing the sarcasm concerning his opponents, Menzies contrasted his united Government with a snapshot of chaotic dissension among these opponents. He revived in this brief sketch his earlier more detailed portrayal of 'a collection of people who haven't been able to live together, politically, haven't been able to govern themselves, politically'.474

The strengths of disparaging sarcasm and cutting wit served Menzies best when, in the role of an advocate, he could spin off or react to people, situations, or events. He was at his weakest on some occasions when trying to manage dramatic or created images, as if the analytical and evaluative abilities needed from his legal background found best integration in a type of dialectic concerned with specific facts or concepts. When he included listeners in his recollections, though, he could sustain a story at his own or others' expense. At times, these were somewhat dry.

Shared Understandings

At a National Press Club luncheon address, Menzies used this approach to keep relationship with listeners, by tapping shared understandings. He began:

> Mr Chairman I've been misled and I've been misled by that deplorable character Maley [*Laughter.*] [his press secretary] ... I understood from him that today was my 30th anniversary. I am no doubt quite wrong, but there you are. But I thought it was I didn't look it up, and when I had people coming to me earlier and saying 'Many happy returns of the day', a somewhat fantastic wish you will agree, I was still under the illusion that it was today, but now it's tomorrow. So I suppose I'll have to make a little speech and then make it a retrospective tomorrow, hoping that I survive so long. Now I was told that what you would like to hear, as briefly as possible would be some retrospective views of affairs, people, since I came here first in 1934. Or as Ray Maley, with that exquisite capacity for an original phrase that characterises the Press, said to me 'Wandering Down Memory Lane'. [*Laughter.*][475]

In addition to including listeners in his recollections in this way, Menzies varied how he established mutual understandings. He would:

- Implicitly or explicitly declare his own human weakness.
- Project humility, sometimes humorously or evidently feigned.
- Refer to his own role as prime minister.
- Identify just two points at a time, about which he intended to speak, thereby keeping a simple structure.
- Refer to or establish his personal credentials to be speaking.
- Mention the reason for his presence before listeners.
- Refer to reasons why everyone was assembled.
- Concentrate on the senses: 'I found ... looked ... hear'.
- Identify his own knowledge of the topic of the speech.

He frequently made use of parallel phrases and repetition to identify priorities, emphasising connotations of words in successive phrases. Menzies showed preference for particular words as reinforcement or emphasis, such as 'remarkable' in variant uses. From the early stage of most speeches, he entered a personal 'I-you-me-we' relationship with listeners, modulating his use of pronouns to distance or envelop the audience.

As do many other politicians, ranging from the conservative to the radical, Menzies used the clichéd and weak time reference 'in point of time', as well as the assertive 'I firmly believe', and the vacuous 'as a result'; and he included common clichés, such as 'I'd hasten to say', often making a complicated language structure appear simpler and colloquial. He moderated his long sentences with such insertions, which needed to be heavily punctuated when reduced to writing.

A common way Menzies achieved an apparent simplicity reminiscent of conversation was by heavy use of the conjunction 'and', so that a succession of ideas was strung together as in conversation. Also contributing to a conversational effect were his interpolations, even within short sentences. Some complexity in his language structure at times derived from parallel structures used for emphasis, with repeated verb forms ('have been ... have given'), or triads, 'we talk too much, we read too little and as for thinking, we are getting quite rusty'. One way that he simplified the parallel and triad structures was by using every day simple words common in conversation.

Adherence to Traditions

Against such largely personalising features, Menzies also showed commitment to formalism, including formal argument and logical processes, as well as arguing from established principles or positions. He was devoted to the formalities of the British Monarchy, and frequently referenced his affinity in speeches. He sustained his self-chosen role as a leading publicist for the British Commonwealth throughout his public life.

Although Australia was a multicultural society in Menzies's time, his projected vision of Australian society seemed to be of a predominantly Anglo-Celtic country, staunchly, proudly, and royally British. This view put aside the national origin of a proportionately small but nonetheless large number of Australians, who migrated in colonial times and increasingly after World War II from a diversity of countries, including Europe, the Middle East, and Asia.

For most of his political career, what Menzies meant by national unification was likely the continuation of Australian government practices, which continued after his time to at least the early 1970s of seeking to assimilate or integrate First Nations and people from other nations. Considering this from the point of view of the many citizens who sought equivalent recognition for their cultural origins, it might be a stretch to describe Menzies as a *rhetor* who interiorised all that was best in the culture.[476] He implicitly and explicitly sought people's support for a Westminster democracy, based in a culture of Britain transported.

Remarkably to some of us then growing up in Australia, it was not until 1962, albeit during Menzies's Government, that the country's First Nations were granted the right to vote and further rights were secured in 1967, thanks to a national referendum.

Worldwide Spotlight

Menzies's ceremonial and deep commitment to British tradition was in full view when he presented the apparently simple eulogy to honour Sir Winston Churchill, on 30 January 1965. The occasion was broadcast on BBC television worldwide, which put a significant spotlight on not only the remembrance of Churchill but also Menzies and his rhetorical stance. Within the speech, he included references to his friendship with Churchill and revived a full picture of the man, even producing 'his own imitation of the famous leader's language'.[477] While catering to specific requirements for the circumstance of the speech, Menzies positioned himself in a commanding and dominating stance relative to his listeners:

> Some day, some year, there will be old men and women whose pride it will be to say, 'I saw him, and I heard him—the unforgettable voice and the immortal words'. And some will be able to say, 'I knew him, and talked with him, and was his friend'. This I can with a mixture of pride and humility say for myself.[478]

Listeners sympathetic to or at least not objecting to Menzies's placing himself on so friendly a basis with Churchill would likely permit him to add to his own ethos by this association. Some, particularly in the British audience, might not have welcomed the stance, perhaps feeling that this chatty association by someone of lesser standing was not appropriate.[479]

Menzies would within a few months announce Australia's first major military commitment to the war in Vietnam. Six months before the speech, the Menzies Government had introduced compulsory conscription of Australian 20-year-old men to military service, using a 'birthday lottery' system of selection for what was called 'National Service'. During this time, 'What Menzies did not say was that his Government had approached the United States requesting... an invitation' to expand substantially Australia's commitment of soldiers to the war in Vietnam.[480]

War Leader

Menzies's reminder in this eulogy of the danger of a tyrannical presence near a nation's shores pre-empted later claims by some politicians, including Menzies himself, that the communist 'scourge' to the north of Australia was about to engulf the country. Unlike Pericles's famous Funeral Oration, Menzies made no direct call to arms,[481] but he certainly framed the moment, recalling the dangers experienced in Churchill's time. He recalled with intensity Churchill's most notable accomplishments in war, by providing a vivid reminder, as well as rekindling some insights into aspects of the foreign threat that the Allies faced in World War II, and the scale of that challenge.

Menzies recalled the World War II example vividly, reviving for listeners striking memories that might overcome inertia or any opposition to the proposition for a nation to be militarily prepared. He set the framework for such a proposition by recalling the strong evidence[482] of Churchill's historical success, despite Britain initially being unprepared for war. The speech refreshed the value of sustaining preparedness against a foreign adversary. Menzies directed the attention of any audience members interested in but undecided about such a proposition to the lesson from history. The extent of the threat and the difficulties Churchill had faced were parts of emotional evidence, on an emotion-filled occasion, to recall the importance of national preparedness and leadership.

While honouring Churchill, Menzies also came perhaps as close as decency might allow in a memorial speech to echo the famous war leader. He stated:

> Many of you will not need to be reminded, but some, the younger among you, the inheritors of his masterstrokes for freedom, may be glad to be told that your country, and mine, and all the free countries of the world, stood at the very gates of destiny in 1940 and 1941, when the Nazi tyranny threatened to engulf us, and when there was no 'second front' except our own.[483]

The entire speech of course celebrated Churchill who, more than any other person in contemporary British history, marshalled the efforts of the whole British Commonwealth to resist a foreign invader of Britain.

'Just Two Points'

Typically, as here, Menzies developed a clear structure in the opening of a speech by addressing the occasion and outlining the points to be developed; he related facts and events that established the significance of the occasion, elaborated his own and Australia's role, and finally summed up.

Through this approach, he called his listeners' attention to two points and then elaborated one of these before moving to elaborate the other, as described in Chapter Seven. In this speech and on other occasions, one of the points was to establish Menzies's own credentials. The structure of this *Eulogy for Churchill* shows how he progressed from such an opening:

    Introduction
    Statement of place ('streets of London and St. Paul's Cathedral')
    Occasion ('historic procession')
    Speaker's authority ('Senior Commonwealth Prime Minister' and 'personal acquaintance')
    Introduce topic (honouring Churchill)

Body
(i) Formal Recollections
Memory of past achievements ('overcame Nazi tyranny')
Leadership (heroic figure and inspiration)
Re-creation of a daring and courageously strong figure
Unification under religion (CLIMAX)

(ii) Personal Recollections
Memory of personal voice ('strive to be worthy of his example')
Devotion of wife and her loss ('to share with her those rich remembrances')
'Light of hope' reminder (CLIMAX)

Conclusion
Restatement of place
Occasion
Churchill's rugged authority
Formal close: 'enriched by splendid memories'[484]

Evident in this outline was how Menzies managed both formal and informal elements as the basis of the speech. Even within the rhetorical genre of the predominantly epideictic discourse of the eulogy, Menzies created a sense of conversation and simulated dialogue for his listeners. The speech focused attention on widely shared symbols of religion and culture. He referred to the *free world*, 'God Almighty' and religion, British heritage, and national pride pitted against enemy forces from outside the Commonwealth. Menzies portrayed these forces, as Churchill had, as images of 'darkness'. He made frequent reference to the attractive model of courage and authority that Churchill provided, recalling for listeners Churchill's role as a leader, and then he swiftly and powerfully aligned himself with Churchill.

'Light and Hope'

Menzies reminded listeners that, unlike 'some men of power who have cast shadows across the world, Winston Churchill, on the contrary, was a fountain of light and hope'.[485] Churchill's own war speeches were characterised by this image of light and brightness. Especially when speaking of the allies, this was so in Churchill's most powerful speeches, as in 'all Europe may be freed and the life of the world may move forward into broad sunlit uplands'.[486] Menzies's use of balanced *polysyndeton* in the first and second half of the following sentence reproduced an echo of Churchill's speaking style:

> With courage, and matchless eloquence, and human understanding, he inspired us and led us to victory.[487]

and his parallelism of 'one' to play on the similar sound (*homophone*) of 'won':

> In the whole of recorded modern history, this was, I believe, the *one* occasion when *one* man, with *one* soaring imagination, with *one* fire burning in him, and with *one* unrivalled capacity for conveying it to others, *won* a crucial victory...[488] *[my italics]*

Unified Nation

The reminder of the value of a unified nation was clear. His focus on the unit 'one', with direct references to 'oneness' in the context of national unity under God and monarch, reflected a central theme of monarchist theory. While this is at odds with popular democracy, Menzies also celebrated Churchill's efforts as being 'for the very spirit of human freedom'.[489] He stressed that success came from the unity ('with one heart ... [and] ... with one mind') that Churchill had forged. Throughout the speech, of course, Menzies repeatedly alluded to the obvious religious basis of the entire ceremony. In a memorial eulogy, the religious appeal will often be referenced, unifying many listeners. Unsurprisingly, Menzies incorporated appeals to 'God Almighty', to the British Commonwealth, and to national pride.

The reassurance of Menzies's 'voice', respectful of tradition, vividly revived a sense of the famous war leader, through associations from the language, the history, and the recalled accomplishments of Churchill. Menzies so closely simulated Churchill's language at certain moments that he was barely distinguishable from the institution that Churchill had become in people's memories, and he emphatically recalled the 'great man's' victories. Menzies recalled not only the spirit and strength needed in war, but he more than subtly echoed Churchill by using the signature words from one of his most famous speeches, 'battle, air, sea, and field'. Menzies recalled:

> That *battle* had to be won not only in the *air* and on the *sea* and in the *field*, but in the *hearts* and *minds* of ordinary people with a deep *capacity for heroism*.[490] *[my italics]*

The parallelism in this sentence simulated a sense of the formal yet conversational style of the wartime leader. Menzies's own ability to combine formal and conversational language in this way enabled him to seek a very personal relationship with listeners for himself, reviving memories of the rhythm and sensation of Churchill's distinctive language.

Rhetorical Patterns

This use of balance and parallel language was consistent with Menzies's own inclination to ornateness and formality. He used a full battery of rhetorical patterns to emphasise his main points. These included *anaphora* ('with one fire burning in him, and with one unrivalled capacity for conveying it to others'), parallel structure ('I saw him and I heard him' and 'in the air and on the sea and in the field'), *antithesis* ('what was at stake was, not some theory of government, but the whole and personal freedom of men and women and children') and *polysyndeton* ('I knew him, and talked with him, and was his friend').

The collective effect of these and other rhetorical patterns and the high tone references, such as 'hearts, immortal words, fountain of light and of hope', directed the rhythm and pace of his speech, while also echoing the rhythm of Churchill's speech. This enabled especially refreshed experience of the wartime leader, virtually bathing listeners in an immersive reminiscence of events in Churchill's time. Through this shaping of resonance with Churchill's words, Menzies crafted a renewed experience of the poignancy of Churchill's addresses in his 'finest hours'. Menzies thereby recreated a celebration of the forces of 'light' (the Allies of the Free World) conquering the forces of 'darkness' (Nazi Germany), putting a strong spotlight on Churchill's strength.

And, by the close of the speech, Menzies so closely simulated Churchill's speaking style that it is easy to have the impression that Menzies might readily step into any needed leadership against a new 'tyranny'. He appeared to be setting the scene for that time, to be also identified as the one person who could lead his own country to victory against the 'communist tyranny', presumably as a new defender of freedom. Although Australia had only about 100 soldiers in Vietnam as 'advisers' at the time, the Vietnam War was in Australians' consciousness. It is scarcely much of a stretch to speculate that Menzies would have welcomed being seen on Churchill's coat tails of credibility as a war leader, through this association with the charismatic war leader. It seems likely that Menzies developed this ceremonial occasion as political 'stage-setting', as well as fulfilling its overt purpose as a eulogy.

A Personal Voice

Even on such a formal occasion, Menzies sustained the sense of his personally talking with listeners. He continuously used markers of conversation, including personal pronouns in support of his 'chatty' stance. Notable markers of this conversational undercurrent were:

- Interrogatives
- Repetition
- Personal pronouns

- Interpolations and other interruptions to the logical flow of ideas
- Omission of pronoun subjects
- Apposition of ideas in brief sentences and phrases
- High proportion of function versus lexical words.

In the printed texts of Menzies's speeches, he also occasionally used one of the most characteristic indicators that distinguishes spoken from written language, namely the sentence fragment.[491]

Individual Ethos

The figure of Menzies dominated the Australian political landscape for decades. Through the transitions from public hall to radio to television, he remained virtually unchecked in his ability to connect with listeners, whether they agreed with him or not. With an ability to anticipate and respond to interjectors effectively, combined with flexibility across a range of rhetorical speech forms, he described a simple dictum guiding his speaking that:

> ...the speaker should have something to say which he has resolved to convey to his listeners in the simplest, most intelligible, and most persuasive language...[492]

Frequently he went well beyond such beguiling simplicity in word and syntactic choices. His goals, method, and speaking accomplishments were more sophisticated by far.

Menzies drew largely on a unitary view of Australia's origins from Great Britain and an Anglo-Celtic heritage, subsuming the multicultural reality of Australia. Although Australians gradually found such a stance less appealing in times following his time in public life, this was the basis for Menzies's predominant rhetorical positions, to tell, to reassure, to challenge opponents, and to encourage listeners to follow his patriarchal leadership. In artful ways in his time, he sustained devotion to monarchy and the motherland as Australia's positioning in the world, while cultivating relationships within and beyond the Commonwealth, including alliance with the United States.

Along with the British, Menzies well understood how to reinforce feelings of loyalty to the Crown, with ceremonial royal tours during his leadership attracting large crowds of adults and schoolchildren lining the streets and filling sports fields. This stimulated many Australian families to visit wharves or riverbanks to seek a glimpse of *HM Yacht Britannia*, or a royal. Many households had at least some of the vigorously promoted royal paraphernalia, present in many households long after the elaborate *Queen Elizabeth's Coronation Book*[493] which was specially printed in 1953 as a pictorial record in the format of a coffee-table book.

In 1963 when the young Queen visited Parliament House, with an established reputation as Australia's longest-serving prime minister, Menzies sought to capture the sentiment of Australians in his admiration for the British Monarchy. He famously quoted the English poet Thomas Ford's poem, *There is a Lady Sweet and Kind*, waxing eloquent in his effort to honour Her Majesty, 'I did but see her passing by, / And yet I love her till I die'.[494]

The response of even some of his strongest supporters to the front-page news reports of this speech at the time was not universally positive. On this occasion, he seemed to be 'out of step with the public mood'.[495] Nonetheless, during the 1950s and for much longer, Australia remained enamored with its British origins and Menzies remained a committed and adroit publicist for the British Monarchy.

12: Action Calls of Kevin Gilbert and Oodgeroo Noonuccal

'Our values need to be good and fine for us'.[496]

– Kevin Gilbert

In speeches, articles, and poems, Oodgeroo Noonuccal [Kath Walker] and Kevin Gilbert held a mirror to Australians, highlighting conflicts of values within as well as between First Nations and people with family origins in other countries. Each creatively used language to ask all Australians to consider the injustices to which people of the First Nations are subjected, and to take action. Each informed and educated audiences about the specifics of life in First Nations and the impact of the actions of Australia's governments, immigrants, and other Australians with heritage outside Australia.

Even into the 1970s, government policies and the assumptions or misinformation in educational curricula, popular history, and the news media had the effect of segregating First Nations and others in the community. As someone growing up in Australia in a European suburban cocoon, for example, I first found the poetry of Oodgeroo and Gilbert only after graduating with a degree in English language and literature, and reviewed their writing narrowly then, compared to how I have since come to view their work.

Gilbert indicated in a speech to teacher trainees in the early 1970s at the teacher training college in Armidale, a city in the Northern Tablelands of New South Wales, that he would outline 'some of the needs' of First Nations.[497] Along with presentations at the same event by other accomplished individuals, the speech directly confronted stereotypes and the mistreatment of First Nations, describing how indoctrination caused differences in values. He addressed the attitudes, actions, and inaction causing abuse and neglect. He challenged materialism, called for recognition of living conditions, and advocated to listeners that they allow people in First Nations to 'come up with their own values'.

Gilbert placed realities directly before his listeners, addressing them in terms of 'you' and 'we', while calling out materialism, 'You're all God, you're dictated to by money, you obey money and possessions…' From start to finish, the speech is a strong plea to change attitudes and actions, specifically calling for recognition of land rights.

Gilbert specified failures and set a path for commonsense practical change. From my first impression and subsequent close readings of his speech, it stands as one of Australia's most powerful cases for social change.

Continuing Imperative

In Gilbert's close to the speech, he focused the imperative for his audience:

> It is a *big country* and a *good country*—one that each of you *should be able* to look up to, *should be able* to respect, be *big enough* to meet, *big enough* to handle, *big enough* to preserve your image. At the present moment *you're not*—and you can see people dying because *you're not*.[498] *[my italics]*

Here his parallel repetitions spotlight the prospect that lives will be saved through a changed morality, to be found in reaching for understanding and respect in a genuinely pluralistic Australia. For the audience, Gilbert also wisely highlighted this as being within the future interests of all Australians to 'Advance Australia'.

Through the speech, Gilbert broadly and specifically illustrated past and contemporary mistakes, as well as the neglect and outrages that had failed to meet the needs of both the peoples of First Nations and other Australians. In closing, he stated his implicit proposition that it was through improved treatment of First Nations that the legacy and future vision for everyone would improve. He called for action to live up to the values advocated for so long by Australians more broadly. His speech called for major shifts in understandings, attitudes, and actions throughout the community.

Presumptions and behaviours of conquest and colonisation, which were established from the arrival of the First Fleet in 1788, disastrously impacted the lives of Australia's First Nations into the latter part of the twentieth century, before any real shift in official government policy started to occur. For 60,000 years or so, peoples of an estimated 600 First Nations had lived in harmony with the environment, yet successive policies of colonial and later governments set them to live mainly on remote reserves or on the fringe of cities and towns, out of sight of most of the population. An Australian Law Reform Commission account in 2010[499] of the sorry history of European interaction with First Nations touched only some of the harm.

Until 1962, the federal government policy was to assimilate peoples of First Nations. This mandated the surrendering of heritage and daily life to the Australian-European culture. While some in Australia confused and melded this policy of 'assimilation' with a subsequent 'integration' policy, Oodgeroo noted that government did not consult the First Nations about either policy and neither policy assured the independence and self-determination that people of First Nations sought.[500]

Some Rights Recognised

In 1962, the Menzies Government amended the Commonwealth Electoral Act to give people of First Nations the right to enrol and vote in Commonwealth elections. In 1965, the media covered a bus tour through communities of First Nations in New South Wales, led by Charles Perkins and students from Sydney University. Reportedly 'for the first time', this exposed Australians to the cruel realities of the lives of people in First Nations.[501] Following this and much additional pressure, a national referendum held in 1967 resulted in more than 90 per cent of the voting population approving citizenship rights for peoples of First Nations.

From 1972 onwards, the nonviolent protests at the Aboriginal Embassy established on the front lawn of the national Parliament House in Canberra[502] helped rally calls for land rights for First Nations. With the election of the Whitlam Government in December 1972, federal legislation abolished discriminatory treatment, overrode the Queensland State Government's discriminatory laws, and advocated land rights for First Nations.[503] But this Government was not in power long enough to implement their recommendations on land rights.

Oodgeroo, Gilbert, and many other leaders stepped forward through these events and more, committing much of their creative lives to efforts to seek rights that would be mutually acceptable to First Nations and government.

Arousing Conscience

Gilbert, in his speeches and wider creative work, including poetry and other writing, protested the inappropriate actions and the inaction in the broader Australian community, likely in hopes of arousing a dormant conscience. Oodgeroo in her speeches mainly accumulated facts, shared truths, and discussed the implications of these. She showed consideration in recording what individual 'white Australians' had sought for First Nations, keeping her criticism focused on un-named government heads and specific behaviours, as well as their wrong actions and mistakes that had resulted in the ongoing harm that needed remedy. She detailed conceptually and concretely the actions and events that affected life.

In a speech in 1970, Oodgeroo described her childhood and the life that her parents provided, sketching their home, sources of income and food, and other living conditions that enabled her family to be 'very healthy though financially poor'.[504] Her descriptions of family and living circumstances or other life events used vocabulary with tangible referents, such as describing living in an 'assimilated gunya' of 'discarded hessian, canvas and corrugated iron' or working 'for a pittance as domestics or labourers.'[505] Both Oodgeroo's prose and poetry set such scenes as the backdrop to recording wrongs, on occasion sharing strong emotions, and she tended toward progressively educating to solve problems and seek a better future.

Some of Oodgeroo's poetry highlighted and objected to both moral and government failures. She was wide-ranging in her poetry. She reflected on the significances of nature, or First Nations' traditions, or ancestors' tribal lives and death, or a mother's love, or focused on appeals for equality at law, mateship, tolerance, integration, and shared humanity, sometimes with light humour.

Her poems ranged from the lyric to humorous to protest, seeking to touch a reader's emotions, often with deft description of place, people, nature, or events. As Adam Shoemaker notes, Oodgeroo's poetry celebrated 'survival in the face of adversity, lamented prejudice and oppression, and offered an optimistic view of the potential for interracial harmony in the country'.[506]

Stance as Reporters

In three of Oodgeroo's speeches that were reviewed,[507] she adopted a reporting stance with some variations to suit the different occasions. In Gilbert's Armidale speech, while also in a reporter's mode, he recounted dialogue and actions, and he tackled head-on the misunderstandings and clash of values in the expectations and lives of people, incorporating a mix of deliberative and judicial rhetorical genres. He specifically named the struggle needed. Gilbert and Oodgeroo were aligned on the main topic for these speaking occasions, calling plainly for the recognition of land rights. Gilbert related graphic specifics, while moderating some controversial features of his speech through the reporting stance.

His briefly neutral opening to the speech perhaps set an expectation for listeners that a list of needs would follow, possibly in the dry mode of report that seminar presenters in an academic setting will often provide. Instead, he moved quickly to state strongly that spokespersons of First Nations '…are pretty loud and clear in claiming that all white people are bastards'.[508] The statement likely helped to gain the undivided attention of Gilbert's audience. As David Headon points out:

> ...his confrontational tactics usually made a strong political point, and one which symbolically reversed the established historical patterns of behaviour in this country since 1788.[509]

Headon makes the convincing suggestion that Gilbert was the '"conscience" of many Australians, both black and white–an often unpalatable yet vitally necessary voice'.[510] Certainly in this speech, there is no sign of what one commentator had asserted[511] that Gilbert mocked the racial groups among listeners. Rather, he simply shared tangible and real-life experiences, albeit as challenges.

Gilbert grew up with direct experience of life in First Nations, as the youngest of eight children, born to a Wiradjuri mother and an Irish/English father. He was orphaned at seven years and raised by his eldest sisters and extended family on an 'Aboriginal Reserve' in a rural area. He described that, in springtime, cherry picking allowed:

> ...some freedom, from under the crucifying heels of the local police and the white 'station' managers; an escape from the refugee camps called 'Aboriginal Reserves'.[512]

Comment and Interpretation

The Armidale speech was lively and strongly passionate, assembling details about people, places, and Gilbert's own direct experiences, to vividly illustrate the mistreatment that caused frustration and worse. Consistently in the speech, he was straightforward in using the reporting stance, but his sequenced anecdotes also enabled continuous commentary, to interpret the frustration and outrage reported. Gilbert's description of indoctrination and his metaphor for predation were powerful in outlining the conditions of the time:

> Very few people get to the root cause. *They* don't realise that *your* whole society is based on indoctrination, especially at school. *Your* people are taught to be sharks, to use *your* initiative and *your* competitive spirit in order to advance, and particularly to advance above *your* fellow man. The Aboriginal people have, since *their* de-tribalisation, been indoctrinated with the handout system: *they* are there only when the boss calls, *they* will earn only when the boss dictates. *They* will live and construct *their* society only as the European decides.[513] *[my italics]*

Gilbert used words precisely, as the poet and visual artist he was, to highlight contrasts and draw conclusions, laying down words and brief phrases one after another in quick succession, to visualise some interactions between people or to state a perspective or both. The following was only one of many times that, by this analogy, he layered words and phrases, much like well-placed touches of paint on a surface, to build the visual scene:

> When I was going to school, I went to fourth class primary before I finished. Every time there was an English lesson, or whatever, four or five Aborigines were sent out to clean the yards and do the sweeping up. They were thought to be generally useless; it was assumed that education served no purpose–it was merely the letter of the law that needed to be applied.[514]

With an echo of casual arbitrariness in the throw-away interpolation 'or whatever', this scene starkly noted the termination of education at grade four, the exclusion from learning, and use as child labour. He compiled a picture that was the *antithesis* of education–rather, it was a damning picture that showed failure in the execution of policy to deliver for people.

Recommended Action

Some part of Gilbert's artfulness was to create a mix of description, narration, and persuasion, to recommend action. He introduced a theme of inviting his student teacher audience to look afresh at existing assumptions between peoples, to review how the conditions of living set different attitudes and ways of life. He provided an incentive that with 'the Aboriginal voice…rising for better conditions', all Australians would be wise to become educated at allowing people of First Nations to help themselves and grow at their own pace. He rejected stereotypes of the European, government policy, and the handout system, calling for all to 'try to communicate'–sincerely! Then he recalled the heritage of thefts of land, identity, gods, god-heroes and spirit-beings, and medical aid that resulted *de facto* in a 'policy of genocide'.

Gilbert sequenced case after case to show the realities of lives that were contrary to what was acceptable living, such as:

> The child will go to third or fourth year [of school] and will return to the mission or settlement because opportunities have been denied them in society…

And elsewhere:

> It is the policy of the government to allow these houses to fall into disrepair.[515]

After describing the ways of living among divided Australian communities, showing what thinking and actions had not worked or were still not working, he called for more understanding and more action to secure land rights.

Both Oodgeroo and Gilbert likely faced audiences often enough who were apathetic or opposed to their propositions. Nonetheless, while incorporating concrete and even startling comments to report what they had witnessed and to attract attention, they sought engagement with audience members who might range from the interested but undecided, all the way through to any apathetic about the situation, and inevitably some who opposed land rights for First Nations.

For each group within their audiences, both sought to demonstrate basic causes of the problem and secure common ground. To motivate engagement, they used visualisations that hit vital spots and provided a basis for seeking agreement on general principles[516] of humanity applied to granting land rights. Oodgeroo and Gilbert drew on defined experiences to state defined solutions and to request definite action.

Better Policies and Conditions

The reporter/narrator stances that Oodgeroo and Gilbert adopted in these speeches also helped moderate the challenge implicit in their advocacy of better policies and conditions for First Nations. Although Oodgeroo and Gilbert showed some similarity in this stance, each had a distinct style. Gilbert tended to confront strongly, whereas Oodgeroo spoke with a quieter though still penetrating 'voice'. In contrast to Gilbert's challenges, Oodgeroo used less *dispute* polemic, while still contesting differences of attitudes and feelings.

Like Gilbert, she moderated her use of *discussion* polemic[517] by detailing actions, insights, and understandings of the lives of people in First Nations under Australia's governments. Her mode was to seek solution to the problem. As Libby Connors notes:

> Oodgeroo was an experienced political activist who also appreciated the need for white support... she always sought to maintain communication with the white power structure even while she was fighting it...she always rose above the internecine warfare that besets all social movement politics.[518]

Oodgeroo incorporated features of the deliberative and judicial rhetorical genres in her 1968 paper on *Integration and Queensland Society*[519] and her 1970 speech titled *How Well Off Are Aborigines in Modern-day Australia?*[520] with both events held in Brisbane. In 1988, at Macquarie University in Sydney, when accepting the award of an honorary degree,[521] Oodgeroo adhered to a ceremonial genre, while incorporating some deliberative features to advance the cause for land rights. Despite some differences among these three speeches in tone and how she appealed to the emotions, her consistent deliberative objective was to seek land rights.

Seeking Land Rights

In the seminar paper in 1968, Oodgeroo noted that, one year after the referendum to recognise citizenship for First Nations, little had changed. Her opening questions in the speech inferred this, then asked bluntly, 'When can we expect some action?'[522] Like Gilbert, she tackled head-on the failure to deliver on the new law or do more than talk. Yet, Oodgeroo immediately moderated this challenge by relating some earlier history of the Assimilation Policy. For the failures in delivering change, she did not blame Professor Elkin, who had introduced the policy, but directed attention to the sequence of actions of un-named government heads who failed to execute the policy.

She pulled no punches, with her language ranging in a single line in the printed text from a balance of everyday language, 'the biggest farce of all times' to some specialist language, 'social equality'.[523] As Oodgeroo recounted actions that impacted the missions and reserves, as well as the 'fringe settlements', she managed her stance as a narrator cum reporter by sharing considerably more detail than might already be known to her listeners. She appeared objective, in part by not calling out individuals by name for any failures.

To frame the speech in 1970 at the Pius XII Seminary in Brisbane on how lives in First Nations compared in 'modern-day' to 'yesteryear',[524] she pursued a task-oriented reporter's approach. Initially, she described the realities of her family life, growing up on a subtropical island near Brisbane, living off the natural bounty of the island, with some addition of limited government supplements. Following this first quarter of the speech, she stated flatly that the three years since the referendum had done 'nothing for the Aborigine'.[525]

The opening to her *Acceptance Speech* in 1988 at Macquarie University for the award of Doctor of Letters was gracious, subdued, and more formal, commencing by gratefully acknowledging the award as 'a milestone in the history of this land now known as Australia'.[526] She then recorded her perspective on the arrival of the white Europeans, 'we admired and marvelled, but with foreboding'.[527] This was one of ten parallel appositions (with 'we' repeated ten times) in which she sketched in the short speech, a sharp contrast between the outlook and lives of peoples of First Nations compared with most of her audience. Oodgeroo sustained a narrator's stance, while emphasising these extreme contrasts.

More formal than Gilbert, in length and complexity of sentences and in other ways, Oodgeroo used relatively fewer:

- Interrogatives
- Repetitions
- Personal pronouns
- Interpolations and interruptions of logical flow of ideas

- Oppositions of ideas in brief sentences and phrases.

She also used very few sentence fragments, few short lively phrases, few contractions, little slang, no invective, and few short words with tangible referents. These all featured more frequently in Gilbert's speech, characterising his language as a form of conversational challenge that he sought to have very directly addressed.

Oodgeroo incorporated little of the *anaphora* or other parallelism that underpinned Gilbert's emotive argument in his Armidale speech. Although the academic and seminar settings might be situations that encourage a formality of a particular type, Gilbert's interpretation of a reporter cum narrator stance offered more frequent contrasts and comparisons with quick conclusions than did Oodgeroo.

Calling for Correction

In the context of presenting a speech or paper especially, Oodgeroo's tone was generally low key when expressing raw feelings about the losses that First Nations experienced. Nonetheless, in each of her three speeches, her voice of criticism and correction was still present in brief assertions. In 1968, she called out the 'humiliating policy of segregation', countered 'we'd rather live on your rubbish dumps', pointed out that peoples of First Nations were not helped by 'talking to a sea of European faces', and corrected a government minister that 'we are not "his Aborigines"'[528]

In the 1970 paper, she was similarly forthright and recorded that the peoples of First Nations were 'banned from most social activities', assessed the Queensland Act governing First Nations as the 'cruelest policy', charged Australian governments with 'desire for greedy gain' and clarified that for people in First Nations 'Poverty is already here'.[529]

Almost two decades later, at her honorary degree award at Macquarie University, Oodgeroo presented a series of *antitheses* of the lives and expectations of peoples in First Nations and other races, to call for the changes needed to assure happiness for all groups in a multicultural society. She had noted the European 'sacred tokens of lord and lady' and a 'strange cult of uniformity', pointing out the adaptations that First Nations had already made to deal with 'gaols and orphanages, rents and taxes.'[530] She used these observations to call upon her audience to make change themselves, whatever the obligated laws of the day were.

By the time of this speech in 1988, the call for land rights had a unity of purpose for First Nations in Australia. Oodgeroo now clearly stated the importance of granting land rights in the context of the culture of First Nations. She described the land as '...our mother ...she owns us.'[531]

Case for Land Rights

While Oodgeroo and Gilbert both focused on the goal of securing land rights, Gilbert's speech to the trainee teachers in Armidale illustrated very specific features of life in First Nations. He also asked people outside First Nations to look differently at their own lives. He presented his observed truths that contested existing attitudes, feelings, and presumptions. He sustained the thread of his case while disputing the purpose or the effects of actions taken in the treatment of First Nations.

An initial climax in the speech called for those outside First Nations to get their own assumptions in order. A second climax called for the education not of First Nations but of 'Europeans'. A third called for efforts to communicate. The fourth climax put on record a 'genocide' of peoples in First Nations. This set the platform to ask the trainee teachers to take up the cause for land rights by helping to defeat discrimination in their work and life. His penultimate climax was to indicate that land rights meant '...that all Aboriginal reserves be immediately deeded in perpetuity to the Aboriginal people as a whole'.

Gilbert had shaped an argument that might enable listeners to modify their positions on the weight of evidence. He used all three types of polemic, *discussion*, *dispute*, and *controversy*,[532] to challenge listeners with a cascade of illustrative life stories touching raw emotions. He used everyday earthy language. He seemed directly familiar with real situations and used these stories to illustrate, to stimulate, to challenge, or to urge action. His illustrations were clear and tangible:

> I asked a woman at Purfleet Mission what there was in the community for the children, and she said, 'nothing', 'What have the men got?', 'Nothing', 'And what have the women got?', 'Nothing'.
>
> ... to vote for politicians who couldn't give a damn about their kids dying, who couldn't give a damn about the houses, who, in fact, will not allow any houses to be built on reserves. As soon as the houses are vacated, they are bulldozed into the ground in order to try and get them into your society.[533]

His stimulation specific:

> Today the Aboriginal voice is rising for better conditions, better opportunities for their children, opportunities which are not provided by education.
>
> ...try and see that black person down the street not merely as a drunk, as a problem and an embarrassment. The man is not a problem, he is a victim: a victim of colonisation, a victim of government policies that have been wrong, and a victim of discrimination.[534]

His challenges were personalised:

> What we have to do is allow a people to grow: allow them to grow at their own pace; allow them to make the decisions in their own community.
>
> …Is your society so good? As you can see by student demonstrations, there is a lot that's wrong with it. While we cannot expect the 'perfect', we can work towards human dignity, we can work to give some justice to a people…[535]

His urgings of action were strong:

> …we have to try to communicate. People have to be sincere…
>
> There is discrimination in Australia. This is your part—being sincere—that whatever you teach, wherever you work, try to stop this. Another vital role you can play is asking for the recognition of Aboriginal land rights.[536]

Conversational Narrative

In addressing student teachers, Gilbert could perhaps confidently focus on their wanting to improve their society. Aristotle's perception of the young was that they were 'strongly ruled by their desires, impulsively angry, idealistic, and excessive in all that they do'.[537] Gilbert did not seem to assume all these qualities in his listeners but focused more on their idealism and desire for change. He provided a simple path to reassess existing views through his observed truths and enabled his listeners to reconsider what they understood. He framed observations within what he reminded were their own moral values, 'you profess—justice, humanity, decency'.[538]

In recommending such self-reflection and in other ways throughout the speech, a notable strength in Gilbert's personal appeal was his conversational narrative mode. As do other speakers who accentuate a conversational effect, Gilbert used a high proportion of:

- Interrogatives
- Repetition
- Personal pronouns
- Interpolations and interruptions of logical flow of ideas
- Omission of pronoun subjects
- Opposition of ideas in brief sentences and phrases
- Function versus lexical words.

His speech contained a lively series of interrogations, often with interpolated dialogue and contrasts, apposition of ideas in short phrases, a high density of sentence fragments typical of conversation, with mostly short words, much parallelism for emphasis, and many short sentences. These features accumulated to characterise the speech as a 'conversation'. From the introduction and throughout, Gilbert included interpolation and slang:

> ... most Europeans see the Aborigine *as* 'Jacky'—*as* a drunk, *as* a man who will not work, *who* goes on walkabout and *who* will not help himself. There seems to be a difference in values.[539] *[my italics]*

Gilbert also offset this colloquialism with some features common in more formal argument. His language incorporated features of conceptual thinking or formality, such as parallel phrases and clauses within predominantly complete sentences. His clarity of reasoning provided perspective on the realities that he described, with language features suggesting a mix of the formal and the personal.

Values of First Nations

As in the excerpt below, Gilbert emphasised the need to respect distinct culture, repeating 'in their own right' and closing the sentence with *antitheses*:

> They want to be *Aborigines* in their own right, to be *people* in their own right, rather than *imitation white men, pseudo-white men*.[540] *[my italics]*

He underscored a core tenet of his case that 'white values' are not and ought not be imposed as values of First Nations.[541]

By using sustained *controversy* throughout the speech Gilbert had confronted some basic misalignments of perception between First Nations and other Australians. The final challenge he restated was to recognise land rights. In the close to the speech, Gilbert emphasised with parallelism and repetition what specifically his listeners could do—to teach, work, stop discrimination, and ask for land rights for First Nations in Australia.

The main differences between the arguments of Oodgeroo and Gilbert were in tone, organisation, some language features, types of polemic, and vocabulary. They illustrated distinctive ways to approach listeners on a similar subject. Gilbert's connections and transitions for the flow of the argument were made mainly through the relevance to each other of the successive points he stated. To connect points in the argument, he also frequently used parallelism, and questions, with colons and dashes to represent speech pauses, and some conversation-like connectors, such as 'but', 'so', and 'now'. Less evident were complex and compound sentences or qualifying clauses that were more common in Oodgeroo. Both sustained effective stances as compelling conversational narrators.

Since the times of the speeches reviewed here, thanks to the efforts of Oodgeroo and Gilbert and the efforts of many more from First Nations and more widely in the community, Australia has advanced further in recognising rights. Important advances include the result from ten years of litigation, with a High Court decision in the Mabo case in 1992, and the landmark Native Title

Act 1993 to protect native title in co-existence with the national land management system. Yet despite these advances, and some public recognitions from the prime ministers Keating and Rudd that will be assessed later, self-determination and cultural identity expectations are still to be fulfilled.

Colin Tatz wisely notes, 'We are entitled to turn the page, move forward, to celebrate achievement, to engage in some triumphalism, but...Moving on is only possible when we face our history and ourselves: This surely is a measure of our maturity as a nation.'[542] Still walking in the footsteps of Oodgeroo and Gilbert are many others, who seek to advance human rights for First Nations in Australia.

13: 'Revolution' Rhetoric of Germaine Greer

Sexism should always be unacceptable.[543]

– Julia Gillard

Arguments for social revolution often have a short life. They are quickly realised or nearly as quickly forgotten. But the movement to advance women's rights, like some other enduring struggles for rights, has had to sustain efforts continuously for centuries. The movement has produced imaginative speech and writing to keep attention and move the cause forward. Germaine Greer's book *The Female Eunuch*[544] continues to be in print since it was first published in 1970 and captured international attention, holding readership and thoughtful attention more than 50 years following publication.[545]

The book was a very personal argument for a social revolution to free women to live individually fulfilling lives. Greer covered a wide range of topics. She backgrounded the preconceptions and misconceptions of society (including employers, spouses, parents, politicians, reformers, writers, journalists, and others) on the perceived roles of women. She commented on women's employment in secretarial, nursing, production-line, academic, business, and other jobs. She discussed the proliferation of stereotypes, half-truths, and lies about what a woman should do, be, say, and appear to be. The book was garnished with brief supportive quotes from a variety of writers and commentators. Most importantly, Greer's writing provoked responses from a wide range of people.

Straightforward Approach

As one reader puts it, Greer said 'the unsayable'.[546] Many men and some women did not want to hear her. Greer was not to be silenced, as shown by her range of public interactions before and after the publication of the book. She is well able to express a different way to look at matters, stand her ground, and speak out with a candour, wit, and sharpness that women were not supposed to show. Most commonly she asserted alternate ways to view established norms and actions in areas of personal life. She conveyed a sense of practical wisdom through her generalisations, which sometimes did not align with a specific reality, as well as through her reinterpretation of perspectives.

Unsurprisingly, as an advocate of change Greer attracted much criticism, along with praise and gratitude from many readers with whom her case resonated. In the 1970s, there were readers as prurient as in earlier times. Although she pushed some people's tolerance for earthy language, expletives were not as frequent in *The Female Eunuch* as criticisms of her implied. This was a time when the ages-old bluff of a patriarchal society continued to use 'threats and violence to try to frighten women into silence or try to make the debate about something else altogether to distract attention from the main issue'[547] of concern to many women.

At that time, public communication almost uniformly talked about men and mankind. Even the first sentence of Greer's book was subject to use of the masculine pronoun 'his' in place of 'person'. In addition to being invisible in the language of public and everyday conversation, women were mostly stereotyped as weak and submissive, along with even more pejorative portrayals, in life, news media, and literature. It was still signalled in society that women were incorporated in a status quo, as being dependent legally, financially, and emotionally, on fathers, husbands, or other men. Greer described these representations as oppression, along with the reality they often represented. Although the women's movement had made some gains, including the right to vote in the early twentieth century, much had yet to occur for women to be free from the oppression Greer addressed. She reassessed presumptions that persisted. She vigorously pursued a logic of correcting 'some of the false perspectives which our assumptions about womanhood, sex, love and society have combined to create'.[548]

She critiqued norms governing perceptions of self, family, marriage, child-rearing, and social interactions, which she said denied women's freedom. At the time of the book's publication, Greer's audience included male readers, but caught the attention especially of women in a range of circumstances. To appeal to this wide audience and to change attitudes, the writing had to be interesting, impassioned, and intelligent.

Greer built her case by incorporating intuitively or consciously[549] principles and techniques of rhetoric to create a suasive informality. She commonly used a variety of rhetorical features and integrated figurative language, especially to frame thinking. This review explores ways that Greer built her case with a provocative conversational language that incorporated humour. A close study of the book's final chapter here details her rhetorical stance, some consistencies in language style, and ways that her language compared with the influential writing of George Orwell and the writing of two contemporary protest writers, Kate Millett and Ronald Segal. An important characteristic of Greer's language was that, while sustaining an engagingly lively conversational tone, she smartly combined polemic and humour to surgically eviscerate nonsense-talk.

Provocative Case

The Female Eunuch presented a provocative but cogent case for women's liberation. Greer stated that the earlier suffragette reforms had 'opened the cage door... but the canary had refused to fly out'. She stated that 'reforms are retrogressive' and noted that 'now ungenteel middle-class women... [were] ...calling for revolution'. She encouraged newcomers to feminism to overturn the patriarchal system through 'revolution'. Greer described the earlier approaches of the suffragettes as inadequate and sketched out alternate ways for women to find individual freedom in company with and encouraged by sisters. She advocated that this required changes to manners and behaviours. Her approach negated violence and advocated finding, through a better consciousness of the situation, a 'festival of the oppressed'.

The title and subject of the book put attention on sexuality, the relativities of women and men, and the emasculation of women. The genre of the book was largely deliberative. It incorporated both *discussion* polemic to seek truth in the problem being considered and *dispute* polemic to contest attitudes, feelings, or preferences—in this case to win justice for women. Greer's commentary was irreverent, using trenchant wit to outline her view of the history of women and their treatment up to 1970, together with a model for a different future.

Controversial Humour

Greer's humour integrated her dynamism and intelligence, continuously underpinning the thrust of her argument, at times bawdy, sometimes making fun of a presumption, and other times resonating with earthy insight to make a point. Her humour suggested a grounded cleverness that influenced an audience's feelings about Greer and her treatment of matters. Her humour was woven throughout much of her writing and was empowered by ambiguity, allusion, hyperbole, parody, overstatement, and understatement, helping to sustain variety and liveliness in her treatment of topics.

She often used humour to shape the lens through which a reader was to look. Greer illustrated one denial of self as the giving to others imposed at her Catholic convent school when growing up, 'we put our pennies in a red and yellow box… for the missions, if we were holy that is'. Likewise, to make a point about the 'Cinderella profession of teaching'. Or, to debunk popular mythology, 'The orgies feared by the Puritans have not materialized on every street corner'.

By taking a different tack to what was expected, Greer would trigger a surprise punchline as a reality check, sometimes also making a point through what was not said, 'The occupational hazard of being a Playboy Bunny is the aching facial muscles brought on by the obligatory smiles'. Hyperbole and mild exaggeration were commonly used to put on display and reassess assumptions, such as the facile romance novel where 'everything happens in a swoon or a swamp of undifferentiated sensation'. Following this, she commented on 'how deeply we believe in the concept of male mastery'. Her inclination to puns included creating neologisms, to make fun of a perspective.

At times, she used exaggeration as throw-away mockery, referring to men's 'chicken legs which they expose on any British resort beach'. Other times, Greer drew on parody of a stereotype to make a point, 'communication is not advanced by the *he talk, me listen* formula'. A special power in her humour was to encourage reassessment of an assumption which, when presented humorously, became self-evident as an 'artificial' or 'unattainable' idea.

Compared with Speech

Greer sustained a lively moderated conversational tone well-suited to dealing with the range of her topics. Her welding of the colloquial into her language enabled an amiable relationship with an audience, fostering willingness to learn more.[550] She balanced the formal and the colloquial, as do other public figures who seek a wide audience. Her consistency in using some language features typical of lively conversation was apparent in a comparison of the initial 600-words of the final chapter of the book with a same-length sample of her speech at the Washington Press Club.[551] Among these language features recorded in the writing/speech samples were:

average words per sentence (27/30)
compound clauses (7/10)
action verbs (26/24)
'to be' verbs (28/29)
present tense (49/51)
infinite verbs (8/9)

clichés (4/3)
slang (1/2)
interpolations (12/8)
pairs (41/37)
ellipses (5/3)
monosyllabic words (64%/69%)
bisyllabic words (16%/16%)

In many respects, Greer wrote as she spoke. She showed preference in both this writing and speech for personal pronouns (24/44) and proper nouns (10/18), with some of the varied frequency of these features in the short samples dependent on the subject matter.

Noticeably fewer in the writing compared with the speech were the number of verbs relative to nouns (44%/62%). Within the writing sample, she used complete sentences as a nod to formality, but also incorporated brief sentences typical of conversation. In both writing and speech, Greer also struck a balance of everyday and abstract words. She used lists in the writing but not the speech (3/0). And she did not use in either sample some features that occur in conversation, such as question sequences which she used elsewhere, or sentence fragments and exclamations. Her use of earthy slang or expletives was one of the more striking reflections of lively colloquial conversation.

Earthy Slang

Greer grounded discussion of everyday matters in *The Female Eunuch* in the language commonly used in the everyday rather than 'polite' society. When she used expletives, it was not only for the shock effect to attract or hold attention. She confronted readers with the language that some so-called polite individuals also used when speaking among themselves to demean or disparage women. Her tackling this hypocrisy was consistent with and supported a central purpose of the book. Likely, the use of expletives did not greatly impact Greer's ethos in any direction different from what was assumed from her public persona.

She used a common expletive for women's genitals in different ways 14 times throughout the book. In a single use in the final chapter, Greer asserted that the vulva '…must come into its own'. Public acceptance of linguistic taboo was durable concerning the use of a word largely avoided since the fifteenth century in written and polite spoken English,[552] and classified as illegal to print for a long period since about 1700—with continuing legal ambiguity in some jurisdictions. Criticism of her using the expletive ignored the wisdom of linguists as far back as Brander Matthews in 1893, who commented on presumed offences in language use:

> One of the hardest lessons for the amateurs in linguistics to learn…is that affectations are fleeting, that vulgarisms *(solecisms)* die of their own weakness and that corruptions do little harm to the language…Slang and all other variations from the high standard of the literary language are either temporary or permanent. If they are temporary, the damage they do is inconsiderable. If they are permanent, their survival is due solely to the fact that they were convenient or necessary. When a word or phrase has come to stay… it is idle to denounce a decision rendered by the court of last resort.[553]

Given that Greer's use still aggrieved or startled critics in the 1970s, it might be argued that she performed a reversal of the *Oxford English Dictionary's* supposed injustice to women,[554] that excluded this word but included the slang, male equivalent.

Her single use of the expletive in the final chapter redirected attention from 'male genitality' but left ambiguity whether she was referring to the female pudendum as a symbol of woman, or sexual intercourse itself and woman-as-sex, both physically and spiritually. Greer then probed at a more intellectual level 'The question of the female attitude…'. To advance her case for women to come into their own, she put a strong focus on women's sexuality and challenged perceptions of 'sexuality', 'genitality', 'lesbianism', and 'sex', amid formal language and accumulated passive voice verbs ('were relieved', 'should be adopted', 'should be taken off' and the elliptic 'replaced'). Returning to abstraction of the sexual might have assisted the continued attention of possibly all except the most prurient readers.

Rhetorical Argument

In the final chapter of *The Female Eunuch*, titled 'Revolution',[555] Greer brought focus to the case that she had unfolded throughout the book. Her closing argument addressed what revolution meant to her and set out actions she considered would help women change from established roles in society. She provided a framework for a reader to determine an individual personal direction going forward. Like the classical *peroratio*, this chapter summarized and re-evaluated the main argument of the book to offer a passionate call to action.

In the previous chapter, Greer had described how she believed some women had mistaken the reaction in rebellion for revolution. She now urged women to reject violent displays, to love rather than admire a man, to think, to be independent, to listen to 'experienced sisters', to learn from mistakes, and to choose a 'right' course of action. At the close of the chapter and book she would challenge women finally by asking 'What *will* you do?'

Beginning this final chapter with a correction of the popular confusion between rebellion and revolution provided Greer's springboard to an argument that incorporated a range of rhetorical approaches, figures, and tropes.[556] She began the final chapter:

> Reaction is not revolution. It is not a sign of revolution when the oppressed adopt the manners of the oppressors and practise oppression on their own behalf. Neither is it a sign of revolution when women ape men, and men women…[557]

By contrasting revolution with the reaction of rebellion, Greer sharpened the focus for readers. In the abruptly simple first sentence, she introduced the theme in a pithy self-assured statement that strongly resonated a sense of wisdom, or *sententia*. This first paragraph swiftly introduced the reader to major ideas of the book's conclusion. Her simple distinction of 'reaction' from 'revolution' along with a recap of prejudices and stereotypes were ideas easily grasped.[558] Greer also incorporated a simple and much-used way to attract audience attention, by listing what was ostensibly not to be the subject of discussion but was merely being called to mind (or *praeteritio*). This rhetorical approach found expression as far back as Cicero's first oration *Against Verres*.[559]

She also sustained simplicity through a conversational narrator's language, with the narrative approach offering the advantage of natural sequential development. She mainly used monosyllabic words. Repetitions also reflected a sense of conversation, such as with the root word 'oppress' (or *polyptoton*), the connective 'when' (or *anaphora*), and the inversion of 'women' / 'men' (or *antimetabole*), all of which provided emphasis while contributing to the conversational effect. In the complete first paragraph, Greer used simple sentences of the standard SP (Subject, Predicator) structure, in sentences *i, ii, iv, v, vi, viii, ix,* and *x*.[560] In addition, the disjunction in clauses[561] (*viii, ix*) and the form 'Neither is' contributed to an informal tone, in association with the *ellipsis* of 'when' and 'ape' in this context,[562] in the phrase 'and men women'.[563]

Continuing a provocative, conversational style through the paragraph, Greer highlighted apparent contradictions. She used *paradox* cliché, the *simile* 'like the white man's black man', corrected this with a pejorative for an African-American, and provided a swift series, 'the susceptibilities, the guilts and hidden desires of men'. She then drew on the pejorative connotation in 'creature', when referring to the pioneering British politician Barbara Castle, who had indicated that feminism offered no assistance in her fight for rights. Each of Greer's language choices raised the emotional level of the discourse and reflected what was common then as everyday earthy conversation.

Countering Opposition

Following this opening paragraph, Greer presented an emotionally charged series of opinions about the role of career women in society. These ideas might be accepted by some readers, but in the second paragraph she anticipated militant women's rights advocates, who might oppose her claim that women should not use violence as a way out of the existing situation.

Heading off the possibility of objection, by analogy Greer related violence to war. And she quickly asserted that men training for war was an inappropriate model for women, since 'wars cannot be *won*'. Using World War II as an example, she re-stated a view popular with some who believed England lost that war, when the country's fortunes were compared to the 'post-war fortunes' of Nazi Europe–which supposedly lost. Once Greer had swept the reader into the subject of war, she set up reassessment of the popular identification of Nazism as 'bad' and Winston Churchill as 'good', while incorporating a guarded criticism of the British war leader. Greer followed a pattern of setting up an assumption, to contradict it with new information or with an insight different from what was commonly considered.

Greer then concluded that war failed to solve problems and further suggested that militarism simply 'dehumanised manhood', resulting in the 'specifically masculine end of suicide'. Here she used a series of words connoting 'badness' ('condemn', 'perversion', and 'dehumanised') to conclude with the most 'bad', 'specifically masculine' and 'suicide'. In what sense suicide should be regarded as 'specifically masculine' was left unclear, since, as Greer herself stated (page 281), more women committed suicide than men. Nonetheless, her primary perspective of strongly discrediting violence became the platform for her to tackle the realities of dealing more directly with its effectiveness for women who see violence as the way forward.

These first two paragraphs of the chapter showed marked similarities in number of words and sentences, and in other ways. Some underlying similarities might illustrate broader consistencies in her language style. In both paragraphs, the conventional order of a Subject/Predicator sentence and clause structure predominated. She alternated between active and passive voice verbs, with active voice verbs in the opening and closing sentences of each paragraph [a = active voice; p = passive voice, with embedded clauses noted by subscripts 'b', 'c', *etc.*]:

I a i, ii, iii; p iii_b, c; a iv, p v, v_b; a v_c, vi, vii; p vii_b; a $viii$, ix, x.[564]

II a i, ii, iii, iv, v_s; p v_b, vi; a vii; p $viii$; a ix.

She also had only one use of the plural first-person pronoun 'we' in each paragraph (I vi; II vii). Of contrast was the number of words in the opening and closing sentences of paragraph II, at almost nine times the number of words in the closing and opening sentences of paragraph I. Similarities predominated though, including the number of occurrences of 'it' (2,3), 'the' (16, 19), noun clauses (1, 1), infinitives (3, 3), possessives (4, 4), non-proper nouns (59, 60), determiners (26, 26) and monosyllabic words versus others (64%, 60%).

In the second paragraph (II), Greer increased her use of polysyllabic words (I 12%, II 21%), with a decrease in bisyllabic words. Her change of subject to 'violence', her beginning to use adverbs with a tendency to polysyllabic words with '-ly' suffixes, and her assumption of an official reporting stance using vocabulary from the register of officialdom to discuss the World War II example were likely the main reasons for the increase in polysyllabic words. The changed subject matter also resulted in the use of more proper nouns (2, 6) and perhaps also a marked increase in adjectives (12, 23).

Contrasts and Parallels

In the third paragraph, Greer condemned women who learn karate in order to be free from threats of violence. She suggested these groups were deluding themselves. She would later call 'fools' those who fancied 'that they manipulate the world'. Greer pursued at length multiple meanings or nuances of the word 'violence', using examples and insight to illustrate what she urged was a better or wiser approach. She developed the discussion around the meaning of the one word 'violence', which was a technique that she was fond of, and possibly derived from her academic background.

Whereas the previous discussion of violence in war was with a detachment akin to historical commentary, she now used more animated figurative language to make her point. Her uses of 'violence' and its euphemisms up to this point were only in association with 'sham' or impliedly non-dangerous situations. The adjustment of her description in the final two sentences in the paragraph emphatically outlined the character of someone who was truly dangerous.

She identified this person unambiguously as the 'genuinely violent man'. Greer shrewdly observed:

A) The genuinely violent man does not play

about with karate or the Marquess of Queensberry's rules–

B) he uses a broken

bottle, a wheelbrace, a tyre lever or an axe.

C) He does not see the fight through,

D) but seeks to end it quickly by doing as

much harm as he can as soon as he can.[565]

She contrasted in this brief narrative the reality that karate was no match in defending oneself against such a man. Greer used mainly colloquial words that reflected the reality of the situation described. She pointed out that this man does not 'play about', then swiftly listed a catalogue of his tools for doing violence, with the most brutal ('the axe') in the emphatic final position. Her graphic perspective illustrated how karate and 'Marquess of Queensbury rules' belong to a different world and were ineffective against the 'genuinely violent'. The dramatic contrast of both the content and the language in the phrases 'A' and 'B' highlighted the very real, non-theoretical, non-theatrical, everyday tangible implements used in such a fight. Greer's colloquial voice underpinned her perspective, and she implicitly mocked the formality of the rules-based methods of fighting.

In addition to the parallelism used for contrast in this narrative, Greer reminded of Lysistrata's approach, also using parallelism for emphasis and contrast. This illustrated sexual 'reward' (or more accurately, the denial of it) as one weapon available to women to minimise the incidence of violence. She then contrasted male v. female within the parallel clause structures of multiple 'if' clauses, the doublet 'the brawn and the bravado', a catalogue of 'soldier, wrestler, footballer or male model', using feminine and masculine subjects.

These patterns of balance and form potentially conditioned a reader to expect an organised sequential approach. But concurrently Greer incorporated some sharp contrasts that sustained a sense of movement in the language. She used rhetorical questions, interpolation of a parenthetic clause, the mention of Lysistrata, and *polyptoton* of the root word 'withdraw',[566] which produced variations of rhythm and pace. Also, in these middle paragraphs of the chapter, Greer repeated her practice of leading a discussion by concentrating the reader's attention on the meaning of a particular word. In contrast with the earlier treatment of 'violence', she was more subtle in focusing on the sensitivity of problems that women face from domination and sexual blackmail. The perversion of sex as violence was gradually seen here in her argument as an entwined unit.

Rhetorical Interpolations

At various points in the final chapter, Greer used interpolations such as the parenthetical clause and the rhetorical question that provided impressions of movement, building the cut-and-thrust of debate into the language flow. Three occurrences of parenthetical clauses (IV *iii*; XII *v*; XX *xviii*) and six occurrences of rhetorical questions (IV; VI; VIII, *v*; XX), and uses of a type of question and answer for rhetorical effect (VIII; XVIII) caused sometimes lengthy interruptions that strengthened conversational effects.

Her use of the rhetorical question carried the risk of having the reader supply an answer that might have interfered with the argument or potentially redirect the language rhythm in a way that a parenthetical clause did not. Other than the exceptional final rhetorical question, XX *xx*, which had the entire book behind it to condition the desired answer though, all of Greer's questions in this chapter had the required answers implied within the question or within the text or context. Her first questions about the institution of marriage, VIII, Greer answered herself. The most probable response to why a girl marries–'love'–was turned about and shown to be in fact no answer at all, by presenting the *interrogatio*:[567] 'why must it [love] be exclusive?' The single word 'Security?' as an alternative reply to the original question provided Greer with the opportunity to dismiss 'security' as a 'chimera'.

Although such question-and-answer form provided forward thrusting then arresting of the reader's thought process, the more predictable patterns of other rhetorical devices acted as stabilising features (such as *anadiplosis, parison*, and *anaphora* of 'love', *ii, iii* and *iv*, and *anadiplosis* of 'security', *vi, vii*). Time and again, such rhetorical features as these occurred within the middle paragraphs. A surface interpretation might consider these sentences merely to be making an outline of matters with few rhetorical effects. Although certain paragraphs require close examination to observe their rhetorical components, the extensive occurrence of these features throughout reflected the constant presence of Greer as rhetorician.

Reinforcing the *Peroratio*

Just as the final chapter on *Revolution* summarized and reassessed the book, the final paragraph in the chapter very directly focused the reader's emotions to bring Greer's peroration to a close. Within one paragraph, she neatly summed up the final chapter by relating what revolution meant to someone taking on this challenge. She provided a model of *'joy in the struggle'*, for women to take into their own lives.

The rhythmic final sentence of the penultimate paragraph (XIX) had suggested that the world must now listen to women. Greer thus prepared the way to state particulars in the final paragraph (XX) of the book at an intense emotional level. She referenced strong emotions, using *paradox*, the superlative adjective 'surest' (*i*), and the repetition of the verb 'is' (in a slightly shorter than conventional average-length sentence, at 18-words and a short 7-word sentence). The *paradox/sententia* 'Revolution is the festival of the oppressed' (*ii*) strongly restated the thesis behind the chapter and book. It echoed the second sentence of the chapter that had so strongly adumbrated with *polyptoton* of the root word 'oppress'. She now telegraphed a forcefulness in outlining what women should not do. Along with the earlier specific reminder, in XVI, on what women might also do to make even housekeeping enjoyable for example, in XX ii, Greer recalled her practical advice to make *fun* from work.

Lasting Power

The lasting power of the book's final paragraph came from its close combination of emotional forcefulness, partly due to prescription in a guise of description. Greer provided a setting for the final rhetorical question through the progression of her main topics in this paragraph:

what is the test of 'correctness' of action?
what will be experienced
what will be achieved
what revolution means
what is not relevant
what will be discovered
what must be avoided
what must be done
what will be distracting, thus
what *will* you do?

These topics tracked the earlier propositions of the chapter: that reaction is not revolution, that violence must be abandoned as a revolutionary tactic, that admiration of violence ought to be eschewed, that rationales for one's life must be examined, that social pressures that required set behaviour from women must be fought against, that realities should be faced, and that the experienced 'sisters' should be listened to. She indicated that the realisation of 'genuine revolution' depended on her readers taking action to move the cause forward.

Whereas earlier propositions had detailed how revolution might be achieved, the final paragraph recalled and reinforced a blueprint of the joy in revolution, against which women could easily compare their present lives. Concentrating personal pronouns with effect, she returned to echoes of language at the start of the chapter when she distinguished reaction from revolution. Perhaps this subtly flagged that Greer seemed to know where she was headed from the start of the chapter, with her language giving a sense of unity to the chapter, and perhaps to the book.

Comparisons

Comparison of this conclusion with the final paragraph of Ronald Segal's book, *Race War*,[568] showed a contrast in the approach of these writers. Segal focused attention on 'them' rather than Greer's use of the personal pronoun 'you', with which a reader might easily identify. Segal also posed an apparently more remote and ambiguous problem in his close, with his series of rhetorical questions providing a different emotional force. Segal addressed the broader, more intellectual question of whether there was any point to people's existence if they could not be trusted to take part in the search for 'freedom, knowledge and peace'. In contrast, Greer revived her variety of concerns to propel her reader to action. Whereas Segal focused a single perspective in conclusion, Greer framed opportunity for individual choices for action going forward. Kate Millett in *Sexual Politics*[569] seemed also to argue there was only a single way forward.

Although all three protest writers used hybrid types of polemic, Segal and Millett closed with *dispute polemic*, which is primarily concerned with a sole solution of winning. In contrast to the approach of Segal and Millett, Greer is more similar in this aspect to the approach of the well-regarded and lucid writer, George Orwell, in his essay 'Politics and the English Language'.[570] Orwell illustrated disparate influences or views, typified in his often-quoted sentence, 'Political language—and with variations this is true of all political parties, from Conservatives to Anarchists—is designed to make lies sound truthful and murder respectable, and to give an appearance of solidity to pure wind'.[571]

Whereas Millett heavily used words connoting 'good' and 'bad' ('to rebel...be broken, stigmatised and cured') as absolutes, Orwell compared the 'good' and 'bad', weighing up extremes with qualification and moderation—such as 'with variation', 'sound', and 'appearance'. For Greer's qualification and moderation in the final sentences, she used balance, *antithesis,* and ellipsis ('The old process must be broken, not made new' *xviii*) and ('slaves enslave their masters' *xvi*). Akin to Orwell, she sounded like someone attentive to multiple considerations, while nonetheless asserting a prescription for revolution and recommending a model for action. Compared to Orwell's clarity however, Millett, and Segal, and to an extent Greer, to some readers would 'border on pure wind'.[572]

The 'Conversation' Effect

With a growing expectation, especially since the latter half of the twentieth century, for public communication to reflect the liveliness of personal interaction, the reflection of conversational effects in writing has enjoyed progressively increasing importance. Language style analysts and linguists have long thought verbs and verbals enhance a sense of lively conversation.[573] Verbs suggest action, immediacy, or connectivity, and some research has refined clues about verb and noun ratios and some other language features to help diagnose and treat psychological conditions.[574] This research built on earlier projections that higher occurrences of verbs might coincide with greater emotional stability.[575] Verbs are thought to have high value relative to nouns,[576] which are static and less vivid than verbs, lead to longer and less vivid sentences, and do not provide a diversity of sentence patterns.[577] Some other language features that occur frequently in conversation[578] are compound clauses, sentence fragments, contractions, parentheses, pauses noted by dashes, interpolations, interrogatives, articles, and some function words such as personal pronouns.

Three quantitative analyses of Greer's writing noted language features thought to contribute to her conversational tone, by comparing occurrences in Millett, Orwell, and Segal. Counts of language features in the 5,980-word final chapter of Greer's book were divided by 10, to compare with 600-word writing samples by Millett, Orwell, and Segal. Firstly, language features were counted that Walker T. Gibson listed for a prototype 'style machine' he developed to compare tone in language,[579] as noted in Appendix Two. Secondly, the four writers' use of verbs, nouns, and their derivatives were compared. Thirdly, the total counts of a variety of language features were surveyed to observe commonalities among the writers that might reflect conversation.

The 'style machine': This early 'instrument' was developed largely to illustrate what language features suggest colloquial conversation.[580] Its creator, Gibson, acknowledges its limited development, with the tongue-in-cheek name as a 'Model-T style machine'. Idiosyncratically, he named his overall categories of language types as 'tough/sweet/stuffy'. He acknowledges a defect in his approach that, while identifying mixtures in style, the scores did not discriminate between the dreary and the artful. Possibly limiting also is his use of a triad rather than four qualities as descriptors, which would enable comparison of coordinate axes. Despite these considerations, the supposition that the general reader might be more engaged by 'tough' or 'sweet talking' writers, rather than writers with higher scores on 'stuffiness' is interestingly plausible.

The writers were found to be only marginally different, because all had 'mixed' styles with a tendency to be Tough and Sweet. The summary of scores on *The style machine's* Tough : Sweet : Stuffy ratio were: Greer 5 : 5 : 3; Millett 5 : 6 : 4; Orwell 7 : 6 : 3; and Segal 7 : 5 : 4. All the writers appeared to be prescriptive ('Tough') and yet responsive ('Sweet') to readers. Greer and Orwell both scored slightly lower on the 'Stuffy' scale, perhaps indicating that their similarities in language features could be suggestive of conversational effects.

High use of verbs: As noted previously, the heavy use of verbs can give a sense of liveliness, with verbs making connections among and perspective on actions, thoughts, people, objects, or events. A nominal/verbal ratio was obtained by including features that have nominal function (nouns, true/isolated adjectives, adverbs modifying adjectives, determiners, and prepositions) and then dividing the result by the sum of the features with verbal function (finite and infinite verbs, total adverbs minus those modifying adjectives and intensifiers). The Ratio of Nominals to Verbals (N/V) for the writers was Greer 2.4 / Millett 3.0/ Orwell 1.9 / Segal 2.3. Millett and Orwell are at opposite extremes of the group, with Greer and Segal about the same, but slightly closer to Orwell at the verbal end of the range.

Common features: Three features with some commonalities of occurrence were noted, namely compound clauses, ellipsis of verb or auxilliary, and non-present tense. The occurrence of these features in Greer/ Millett / Orwell / Segal were: Compound clauses: 10.7 / 1 / 16 / 3; Ellipsis of verb or auxilliary: 2.6 / 7 / 1 / 5; and Non-present tense: 4.8 /6 / 5 / 8.

On the counts of ellipsis, compound clauses, and non-present tense, Greer and Orwell were most similar. As discussed earlier, compound clauses simplify, compared to subordinate clauses, and are thought to suggest a conversational effect. Ellipsis of a verb or an auxilliary is also thought to produce a predominately colloquial effect. Non-present tense has doubtful value to suggest the liveliness and immediacy of conversation, since a common effect of past and conditional tenses is to distance a speaker/writer and/or a subject. Greer and Orwell were similar in the occurrence of ellipsis and of compound clauses in their writing, which offers some further support to consider the effect of these features as contributing to a conversational 'voice'.

Conclusion

Greer's high use of verbals, in addition to possibly implying assuredness and emotional stability, strengthened both her conversational tone and the vigour of her assertiveness. Women in literature were often portrayed as weak, dependent, reactive individuals, whose language style contained a concentration of nominal features, especially adjectives. Greer's language use provided a different and potentially enduring model. Since she integrated some language features that were previously considered more characteristic of males, the book required readers inherently to reassess how they viewed male and female.

Research in organisational communication has shown how women in the workplace have overtly challenged men's fantasies about their supposed dominant and aggressive position during work activity,[581] so that women might be included as people with valuable contributions to make. Gradually, the use of 'he' and 'she' has also changed. Language forms that include women, such as 'person', 'people', 'worker', and 'operator' were becoming part of the real world of everyday speech[582] when *The Female Eunuch* was published. Older exclusionary forms such as 'chairman' and 'workman' have gradually diminished in use to describe jobs performed by women and men.

Beyond language adjustments, changes have occurred that overcome some aspects of sexism, yet many people would acknowledge that much remains to do. Greer provided a valued model for women who sought an appropriate stance and language to persuade society to take these matters seriously. She created an apparent simplicity in her writing, while maintaining an often subtle, yet strong persuasion of the emotions. These qualities ensured that Greer's book *The Female Eunuch* was a model in persuasive language–written by an effective modern rhetorician.

14: Winning on Television–Bob Hawke

'...this is a fight for the future of Australia,

for the true heart and soul of Australia'.[583]

– Bob Hawke

Television allows the accomplished communicator in this medium to shine, but also magnifies awkwardness for anyone less adept. Ever since the 1960 Kennedy-Nixon debates in the United Sates, which were considered a key turning point in that year's presidential election, the value of television has loomed larger in the minds of public figures, promising direct transmission into the domestic living room or now also via mobile devices anywhere into daily lives.

In Australia, the 'core democratic rationale for leaders' debates is to provide voters with comparative information about the rival leaders, parties, and policies on offer'.[584] For whichever of the various formats for debates used over the years, it is the combination of the public figures' performance, along with the powerful impact of pundits' analyses, that shape an impression of the relative political and communicative competence of the contending individuals.

This chapter examines public speech in the 1983 Australian Federal election of the Labor Leader, Bob Hawke and the then prime minister, Liberal Leader Malcolm Fraser, including nightly television news during the period 2 February to 2 March 1983. It examines the approaches of the party policy speeches, together with speech segments of the two leaders on the ABC television news at 7 pm and Channel 7 at 6 pm, the then highest rating evening commercial news programme. Both the language and nonverbal features of the leaders' speaking styles on television were reviewed. Comparison was also made during the 1984 Federal election of leaders' communication styles, in the first Australian televised leaders' debate between the prime minister Bob Hawke and his challenger, the Liberal leader, Andrew Peacock.

Media Events

The 1983 and 1984 Federal elections presented Bob Hawke more visibly than ever before to Australians, successively positioned against opponents in special media events. Each of the contenders for the nation's highest political office of prime minister were acknowledged as 'achievers' in their respective spheres. Each used television heavily in emotion-filled campaigns. These were campaigns that foregrounded the leaders and called for sophisticated abilities in television performance.

Media commentators have long recognised the importance that television gives to an election, as leaders and voters are afforded special treatment involving upheavals in programme scheduling, the use of special programme formats, and so on.[585] This chapter outlines aspects of communication competence required of political leaders to be in the foreground as performers on television. It assesses particularly how in the 1983 and 1984 Federal elections one leader, Bob Hawke, deployed his communication competence in dealing with television.

The capacity of politicians to attract viewing audiences will often vary. But the on-screen contests of candidates in the 1980s appeared to resonate sufficiently with media audiences to link voters into the unfolding, sometimes dream-like sequence that modern elections deliver as media events, interrupting favourite sports and other on-screen entertainment.

With personal style being core to a leader-centred campaign, in 1983 the leading figures were front-of-stage early in this short election campaign. The media focus and magnification of the leaders' actions and idiosyncrasies substantially shaped roles akin to characters in a narrative. It was tempting to see analogy with other tales, even a fantasy tale like the story of Peter Pan. Without much squinting, these sharply different leaders in 1983 aligned with the vastly different characters of Peter Pan and Captain Hook—with a voter's ideology perhaps inevitably determining who in the fantasy tale might represent whom.

By stretching the Peter Pan analogy, the siblings Wendy and John might represent the Australian public, being shaken awake quite suddenly, with little warning of what was to happen; and as usual, left to figure out the plot lines in the campaign's progress; it remained unclear how John's leadership interests that were within the original tale might fit the election reality. Sharply defined though was the Crocodile, as the media. But later in the campaign story, some of the media changed role to become Tinkerbell and went about dispensing pixie dust on the media audience, mainly for Hawke.

Choice

For many in 1983, Fraser's much publicised comment more than a decade earlier that 'life was not meant to be easy' was apt framing for the choice between Fraser and Hawke. To some Fraser was aloof and impersonal, a professional politician, not a complimentary description in Australia. Hawke was well-known as a union leader, unproven in leading a national government, whom some considered volatile and showy. Among segments of voters, each was both respected and disliked. According to Brooke Gizzi-Stewart:

> ...both leaders were perceived to be "strong and tough", but Hawke was seen as a "unifier and bridge-builder" ... [committed to] national reconstruction and recovery'.[586]

Fraser was viewed by some as carrying baggage left over from his role in 1975 that had resulted in Whitlam's dismissal. In Gizzi-Stewart's view, the Liberal Party seemed convinced:

> ...that votes could in effect be "bought" with the wage pause, ... [preventing] it from noticing the growing disillusionment of a nation faced with higher unemployment, inflation and continually high interest rates'.[587]

In this short, emotion-filled campaign, it seemed that many voters might decide late which leader was least risky for them.

Accordingly, the stylistic features of language and nonverbal communication of the leading political protagonists were important for projecting competence and caring about the voting audience. Judgments by the audience about any apparent *competence and caring* in Hawke, and the sufficiency of these qualities in his opponent, were to become more pertinent as their respective political images took shape during the campaign. These images of the leaders were of course constructed by the audience, played out particularly through the accumulated impact of some nonverbal assumptions.

Unfortunately for Fraser, during the campaign he committed some obvious errors, of:

- Endorsing his opponent's political strength by accepting the assumptions in what Hawke was saying.
- Making repeated mention of his opponent's name.
- Relating his opponent to a then popular stage personality, albeit in a derogatory fashion.

- Giving attention to his opponent constantly.

By way of comparison, what did Hawke do? Hawke was not declarative, nor absolutist, but responsive, yet he was clear in drawing a line in not accepting Fraser's assumptions at all. From the beginning, the roles were taking shape in ways that were to largely continue throughout the campaign. Bob Hawke became the champion of jobs for Australians, working for all Australians, as a polished media presenter within the campaign, and it was a characterisation to which people responded.

Fraser's Televised Policy Speech

From the opening words of the two leaders' televised policy speeches, differences were clear. Fraser said:

> Ladies and Gentlemen, Australians have never had a clearer choice than at this election. It is the Liberal Party that is preserving and building a free society. It is the Liberal Party that is working to fulfil the hopes of all Australians. It is the Liberal Party alone that can keep building the future. [*Applause.*] We govern for all Australians whether their families have lived here for generations or only a few years. It encourages all Australians to contribute their best for the best nation on Earth. [*Applause.*] This election gives Australians a choice between the certainty of recovery under this Government and insecurity under the riskiest and most divisive Labor Party in our history. It presents a choice between the Wages Pause supported by eight governments and the nation's wage tribunals and Labor's attempt to destroy the Pause. The nation asked for Labor's cooperation but got a callous rebuff. This is an election about responsibility, about the security that only responsibility can bring. Australia can't afford the turmoil and insecurity of the Federal Labor Party. [*Applause.*][588]

In common with most party rally speeches, Fraser's had a fair share of party 'flag-waving' reinforcing the party's stance. Fraser told his followers in instructional terms what he believed the situation was, repeating even in this brief opening passage the declarative 'It is the Liberal Party…' three times, along with emphatic words, such as 'never… a clearer choice'. Perhaps seeking to emulate Menzies in an earlier time, Fraser described the Labor Party as divisive. He mentioned 'insecurity/security' and 'risk' as fears, seeking almost as a logical sequence, to show how the Labor Party was insincere because it had not supported the Wages Pause.

For this approach to work, his speech needed to bring listeners on board emotionally as Menzies had. As noted earlier, Menzies was able to portray his opposition emotionally as 'a collection of people who haven't been able to live together, politically'.[589] For this occasion though, Fraser also needed to develop some commitment that giving up wages was good for his listeners—surely a hard sell. Fraser appeared unconvincing on these points. Additionally, he positioned himself and his immediate listeners, the gathered Liberal Party faithful, above 'all Australians', saying 'We govern…', meaning 'We' as the Liberal Party. As a speech to the Party faithful, such a positioning might work with his first audience of the Party, but to many in the wider, second, and most important audience listening to the televised speech, Fraser's observations had the sense of the ruling power of an elite group wanting to retain its exclusiveness.

Hawke's Televised Policy Speech

In contrast, on the next night when beginning his speech, Hawke said:

> My fellow Australians. Today we set out together on a task much greater than winning an election. The task is to win the future for Australia, and all Australians. The real fight, the fight for Australia is not just between competing parties or competing policies, important as they are. Much less is it a contest between personalities. There are tremendous issues involved in this historic election on the 5th of March. First, and foremost, the right of all Australians to a job. [*Applause.*] And whether the disastrous economic policies, the political opportunism, and the divisive leadership which together have produced Australia's catastrophic unemployment are to be changed. For the sake of the one million and more of our fellow Australians who face unemployment unless there is a change, these policies must be changed and will be changed by the Australian Labor government after the 5th of March. [*Applause.*] But above all, this is a fight for the future of Australia, for the true heart and soul of Australia. For we are asking on the 5th of March for a decision from the Australian people which will declare to the world that the politics of division, the politics of confrontation, the deliberate setting of Australian against Australian which have debased the national leadership and disfigured the national life for so long have no part in the Australian way. [*Applause.*]590

The context Hawke set for his speech suggested that events larger than an election mattered most. This was especially apt in the context of that day's dominant news of widespread bushfires across the southern states of South Australia and Victoria. There was so much destruction and loss of life that both candidates soon afterwards briefly suspended their campaigns.591

In contrast to Fraser in his speech, Hawke reinforced the support of followers but made no reference to his own Party, other than its incorporation as the new government. While 'we' were unmistakably his supporters, the avoidance of as much party drumbeating enabled Hawke to take a position that sought the involvement of all. Unlike Fraser's 'Ladies and Gentlemen', Hawke's language, 'fellow Australians', 'set out together' and 'fight for Australia', projected a leader with a cause to be shared by and implicitly in the interest of all Australians.

When Hawke then identified the first issue, which touched most workers from all sections of society directly as 'the right of all Australians to a job', he did so from a framework of concern for all. Thus positioned, Hawke's attention to issues became one as a champion, yet fighting together with and for all Australians, very much as a member of the group himself. By following with abstract references to Fraser, who remained unnamed, as the one whom he cast as politicking and destroying, Hawke dismissed Fraser's whole approach as irrelevant to the real concerns of people. In this, Hawke recognised that a credible promise of employment was far more powerful than Party point scoring and a 'wages pause'.

Credible Style

Much of the credibility of a leader is stimulated in the mind of listeners through personal style. The perceived image of a political speaker has long been regarded as central to political efficacy. Whether Hawke or Fraser was to be more successful in winning support depended very much on what Aristotle described as the appeal of personality or character (*ethos*).[592] The appeal of *ethos* is considered central to how speakers persuade others. As a mode of proof or appeal, personal image has remained central to effective communication.

Much work in political communication has investigated contemporary political speech in election campaigns through the framework of image construction. Political image incorporates the idea of a person that listeners construct in their thinking, based on verbal and nonverbal features of the politician's speaking performance. Paul Corcoran maintains that 'contemporary kinds of rhetoric are most concerned with political image, and projection of image is the dominant mode of today's political campaign'.[593] This remains as true as ever. The relative ability to construct a communicator style that matched with listeners' desired image for their political leader is central to successful persuasion.

For Fraser to be truly credible, he needed to overcome the criticisms of his Government as having had the opportunity to remedy the high unemployment and economic difficulties experienced during his Government's time in office. By not providing a credible promise, but simply relying on a projection of his right to rule, Fraser left himself vulnerable to attack. Hawke obliged, negating Fraser's party politicking and then shifting attention to other concerns which concerned 'all Australians'.

Tactically then, Hawke was able to construct a positioning whereby his image had potential for growth. Fraser was left behind drumbeating and providing 'scares', including even a 'communists under the bed' reminder, serving to project Fraser as concerned with the negative. A negative was also unfortunately included in the Party's campaign slogan, 'We're not waiting for the World'. In contrast, Hawke set about developing a positive image as someone concerned with 'Bringing Australia Together'. This seemed to be an occasion where campaign slogans and the respective leaders' communication styles aligned.

Televised News Clips

As the campaign got underway, throughout the televised news clips that reported Fraser's comments, Fraser was shown attacking Hawke and his 'policies' or claimed lack of them. Fraser thus publicised his opponent repeatedly, while reviving an impression of himself as negative. Hawke, on the other hand, in the clips of his comments, largely declined any direct attack on Fraser and instead invited debate with the then prime minister, saying that Fraser kept getting himself into trouble.

On being told that 'Mr Fraser this morning described you [Hawke] as unpredictable, what's your reaction to that?' Hawke coolly replied, 'Very strange coming from the greatest breaker of promises in the history of Australian Federal Politics, isn't it?' Fraser was thus portrayed as someone making unprovoked personal attacks that Hawke ably swept aside or returned like a boomerang, with added injury.

It is likely that this overall nonverbal dynamic of the campaign was potent in determining the election outcome. Nonverbal characteristics are important, firstly because they have more influence than most people credit. If only because the nonverbal characteristics are usually not noted consciously, they have potential to be very persuasive. Secondly, nonverbal features can repeat endlessly for reinforcement, exploiting an effective means of persuasion, of repetition with variation. Thirdly, nonverbal framing constructs promotional events and provides the context for news reporters' questions and commentary.

Initially, Fraser did many of the right things in nonverbal terms. News reports of him were often set against a backdrop of his moving about in the electorate. Interviews showed him out in the open, under trees, climbing on machinery, on street walks in the community, and clearly on the campaign trail. The camera angles were always pointing upwards at him. He was a tall man and perhaps to take advantage of this physical difference from his opponent, he conducted many of his interviews standing up. Yet he remained set with that mode throughout much of the campaign.

At one stage, for reasons not entirely clear, he returned to being interviewed in his office. A significant feature of the process of a political campaign is that one must 'progress' in nonverbal settings. Hawke still had somewhere to go—into Office. Fraser as he started on the campaign trail, however, gave himself scarcely anywhere to progress to, since he was already the formal figure. He seemed to reinforce his projection as a patriarchal and aloof leader. He appeared to expect listeners to accept his judgment about the fairness and soundness of the performance of his Government on his say-so, while other voices from the opposition challenged this. He appeared to want to project an image of experience, toughness, and coolness under pressure, as a safe and known quantity.[594] Fraser's language and nonverbal style took shape as that of a leader who considered he ought to be followed because of his record and potentially his 'right' to lead. To identify with Fraser, the listener would need to see him as one who had special knowledge and understanding and whose position was rightly leader, with his listeners as followers.

Hawke, in his presentations, projected the figure of someone speaking more about human concerns, such as having a job in an economically difficult time. He appeared to expect listeners to acknowledge the country's economic discord and the claimed poor performance of the Government. He projected an image of conciliation, firmness, and control, as a popular and caring person. Hawke's language and nonverbal style took shape as a leader who would set up a system where people could work together to construct a better environment for living. To identify with Hawke, the listener would need to see him as one who had special knowledge and understanding. Unlike Fraser, Hawke positioned himself physically among his listeners, commonly with people around him. His communication style sat well within a prevailing communication mode for leadership, of providing a consultative approach.

Distinct Communicator Styles

Television viewers could thus construct two distinct sets of communicator styles for the two leaders. Hawke was predominantly the consultative leader from among the people and Fraser mainly the instructing leader positioned above the people. Even though some listeners might construct different communicator styles from the same stylistic features, these two styles seemed to dominate.

Early in the campaign, Fraser was addressing what people were concerned about and to an extent appeared concerned about people, with a suggestion of his protection of the economy with a wage pause. Hawke initially gave an impression of being on stage as a remote showman. After week one, though, this changed as Hawke moved into a high-backed chair with nonverbal reinforcements of his changing role. Soon Hawke was most often shown more like a media celebrity with a battery of microphones and eager questioners seeking his opinion.

From this point onwards, Hawke was frequently pointing, thumping the table, the authoritative individual, knowing where he was and where he was going. He was placed in front of the Australian flag very early in the campaign– by day four. This became a consistent framing for Hawke, who thus exploited the latent Australian nationalism that the Liberals ironically knew about from their research.[595] The Australian flag was ever-present in the Australian Labor Party's and Hawke's publicity and media interviews, perhaps also helping to allay fears of republicanism and a potential flag change. Most people were likely unaware of the ironic reality that the easiest substitution of a national symbol is made when the symbol being replaced is already most prominent.

The nonverbal cues to Hawke's growing signs of authority continued with his being interviewed in the high-backed executive chair and always appearing in front of a bevy of microphones on a table. He was often viewed from the side or at an angle of the table that put him directly in the frame of the camera, without the microphones forming a barrier. Fraser, on the other hand, was mostly photographed at a distance from his audience, with any microphones separating him from the viewers' gaze through the camera, which pointed up at him. Because he was tall, this was somewhat guaranteed by his standing for many interviews but, given his perceived personal style as aloof, this might have increasingly exaggerated a negative feature, rather than accentuating an impression of leadership. With Fraser, viewers had to look over the barrier of microphones to see him. For Hawke, viewers were there with him, as if viewers were at the table and being involved in discussions and decision.

Hawke thus appeared to be very much the person whose opinion was sought. Throughout the campaign, he repeated gestures of hitting the table on which the microphones were located and waving his finger in the air, sometimes 'fiddling' with a shiny wedding ring. The display of the wedding ring on Hawke's hand was a nonverbal feature with potentially greater than usual importance. That wedding ring was held up, moved, and shone in front of the camera, amid the generally known context of media speculations about it. This became an accepted part of Hawke's style.

As the campaign progressed, he also progressed from open neck shirt and shirt sleeves into a formal lounge suit. Soon in the campaign, Hawke's hair lost its hair-oiled larrikin look. Progressively, his craggy face became softened by the silvery tones of fluffed out wavy hair, reminiscent of Whitlam in his 1972 campaign. The nonverbal signs mainly pointed toward Hawke's moving into a statesman role and into office, whereas Fraser's campaign lacked any such dynamic.

Image Construction

As noted earlier, some journalists contributed to the image construction of Hawke, either consciously or not, as shown in comments such as 'Not even Bob Hawke has enjoyed so much media attention as he's had in the last 24 hours', and from the same journalist, 'Apparently in the belief that if he says it often enough, Australians will come to believe it, Mr Fraser repeated his claim that

Labor has no set policies'. But the tendency to treat Hawke as a media star came from Fraser too. As early as 2 February, he referred to Hawke's television celebrity appearance relative to the then popular entertainer, Rolf Harris. When seeking to debunk Hawke three days before his formal election as leader of the Labor Party, Fraser had entered the dangerous field of referring to his potential opponent twice by name and aligning Hawke with a popular entertainer. The attempted debunking appeared to backfire.

Within the image formation for this campaign, other less visible but nonetheless powerful messages were found in nonverbal events, language features, and actions. For example, what might be called the wife 'emergences'– spouses always *emerge* in a campaign. In some elections, their emergence will be as if out of an invisible cocoon, often at some special event, with 'wings' spread like butterflies appearing for media attention. Cynics might observe that this frequently occurred when it was time to shake the hands of little children.

In this campaign, as usual the candidates' wives were shown at events, as if in some serene, decorous simulation of royals working the crowd. But it was also in this campaign that one wife unusually for Australia at the time emerged rather differently from the cocoon, in a bikini. It mattered little that some people apparently took offence at this. By that stage, the judgment that Hawke and his wife were different, and perhaps therefore considered interesting or dynamic to gossips, were beliefs that were set, and likely reinforced by such 'dynamism'.

Reinforcing Beliefs

Hawke demonstrated understanding of how to reinforce beliefs again and again throughout the campaign. He capitalised on his strengths and could afford to appear dynamic, even 'flashy'. Fraser, however, was caught in the position of being the person who walked under the cloud of his Government's troubles. As the campaign continued, he was shown periodically in active roles, still moving around the community, yet even with such signs of activity and potential dynamism, the media especially kept probing the cloud of troubles around his head. These included such matters as the non-delivery of promised taxation cuts, which plagued him for some time. These eventually were put in place, only after considerable pressure from the Liberal Party organisations throughout Australia.

Both during the close verbal infighting and in the planned and unplanned nonverbal dynamic of the 1983 campaign, Fraser had met his match. While Fraser had exploited electronic media brilliantly in earlier campaigns,[596] in 1983 he faced a verbally accomplished opponent, who also ably exploited the nonverbal capacities of television.

Although each leader identified and emphasised his own goals, while also orienting himself toward others,[597] Hawke appeared to construct his goals with his listeners as one of them. In contrast, Fraser appeared to be somewhat imperious and unable to adequately answer questions concerning the economy in terms pertinent to everyday people. Hawke seemed proficient in showing his communication competence[598] and developed a style that permitted listeners to identify with him. For Hawke to accomplish his election goal, enough voters believed him to be the more effective representative of their interests and identified with this more communicatively responsive political leader.

In Office

Following the 1983 election, while sustaining a strong media presence, Hawke conducted a high profile National Economic Summit Conference. Just seven days after his successful election, in a speech at a Labor Day Dinner in Melbourne, Hawke signalled again his intention to further strengthen a consultative approach, partly through the Economic Summit Conference:

> One of the most important things, not only for the success of the Conference but for all our efforts towards recovery which will flow from and follow the Conference, will be the capacity of the Labor movement itself–political labor, industrial labor to work together, in cooperation with all the other sectors of the community, until we have restored prosperity to this nation and health to its economy.[599]

Amid the inevitable 'buyer's remorse' that occurs following most elections, Hawke sought to offset challenges to his Government's delivery on election promises. Before the Conference was held, less than a week after this Melbourne speech, the visit to Australia of Britain's Prince Charles, Princess Diana, and their infant son William occurred. The extraordinary popularity of Princess Diana with the Australian population could have potentially put a bright spotlight on Hawke's preference for Australia to become a republic. With Australia's main political concerns at the time being economic, Hawke kept attention on what his Government would do for the enduring economic and social health of the nation. He firmly framed this focus, keeping consistently in public attention both his longer view of people's concerns for the economy and his consultative approach. He sustained popularity. He continuously promoted the desirable image of concern, activity, energy, and being 'on the go', of being in control.

During his welcome to participants at the National Economic Summit Conference itself, Hawke continued the focus from his election campaign on the united effort needed to address the economic challenge. He made analogy to the united effort that the prime minister John Curtin rallied to face the external threat of invasion in World War II. Hawke said:

> Of course, the two are very different in nature and scale. Survival itself was at stake in 1942. But in one sense, the present crisis is more complex and at least as challenging to our resourcefulness as a people. Then, the challenge

was clear, identifiable and external. Today, the chief challenge comes from within.

But now as then–every bit as much as in 1942–the essential requirement for victory remains the same–the united effort of a united people working together to achieve goals and common objectives.[600]

Along with this high-profile event, Hawke continuously directed attention towards his appearing competent and caring for people's wellbeing.

Election 1984

It was just 20 months following the 1983 election that Hawke set the time for the 1984 national election, which was preceded by a long campaign. This was a campaign in which Hawke would build on his successes in projecting a sense of being on the move and well suited to lead 'the nation into the 21st century... [while the] Liberal Opposition was personified as having deep inter-party divisions, a "crisis" in their capacity for economic management and an inability to demonstrate strong leadership'.[601]

During this campaign, the first Australian television debate of national leaders was one of the highlights in the lead up to the election. The debate emphasised how influential a single television appearance could be in shaping personal images. Consistently throughout the 1983 campaign and subsequently as prime minister, Hawke was applauded for his command of television. Yet, in one historic television event, which attracted a huge viewing audience, his challenger showed a great ability to control the medium. Not everyone of course believed that all the telephone polls conducted by the television stations were precisely accurate, in generally placing Hawke as lagging Andrew Peacock in their performances. (Channel 9: 44% and 56%, Channel 0-10: 49% and 51%, Channel 7: 49% and 51%, and Channel 2: 28% and 72%)

That many people talked about Peacock as having won, however, shifted him from underdog to potential top dog in a way that few thought possible just weeks earlier. The lasting importance of the debate was that the Australian voting public saw their public figures make sophisticated use of television. In summary, key communication techniques the two leaders deployed to maximise their impacts were:

Eye contact with the camera

Effective eye contact inferred audience inclusion and concern. Here Peacock overshadowed Hawke in addressing comments and answers to the camera directly, rather than to the journalists in the television studio. As prime minister, Hawke, perhaps out of habit, tended to engage in dialogue with the journalists who were questioning the candidates, rather than looking toward the television viewers. This was a surprising flaw, perhaps a legacy of the 1983 campaign or later media conferences situating a leader among a gaggle of reporters.

Personal space

Wide angle shots that included Hawke in cross-chat with journalists or others in the studio were more common than for Peacock. These had potential to make the audience feel detached from Hawke, accentuating further his apparent involvement with another group and not connected through the camera with viewers.

Revealing reaction shot

Finally, although opportunity for influence or control of this shot is minimal, where one person answers a question and the camera switches back to the other person for nonverbal reaction to the first person's words, an advantage is available. The person who receives more frequent and longer reaction shots has the advantage in gaining some sense of command, ordinarily contributing to a more favourable image.

The prime minister had more reaction shots than Peacock (27 to 19), but Peacock's were longer. Most importantly, Peacock was mainly looking at the camera during these shots, giving various animated facial responses and smiles, whereas Hawke mostly looked down, wrote notes, or looked to others in the studio. Accordingly, Hawke likely lost out on this feature.

Though a first televised experience for Australia, the liveliness of communication contributed more punch than many had thought possible for what was soon called in some places a 'Great Debate'.

Television Roles

These two televised elections in 1983 and 1984 advanced substantially Australian public figures' use of television since the early use of the medium– mainly by Sir Robert Menzies prior to his retirement in 1966, and the inconsistent use of the medium by most others since then. On those first occasions, Menzies was recorded as seeming:

> ...to yearn for a public communications model reminiscent of classical democracy, where direct and unmediated communication between politicians and the public was feasible, where parliamentary debate was 'uncorrupted' by intrusive media, and where modern technology generally had no room to distort or contaminate.[602]

As Katherine McCabe notes, skilled orators such as Menzies were less impressive on screen than in person or on radio.[603]

From the 1983 and 1984 experiences, some lessons were clear for future prime ministerial aspirants. The strength of appeal through a consultative approach in Australian politics was firmly established. Well-worn and previously successful assumptions about election campaigning were adjusted. Going forward, televised political communication in Australia would remain important. Success using television though would require a sense of two-way exchange with an audience, at least as much as the personal interactions that had predominated in earlier times. Going forward, the effective communicator would have to understand this intrinsically to win the television election.

15: Reform Advocacy of Michael Kirby

'...we should show Lalor's resolution to reform the law

to meet the requirements of our new, diverse,

more interesting and multi-cultural community'.[604]

– *Michael Kirby*

Evident throughout Michael Kirby's voluminous public speeches and writing[605] are many thoughtfully creative approaches to engage with people's minds and hearts. Kirby served from 1996 to 2009 as a Justice of the High Court of Australia and then remained active as a jurist and academic, with some key contributions in international law.

His communications demonstrate a commitment to justice and fairness through law reform that required uncommon clarity of thinking, along with a developed ability to show how the substantive and procedural aspects of the law affect people. Kirby's versatility and range as a public communicator to encourage listeners to focus on what matters is a continuous thread in his advocacy of law reform.

In 2016, when reviewing *Academic and Institutional Law Reform in Australia: Past, Passing and To Come*, he remarked that:

> …if a systems and management expert were to assess the Australian constitutional system as it presently operates, they would be horrified by its inadequacy and indifference to orderly law reform.⁶⁰⁶

He concluded his detailed review of the status of this field by urging:

> The voice of persuasion should be heard in the land. Until, in due course, the hostile forces are once again overcome and the optimism and idealism about systematic law reform in Australia is rekindled in a new generation of lawyers and citizens alike.⁶⁰⁷

Through the advancement of law reform, Kirby determined to make the world a better place, living and advocating the principle, 'Never give up, never give up, never give up'.⁶⁰⁸

New Perspectives

He commonly invited listeners to accept new ways of looking at circumstances by assembling a sequence of briefly stated facts, ideas, or opinions that clarified circumstances. Through insights or assumptions in what he outlined, he thereby encouraged listeners to reach a different view from currently held beliefs. Kirby often used the type of polemic that Dascal described as *controversy*, which is between the other types of polemic of *discussion* and *dispute*. *Controversy* is used to persuade, by seeking resolution of competing positions through persuasion based on the weight of evidence, to find modified positions that might prove acceptable.⁶⁰⁹

On different occasions, Kirby used *discussion* polemic also, alone or in concert with *controversy*. This was so when he hosted the United States Justice, Antonin Scalia with a judicial group in Australia.⁶¹⁰ While welcoming Scalia and observing appropriate courtesies and formalities for such a visit, he invited Scalia through a problem-solving approach to acknowledge mistakes. Kirby pointed out that 'originalist' thinkers, such as Scalia, had not recognised the expressed original intention of the founders of the United States who developed its constitution. He shared suggestions from the founders that the document would need to be interpreted, adjusted, or changed to accommodate unforeseen or unforeseeable circumstances.

In this speech, too, Kirby outlined a case for United States judiciary to make use of the intelligence and experience of justices in other countries within the established terms of comparative law, concluding:

> This is why an Australian lawyer will reject the 'original intention' notion of constitutional interpretation advocated by Justice Scalia and why Australian

law will not deny, but will acknowledge, the utility of international and transnational law. It is not 'precedent.' But, by analogy, it may sometimes be useful to our reasoning and helpful to our law.[611]

Kirby's speeches and writing show his commitment to the combined power of facts, ideas, and opinions that unfold as reasoned and emotional evidence.

He sustained discussion through conventional, declarative, mainly simply structured sentences, packed with novel information or new ways of viewing matters. He showed a readiness to emphasise points using interpolation, or short sentences, or short breath groups, sometimes as brief as one or a few words.

Coherent Humour

Kirby often invited an audience to reconsider beliefs within a framework of human decency, sometimes drawing on his sense of humour. He showed a developed ability to use humour in speeches, well beyond the ability of many other public figures, as briefly described in Chapter Five. His use of humour is varied in type and purpose.

Unsurprisingly, he did not appear to use the favoured barbs of politicians, who will make a quick reply to mock someone, or cause injury to another, or seek to divert attention from their own actions. Rather, Kirby's inclination to humour in his speeches took shape as a form of *meiosis*, sometimes euphemistically describing his own profession and by extension himself, as evident here highlighting Australia's origins as a penal colony:

> My only claim to address you today is one of historical title. In a sense, I am the descendant of a singular group of elderly gentlemen who played a vital part in populating Australia in its earliest years. I refer to the Judges of England.[612]

Later in the same speech, following amusing well-known quips, such as 'The French poet Paul Valery says that the future is not what it used to be', he shared an incongruous coincidence of history to make a serious point:

> When the First Fleet entered Botany Bay, they were not two days before the first perceived overseas threat to the infant colony arose. It did so in the form of French vessels under the command of Captain de la Perouse… The real challenge soon proved to be from within: from a hostile continent and the need to develop it.[613]

Kirby could also make light on a serious point about his own commission, such as in an interview on the radio with John Laws. When Laws asked him to explain why he called his seven years as Chairman of the Australian Law Reform Commission 'the lean years', Kirby replied:

> Well I think reforming the law is a difficult task, the law inevitably tends to get out of date and trying to drag it into the 20th century before the 20th century is over is not an easy task.[614]

When seconding a toast moved by the State's Premier for his friend Sir Asher Joel's 80th birthday, Kirby lightly made a point about getting facts right. He described how an oversight in a *Who's Who* supplement caused him to write as Chancellor of Macquarie University to the 'widow' of a distinguished parliamentarian who had served for many years on the University Council. Accordingly, a few days later to his surprise he received a response from her to the effect:

> Somehow a rumour has spread about my husband's untimely death... I am pleased to tell you that my husband is very much alive. In fact, he is sitting here with me, still opening letters of condolence. We will put your letter aside and accept it contingently–to be brought out on a future date: hopefully far away. Please believe me that we both appreciated the generosity of your sentiments–though not as much as their prematurity![615]

After relating this personal story, Kirby sustained his speech to honour Joel by sharing personal reflections on Joel's public and private kindness and thoughtfulness.

Visual Language

In a variety of ways, Kirby's communications show his ability to integrate visualisations of people and circumstance to advance or to emphasise the significance of a matter. He deftly recollected a vivid childhood memory during World War II, when at six years of age, he was 'commandeered' with other school children to line the street and wave a flag to honour the visit of a remarkable woman, Eleanor Roosevelt. He recalled this childhood experience to remind of her powerful role to spearhead the passage of the Universal Declaration of Human Rights (UDHR):

> These high aspirations were probably going through the mind of Eleanor Roosevelt, that great champion of humanity and human dignity, as her car approached Concord in Sydney, Australia in 1944. The young school children waved to her. Even they knew that she was an important messenger that the future need not be like the past. And it was a duty of new generations to make it so.[616]

The conclusion of this description with the imperative 'make it so' was interestingly emphatic, not only in its message but also in its resonance. Within long cultural assumptions, the phrase has connotations of authority in the military, from association with one of the most definitive orders that draws on a ship captain's authority, having a long history in the Royal Navy. The phrase has also mustered some additional popular authority since 1987 as a favoured command of the captain of the iconic starship *Enterprise,* in the televised Next Generation version of *Star Trek* the popular culture phenomenon.

In 2015, for an Op-Ed in the *Sydney Morning Herald,* Kirby recounted his student days in the 1960s to reflect on his *alma mater's* finally welcoming 'gay' and 'queer' students. The Op-Ed began:

> What would Sydney University's long-time, and formidable, Registrar (1955-1967) Miss Margaret Telfer, make of an occasion celebrating 'gay' and 'queer' students arriving in droves at the University of Sydney? Of the Chancellor and Vice-Chancellor actually welcoming them in the hallowed precincts of the Great Hall? And that strange rainbow flag floating above the clock tower in the quadrangle? 'Has the world been turned on its head, Sir Stephen?' she would no doubt ask Sir Stephen Roberts the University's grumpy Vice-Chancellor.[617]

He followed the imagined reactions of these university leaders with perspective on the rhetorical questions:

> We are now affirming the fact that the world has moved on, at least in Australia. We now know that homosexual, bisexual, transsexual and intersex people are part of the scientific reality. Pretending that they are not (and demanding that they should also pretend) is a game that is over... This leap took a long time coming. But at last, the nation's oldest university has accepted and even welcomed the truth about this matter. Gay people are everywhere. Get over it.[618]

Kirby's Op-Ed recalled and parodied the stance and behaviours of a long-endured pretence that harmed 'gay' and 'queer' people and then recounted the different reality that now pertained.

Personal Ethos

For the very different genre of a eulogy for his former senior colleague at the bar and State Premier, Neville Wran, with apt sense of occasion Kirby said:

> In his sense of personal reserve, energetic labour and cautious reform, Neville Wran held up a mirror to some core features of Australian society. That is why he was so successful in public life. We saw in the mirror talents that most of us aspired to in ourselves. Most liked what we saw. His comet has run its course. But the dazzling tail of bright light will last long hereafter.[619]

Kirby has sustained a developed capacity for appropriate imagery, particularly by drawing on metaphors that dignify and celebrate the best in people and in humanity.

In 2016, for a speech in memory of the portrait artist Judy Cassab AO CBE, he was asked to keep the speech brief, so he first shared a vignette that reimagined an exchange reflecting this request. He then said:

> And so, craving your indulgence and supplementation by memory and imagination, I offer a pen portrait of Judy Cassab. I will try to do it, as the Lord Protector Oliver Cromwell once commanded, 'with warts and all'. And I will offer it in the impressionistic style. It will be no more than a stringbag of adjectives that come flooding into our minds when we think of Judy Cassab. She was one of Australia's greatest artists—a mighty portraitist. Winner of this and that. But I want to speak of Judy the person. Judy the refugee. The mother. The human being.[620]

Accordingly, he crafted a word-portrait of the artist's qualities, interwoven with adjectives as the lens through which to view her life fondly:

> ...joyful... Eyes and heart were smiling... professional... organised... disciplined... worried about faults of omission... concentration and devotion to the task were formidable... surprising... smart and determined... adaptable... proud... praise rained gently down on her... formal... inspirational... calm, self-contained and open to new ideas and challenges... Like the art of our beloved Aboriginal artists... Those who are looking at ... [your portrait] ... will join the dots together in their own minds... God will add the magic... God will be kind.[621]

In the spirit of an observed wisdom, that words chosen to describe another often tell as much about the person choosing the words as the person described, these adjectives captured some of Kirby's own qualities and capabilities so evident in his public address.

Values, Needs, and Priority

Likewise, for a nation, words in the public sphere tell much about the values, needs, and priorities of its people. As Chairman of the Law Reform Commission in 1980, Kirby reviewed historical situations to propose some areas of the Australian law requiring remedy, in a speech titled *The Australian Community and Anti-heroes*.[622] This was the Lalor Community Relations Address in Canberra, for which a notable speaker is invited annually to commemorate the significance of Peter Lalor and the Eureka Stockade in Australia's history. Kirby built the metaphor of the anti-hero that served to animate[623] some human qualities needed to reform the law, concurrently illustrating the multicultural character of Australia from colonial days.

In 1980, while the foment and reexamination of cultural assumptions brought to some focus through the policy reforms of the Whitlam Governments of the early 1970s were continuing, Kirby began his Lalor Community Relations Address:

> Foreign observers and newcomers to Australia must find some of our objects of national pride and celebration curious, to say the least.
>
> We commemorate the modern history, in the knowledge that it began very largely by accident and as a direct outgrowth of Britain's loss of the penal colonies in America, following the American Revolution. Our colonial history started with nothing more than the establishment of a prison colony. The rough early settlers showed little tolerance and less respect for the Indigenous people of the continent, who had lived thousands of years in harmony with its special environment.[624]

He invited listeners to see their nation as others might see it, foreshadowing a framework to view both our nation's history and its future differently from conventional views. Kirby had set his purpose with a pattern of contrast and contradiction, to encourage a fresh look at history and the future.

Discursive Controversy

From the outset in this address, Kirby readily embraced controversy in a discursive mode. Evident were his versatility, creativity, and sense of humour, deployed to invite listeners to think afresh about laws to ensure justice and fairness. Through *discussion* polemic, he effectively described historical events to point toward changes needed to avoid mistakes in the future.

This constituted an effort to seek the truth through consideration of issues in Australia's problematic past, which included preoccupation with anti-heroes. Kirby incorporated and examined a range of nationally symbolic events, swiftly reassessing how to view them. He established a deliberative stance to assemble the weight of a case for persuading listeners of the need for ongoing law reform, which would accommodate human dignity within the needs of a multicultural nation:

> So here we have it. A country began as a prison, over long contemptuous of people here thousands of years before, celebrating a pathetically unsuccessful and short-lived revolt, idolising a 'desperado', annually commemorating a failed military enterprise and dealing out a generally poor hand to many of its leaders: all to the tune of 'Waltzing Matilda:' a stirring song which itself condemns lawful authority. Do we have here a contra-suggestible nation of anti-heroes? Is it all as simple as this?[625]

In his brief individualistic review to focus Australia's self-perception of national values, heroes, and priorities, Kirby set the stage to recommend a reassessment of some of the nation's laws through the remainder of the speech.

He risked sharing a new way for us to view ourselves by highlighting concepts, emotions, and priorities, to open an audience's eyes and hearts. From this, Kirby outlined needed efforts in law reform to ensure that the law respected human values, to accommodate changes in circumstances or the ethnicity of citizens.

His language was direct, focused tangibly through proper names and recollected scenes, in shorter-than-average, mainly simple sentences, compared with 600-word passages of others noted in Appendix Two. Nonetheless, he used more than double the average number of past tense verbs and passive voice. This distanced material and helped to cast Kirby as an historical or neutral commentator. As he qualified matters, Kirby was inclined to use pairs, that is, two grammatical items together, such as two nouns or two adjectives together. With limited *anaphora*, namely the repeat of the same word at the beginning of successive grammatical units, and little other parallelism or use of compound clauses, he appeared simply to outline matters, while relying on contrasts and comparison to articulate a reevaluation of facts and opinions.

Historical Contrasts

Kirby used the formal vocabulary characteristic of historical review, 'objects of national pride and celebration', which was immediately and carefully evaluated as 'curious, to say the least', thereby establishing an overall pattern in the speech. The pattern was to follow up statements of shared understanding with contrast, antithesis, or contradiction, often at the emphatic end point of the sentence or passage.[626] He commented about the stimulus for the annual address:

> The Eureka Stockade in 1854 is celebrated. Yet this is a tale of a group of gold diggers who defied the legislative authority of government. *They broke the law*...[627] *[my italics]*

which is followed with graphic, brief observations to recall and then reassess the event:

> The leaders of the rising were tried for treason, though even in this there was an element of fiasco *as each accused was acquitted.*[628] *[my italics]*

Again and again, in his quick succession of sub-narratives, Kirby stated a shared understanding, then outlined facts and observed contrasts to encourage reconsideration:

> ...In the very month of the Stockade, there was born the archetypal Australian anti-hero, Ned Kelly... *guilty* of the murder of three policemen and other innocent civilians. Yet *Ned Kelly* is *celebrated* today and *the judge* who tried him is *burnt in effigy* in Melbourne streets.[629] *[my italics]*

Or further:

> ...at Gallipoli, showing... courage... fought bravely, *but unsuccessfully*...[630] *[my italics]*

Then he interspersed a personal note of seeing this significant site of Xerxes's historic crossing of the Hellespont, to state an historical opinion that:

> We celebrate Anzac because it was the first great battle, after our country was united in Federation, in which the spirit of its soldiers was tested.[631]

A first impression from the opening of the speech was to expect a fresh view of well-known historical events.

Tangible Description

The descriptions in this opening included the settlement of Australia, events at Eureka, Ned Kelly's exploits and perception in popular thinking, and Gallipoli, along with the remembered failures and frustrations of prime ministers. Each was sketched using concrete nouns, including proper nouns (*observers, accident, settlers, prison, people, diggers, stockade, soldiers, rebel flag, Australia, Britain, America, American Revolution, Eureka Stockade, Queen's troops*). From the outset, many largely evaluative nouns that lack concrete referents also occurred (*pride, celebration, nothing, knowledge, outgrowth, loss, establishment, tolerance, respect, harmony*), which underscored the evaluative nature of his historical narrative.

Sentence lengths in the opening 600-words of the speech ranged from 37 words to just three, with eleven of the 35 sentences or short breath groups at twelve words or less—notably below a generally preferred average sentence length of 20 words. These contributed to Kirby's own short average sentence length of 18 words in this opening passage. The shortest sentences often highlighted key facts for emphasis, and, in the passage below, were combined with *anaphora* of 'they' that provided further emphasis. This also distanced 'them' (the anti-heroes) as 'others', through the repetition of this third-person plural pronoun:

> *They* broke the law. *They* refused to pay taxes. *They* hoisted a rebel flag over a stockade. *They* resisted, with arms, a body of the Queen's troops sent by the lawful government. *They* were defeated in the assault. In fact it was all over in a matter of minutes.[632]

Kirby later in the speech described additional interpretations of the nation's search for heroes, including in the more contemporary events surrounding the dismissal of prime minister Whitlam in 1975.

Then he summarised these opening descriptions, to follow with a detailed outline of 'The Facts of Eureka' and a variety of interpretations of the event. He related that:

When Labor and Liberal politicians agree that this was an event important for Australia's national identity, democratic aspirations and resistance to unfair authority, we can safely assume that Eureka is a national and in no way a class, sectional or partisan event.[633]

This permitted further connection of his interpretation of the event as significant to the Australian legal system. He identified that '…one of the causes for which they [at Eureka] died was reform of bad, out-dated laws'. This led to Kirby's overtly drawing on the popular authority of the colonial poet, Henry Lawson '*Reform your rotten law*, the diggers' wrongs make right…'[634]

Pathways from the Past

Accordingly, through an accumulation of emotional 'precedent' in Australia's history to support law reform, further supported in the iconic poet's words, Kirby had developed a platform for the remainder of the speech. He thereby accentuated the practical need for law reform to meet the needs of the increased number of migrants from a variety of ethnic origins in the community. He illustrated how details in the specific circumstances of migrants necessitated reforms of the law, to ensure justice for multicultural groups within the community. This constituted an artful and fresh approach to bring the emotional 'evidence' of deeply felt history, buttressed with popular literary support, to recommend a case for law reform that seriously considered the needs of migrant communities.

By assembling a combination of narrated facts interspersed with evaluation, Kirby revealed the harm to migrants' lives. He immediately interpreted and explained these specific cases to draw conclusions for recommended attention or action:

> The distress experienced by women in illegal migrant situations, where there is family breakdown, violence or abuse is even more acute. These women are a silent group who through fear and sometimes through ignorance are unable to go to recognised authorities for protection and guidance. They are susceptible to blackmail, including from amongst their own number. It is for that reason that amnesties may be specially desirable to remove the causes of such injustice.[635]

This inductive assembly of facts, leading to a reasoned conclusion, was made more powerful by the understated nature of 'may' and 'desirable' in the recommendation, and supported by the pointed 'specially' to amplify the desirability of amnesties.

Reassessing Laws

Building a perspective for viewing historical and contemporary Australia, the entire speech was structured to focus on encouraging the reassessment of law. After outlining an Australian history of unrest and harm, conceded as important for Australian national identity through the enshrined democratic aspirations and resistance to unfair authority, Kirby also used this narrative to advocate the value of law reform to get ahead of any future harmful outcomes. He turned to self-reference, of why he, a judge, might be chosen for this address that commemorated law breakers, to pivot to motivating listeners, with a specific charge to the lawyers present to take action.

In a multicultural Australia, he noted that beyond legal procedures some substantive change to criminal law might also be needed. He concluded by neatly wrapping together as a cohesive narrative the continuity and value of sustained law reform. By focusing on the rebellion of Peter Lalor, who himself later served as a legislator in the Victorian state parliament, Kirby refreshed a reminder of the need to find ways less dangerous to individuals to reform the law, to meet the contemporary and future needs of a changing Australian society.

In closing, Kirby firmly advocated such reassessment, here using *anaphora*, pairs, and some of the few collective first-person pronouns, 'our, we', to help emphasise areas for us to commit to reasoned personal reexamination of the laws that govern our society:

> Since these early days, the role in Australian life of people from countries other than the British Isles has increased apace... *Our* legal system should be sensitive to these changes. *Its* substantive rules, *its* procedures and *its* personnel should come to reflect, by orderly processes of *reform and renewal*, the changes which have taken place. Whilst clinging to the virtues of the legal system *we* have inherited, *we* should show Lalor's resolution to reform the law to meet the requirements of *our* new, diverse, more interesting and multi-cultural community.[636] *[my italics]*

By immediately preceding his conclusion with a direct extended appeal to the legal profession to 'review our laws and procedures to take account of... changes', Kirby accentuated key responsibilities for 'reform and renewal'.

Advancing Justice

Through the development and advocacy of what he considered was truly important, Kirby honed a compelling language style to advance justice. Distillation of his power and personal approach were evident in a speech at the Charles Darwin University in the Northern Territory in 2012:

> Some may say the media will speak up against such injustice. But the problem with the media is that it is a flighty and fickle champion. Indeed, it is often part of the problem, as the tabloid law and order campaigns against prisoners illustrate. We can do better. Most nations do better. Our record in Australia is not so perfect that we can leave things as they are.[637]

Kirby's varied speech and writing have continuously advanced his commitment to talk with, rather than speak at his audience. In an ongoing effort to ensure that laws evolve to meet the challenge of a changing society, Kirby has shown clearly both the need and a commitment to 'never give up'.

16: Continuing to Speak Out–Paul Keating, John Howard, Kevin Rudd, Julia Gillard, Noel Pearson, and Scott Morrison

We'll get through this together Australia. We all have a role to play.

...I know we'll all do our bit.[638]

– Scott Morrison

Beyond the public communications already assessed, talented Australians keep speaking out powerfully. The most effective speech or writing of public figures in more recent times still draws on the principles and techniques of rhetoric and language style previously proven to be effective for bringing important topics to audiences. Persuasive Australians make speeches that affirm and strengthen cultural values, while calling for action or change.

Yet the former speechwriter to prime minister Paul Keating, Don Watson commented in 2014 that Australians were sick of platitudes that dominated the national debate.[639] He suggests further that:

Words and language in general have been heavily discounted in the last 20 years, and for that reason we really can't expect to hear much from our politicians'.[640]

Another commentator, at the time of Noel Pearson's eulogy for Whitlam in 2014, suggests that Pearson was so well received in part because his eulogy recalled:

> ...a period when policies were not rinsed of real meaning by the misgivings of focus groups, and politics was not dominated by the art of the television non-interview'.[641]

A former prime ministerial speechwriter in Britain, Philip Collins places responsibility more broadly, inferring that the media's search for controversy, combined with a tendency for many more ministers to make speeches that are 'essentially press releases stretched out', has helped to build an 'insensitivity to cliché'.[642]

Redfern Park Address

Delivering one of Australia's more powerful speeches in recent decades, in December 1992 then prime minister Paul Keating presented his Redfern Park address. This was just six months after the landmark High Court decision in the Mabo case, which recognized the land rights of First Nations. Keating's speech was couched within the context of committing 'ourselves to succeeding in the test which so far we've always failed, because, in truth, we cannot confidently say that we've succeeded if we've not managed to extend opportunity and care, dignity and hope to the Indigenous people of Australia.'[643] This speech sharply defined and publicly stated the history of neglect and abuse of peoples in First Nations. Keating said:

> ...we who did the dispossessing. We took the traditional lands and smashed the traditional way of life. We brought the diseases. And the alcohol. We committed the murders. We took the children from their mothers. We practised discrimination and exclusion.[644]

For First Nations and other Australians, this was an important statement from the leader of the national government. The speech acknowledged and detailed the violations of core values of life, land, and families, plainly recording the stark reality of harm and cruelty. Keating gave the speech extra impact with a very specific list of realities in short sentences, each item packing sufficiently stark acknowledgement of harm to stand on its own.

Reconciliation

As Tom Clark points out in his review, Keating's speech was remembered for fashioning 'its most compelling narratives with very little sentimentalising'.[645] Keating addressed the past not only to highlight that 'the past lives on', but also to advocate the continuing need for reconciliation with First Nations, stating:

> It was *our* ignorance and *our* prejudice. And *our* failure to imagine these things being done to *us*. With some noble exceptions, *we failed* to make the most basic human response and enter into their hearts and minds. *We failed* to ask— how would I feel if this were done to me? As a consequence, *we failed* to see that what *we* were doing degraded *us* all.[646] *[my italics]*

The core message to think and act differently was strengthened by Keating's calling on his listeners to imagine how they would feel if this was done to 'us'. He used repeated forms of 'imagine', especially in the imperative form of the verb, which occurs infrequently in conversation, and thereby carried special power here. In addition, Keating accentuated his personalisation of the tragedy. He used the first-person collective pronouns, the *anaphora* of 'we failed', the repetitions of both 'our' and the strong verb 'failed' while recalling events that produce deep feelings.

The rhetorical question and the ellipsis of an object for 'failed' enabled a swift wrapping of listeners into the degradation historically dealt out to First Nations. The premise for the failure, 'ignorance and prejudice', are in just a couple of sentences linked to a new view of the consequences, and the change that he proposed.

The venue in Redfern in celebration of the International Year for the World's Indigenous People was important symbolically and substantively, for the prime minister to be addressing an audience of mainly people of First Nations. Overcoming some physical challenges of the setting at an open-air festival, with continuous background noises and distractions, Keating made his case firmly. This was representative of the rhetorically strong speech style and substantive content for which Keating became known.

Port Arthur Aftermath

It was four years later, in the sad context of a tragedy at Port Arthur, Tasmania, in which a gunman killed 35 people that another prime minister, John Howard, presented a sequence of powerful speeches. It was just two days following the tragedy, on 30 April 1996, that Howard elected to address the Parliament and the nation. He not only expressed shock, extended the deepest sympathy to families and friends of those killed and injured, and urged the bipartisan cooperative action of governments, but also repeated his commitment from the previous day's press conference, 'to bring about significant improvement' to gun control. He said:

> I think Australia has been shaken to the core. I think these events removed any vestigial sense of innocence that this country may have had that in some way it was untouched by some of the individual insanities and crimes that beset other societies and beset other nations.
>
> It is an occasion for all of us to reflect upon the humiliation that it brings to us as a nation and as a people, for us to try in a constructive positive way to learn lessons from it, to address those issues which such a tragedy produces. And, not least of course, is the vexed issue of gun control laws. And, whilst this is not an occasion for me to initiate a debate on that, but I would not be doing the right thing by this parliament if I did not repeat to it what I said to the press conference I had yesterday, and that is that I will do all that I humanly can as leader of the government to bring about a significant improvement and to address some of the great deficiencies that exist.[647]

This address made clear Howard's intention to act on gun control. By recalling the tragic event in a subdued but firm speaking voice, in short breath groups, with thoughtful hesitation at times, Howard shared his own shock, sympathy, and empathy, and he underscored his determination.

At the close of the speech, amid his recalling with emotional recognition the suffering and, with thanks for the efforts of survivors, health workers, and police, he restated his determination to try in:

> ...a constructive, if possible bipartisan fashion, and *I don't say that lightly*, but I mean it, to address some of the difficulties that arise and some issues that have been thrown up by these dreadful events...[648] *[my italics]*

At that time of initial grieving, Howard simply called for thoughtfulness for future cooperative effort. But, by framing the need for action within the emotional narrative of Australia's humiliation in having lost its innocence, he accentuated generally shared feelings about the tragedy for all Australians.

He foreshadowed that he would require the anticipated opponents of gun control to face squarely the desire of most Australians to restore, as a treasured part of national identity, some sense of the 'innocence' that characterised Australia as a place of safety, distant from 'insanities and crimes that beset other societies'. The highly emotive vocabulary and the cautiously stated but unambiguous statement of Howard's intent was soon to be put into action.

Agreed Gun Controls

Within 12 days after the massacre, on 10 May, Howard announced the agreement of Commonwealth, State, and Territory governments to far-reaching gun control that also required the surrender of many weapons newly made illegal.[649] Then, little more than a month after the tragic event, he addressed opponents of the new legislation at a Gun Rally in Sale, Victoria, opening with a statement that sought some common ground, while reasserting his own position:

> Last night I saw on national television Mr Ted Drane, the National President of the shooters' organisations in Australia–And he said something with which I totally agree. He said that he and his fellow shooters were not criminals, they were Australians, And I want to start my address to you today by saying *at no stage* in the weeks that have gone by since the decision taken by the Federal Government and the Police Ministers in that decision, *at no stage* have I sought to describe or categorise the attitude of people who enjoy shooting or people who are shooters as being in any way criminal or un-Australian.[650] *[my italics]*

This was a plain-spoken approach to seek a rational framework for the speech, with little emotional embellishment. Underpinning Howard's everyday language on this and other occasions was a formulaic rhythm reminiscent of traditional spoken verse. Clark describes this as occurring more widely in Howard's speeches.[651]

Howard used occasional *anaphora* to emphasise a point, such as with 'at no stage' in this opening passage. He also related the commentary of Mr Drane as a tangible start to frame, in an understated and personalised way, some sense of the conversation that Howard sought with his listeners. In an effort to remove an emotionally charged allegation of his feelings toward his listeners, Howard stated that the Government decision was taken without any 'thought to label or smear you or other tens of thousands of law abiding citizens'.

He stepped on from this principle, to put firmly on record what motivated the Government decision, as well as to detail his regret for the 'inconvenience' to law-abiding citizens caused by the legislation to remove their guns, to protect the interest of the greater good. To focus this rational strategy for addressing an emotionally charged audience, briefly stated, the main points of his case were:

> National interest for 'dramatic reduction in number of… weapons'
> Acknowledge and apologise for inconvenience to law-abiding citizens
> Link 'volume of powerful weapons' and 'indiscriminate' use
> Show mindfulness of the differing impact on weapon owners to others
> State that some occasions require Government to act for a 'national good'
> Apologise for 'disproportionate deprivation'
> Outline Government responsibility to weigh up gains against losses
> Acknowledge no guarantee that there won't be future 'mass murders'
> Commit to investigate impact of early releases from mental health institutions
> Society must examine any cause of violence on television screens

> Come to explain directly to people who are unhappy with Government decision
> Care taken to 'ensure… [maintenance of] legitimate use of farmers, of weapons…'
> Buy-back of illegal weapons to be funded from a one-time tax
> Commit to 12-month amnesty for buy-back, enabling fair compensation
> Compensate properly for weapons based on fair value at time of decision
> Assure decision was not part of any attempt to deprive of liberty
> Sympathise with people no longer able to pursue a sporting commitment
> Government must commit to act for the aggregate national good
> Come to explain directly and simply the basis of the decision in good faith
> Government and prime minister responsible to benefit national good
> Thanks for coming and happy to answer questions

This disarmingly straightforward sequence of topics stated the basis and details of the decision, while acknowledging the difficulties for his listeners, and thanking them for coming. Most appropriately for his listeners, Howard expressed repeatedly his apology, sympathy, and regret for the inconvenience and difficulty caused to them.

Nonetheless, he also firmly asserted the larger principle of the Government's obligation to act for the common good, thereby reasserting the basis of representative government. This was 'straight from the shoulder' plain-speaking, while addressing any potential distractions from Howard's case. He used short statements for emphasis of key conclusions, 'And that my fellow Australians is the basis of the decision that we have taken'.[652]

Plain Speaking

Howard sparingly incorporated *anaphora* and other parallelism throughout the speech, particularly to emphasise his own feelings in understanding listeners, such as 'I acknowledge and I have acknowledged', 'I know that, I regret that, I apologise for that', 'I know that, I regret that', 'to explain directly… to go to explain directly… to remind you', 'I understand why… I understand why… I understand why… I fully understand and I can sympathise… I deeply regret… I do deeply regret it'. Sometimes he simply reassured that 'the intention is to pay fair compensation… That is the intention and that is the commitment…'.

He also used *antithesis*, such as 'not the basis of the decision. But the basis of the decision… is'. With artful clarity, he acknowledged listeners' concerns and complimented views that might align with their views, demonstrating that he was also listening and cared about what they said:

> I have read during the past few weeks some reactions to the decision taken by the Government. I acknowledge that many of those reactions, although

very strong and *very vigorous* and *very determined* have been *absolutely measured* and the sort of reaction that you would expect in a strong, robust, democratic country such as Australia.⁶⁵³ *[my italics]*

Howard then contrasted other views that were extreme, contradicting some of these, while showing understanding. He sought to have his listeners recognise the greater good that he advocated the Government must serve–in service of a government's role to ensure safety for everyone. Howard referenced democracy in the close of the speech, inviting recognition that, while understanding why many felt angry, his Government's decision will 'bring about a safer Australian community, and that my friends is a proper objective of Government. It is a democratic objective of Government...'⁶⁵⁴

A great strength of this speech was Howard's unwavering effort to moderate the deep feelings of people. It was much later noted that his dealing with some of the newer media was handled less effectively during an election.⁶⁵⁵ For the successful negotiation of gun control though, Howard used established communication modes well to outline empathetically and emphatically the national need for action. Throughout his speeches in the House and at a rally, combined with press conferences, he illustrated his very developed competency in these modes. Given the depth of feelings of the divergent groups within the community, Howard's accomplishment was substantial in handling the gun control issue, with understated and responsive communication, at a time of national challenge.

An Apology

In a context differently charged with emotions that had accumulated for more than two centuries, on 13 February 2008⁶⁵⁶ then prime minister Kevin Rudd offered apology from all current and past Australian governments to the peoples of the First Nations of Australia. He did so with emphasis by using the everyday common apology that Australians often spoke in conversation, 'Sorry, mate'. He acknowledged the mistreatment of First Nations 'to turn a new page in Australia's history by righting the wrongs of the past and so moving forward with confidence to the future'.

Rudd made an historic acknowledgement, melding language appropriate to the ceremonial occasion, with touches of the Australian common vernacular that he incorporated within the primarily epideictic genre of the speech. Early in the speech, he made the *ad populum* appeal for the apology to 'be received in the spirit in which it is offered as part of the healing of the nation'.

Rudd's apology as prime minister was framed as an expression of regret to First Nations, past and present, from Australian governments, past and present. This approach seemed somewhat compatible with an expressed philosophy of

First Nations, which emphasised that 'individual wellbeing is always contingent upon the effective discharge of obligations to society and the land itself'.[657]

In the powerful opening, Rudd left no doubt concerning the scope of the speech. He used *anaphora* of *'we'* in successive phrases and sentences, *'we honour'*, *'We reflect'*, *'We apologise'*, and *'we say'*, sorry', to highlight his purpose–followed by *anaphora* of *'their'* at the end of the opening passage, to focus the extent of the harm. He moved from the general to the particular at each stage of the opening passage, making clear his metaphor of 'turning the page', to move on from the *'blemished chapter'*. The choice of 'blemish' softened the severity of the challenge to the nation's history, for the benefit of listeners who were not of First Nations.

Yet, Rudd soon addressed harder evaluations, using the powerful contrast *'righting the wrongs'* to anticipate the more significant harm listed in the triads, *'grief, suffering and loss'* and *'pain, suffering and hurt'*, and in the climactic parallelism of the pairs, *'mothers and the fathers'*, *'brothers and the sisters'*, *'families and communities'*. He emphasised in one sentence the tragic extent of the harm done to *'our* fellow Australians'. Rudd made the speech as a motion to the House, so that as prime minister, he moved:

> That today *we* honour the Indigenous peoples of this land, the oldest continuing cultures in human history.
>
> *We* reflect on their past mistreatment.
>
> *We* reflect in particular on the mistreatment of those who were Stolen Generations—this *blemished chapter* in our nation's history.
>
> The time has now come for the nation to *turn a new page* in Australia's history by *righting the wrongs* of the past and so moving forward with confidence to the future.
>
> *We* apologise for the laws and policies of successive Parliaments and governments that have inflicted profound *grief, suffering and loss* on these *our* fellow Australians.
>
> *We* apologise especially for the removal of Aboriginal and Torres Strait Islander children from *their* families, *their* communities and *their* country.
>
> For the *pain, suffering and hurt* of *these* Stolen Generations, *their* descendants and for *their* families left behind, *we* say sorry.
>
> To the *mothers and the fathers*, the *brothers and the sisters*, for the breaking up of *families and communities*, we say sorry.[658] *[my italics]*

Specifics of Apology

With the sincerity of regret, explanation of what went wrong, acknowledgement of responsibility, statement of repentance, offer of remedy, and request for forgiveness, all required for the apology to be considered authentic, Rudd focused on some specifics in these areas. His making the Stolen Generations the primary focus for detailing the commitment of wrongs put attention on one of the most emotional events that tore families apart and caused much suffering across multiple generations. This focus therefore delivered potential for substantial emotional impact on listeners, and highlighted horrific events perhaps not understood previously in much detail among the population beyond First Nations.

Having addressed past failures, Rudd 'respectfully' requested that the apology be accepted as a basis to resolve a different future. He quickly contrasted with the past, the proposed undertakings for the future, each introduced in five sentences commenced with *anaphora*, 'A future…'. He then dealt with the reasons for apologising. He chose to illustrate the pain and suffering imposed on First Nations by graphically and extensively relating (at over 16% of the speech) one personal story of a woman in her 80s who was present, Nanna Nungala Fejo. He shared some stages of her life and how the stealing of children impacted her, as one of the children stolen at age four.

By focusing tangibly on one of the experiences of one of the mistreatments of First Nations, Rudd managed a searing emotional focus on the inhumanity. He then contrasted the cruel words of individuals in the roles of 'Protector of Natives', to dismiss earlier assertions by bureaucrats of claimed 'good intentions'. From relating this sad story, Rudd stated general principles to 'turn this page together'. He reminded that 'Australians are a passionate lot. We are also a very practical lot', appealing to Australians' feelings for a 'fair go'. While introducing some specific actions for the Government and the Opposition, Rudd neatly balanced vernacular in a mix with formal language, 'Today the parliament has come together to right a great wrong'. He mainly used everyday language, including the clichéd metaphors, 'building a bridge' and 'So let us seize the day'.

Identity and Rights

What Rudd offered for measuring the success of his offered proposals to 'Close the Gap', however, showed little attention to enabling peoples of First Nations to strengthen their identity as First Nations. Nor were there specifics to address the well-articulated desires of activists, such as Oodgeroo, Kevin Gilbert, and others over many years previously, to refresh the cultures of First Nations.

The metaphor on which the speech was based was of 'turning the page' of history, a Western-European concept. This was a metaphor that served Rudd well to frame past events as part of history, potentially with the inference that these could be 'filed away' or distanced, to allow a new beginning. By doing so, a wide variety of harmful events were relegated to the responsibility of earlier individuals. Accordingly, Rudd was not making acknowledgement of personal responsibility, other than for government policies in the future.

The accomplishment of the speech was to address some very specific concerns about Australia's long-troubled treatment of First Nations. It provided a symbolically important and unique experience for all listening. It could be argued that this would also have been an opportunity to enhance the Australian government's decades-long espoused policy of multiculturalism. This was an opportunity to include mention at least of specific targets for First Nations' long-requested self-determination, cultural identity, and respect for values and rights as First Nations. Yet, within the framework that Rudd provided, as no government leader of Australia had previously, he offered opportunity for emotional catharsis between peoples to provide a basis for beginning a new future.

The enduring power of the speech comes in part from an ongoing tension between the graphic illustrations of stolen lives, with specific focus on this one area of harm done to First Nations, amid a continuing reluctance more widely of some Australians either to acknowledge the wrongs or the need to remedy wrongs in the way Rudd proposed. He recorded potently both the past harm, 'often bloody encounter', and a sense of the future, 'new possibilities for the future'. The speech from the Opposition Leader that immediately followed Rudd's speech appeared to be largely ignored or panned, including boos in some venues to which that speech was broadcast. Rudd concluded by inviting combined effort 'to craft' a better future, calling on key representative groups to unify, returning to his pages-of-history metaphor:

> *Let us* turn this page together, Indigenous and non-Indigenous Australians, government and opposition, Commonwealth and state, and write this new chapter in our nation's story together. First Australians, First Fleeters and those who took the oath of allegiance just a few weeks ago—*let us* grasp the opportunity to *craft a new future* for this great land, Australia. Mr Speaker, I commend the motion to the House.[659] *[my italics]*

Throughout the speech and in the close, Rudd incorporated appeals to listeners' emotions. He narrated tangible events and shared feelings of personal and national responsibility, modeled from a stance he took on behalf of Australian governments.

'Will Not Be Lectured'

Yet another powerful speech in recent decades was by prime minister Julia Gillard, in her so-called misogyny address in 2012 in Parliament, which delivered strongly deliberative rhetoric. In full control of her pace of delivery, modulation of voice, and the speaking environment, Gillard said:

> I rise to oppose the motion proposed by the leader of the opposition. And in so doing I say to the Leader of the Opposition, *I will not* be lectured about sexism and misogyny by this man. *I will not*. And the government *will not* be lectured about sexism and misogyny by this man. *Not now, not ever…* On the conduct of Mr Slipper, and on the text messages that are in the public domain, I have seen the press reports of those text messages. *I am offended* by their content. *I am offended* by their content because *I am always offended* by sexism. Because *I am always offended* by statements that are anti-women. *I am offended* by those things in the same way that *I have been offended* by things that the Leader of the Opposition has said, and no doubt will continue to say in the future. Because if this today was an exhibition of his new feminine side, I don't think we've got much to look forward to in terms of changed conduct.660 *[my italics]*

From the first words, with the parallelism of 'I will not', which is swiftly emphasised by the further *anaphora* in 'Not now, not ever', Gillard firmly established her stance. In one analysis of the speech, Clark explained the congruence of Gillard's substantive stance and choreography in delivery and pointed to the media recalling the power provided by this congruence.661 Gillard's forcefulness captured much attention, standing her ground and pushing back using evidence of hypocrisy in the Leader of the Opposition Tony Abbott. She infused vitality in an interchange that became analogous to a gladiatorial cut and thrust, in which audience members might settle emotional alignment behind a champion advocate.

Her six uses of the *anaphora* 'I am offended', including a variation in which she inserted 'always', provided a structure that enabled her to turn Abbott's comments back on him and to progressively deal strongly with his own behaviour. The emphasis sharpened the degree of her feeling, but the changed pace and sentence structure that followed helped to highlight Gillard's polemical mockery of what she called the Leader of the Opposition's 'new feminine side'.

She plainly stated the context for what listeners might anticipate from him in the future. Her entire speech was a strong attack-in-reply, within the constraints of social conventions and the context of a formal speech from the floor of the House of Representatives in Parliament.

Strength of Narratives

Gillard sequenced the increasingly damning information against the Leader of the Opposition. Fully in debate mode, she foreshadowed early what was to be unloaded on him, by saying that she hoped he had 'a piece of paper and he is writing out his resignation'.

In relating each narrative, she set the pace for stating and qualifying information, such as in the sequence '…said *when* he was a minister under the last government–*not when* he was a student, *not when* he was in high school *but when* he was a minister under the last government'. *[my italics]* She directly quoted Abbott and followed with her tangible assessments, 'he needs a mirror. That is what he needs', 'This is the man from whom we are supposed to take lectures about sexism', and 'something that would never have been said to any man sitting in this chair'.

By coolly recalling that Abbott 'stood next to' offensive signage that had referred to her, namely 'Ditch the witch' and another describing her as 'a man's bitch', Gillard comfortably responded that 'It is misogyny, sexism, every day from the Leader of the Opposition'. She repeated 'Every day, in every way', to underscore her case of his hypocrisy by bringing the motion to remove the Speaker of the House. By calling out her opponent through the recall and turning back of his own words and actions, she systematically eviscerated his credibility, while concurrently advocating her case against sexism and misogyny.

Standards of Behaviour

Gillard provided a structure to her case overtly, with numbered reasons for 'why the Leader of the Opposition should not be taken seriously on this motion'. A strength of her case comes from the vitality and precision of her portrayal of specific scenes that implicitly urged listeners to 'get real' in looking behind her opponent's claims.

Much power also came from her multiple neat counterpoints of formal rebuke and conversational mockery to define standards for behaviour, as evident below in a structural outline of the speech:

Introduction ('will not be lectured about sexism and misogyny by this man')

Proposition ('people who hold sexist views... not appropriate for high office')

Negate sincerity ('does not need a motion... he needs a mirror')

Body
(i) Repulsive double standards ('I was offended')
What he said ('men have more power... than women... is that a bad thing?')
What he did ('catcalling across the table... here' / 'stood next to a sign that said "Ditch the witch"')
Mockery ('wants to be taken seriously... suits... political purpose')
Dismissal ('This kind of hypocrisy should not be taken seriously')
(CLIMAX)

(ii) Giving lectures ('keen to say others should assume responsibility')

What he did ('track record [preselecting Speaker for multiple elections]
What he said ('congratulate... a friend of mine for a very long time')
What he did ('attended wedding as a friend')
On the offending text messages ('I am offended...')
Recognition of legal consideration ('this parliament should see that conclusion')
What will not stand for ('peddling double standard')
What should ensure ('Good sense, common sense and proper process')
Not tolerate ('political game')
'Looking at his watch' ('a woman has spoken for too long – I have, in the past, had him yell at me to shut up.') CLIMAX

Conclusion
What should do ('reflect on standards')
Motivations ('reject the motion')
What should do ('think seriously about the role of women in public life')
Formal close: ('entitled to a better standard than this')[662]

Gillard drove her argument to reassert 'proper process', using a combination of formal and informal vocabulary, with longer complex and compound sentences complemented by short aphoristic statements, and frequent interpolation:

> ...he could apologise for standing next to signs describing me as a witch and a bitch–terminology now objected to by the frontbench of the opposition. He could *change standards himself* if he sought to do so. But we will see none of that from the Leader of the Opposition, because on these questions he is *incapable of change*. He is capable of double standards but *incapable of change*. His *double standards* should not rule this parliament.[663] *[my italics]*

With debating strength, Gillard powerfully pushed back on the underlying assumptions that stimulated the motion, which she moved be rejected. Viewers of her speech on YouTube in Australia and worldwide acknowledged the power of the speech, as did the media apparently, playing the event up into 'war' and 'battle' metaphors.[664]

Powerful Eulogy

Yet another powerful speech, inarguably one of the most powerful public communications in recent times, was the widely well-regarded eulogy for former prime minister Gough Whitlam in 2014, by Noel Pearson.[665] Pearson's eulogy was firmly in the epideictic genre. While praising 'this old man', he eloquently reaffirmed some social values for many listening. Pearson, on a national platform for the significant eulogy for Whitlam, presented a speech that, more than most, might be said to have reached beyond Kosciusko to the heights of Olympus.

Pearson began with command of the context and direction for the speech, by expressing 'immense gratitude for the public service of this old man'.[666] Within little more than the first 100 words, he focused the key concerns of the special character of Whitlam's commitment to public service and the benefits that the reform prime minister brought to Australians. Pearson also introduced himself through recall of his own origins, stated the significance of the occasion, noted his purpose to address Whitlam's 'legacy with no partisan brief', expressed his feeling a sense of honour in presenting the eulogy, and touched on the change that he personally experienced because of Whitlam's life.

Through this early part of the speech, Pearson drew on specifics of his own growing up under severely discriminatory laws enforced by 'a cold and capricious bureaucracy'. He swiftly recalled a tour of his village with Whitlam, noted the changes he set into law, and observed Whitlam's strength to understand discrimination and 'the importance of protection from its malice'.

This set the scene for Pearson to recall the changes that the Whitlam Government brought, with a list of 23 items of accomplishment that touched off listeners' multiple pulses of applause. Then Pearson deftly sustained a humorous allusion, to question 'what this Roman ever did for us', and recreated a vision of Whitlam as the imperious yet self-mocking figure who 'played no small part in the progress of modern Australia'.[667]

Command of Words and Delivery

Pearson's command of pace, phrasing, and adjustments of volume and tone matched well the precision of his language. For an intelligent review of the rhetorical features and power of the speech, including aspects of its delivery, an article by Matthew Sharpe provides a detailed perspective.[668] Pearson recalled and visualised specific events in concrete language and sustained his avowed non-partisan stance to commend Whitlam's reform policy agenda and its effects to change the country forever.

Pearson illustrated the emergence of today's Australia 'like a technicolour butterfly from its long dormant chrysalis'.[669] He followed this comment by touching a memory of Monty Python's parody of Mark Antony's funeral speech that lightly, but amusingly, reframed the ceremonial praise. In doing so, Pearson recalled a hint of the frequent twinkle in Whitlam's eye that would be so well remembered by many listeners.

Through a conclusion that merged reminiscence, perspective, and a touch of incantation, a pin could have been heard to drop as listeners engaged personally with individual recollections of 'this old man', which Pearson had so movingly stimulated. He powerfully saluted Whitlam, concluding formally that 'he truly was Australia's greatest white elder and friend without peer of the original

Australians'.[670] This remarkable speech reaffirmed in multiple ways the power of Australians who speak out, including by the power in its very presentation.

Reassurance in Crisis

Within the unique context of the global coronavirus pandemic on 12 March 2020, the prime minister of Australia, Scott Morrison faced a very different speaking challenge. His opening words for a less than five-minute, nationally televised address early in the pandemic sought to reassure Australians that the Government was well prepared to deal with the still little-understood virus:

> Good evening, Australia. Tonight, I want to talk to *you* about the global coronavirus. *What* it means for *you* and *your* family, and *what* the Government is doing to see Australia through… While this is a global health crisis, there are very real and significant economic impacts. For all of these reasons, *we* have been taking the coronavirus very seriously. I want to assure *you* and *your* family tonight that while Australia cannot and is not immune from this virus, *we are well* prepared, and *we are well* equipped to deal with it, and *we do have* a clear plan to see Australia through. *Our* plan has three goals. One, *protect* Australians' health. Two, *secure* Australians' jobs and livelihoods. And three, *set* Australia up to *bounce back* stronger when the crisis is over.[671] *[my italics]*

Making use of *anaphora* with 'what' and using simple sentences, some parallelism, and strong action verbs, Morrison put prominence on the actions of his Government, as well as a glancing emphasis on a promise to 'bounce back stronger'. He set the path of actions that were ahead for the nation and the Government, with specific steps and reassurances throughout his speech. He closed by saying:

> …*we* do still have a long way to go. But, be assured, *we* are taking action and *we* have a clear plan. The months ahead will present many challenges, but *we* will respond. *We* will continue to keep *you* updated, and take decisions based upon the best possible medical advice… *We*'ll get through this together, Australia. *We* all have a role to play, employers, nurses, doctors, teachers, scientists, friends, family, and neighbours. I know *we*'ll all do our bit. Thank *you* for listening tonight. Goodnight, Australia.[672] *[my italics]*

Important Choices

Morrison made important choices about where and how to put his emphasis. Firstly, his plan to handle the problem of the virus was framed in simple logical steps that appeared to emerge from situation analysis. He made clear that the ongoing response to the virus would be 'based upon the best possible medical advice'. Secondly, he addressed his audience directly in terms of 'you' and 'we'.

His everyday language foregrounded nouns, verbs, adjectives, and adverbs that referred to specific facts, figures, and actions, as well as to his listeners. Thirdly, Morrison had no exaggeration, few prepositions and few nonreferential adverbs. Fourthly, he used complete short sentences, at 12 words average. He underscored precise details and actions in a rational approach, which can provide reassurance and confidence during a crisis. He empowered a logic to address emotional uncertainties, thereby strengthening his *ethos* in the eyes of the audience.

Direct Appeal

His was an appeal directly to the emotions of the audience both by sharing concern for their wellbeing and by using language suggesting a 'folksiness' of conversation. To secure common ground, Morrison presented information and perspective that emphasised points of agreement, drawing on attitudes, beliefs, and experiences common to Australians' preference for laconic, understated speech and an inclination to seek solutions to a problem.

Helpful to accomplishing a primary challenge of keeping listeners calm was Morrison's sharing the Government's plausible plan for moving forward,[673] while appealing colloquially to an Australian habit of doing one's 'bit'. He made frequent use of a connector commonly used in conversation, 'and', with 12 occurrences in the little more than 200 words just quoted. His many uses of personal pronouns 'you' and 'we' were positioned for emphasis, including as *anaphora*–also, he transitioned 'we' from being the Government, to conclude the address with 'we' to mean all of us together. At least as importantly, Morrison's speaking voice was moderated in an understated personal tone at a volume suitable for conversation, contributing to a sense of ordinary calm, and boosting a sense of authenticity.

The Morrison Government subsequently received criticism for the rollout of vaccine availability, earning the dubious honour of the Macquarie Dictionary recognising 'strollout' as word of the year–a neologism that emerged into wide use to describe a 'perceived lack of speed' in Australia's vaccine rollout[674]. Yet, for the difficult time of initially addressing the fears and confusions caused by the pandemic, Morrison's speech set out a clear, calming approach, especially when compared with the haphazard national responses to the early awareness of coronavirus in some other places. Morrison's speech content, vernacular, genre, passage development, sentence shape, and vocabulary seemed apt. His speech illustrated some sound choices for public talk to be effective for its purpose.

17: Conclusion

The public communication reviewed in this book glimpses the good minds of Australians who advanced important matters, using truthful, lawful, and just speech. Each advocated ways to improve people's lives by enhancing a civil society that respects free speech and other personal freedoms. Each helped to strengthen democracy in Australia through their efforts, and underscored that democracy is more than a government structure. It is a way of life that furthers tolerance, respect, choice, diversity, and so on.[675]

Understandings of democracy will inevitably differ within and between societies, and democracy itself is a 'contested concept open to continual debate and dispute'.[676] How to assure citizens' respect for each other will also likely remain a contested process. The constancy in the democratic ideal that modern communities have inherited from classical times is that democracy persists because people make the effort to see that it does. Words also persist as the mightiest tools to advance this way of life, invisibly joining us with others committed to do well by people. By listening to and talking with others, we can learn much and do much to advance individual freedoms, especially freedoms of thought, speech, and association, for pursuit of the common good.

Danger of the Demagogue

In recent years, during the rising noise of pseudo-populist rhetoric worldwide, the former prime ministerial speechwriter from Britain, Collins alerted to the dangers of autocrats who use propaganda to sound democratic.[677] Collins identified the hazard of populist-propagandists' oversimplifications. He reminds of the virtue in 'going high' to advance what is best for people, thereby helping to sustain democracy. He warns that autocrats consistently self-indulge about how poorly-done-by they are, especially by the media not loving them—

and are forever angry. They promise utopia. Yet their utopia ordinarily requires returning to some mythically better past. They are apparently unable to show us a better future,[678] much less to do so with humour.

Collins warns of the propagandist-autocrat who drumbeats various inventions about conspiracies against the people, by some elite; consistently claiming that 'utopia [is] just around the corner, if only the corrupt elite had cared to venture there'. He notes that this autocrat self-portrays as the leader of efforts to 'rise above the smears, and ludicrous slanders from ludicrous reporters'.[679] Another 'tell' of autocrats is the seemingly innocuous claim heard from such propagandists that 'a lot of people are saying', as authority for some preposterous drivel. Apparently, this is all in every day's 'work' for the self-dealing autocrat.

Ever since democracy proved its value at least as far back as 2,400 years ago, everyday citizens have spoken out every day to sustain democracy as a way of life. From ancient Greece onwards, we know that Isocrates and many other *rhetors* and teachers of rhetoric have encouraged citizen participation. Despite a long period of anti-democratic rule globally until the close of the eighteenth century, democratic systems since have proved their worth. We have all benefited from truthful, lawful, and just speech that has helped to provide our civic foundation. The continuation of this benefit relies on the efforts of each of us to sustain the greatest values of democracy, as the Australians reviewed here have done. By looking closely at how each speaks out, we will be better able to choose what to say, when, and how.

Whether preparing to speak out or to evaluate public talk, many considerations are the same. Each speaker or writer reviewed in this book found an individual approach for advocacy, showing commitment to a cause and to free and open public talk. The future looks likely to present challenges that will increasingly require this responsible use of rhetorical strength. Expected distortions and distractions will include manufactured outrage and the 'por-cken' cacophony of pseudo-populist talk. With public communication trending to short and snappy in an informal or even intimate tone, the challenge to confidently foreground truth, law, and justice has perhaps never been greater.

Guide to Effective Language

Going forward, with audiences attracted to fresh ways of looking at facts, ideas, opinions, and issues, continuous creativity will be needed to appeal to audiences. Much like an outstanding chef, the accomplished speaker or writer will combine the ingredients of language creatively to engage an audience. Audiences are mostly motivated by vivid and lively language, typically with shorter simple sentences, clauses, phrases, and words. Especially helpful too are concrete words, proper nouns, ellipsis, present tense, action verbs, infinitives, forms of the verb 'to be', active voice verbs, greater use of verbs than nouns, as well as moderate use of imperatives, slang, clichés, or neologisms. It will also be helpful to understand how function words not only provide cohesion, coherence, connectivity, and continuity, but also help to project some features of individual style and levels of formality. At times the artful use of personal pronouns or other indicators of conversation will be key, along with knowing how to use, for conversational effect, sentence fragments, interpolations, series or catalogues, and compound clauses or phrases with 'or', 'and', or 'but' as connectives.

But all else being equal, an audience is drawn to the speaker or writer who brings to the foreground matters most pertinent to the audience, in simple catchy words. This requires emphasis, sometimes right up front, of a key solution to concerns. By incorporating thoughtful use of metaphors or other figurative language, humour, and rhetorical tools of emphasis, including *anaphora* and other parallelism, polemic, symbols, slogans, jargon, or sometimes, even slang, a speaker or writer will be better equipped for advocacy.

Australian and International Competence

Such contemporary language can be truthful, lawful, and just, as shown in recent speeches, such as when prime minister Morrison initially dealt with the coronavirus pandemic. When he announced the Australian Government's plan to address the global pandemic,[680] he showed how to address a serious problem. Morrison related his logical plan to the lives of listeners. He developed a personal 'conversation' to make an understated but emotional appeal to the better natures, patriotism, and self-interest of his listeners. He chose issues, framework, language, and a delivery that made a personal connection, while logically addressing how his Government was set to deal with the threat to the nation.

Similarly, it was important internationally as well as for the United States when the American President, Joe Biden, both in his inaugural address[681] and subsequently, visibly and dramatically spoke very differently than his predecessor. The reputedly populist, defeated president Donald Trump[682] routinely used a high proportion of content words with unclear referents and certain function words such as factive verbs and nonreferential adverbs. In contrast, Biden delivered speech that is distinct in content and style, to outline policies that reassert truth, law, and justice as his nation's values. The language of Biden's inaugural address signalled his preference for lively conversational features. Remarkably, he used 38 sentence fragments, multiple interpolations and imperatives, simple and short sentences, phrases, and words, as well as an artful use of personal pronouns to engage the audience. The speeches of Morrison, Biden, and some other contemporary world leaders express commitment to tangible speech to advance principled democratic governance. This is in sharp contrast to the vacuous outrage among pseudo-populists.

Ever since the later twentieth century, mostly gone from popular taste are long, grand rhetorical flourishes, which often made emotive appeals within a noticeably rational framework. These were replaced first by the conversational language and tones required on radio and television, then by the snappy resonance demanded in social media. Going forward, the perversions of brief and snappy into untruthful, illegal, and unjust to deliver whatever is most outrageous will need to be dismantled by strong, capable voices. Each of us will need skills to counter the debilitating effects of those speakers who use outrage to attack democratic ideals. Only rhetorical literacy will shunt aside the outrageous, to empower the rhetoric needed to build relationship with audiences.

Reflect Reality

Perhaps it is reasonable to hope that the renewed prominence of substantive statements from leaders such as Morrison, Biden, and others who refer to people, tangible things, and real concepts might open the way for reinvigorated public communications that reference reality. No one person will be consistently successful, as indicated by the changed perception of how the Morrison Government handled a later stage of the coronavirus pandemic.[683] But effective talk will win out over pious hope to counter the coveys of 'audience-tested' outrage words too-often delivered into talking points—for which the media then provides a megaphone. Speaking up and speaking out will surely require imagination, persistence, and rhetorical sophistication.

Especially before talking or tweeting in response to any public figure whose communication seeks to erode democratic freedoms, each of us in a free society will need to consider how best to address such hazardous talk. For guidance in these efforts, consider ways to address propaganda that were noted at the conclusion of Chapter Four, as well as the ways to frame communications summarised at the conclusion of Chapter Seven. Additionally, Isocrates, George Orwell, Jacques Ellul, and other thoughtful writers mentioned through this book and in the bibliography can teach us much about how to handle such trends.

Drawing on Rhetorical Stylistics

Certainly, improved understandings of how, why, and where to apply the principles and techniques of rhetorical stylistics are as necessary as ever, to help interpret and defeat any bad ideas or harmful actions. In this digital age, as the expectations of listeners and the characteristics of media evolve, the importance of sustaining a flexible facility with language will only continue to grow.

Social media most often use practices also used in advertising, so amply outlined and evaluated since at least the 1950s.[684] Just as advertising stimulates dopamine in the brain to encourage people to act separated from conscious thought, the primary goal of social media is to have more people addicted to spending more time on social media. Understandings from such well-established fields as rhetoric, stylistics, linguistics, semiotics, psychology, and politics make the digital media, to use an old metaphor, an 'open book'. To reveal the specific instances of persuasion in digital media, all that is required is the development of analytic, synthesising, and critical abilities encouraged throughout this book.

The eminent linguistic researcher, David Crystal has published studies on the language of the Internet and texting that are mainly concerned with the impact of these phenomena on language use.[685] Additional studies are needed and will keep emerging to look at how individuals employ language in digital media modes to secure changes in attitude and actions. Especially needed is further investigation that connects persuasive language understandings with computational propaganda and manipulations using social media.[686]

Change Ahead

The path for strengthening persuasive effectiveness will present a journey that will be both challenging and exciting, in which the stakes will be great. As agents for change, communicators will likely evolve new ways to communicate. In earlier times, the literary tradition of building to a climax toward the conclusion of a novel, play, or other communication was complemented by the print and electronic media substantially reshaping popular message norms. In news-reporting, the climax is right up front, in the headline or lead. Social media has prioritised further what is most brief and astounding in words and image.

In a more clipped verbal and visual world, the rhetorical stylistic principles explored in this book will pertain, sometimes with adjustment of techniques. More than just wishing that public communicators were somehow better, each of us will need to keep building personal abilities for public talk. It remains as true as ever that, regardless of occasion or context, an effective speaker or writer navigates differences within an audience to gain attention, define a problem, explore a solution or not, or visualise a solution, or seek action.[683]

Any champion of ideas, beliefs, or actions must choose the issues to address, side-step, or ignore when facing audiences comprising individuals with diverse vested interests and feelings. Some in an audience will favour a proposition, or be interested but not decided, with others apathetic, or opposed. Each of us will need to choose topics, language, and delivery wisely. These choices enable a speaker or writer to relate to an audience, to be seen as authentic, and to move hearts and minds.

# 18: NOTABLE SPEECHES AND WRITING

Sir Samuel Griffith–The Certainty of Australian Federation

ARTICLE FROM THE COMMONWEALTH AND THE EMPIRE
Melbourne: George Robertson and Co., 1895
1845-1919, Queensland Premier, first Chief Justice of Australia 1903-19: As a distinguished jurist, a major contributor to drafting the Australian Constitution, chief justice in the court to interpret that document, a pioneer in the law, including drafting the landmark Queensland Criminal Code, The Rt Hon Sir Samuel Griffith GCMG KC made tremendous contributions to society in the late nineteenth and early twentieth century. In this article, in addition to pointing out the arbitrary nature of lines on a map between colonies, Griffith hinted at the potential for future conflict between separated groups and the possible invasion of one colony as a first step to conquering all colonies, as motivations to advance Australia's federation.

The physical conditions of Australia are unique in the world. It is surrounded by the ocean. It contains no large ranges of mountains, no wide and deep rivers dividing one region from another. In the case of the nations of the older world, the territorial limits are found to coincide, to a greater or lesser degree, with natural features, mountain chains, or rivers, or expanses of desert. In the early stages of civilisation, the territory of a people was small–often little more than the valley of some stream. Then the inhabitants of contiguous valleys combined for defence, and by degrees became a nation: or, in the case of plain country, the nomad populations became associated together. But between one nation and another there was always some physical obstacle of land or water which prevented convenient and rapid communication.

It is impossible to point to a single instance where a people, speaking the same language and occupying a territory over which communication was easy and unimpeded, has remained permanently divided for political purposes by artificial boundaries.

The idea of a country–a fatherland–for which feelings of affection or pride can be entertained, involves the notion of separateness from the rest of the world. It is a conception of some part of the earth as having features that distinguish it from all others and make it worthy of special regard.

If Australia has any destiny as a country, if there are to be Australian patriots, Australia must submit to the common law of humanity as declared by universal experience. A man may be proud of his home or of his ancestral estate. But can anyone conceive of a feeling of patriotism entertained with regard to a portion of territory bounded only by parallels of latitude and degrees of longitude, and which has no natural aspects to distinguish it from adjoining territory on the other side of the invisible and factitious line of demarcation? If so, it will be a new concept, the evolution of which experience gives no warrant for anticipating.

Consider the existing boundaries between the Australian states. Western Australia is divided from the eastern colonies by a great expanse of almost desert country which can only be effectively crossed by a line or lines of railway; but the lines of separation between the other colonies are, with the exception of a few miles of a low range of hills on the northern boundary of New South Wales and a few miles of narrow river on its southern and northern boundaries, separated by purely imaginary lines. Nowhere is there such a difference in the character of the country that a stranger would ever guess on crossing the frontier that he had passed from one state to another.

Moreover, the lines of division, such as they are, are altogether arbitrary, and may be said to be almost entirely accidental. Any others would have been almost equally suitable. Certainly, they are not scientific frontiers.

The territory is inhabited by a people speaking one language, proud of a common origin, and enjoying similar institutions.

Neighbouring nations are always liable to quarrel and make war upon one another, and there is no reason to suppose that human nature on the Australian continent is exempt from this weakness. Is it not the very height of absurdity to imagine two Australian states fighting for the substitution of one degree of longitude for another as the frontier between them?

And with regard to the rest of the world, with which the relations of the inhabitants of Australasia cannot always be expected to remain wholly friendly, can a foreign nation be conceived as paying any respect to these artificial lines?

Every lesson of history, then, teaches that the manifest destiny of Australia is to be one people.

Let this fact be once realised, let the people once recognise their destiny, and the question will not be whether the Australian colonies are to be federated, but what is the best and quickest way to bring about the Federation. And, when the idea becomes familiar, the advantages of union as compared with the disadvantages of the present disunion will become so plain that the only wonder will be why they were not sooner recognised. Those who oppose union are opposing an irresistible force, which, however strenuous the opposition, must ultimately prevail.

Probably if the people of the several colonies had now to rely on their own unaided efforts to protect themselves, instead of relying, as they certainly do, whether they consciously think so or not, on the protection of the British Empire, the absolute and urgent necessity of union would already be apparent to everyone. The danger of invasion may be laughed at—everyone hopes that it is remote; but it is none the less real. If the people could only find time to lift their eyes from the ground and look around them and read what is written in the pages of history, the advocates of Federation would have a very different task from that which now demands all their efforts.

The practical recognition of the certainty of Federal union would have an immediate beneficial effect. Statesmen would no longer devote their energies to measures which in a few years must be futile or worse than futile. And the energy thus set free might be directed with advantage to other channels where it would be of use alike to the province and the continent. The minds of statesmen would be enlarged. The sentiment of patriotism just beginning to show itself would be developed, and in a few years the opponents of union would be regarded as little better than curious survivals of a bygone era.

Louisa Lawson–Womanhood Suffrage

FIRST PUBLIC MEETING
OF THE WOMANHOOD SUFFRAGE LEAGUE
Y.M.C.A. Hall, Sydney, Saturday, 13 June 1891
1848-1920, Poet, Writer, Publisher, Activist for women's suffrage: When Louisa Lawson presented this speech at the inauguration of the Womanhood Suffrage League, her many accomplishments included continuing successes as publisher of *The Dawn*, which she had founded three years earlier, and her role as convenor of the *Dawn Club*, which with the permission of members in this group folded into membership of the League. With visualisation of everyday dangers to family life and appeals to both logic and the emotions, Lawson powerfully challenged men and women to join in efforts to enable the vote for women, which was successfully accomplished in 1902, to be among the first women in the world to vote.

It is said that 'the greatest discovery of the nineteenth century is the discovery of women'. Would we were not compelled to make speeches to induce men to do justice to them. That great hearted worker for the 'world's women', Olive Schreiner, says: - 'If women were the inhabitants of Jupiter, of whom you had happened to hear something, you would pore over us and our conditions day and night, but because we are before your eyes you never look at us'.

Since the time when equal suffrage was first agitated the subject has been grossly misinterpreted and basely caricatured. From the beginning the women who have been its public adherents have been held up by press and people as unwomanly creatures, seeking to stir up strife and dissatisfaction, or at least obtain personal notoriety. More recently, the cause having gained so many friends, public opinion is becoming greatly modified; still, how many newspapers will impartially or faithfully report a woman's rights meeting, or for that matter any other meeting of women. There will be the covert sneer, the attempt at witticism, the unkind comparison calculated to impress the public with women's weakness and inability, or to cast ridicule not only on the cause but upon the members themselves, and the pure heartfelt utterances of true generous women are omitted. From time immemorial we have been told that women's sphere and work was home. Every woman worthy the grand, expressive name woman realises this fact and glories in it, but:-

The hare for her young will fight
The tiny bird grows wild defending its nest;
And dare you think a mother cares less for her child?
Shall we sit still and croon to our baby boy
While a monster lurks without, waiting his chance to destroy?

Is it not a painful fact to contemplate, that according to present conditions it can be looked upon as a miracle should a boy reach man's estate and escape the contaminations of vice which daily example makes him familiar with from boyhood. To be able to smoke, swear, drink, and gamble like a man is the Alpha and Omega of his infantile dreams. Walk down George Street and see the traps laid for our sons and brothers—the sailor boy who has left home and mother for the first time is led into a Chinese gambling den the first night he puts foot upon the soil of sunny New South Wales, where in less time than it takes to tell the money given him by a self-denying parent to spend on land is transferred to the keeping of a Chinaman. And even in broad day light keepers of gambling houses come out upon our footpaths and take half-crowns from little children who sell newspapers upon the streets, and where does the respectable boy clerk get the half sovereign which he stakes upon a horse in our King Street tobacconist shop?

What kind of hearts can the men have who take these boys' earnings from them? Darlinghurst gaol is full of their victims, and Gladesville Asylum is filled with the mothers of them. Useless indeed are women's tears and women's prayers while the votaries of vice hold dominion over our city, and single men may obtain license to open any tottering mass of rottenness as a public-house for the purpose of giving the weak a push hellward. Verily, 'Man's inhumanity to man makes countless thousands mourn'.

Will it be believed a hundred years hence that such a state of things existed, and how but cranks and women had courage to raise their voice in protest? Can we wonder that a woman in defence of self and children smashed the mirrors and decanters in a drinking den where her husband spent his time and money to the neglect of his home and family? Is it to be wondered at that this woman took the law into her own hands, seeing how worse than useless was the outlook for help from any other quarter. If man who is in power and makes the laws has not courage to put down these vices, how can the son be expected to avoid them handicapped as he will be by transmitted weakness?

Here in Australia it is considered more a crime to steal a horse than ruin a girl and should she but have reached the tender age of 14 years she is expected to understand the nature of the advances made to her. Were an illustration needed there lies at this Prince Alfred Hospital one with heart and limbs broken, who when trouble came upon her found that in 'this great cityful home she had none' and the cold iron of the railway line a fitting place to lay her distracted head upon while waiting for 'Death', the only friend she wished for; yes, there she lies for her old mother to weep over, and who knows that black shadow of the betrayer shall not cross our own threshold?

Yes, home is a woman's truest sphere
Its spoilers her deadliest foe;
If a viper coils by your sleeping child
Is the gentlest too weak for a blow?

Men tell us we are responsible for the home and education of children, that the morals of society are in our keeping; they have bound our hands and placed us in the front rank of the battle raging against intemperance, gambling and impurity, they hold us responsible, and yet take away the only weapon with which to fight.

Once in America a body of women presented a petition a quarter of a mile long, bearing the signatures of 200,000 women, with the result that it was rejected as valueless, women having no vote. This, then, is the reason why we want the suffrage; we well know that any petition offered by us for the good of those we love would be valueless because we have no vote, and this is why so many of the noblest, truest women God ever created are quietly and earnestly working to secure the vote.

Our first business, then, is to free ourselves before we can help any good cause; at present we are powerless, and the first service we can render our country and humanity is to get ourselves into a position of independence. If we are responsible for our children give us the power and sacredness of the ballot, and we will lift ourselves and our brothers to a higher civilisation. How many outside the ranks of interested ones realise that it is this fact, borne in upon woman's great mother love, a rare yearning after her own, which none but a mother ever knows, which drives, yes, literally drives, her out into the public arena to work for right and justice, and makes her willing to bear abuse and misrepresentation for the sake of those she loves? This is the reason why we leave our quiet firesides and stand strayed on the side of equal suffrage.

It is the large-hearted woman who realises the universal brotherhood of man, and is willing to set self and self-interests aside, and work and pray for a time when she may go to the poll with her husband, father or son and cast a vote for 'God and home and native land for truth, temperance and morality'; to cast the vote that will protect son or brother from the public-house and gambling den and sister and daughter from infamy and disgrace. When women really understand the relation of home to the equal suffrage work, then will they unite in a body and demand the ballot as a means of protection to that which every woman holds dearer than life, her home and her family.

Many of the new converts to our cause are anxious to know just how far women have advanced socially in other countries, home newspapers are being scanned and records searched to this end, but this is not necessary, we need not follow in the footsteps of others. No land has a government or people a temperament exactly like ours. If this be so then let us be original, not like Martha of old, troubled about many things when but one is needed.

To consecrate ourselves to the just cause of human justice, and press fearlessly onward, well knowing that right must prevail, and to pledge ourselves not to halt until the prize is won, leaving the future to work in the details and supply the means to so glorious an end. Selfishness is easy to teach and easy to learn, and they call it womanliness. To take our ease while gilded hells open on all sides to lure our sons to gamble away their earnings, while lives are blasted, hearts broken and souls damned–shall we because the way is rough and the sun hot be content to sit beneath our own vine and fig tree, to be pleasing to the eyes of men, to pander to their tastes and prejudices as a violet sweet, and as a lute sounding fine harmonies, and bury our hearts and our conscience alive? No, selfishness is not loveliness, weakness is not tenderness, as woman's life broadens and deepens, grows in richness and beauty, grace and power, as women love humanity more, they will give better love to the men at their sides; out of such work and such life men will be the gainers.

There is a movement onward in the world of thought and feeling, and when the nineteenth century shall have passed into history those enjoying the blessings which are the outgrowth of the labours of the pioneers will look back and ponder that such efforts were needed to establish principles so manifestly right. The dark ages gave to women eternal silence and servitude, and as late as 1815 we find in one small district in England as many as 39 wives sold into servitude by their husbands, with the addition of sixpence for the rope with which they were led.

But I see a new heaven and a new earth.

Thank God the day is not far distant. Not only are women in all sections of the country and every condition of life coming to realise their responsibility, but thousands and thousands of men, noble great-hearted lovers of humanity, are coming out on the side of home protection and not only bidding us Godspeed, but doing all in their power to bring about the day that shall see brother and sister standing shoulder to shoulder and heart to heart in the great fight for right, truth and justice, for better laws, for better protection to our sons and daughters, for better and purer homes.

Sir John Forrest–Trans-Australia Railway

CEREMONY AT PORT AUGUSTA TO TURN THE FIRST SOD
OF THE TRANS-AUSTRALIA RAILWAY
Tuesday, 17 September 1912
1847-1918, Explorer, Western Australia Premier 1890-1901, and Member of the Australian Cabinet for much of 1901-18: One of the long-promised initiatives throughout conventions for federation of the colonies in 1901 was improved communication with Western Australia, so physically separated from the remainder of the country by an extensive desert. The Rt Hon Sir John Forrest GCMG was a long-time advocate for the building of the Trans-Australia Railway, extending the commitment he made earlier in life to explore on horseback the routes that improved communications between the population of the west and the colonies in the east, efforts to which he referred here. Within this lively speech were frequent interjections from listeners in approval of both the speaker and the cause that he had championed.

As a representative of Western Australia, I feel grateful for the honour His Majesty The King has done to this historic occasion by sending the gracious message which the Governor-General has received and just read to us. [*Cheers.*] I thank His Excellency the Governor-General and His Excellency the Governor of South Australia and others for the kind references which they have been good enough to make to myself. I have been a constant advocate of this railway on public grounds for many years, and I am naturally proud that the long-looked-for event has come at last. What may be termed the foundation stone of this great undertaking has been laid, and in a few years we shall have East and West connected by these 1,060 miles of railway.

I am glad to be in Port Augusta again, and this is my second visit. Forty-two years ago, I, with a few companions, weary travellers, arrived at this town after an overland journey from Western Australia. [*Cheers.*] I remember the difficulty we had in ferrying our horses across the inlet. Today I had a second look at the same place, and it seemed to be much wider, but I understand there is a tide of 16 feet, and that it was low water when we crossed. I saw a punt, too, and if forty-two years had not passed away I would have said it was the same as that by which I and my companions and fifteen horses came across. [*Laughter.*] We occupied five months on that journey, and were very glad to reach Port Augusta, where we were hospitably received by the residents. One result of that journey was the establishment of telegraphic communication not only between the East and the West of the continent, but with the whole world, thanks to the enterprise of South Australia in erecting a telegraphic line from Adelaide to Port Darwin. [*Cheers.*]

This event represents the consumption of a great aspiration which has occupied my thoughts and engaged my strenuous effort for a long number of years. The connection of the East and the West by railway has been a hope, an ambition, and a determination of mine for twenty years, and I am glad to be here to join in rejoicing at its realisation; to rejoice that the strenuous battle of advocacy has at length ended in victory. [*Cheers.*] I may on this public occasion refer to a promise I made when I was Premier of Western Australia. On the strength of an assurance, before Federation, by leading public men of Australia that, if Western Australia joined the Federation as a original State, this railway would be surely constructed at once, and would be the 'outward visible sign' of Federation, I pledged myself to the people of my State that this assurance would be certain to be realised; and today, although its realisation has been tardy, that assurance and that promise have both been fulfilled.

In my first speech in the Federal Parliament, on 23rd May, 1901, I said–'I look upon a railway to Western Australia as a great, necessary, and urgent work, which will bind together irrevocably the people of the eastern and western sides of this great continent'. [*Cheers.*] Eleven years have passed since then–years of strenuous effort; the people of Western Australia were becoming despondent. The representation of Western Australia in Parliament is small, but there has been no faltering or despair on our part; we have been unanimous. It is about the only thing we have been unanimous upon [*Laughter and cheers*], and the result is our presence here today.

It is indeed a day for rejoicing. In celebrating the commencement of this great undertaking, it is fitting that our first thought should be one of generous and grateful thanks to all those who have helped in bringing this great project to fruition; and I think we should altogether forget those who have been so strenuously opposed to us. At such a time there is only room for generosity and good feeling. Those who have supported this railway hope to see the line constructed quickly and at reasonable cost, and every endeavour put forward to make it a financial success. Those opposed to great projects such as this seem to think that there should be no risk as to their success financially. I have personally no fear whatever in that respect; but there is always an element of risk in all human undertakings. Mr Chamberlain, in writing to me on the opening of the great Goldfields Water Scheme of Western Australia in 1903, said, 'After all, it is the big schemes which succeed; it is no use shrinking and peddling nowadays; those who wish to succeed must risk something, and courage finds its own reward'. [*Cheers.*]

This railway is not going to only join the East of Australia to the West with bands of steel, and to utilise and make wealth producing the country through which it passes. It will do more than that. It will in reality consummate the Federation of Australia, and, when it is completed, will bring into the Australian family probably 500,000 British people who have hitherto been isolated from the rest of their kinfolk, and who are as enterprising and progressive as any in the world.

It is not going to an unimproved and desolate country, but to a country for the most part with a splendid temperate climate, a country much improved, and with vast potentialities. It is going to a State which has already an annual trade of 20 million pounds sterling, and whose total value of exports has already reached 150 million pounds, and its imports 130 million pounds, which has six million sheep and one million cattle, which has already over one million acres of land under crop, including 600,000 acres under wheat, which has raised over two million tons of coal, which has over 3,000 miles of working railways, which has exported 16 million pounds worth of wool, 1.5 million pounds worth of lead and copper, one million pounds worth of tin, one million pounds worth of hides, over one million pounds worth of wheat, one million pounds worth of bark for tanning, 14 million pounds worth of timber and sandalwood, and five million pounds worth of pearls and pearl shells, and which has already produced from the soil over 100 million pounds sterling worth of gold, 600,000 pounds of which was produced last year.

Those who think that any disaster or loss, or other than great advantage, can come to Australia by constructing a railway such as this, can have no faith whatever in the future of their own country. If we look around the world, we will find that, in those lands where means of communication and means of transit are greatest and best, where the free full light of public opinion shines brightly upon them, it is there that liberty and freedom, civilisation, arts and science, learning and culture excel the most, and it is there that the great ones of the earth live and flourish.

If we change the prospect to those lands which have no improved means of communication or means of transit, the dark places of the earth, we will find ignorance and barbarism, superstition, slavery and cruelty. Happily, in Australia we have begun well. We brought with us from the Old Land our free institutions and our love of liberty and freedom; and have during the whole term of our existence lived under the protection and guidance of our beloved Mother Country and have profited and flourished thereby. We are, however, as yet only in the beginning—'in the morning of times'—and the wisest and best policy for us to pursue is to stand shoulder to shoulder with our kinsmen in the Old Land, to extend our railways and all means of transit, to people our immense territory, to extend our postal, telegraphic, and telephonic services, and to provide water supplies wherever necessary, in other words, 'Let us make ways in the wilderness and rivers in the desert'. [*Cheers.*]

It is permissible, I think, for anyone to feel pride in being associated in any degree with great beneficent enterprises; and today, looking back over the forty-two years since I first came to this place as a young man, after travelling for five months from Perth, Western Australia, through an unknown and uncivilised country—looking back also over the many years I have strenuously laboured to establish railway connection between East and West, and thus consummate a real Federation, I do feel a humble pride in being able to be present and in being associated with the commencement of a work destined in my opinion to be of such great advantage and value to the whole people of Australia. [*Cheers.*]

Dame Nellie Melba–Goodbye

GOOD-BYE IN OPERA. TRIUMPHANT GALA NIGHT
His Majesty's Theatre, Melbourne, Monday, 13 October 1924
1861-1931, Operatic soprano: Fervently admired and applauded for her seemingly effortless light, crystal-like voice, Dame Nellie Melba GBE was widely popular in Australia, Britain, Europe, and America. She made many command performances to sing for royalty and national leaders and, in recognition of her series of farewell appearances, 'doing a Melba' entered the language to describe an extended farewell. As *The Argus* newspaper reported after this gala appearance that raised funds to benefit injured soldiers, she 'turned to the speech-making from the haunting beauty'[688] of her performance.

Tonight the curtain falls on my last operatic appearance in Australia, and I have to say to you the most difficult word in life–Good-bye. I shall try to say it with a smile, not only on my lips, but with my heart, a smile that comes not from the memory of achievement, but from the knowledge that I have done my best and that I have tried to keep faith with my art. For all that Australia has done for me, for all the beauty that she has shown me, for all the love she has offered, I wish to say, thank you from the bottom of my heart.

My heart is breaking but I am happy, so happy, that you are honouring me in this way. I am happy too, to think that the darling soldiers, who gave everything, will receive a very large sum of money through your kindness and hard work in this appeal. It is a thing I shall never forget. (Cheers). But you cannot expect me to say too much–you do not want me to break down. (Cheers). You want me to go away with a smiling face, and I am determined to do that. (Prolonged cheers). I thank you more than I can say for your kindness, your fidelity, and your loyalty to me. I cannot express one half that I feel. All that I can say is, 'Thank you, from the bottom of my heart.' And I never was prouder than I am to-night to be an Australian woman.

John Curtin–Speech to America

RADIO BROADCAST
Saturday, 14 March 1942
1885-1945, Wartime Prime Minister 1941-5: Fresh with memory of the surprise bombing of Pearl Harbor just three months before, The Rt Hon John Curtin called directly on the people of the United States to support Australia. With characteristic candour, he pulled out all stops to open the eyes of any in America still holding back from President Roosevelt's commitment to democratic allies in the Pacific.

Men and women of the United States.

I speak to you from Australia. I speak from a united people to a united people, and my speech is aimed to serve all the people of the nations united in the struggle to save mankind.

On the great waters of the Pacific Ocean war now breathes its bloody steam. From the skies of the Pacific pours down a deathly hail. In the countless islands of the Pacific the tide of war flows badly. For you in America; for us in Australia, it is flowing badly. Let me then address you as comrades in this war and tell you a little of Australia and Australians. I am not speaking to your Government. We have long been admirers of Mr Roosevelt and have the greatest confidence that he understands fully the critical situation in the Pacific and that America will go right out to meet it. For all that America has done, both before and after entering the war, we have the greatest admiration and gratitude.

It is to the people of America I am now speaking; to you who are, or will be, fighting; to you who are sweating in factories and workshops to turn out the vital munitions of war; to all of you who are making sacrifices in one way or another to provide the enormous resources required for our great task. I speak to you at a time when the loss of Java and the splendid resistance of the gallant Dutch together give us a feeling of both sadness and pride. Japan has moved one step further in her speedy march south; but the fight of the Dutch and Indonesians in Java has shown that a brave, freedom-loving people are more than a match for the yellow aggressor given even a shadow below equality in striking and fighting weapons.

But facts are stern things. We, the allied nations, were unready. Japan, behind her wall of secrecy, had prepared for war on a scale of which neither we nor you had knowledge. We have all made mistakes, we have all been too slow; we have all shown weakness—all the allied nations. This is not the time to wrangle about who has been most to blame. Now our eyes are open.

The Australian Government has fought for its people. We never regarded the Pacific as a segment of the great struggle. We did not insist that it was the primary theatre of war, but we did say, and events have so far, unhappily, proved us right, that the loss of the Pacific can be disastrous. Who among us, contemplating the future on that day in December last when Japan struck like an assassin at Pearl Harbour at Manila, at Wake and Guam, would have hazarded a guess that by March the enemy would be astride all the south-west Pacific except General MacArthur's gallant men, and Australia and New Zealand. But that is the case. And, realising very swiftly that it would be the case, the Australian Government sought a full and proper recognition of the part the Pacific was playing in the general strategic disposition of the world's warring forces. It was, therefore, but natural that, within twenty days after Japan's first treacherous blow, I said on behalf of the Australian Government that we looked to America as the paramount factor on the democracies' side of the Pacific.

There is no belittling of the Old Country in this outlook. Britain has fought and won in the air the tremendous battle of Britain. Britain has fought, and with your strong help, has won, the equally vital battle of the Atlantic. She has a paramount obligation to supply all possible help to Russia. She cannot, at the same time, go all out in the Pacific. We Australians, with New Zealand, represent Great Britain here in the Pacific—we are her sons—and on us the responsibility falls. I pledge to you my word we will not fail. You, as I have said, must be our leader. We will pull knee to knee with you for every ounce of our weight.

We looked to America, among other things, for counsel and advice, and therefore it was our wish that the Pacific War Council should be located at Washington. It is a matter of some regret to us that, even now, after 95 days of Japan's staggering advance south, ever south, we have not obtained first-hand contact with America. Therefore, we propose sending to you our Minister for External Affairs (Dr H.V. Evatt), who is no stranger to your country, so that we may benefit from his discussions with your authorities. Dr Evatt's wife, who will accompany him, was born in the United States. Dr Evatt will not go to you as a mendicant. He will go to you as the representative of a people as firmly determined to hold and hit back at the enemy as courageously as those people from whose loins we spring... those people who withstood the disaster of Dunkirk, the fury of Goering's blitz, the shattering blows of the Battle of the Atlantic. He will go to tell you that we are fighting mad; that our people have a government that is governing with orders and not with weak-kneed suggestions;

that we Australians are a people who, while somewhat inexperienced and uncertain as to what war on their own soil may mean, are nevertheless ready for anything, and will trade punches, giving odds if needs be, until we rock the enemy back on his heels.

We are, then, committed, heart and soul, to total warfare. How far, you may ask me, have we progressed along that road? I may answer you this way. Out of every ten men in Australia four are wholly engaged in war as members of the fighting forces or making the munition and equipment to fight with. The other six, besides feeding and clothing the whole ten and their families, have to produce the food and wool and metals which Britain needs for her very existence. We are not, of course, stopping at four out of ten. We had over three when Japan challenged our life and liberty. The proportion is now growing every day. On the one hand we are ruthlessly cutting out unessential expenditure so as to free men and women for war work; and on the other, mobilising woman power to the utmost to supplement the men. From four out of ten devoted to war, we shall pass to five and six out of ten. We have no limit.

We have no qualms here. There is no fifth column in this country. We are all the one race—the English-speaking race. We will not yield easily a yard of our soil. We have great space here and tree by tree, village by village, and town by town we will fall back if we must. That will occur only if we lack the means of meeting the enemy with parity in materials and machines. For, remember, we are the Anzac breed. Our men stormed Gallipoli; they swept through the Libyan desert; they were the 'rats' of Tobruk; they were the men who fought under 'bitter, sarcastic, pugnacious Gordon Bennett' down Malaya and were still fighting when the surrender of Singapore came. These men gave of their best in Greece and Crete; they will give more than their best on their own soil, when their hearths and homes lie under enemy threat.

Our air force are in the Kingsford-Smith tradition. You have, no doubt, met quite a lot of them in Canada; the Nazis have come to know them over Hamburg and Berlin and in paratroop landings in France. Our naval forces silently do their share on the seven seas.

I am not boasting to you. But were I to say less I would not be paying proper due to a band of men who have been tested in the crucible of world wars and hallmarked as pure metal. Our fighting forces are born attackers; we will hit the enemy wherever we can, as often as we can, and the extent of it will be measured only by the weapons in our hands.

Dr Evatt will tell you that Australia is a nation stripped for war. Our minds are set on attack rather than defence. We believe in fact that attack is the best defence; here in the Pacific it is the only defence. We know it means risks, but 'safety first' is the devil's catchword today. Business interests in Australia are submitting with good grace to iron control to drastic elimination of profits. Our great labour unions are accepting the suspension of rights and privileges which have been sacred for two generations, and are submitting to an equally iron control of the activities of their members. It is now 'work or fight' for everyone in Australia. The Australian Government has so shaped its policy that there will be a place for every citizen in the country. There are three means of service–in the fighting forces; in the labour forces; in the essential industries. For the first time in the history of this country a complete call-up, or draft, as you refer to it in America, has been made. I say to you, as a comfort to our friends and a stiff warning to our enemies, that only the infirm remain outside the compass of our war plans.

We fight with what we have and what we have is our all. We fight for the same free institutions that you enjoy. We fight so that, in the words of Lincoln, 'government of the people, for the people, by the people, shall not perish from the earth'. Our legislature is elected the same as is yours; and we will fight for it, and for the right to have it, just as you will fight to keep the Capitol at Washington the meeting place of freely elected men and women representative of a free people.

But I give you this warning: Australia is the last bastion between the West Coast of America and the Japanese. If Australia goes, the Americas are wide open. It is said that the Japanese will by-pass Australia and that they can be met and routed in India. I say to you that the saving of Australia is the saving of America's west coast. If you believe anything to the contrary then you delude yourselves.

Be assured of the calibre of our national character. This war may see the end of much that we have painfully and slowly built in our 150 years of existence. But even though all of it go, there will still be Australians fighting on Australian soil until the turning point be reached, and we will advance over blackened ruins, through blasted and fire-swept cities, across scorched plains, until we drive the enemy into the sea. I give you the pledge of my country. There will always be an Australian Government and there will always be an Australian people. We are too strong in our hearts; our spirit is too high; the justice of our cause throbs too deeply in our being for that high purpose to be overcome.

I may be looking down a vista of weary months; of soul-shaking reverses; of grim struggle; of back-breaking work. But as surely as I sit here talking to you across the war-tossed Pacific Ocean I see our flag; I see Old Glory; I see the proud banner of the heroic Chinese; I see the standard of the valiant Dutch.

And I see them flying high in the wind of liberty over a Pacific from which aggression has been wiped out; over peoples restored to freedom; and flying triumphant as the glorified symbols of united nations strong in will and in power to achieve decency and dignity, unyielding to evil in any form.

Sir Robert Menzies–Eulogy for Churchill

SPEECH FROM THE CRYPT OF ST PAUL'S CATHEDRAL
BBC Television Broadcast, Saturday, 30 January 1965
1894-1978, Prime Minister 1939-41 and 1949-66: With exceptional speaking ability to modulate language and delivery to an occasion, The Rt Hon Sir Robert Menzies KT AK CH FAA FRS QC was here at a peak in his political service as Australia's prime minister. Readily challenging the audience to both fittingly remember Sir Winston Churchill and implicitly recall the need for a nation to be militarily prepared, in this speech Menzies displayed his command of language and occasion. He presented a unique eulogy to honour the remarkable life of Britain's wartime prime minister.

As this historic procession goes through the streets of London to the Tower pier, I have the honour of speaking to you from the crypt of St. Paul's Cathedral. I do this in two capacities. One is that I, Prime Minister of Australia, happen to be, in point of time, the senior Commonwealth Prime Minister, and therefore speak on behalf of a remarkable world organisation which owes more than it can ever express to our departed leader, Sir Winston Churchill. He is one of the famous men whom we thank and praise.

My second capacity is more personal and more intimate. I am sure that you, most of you, have thought about Sir Winston Churchill a great deal and with warmth in your hearts and in your recollections. Some day, some year, there will be old men and women whose pride it will be to say, 'I lived in Churchill's time;' some will be able to say, 'I saw him, and I heard him the unforgettable voice and the immortal words'. And some will be able to say, 'I knew him, and talked with him, and was his friend'. This I can, with a mixture of pride and humility, say for myself.

The memory of this moves me deeply now that he is dead, but is gloriously remembered by me as he goes to his burial amid the sorrow and pride and thanks of all of you who stand and feel for yourselves and for so many millions. Many of you will not need to be reminded, but some, the younger among you, the inheritors of his master-strokes for freedom, may be glad to be told that your country, and mine, and all the free countries of the world, stood at the very gates of destiny in 1940 and 1941, when the Nazi tyranny threatened to engulf us, and when there was no 'second front' except our own.

This was the great crucial moment of modern history. What was at stake was not some theory of government but the whole and personal freedom of men and women and children. And the battle for them was a battle against great odds. That battle had to be won not only in the air and on the sea and in the field, but in the hearts and minds of ordinary people with a deep capacity for heroism. It was then that Winston Churchill was called, by Almighty God, as our faith makes us believe, to stand as our leader and our inspirer.

There were, in 1940, defeatists who felt that prudence required submission or such terms as might be had. There were others who, while not accepting the inevitability of defeat, thought that victory was impossible. Winston Churchill scorned to fall into either category, and he was right. With courage, and matchless eloquence, and human understanding, he inspired us and led us to victory.

In the whole of recorded modern history this was, I believe the one occasion when one man with one soaring imagination, with one fire burning in him, and with one unrivalled capacity for conveying it to others, won a crucial victory not only for the forces (for there were many heroes in those days) but for the very spirit of human freedom. And so, on this great day, we thank him, and we thank God for him.

There are two other things I want to say to you, on a day which neither you nor I will ever willingly forget. One is that Winston Churchill was not an institution, but a man a man of wit and chuckling humour, and penetrating understanding, not a man who spoke to us as from the mountain tops, but one who expressed the simple and enduring feelings of ordinary men and women. It was because he was a great Englishman that he was able to speak for the English people. It was because he was a great human being that, in our darkest days, he lit the lamps of hope at many firesides and released so many from the chains of despair. There has been nobody like him in our lifetimes. We must, and do, thank God for him, and strive to be worthy of his example.

And the second thing I will never forget is this. Winston Churchill's wife is with us here in London, a great and gracious lady in her own right. Could I today send her your love, and mine? She has suffered an irreparable personal loss. But she has proud and enduring memories, happy memories, I venture to say. We share her sorrow, but I know that she would wish us to share with her those rich remembrances which the thought of the great man evokes.

There have been, in the course of recorded history, some men of power who have cast shadows across the world. Winston Churchill, on the contrary, was a fountain of light and of hope. As I end my talk to you from the crypt of St.

Paul's, with its reminders of Nelson and Wellington, those marvellous defenders of long ago, the body of Winston Churchill goes in procession through the streets of London, his London, our London, this most historic city, this ancient home of freedom, this place through which, in the very devastation and fire of war, his voice rang with courage, and defiance, and hope, and rugged confidence.

His body will be carried on the Thames, a river full of history. With one heart we all feel, with one mind we all acknowledge, that it will never have borne a more precious burden, or been enriched by more splendid memories.

Kevin Gilbert–Needs of First Nations

SPEECH AT ARMIDALE TEACHERS COLLEGE
Armidale, New South Wales, 1974
1933-93, Author, Artist, Poet, and Activist for First Nations: With forcefulness in this lecture on the needs of First Nations, Kevin Gilbert put a spotlight on the neglect and abuse of the peoples of First Nations since the British settlement of Australia in 1788. With graphic visualisation of how policy and behaviours have affected people's lives, the speech strongly presented a case for land rights and self-determination, along with respect of First Nations' values. With direct language and calling out of stereotyped views, beyond addressing a point of view, the speech urged communication, sincerity, and action.

I would like to try and communicate some of the needs of the Aboriginal community. One of the things we should realise is that most Aboriginal spokesmen are pretty loud and clear in claiming that all white people are bastards. This seems to be an attitude arrived at through circumstances–the conditions under which they live and under which they are raised. On the other hand, we find that most Europeans see the Aborigine as 'Jacky'–as a drunk, as a man who will not work, who goes on walkabout and who will not help himself. There seems to be a difference in values. You seem to think that the Aboriginal person should earn his own house and pay his own rent, buy his own car and to do exactly the same as you do. Very few people get to the root cause. They don't realise that your whole society is based on indoctrination, especially at school. Your people are taught to be sharks, to use your initiative and your competitive spirit in order to advance, and particularly to advance above your fellow man. The Aboriginal people have, since their detribalisation, been indoctrinated with the handout system: they are there only when the boss calls, they will earn only when the boss dictates. They will live and construct their society only as the European decides.

Today the Aboriginal voice is rising for better conditions, better opportunities for their children, opportunities which are not provided by education. Mostly we find the tribal woman, or the person who has been detribalised, who has been on the fringe, is the one to make this effort and send the child to school. The child will go to third or fourth year and will return to the mission or settlement because opportunities have been denied them in society. If the employers have the choice they will hire a European—a migrant or an Australian—before they will hire an Aboriginal: they believe Aborigines are lazy bastards. So we have confusion as to the identity of the people: that *you* are the bastards because you will not recognise the conditions of Aboriginal people, you will not live up to the ideals you profess—justice, humanity, decency. You will do everything to present your image overseas by shelling out for Austcare, Freedom from Hunger, but you never clean up your own backyard.

A good instance of this is in Alice Springs, where the local people gave $25,000 a year to the Freedom from Hunger Campaign. Then Freedom from Hunger decided to start acting within Australia, to give aid to Aborigines. As soon as they gave a number of small grants, the people from Alice Springs withdrew their funds because they said Aborigines would not help themselves, that they would not put their money down the drain to give handouts to Aborigines. There is need for an education programme, but one where, for a change, the European has to be educated, educated in the human values needed to be applied in the Aboriginal community, as against your *paper* education, which get the people nowhere.

The Aborigine who goes to school to fourth year finds he cannot get a job. He likes the close family environment and returns home: where he gains employment digging holes with a brother who has not been educated at all. We need a change in the community, so that Aboriginal people are allowed to determine their own mode and style of life, to come up with their own values rather than the stereotypes of the European. They want to be Aborigines in their own right, to be people in their own right, rather than imitation white men, pseudo-white men. You may believe that your values are good and fine, and so they are. Good and fine for you! Our values need to be good and fine for us. At this moment we are not allowed to bring our values forward. We do have an advisory committee, who do find out what the people need, and then the government says: 'Well, we won't give them that'.

We have to get people, especially you people who are young and who are educated, to try and understand the type of people you're dealing with, the type of environment the people come from. When I was going to school, I went to fourth class primary before I finished. Every time there was an English lesson, or whatever, four or five Aborigines were sent out to clean the yards and do the sweeping up. They were thought to be generally useless; it was assumed that education served no purpose—it was merely the letter of the law that needed to be applied.

What we have to do is allow a people to grow: allow them to grow at their own pace; allow them to make the decisions in their own community. Now this society is geared to earning and to money. Everything costs. (It costs you to die, and it certainly costs you to live.) Because of the unemployment situation and the discrimination in Aboriginal societies, especially in these country areas, we find a lot of people are bigoted because they see, not a human being, but a drunk who will not help himself. They see a house that's virtually falling down–the windows are broken. Because of their 'training', they would have it fixed in ten minutes. But the Aborigines don't worry about the house, because it is built on land that's called an 'Aboriginal Reserve', and it does not belong to them. They own nothing. They're such derelict houses to start with that the Housing Commission will not have anything to do with their maintenance and repair. It is the policy of the government to allow these houses to fall into disrepair and carry out no maintenance, in order to try and drive the people from the reserves, to bring about what is termed 'assimilation'. Now a minimum rental of $4.50 is paid on the houses–and the houses are just not worth it. Many of the people do not earn and they say: 'What is the purpose, why keep the house clean, wire all the fences? We don't own it. The government can kick us out at any time. They are just as likely to put the bulldozers through to knock the house down'.

So we have people sitting around the reserve even when there is some work obtainable, because they're people without a purpose. You have a purpose in life–one is a career, another is to buy your car, your home and to conduct yourself and maintain yourself at a certain level in society–the norm in your society. The norm in our society has always been the handout system, to sit down and wait for some boss to come along to offer you employment at wages far less than the European. And it has been 'found', and indeed it is claimed in New Guinea, that the people do not need equal wages because their standard of living is so much 'lower'.

Whether or not this is a ploy to gain cheaper labour and is the policy of the greedy white man, we can only guess. I believe it is. For instance, in the North we have 'slow worker' clauses where men are paid $24. Now if you were receiving that sum, and a European or an Aborigine was alongside you receiving $56 a week, would you work, or put any effort into it? No! What the Aboriginal people are seeking now is identification in their own land, to try and get some status and some pride. They have pride, but they want it maintained in society, the society you represent.

When Aborigines see you, they don't really see you as an individual who is sincere, who possibly has some feeling for other human beings. They see you as a white face: as one of the people, or as a representative of the race who is oppressing them and often discriminating against them. You are in fact the evil bastard.

Over and above this, we have to try to communicate. People have to be sincere. People go down to the reserves and say: 'Well, right, let's try and do something with the Aboriginal community. Let's try and help them'. And it all seems very good. Often they come away in despair because they cannot realise why an Aborigine doesn't fix his fence, why he doesn't mend the window, why he's sitting there without purpose. Often it's another bandwagon to ride, it's another ego-lifter for the European.

Now in many universities and in a lot of schools, the government is only too ready to give grants for research. It sounds good. It keeps the public on side and the academics are pretty well catered for. They think that at least an effort is being made. When you ask for some practical development like housing, irrigation, drainage, normal sewerage, and grass on the footpath, or general maintenance by the caretakers, you get nothing because the government (or the policy of this New South Wales government) is to try and drive people off the reserves. No more houses are being built on the reserves, no more maintenance is being carried out because the government wants them assimilated. To recognise Aboriginal Land Rights is (according to former Prime Minister McMahon) to risk the security of tenure of every Australian. They try to put this idea in the people's mind so they will become a little afraid their own possessions will be taken from them. They try to play, in fact, on people's greed. You're all God, you're dictated to by money, you obey money and possessions, your material prospects are the ones you cling to. All other perspectives—whether it's integrity or human feelings—you put aside because you must hang on to the only God you have: your material possessions, your identification, your status symbols, your car and your house. What we want—and what we will get, no matter how long it takes or what effort is involved—is land. Because the Australian Aboriginal heritage is based on theft: theft of the land and the oppression of a people, the coming in and taking, by force of arms, the land and an identity from the people.

When the first landing occurred the Aborigine was considered below human level. In school I used to squirm because the teachers used to read out certain passages reflecting on Aborigines—'the most miserable people on earth'—and I would not accept that. I would not accept that embarrassment, so I tried to see what was behind that black face, to see what was behind the tribesman walking across the sand. I saw the culture—a culture that was rich. It was vital to the people and enabled them to survive in a very hard land, it looked after their well-being. Their goals were numerous, certainly their god-heroes. They had one great God, and these god-heroes and spirit-beings who inhabited the earth before man was created laid down the law. They laid down the orderly process for a community to develop and to survive. Then the missionaries came in, of course, and because of ignorance they saw the naked heathen. They saw the man eating grubs, the man without artefacts, the man who did not weave or spin, did not create great pottery and arts and they naturally believed their way was the right way. Perhaps it was. The right way to genocide!

I once attended an Australian Council of Churches Conference where we produced evidence of the people's conditions on the reserves. We told them about the death rate occurring and what was causing those conditions. We told them also that the Australian government in 1969, when the Aboriginal infant death rate was twelve times higher than the European, that the government, in order to economise, withdrew $200,000 from medical aid to Aborigines. By 1972 that death rate was seventeen and a-half times higher and the government at that time, while 'economising', proposed to fly around Australia the South African Rugby Union team—against the wishes of the people who were demonstrating against apartheid.

It is a policy of genocide. It can be no other; for surely common sense and knowledge of the situation would dictate that greater sums of money and greater aid would comfort these people. On the land question, the government denies that the Aborigine has any identification or any cultural significance in areas where he claims the land. It claims we have no boundaries, and indeed the Aborigine has not—according to European concepts. But I believe that every thinking person must recognise that the original inhabitants certainly had prior claim to the land, that these people are entitled to their place in Australia. They're entitled to see the European at last try to live up to the concepts, or at least profess the ideologies, of justice, democracy and human welfare. We can look around us today and see children are still dying, that we cannot get any practical aid, that the Aboriginal people have nothing. I asked a woman at Purfleet Mission what there was in the community for the children and she said, 'Nothing'... 'Have you any halls or youth clubs?', 'No", she said, 'nothing'... 'What have the men got?', 'Nothing'... 'And what have the women got?'", 'Nothing'.

What have they got? They are a people without purpose. They are a people without identity, because that identity has been debased and demeaned. You kick a man, kick a man's culture long enough, debase him and debase his image long enough and he will be ashamed of that image. He will try and pass himself off as a white man. He will try to deny his black heritage, his black association, as I believe is being done here in Armidale, where the Aboriginal people are split into factions—those who dwell in the town and those who live on the reserve. This type of chaos, this human pain and confusion, results in loss of identity, loss of confidence in an identity. They know very well that they cannot be treated as white man, because they are *not*, and they are never treated as white men. They cannot be Aborigines because they don't know what it is to be culturally identified, to be people with purpose and meaning in life. So we have people without meaning in life; we have people struggling for survival; a people who are confused; a people who have suffered so much through the traumatic experience of colonisation that they cannot get on their feet. One of the first things in 'identity' is recognising their right to land, their identity as human beings, giving them status through land and allowing them to own something. They don't wish to be landed gentry, to own a few acres, and say: 'I'm Bill Smith, I own four acres out there. I will go and sell that or I'll build my house on it'.

They want recognition of justice, recognition of their right in the country, the recognition that they be treated on the same level of dignity as your migrants. A work force in generations to come perhaps? But now? No! We see the man on the mission—and what has he? What can he do in society? Where can he go? No clubs are open to him. There is no social activity—only pubs. Why pubs? Because it's a place where he can go, where he can forget a little bit of the misery or a little bit of the responsibility: it's somewhere he can engage actively. What can he buy? An old car, another cast-off of the white man. Usually he holds it. He will work for six months toward buying it. He is impatient, of course. He wants to own something so he'll buy a car. No white man would buy it: he wouldn't be so stupid, but the Aborigine buys it. He's got wheels under him. He tears around for a couple of days and the car falls to pieces because it was a wreck when he bought it. And then he has so much more frustration. He couldn't make it, and even this little wouldn't work for him.

So this is the type of identity we are dealing with. It is a people who are bringing spokesmen forward to try and speak for them. In many cases the speakers are wrong because they say: 'White is bad. Whitey is a bastard'. Where people are bigoted, they certainly are. Where they're sincere it's up to them to try and prove they are interested in bringing practical developments. You showed in the 1967 referendum on Aboriginal rights that you were sincere. But what has it availed the people? Nothing. It's allowed them to go into the pubs. It has allowed them to vote for politicians who couldn't give a damn about their kids dying, who couldn't give a damn about the houses, who, in fact, will not allow any houses to be built on reserves. As soon as the houses are vacated they are bulldozed into the ground in order to try and get them into your society.

Is your society so good? As you can see by student demonstrations, there is a lot that's wrong with it. While we cannot expect the 'perfect', we can work towards human dignity, we can work to give some justice to a people, to try together and communicate, to try and see that black person down the street not merely as a drunk, as a problem and an embarrassment. The man is not a problem, he is a victim: a victim of colonisation, a victim of government policies that have been wrong, and a victim of discrimination. You will see the same thing in your schools. Children are very rarely prejudiced until they're seven or eight years of age, and then the opinions of their parents come in. When we get a lot of children in second and third year especially, discrimination drives them from school. What does school offer bar insult, bar an affront to their dignity because they have not the clothing other children have? They are not on a social level with the other children.

There is discrimination in Australia. This is your part—being sincere—that wherever you teach, wherever you work, try to stop this. Another vital role you can play is asking for the recognition of Aboriginal land rights. There is a moratorium for black rights on July 14. That day is National Aborigines Day. That again is propaganda by the government. They usually bring up some of the trained Aborigines—most of them trying to be pseudo white men—who try to disclaim all connection with the reserves. They usually perform like monkeys on National Aborigines Day to show how educated the Aborigine has become under white tutors, to show how far they've advanced. There are usually photos of the Housing Commission houses Aborigines have been moved into. Very rarely do we see anything of the true situation. We're asking all students and all clubs, all unions and workers to come out on July 14 to ask that land rights be recognised. Briefly, land rights means: a claim that all Aboriginal reserves be immediately deeded in perpetuity to the Aboriginal people as a whole. Should the Aboriginal people from the area pass away, that land should remain as parkland and be developed for the community. Now you know, or at least you should be able to realise, that seventy-one per cent of the minerals and the natural products are vested in overseas interests, that more and more land is being taken, that there are fewer and fewer parks, that there are less and less kangaroos, there are less and less Aborigines (going by the present death rate).

A lot of this, your heritage, is going to disappear. It's going to be an American heritage or a Japanese heritage. I'm not trying to plug the racist line, but it is time that the Australians looked to their own future. This country is a big country. It's too big a country for bigotry. It is too big for injustices and for inhumanity. So far, in fact, it's been too big for the European, who has not been able to live up to the ideologies he professes. There is a placard put out by the National Aborigines Day Observance Committee. It is the 'Aboriginal Embassy at Canberra, 1972'; underneath it says: 'Advance Australia—Where? National Aborigines Day, Friday, July 14, 1972'. I think the vital question is 'Advance Australia—Where?'. Where are we going? What are we doing to make it a country we can live in without embarrassment, without shame and with some sort of pride in our heritage? If I was a white man, (thank God I'm not, because I'd rather be on the side of the underdog), if I was an Australian, I wouldn't like any taint on my heritage. It is a big country and a good country—one that each of you should be able to look up to, should be able to respect, be big enough to meet, big enough to handle, big enough to preserve your image. At the present moment you're not—and you can see people dying because you're not.

Gough Whitlam—Partnership in the Pacific after Vietnam

ADDRESS TO THE NATIONAL PRESS CLUB
Washington DC, United States of America, Thursday, 8 May 1975
1916-2014, Prime Minister 1972-5: Elected on a platform that included bringing an end to Australia's participation in the Vietnam War, The Hon Gough Whitlam AC QC presented this speech in Washington DC two months after the culmination of the Watergate scandal, which saw President Ford take office. The speech proposed new partnership to develop economic and diplomatic strengths throughout the Pacific region.

It is not quite two years since I last had the honour of addressing this National Press Club. In that time, as practitioners of our respective professions, we have all had to cope with tremendous events and tremendous changes occurring with unexampled speed. It was therefore with some little trepidation that I retrieved the remarks I last made to you to see how they stood the test of time. I find, however, that the very first point I made has been amply confirmed in a way few of us could have guessed in July 1973. I said then that I was honoured to address representatives of the world's greatest and most free press in the world's greatest and most free democracy, and that the strength of each was the strength of both. If this democracy had been less free the constitutional upheaval of 1974 would not have occurred. If this democracy had been less strong it could scarcely have survived so traumatic an encounter. So in accepting your invitation for a second time, I again pay tribute to the manifest and enduring strength of the democracy of the United States, of which the press is so fundamental a part.

In the wake of the remarkable events in Indo-China, all of us—leaders in my calling, commentators in yours—are in the process of reassessing basic policies and relations. For the United States in particular, this is bound to be a difficult and perhaps a painful process. In that reappraisal the last thing the Government or people of the United States need are sermons and homilies from foreigners. Certainly, you don't need them from an Australian. It is true that I happen to lead a political party which strongly opposed the intervention in Indo-China: It is also true that I am the Prime Minister of a nation which for many years supported the intervention and encouraged the escalation of the war. Whatever recriminations we might have at home, it is no role for an Australian Prime Minister to lecture the United States.

It is, however, very necessary that we should prevent the creation of new myths about what went wrong. And to do that it is necessary to look at past mistakes–mistakes in which both countries shared. The great danger is that in an atmosphere of deep emotion and recrimination engendered by the suddenness of events in Indo-China, we should fasten upon explanations and self-justification and over-simplifications, which would ensure a return to, a repetition of, the great mistakes of the past. We have, in particular, to resist the same sort of myths which developed after the revolution in China. Those myths, those distortions of reality, perverted our relations with China for more than a generation. They led directly to the debacle in Indo-China.

We should have no truck with any new variation of the 'stab in the back' theory that the war in Vietnam was lost not in Saigon but here in Washington. The truth is that the United States did not 'lose' Vietnam, any more than she 'lost' China. Vietnam was not America's to lose. What was defeated was not the United States and her allies but a policy of foreign intervention which was bound to fail. There was no time in the past thirty years when such a policy could have succeeded. The tragedy for us all, but above all for the people of Indo-China, is that a policy so manifestly doomed from the beginning should have been carried through for so long.

It was never true that the honour and prestige of the United States and her allies were bound up with the survival of the Saigon regime, any more than it was ever true that the honour, or prestige, or security of the United States were bound up with the fate of Generalissimo Chiang Kai-Shek.

When I spoke to you last, I spoke of the 'second opportunity' we had gained because of the moves towards reconciliation with China and with the signing of the Paris Agreement in January 1973. I said: 'For twenty years I have been appalled at the damage we of the West have done to ourselves and to other peoples by our Western ideological pre-occupations, particularly in South East Asia. We are not going to be readily forgiven for throwing away the chance we had for a settlement in Indo-China in 1954 after Korea, after Geneva. We have now been given a second chance. It must not be thrown away'. Unfortunately, my hopes, the hopes of the world, were not fulfilled after January 1973. The gross breaches of the Paris Agreements by both sides–political breaches, military breaches–made it inevitable that the final settlement in Indo-China would be reached by the arbitrament of war.

Yet in the wider sense that second opportunity, that second chance of which I spoke, still remains, the question now is: What are to be our relations and our conduct towards Vietnam whether there be one Government of Vietnam or two? Are we to treat Vietnam after 1975 as we treated China after 1949? Through fear or frustration, because of our failure to impose the will of the West on Indo-China, are we to treat Vietnam as the new pariah, the new untouchable among nations? No-one supposes that it is going to be a simple or easy task to establish meaningful relations with Vietnam, a Vietnam emerging from thirty years of civil war prolonged and deepened by foreign intervention. It is going to be one of the most difficult tasks for statesmanship, for the countries in Australia's region and for the United States.

Two hundred years ago on 22 March 1775–Edmund Burke said, 'Magnanimity in politics is not seldom the truest wisdom'. It was his great speech on conciliation with the American colonies. He was advising another mighty nation which was about to suffer humiliation at the hands of another small band of revolutionaries–not because that nation was wicked or weak but because it was committed to policies doomed to fail. Magnanimity in the face of failure is much more difficult than magnanimity in victory. The present prosperity of Western Germany and Japan attests America's unparalleled magnanimity in victory. The other, more difficult, response lies ahead–in Indo-China.

This is very much a time for a realistic assessment of our strengths and opportunities and for a good deal of confidence in those strengths and opportunities. There are those who feel that because American policy suffered a defeat in Vietnam, we should be pessimistic about American policy elsewhere, and ignore American achievements elsewhere. Dangerous and difficult as the Middle East problem undoubtedly is, taxing as it is for Western statesmanship, it should not blind us to the wider stability and security achieved in the world during the past two decades. Who would deny that the world is a safer place today than it was in the aftermath of World War II? Who would deny–remembering Berlin, remembering Greece, remembering Korea, remembering Cuba–that the threats to peace today are less menacing than those posed by the critical flashpoints and monolithic confrontations of a decade or a generation ago? I hope we shall keep a sense of perspective and reality in these matters, keeping in mind the real progress we have made towards a safer world, and not allow ourselves to be panicked or dismayed by lesser problems than those we have surmounted before.

In the specific matter of Vietnam, I am not going to be panicked by an outcome achieved militarily in 1975 which might have come about politically in 1954. I am intent upon reaching a *modus vivendi*–a meaningful, constructive relationship–with Vietnam in 1975, as we would assuredly have had to do some time between 1954 and 1975, and as with such needless and damaging delay we have done with China.

It is not, however, by focussing exclusively upon Vietnam or even upon Indo-China that we can get the true perspective of our real strengths and opportunities in the region—Australia's opportunities, or America's strengths. There can be no suggestion of wanting to shrug off the events in Indo-China. On the contrary there are great lessons to be learnt. Nonetheless, let's coolly assess both the present and the future.

If we look at the Pacific Basin area, what do we find? The most developed and some of the strongest of the dozen or so most significant nations upon or around the four Pacific continents of Asia, Australia, North America and South America, are flourishing democracies. The United States' most important friends in this vast area, countries like Canada, Mexico, New Zealand, Australia and above all, Japan, have never been stronger—stronger in themselves, stronger in their basic friendship towards the United States.

The Asean Nations Indonesia, The Philippines, Thailand, Malaysia, Singapore are working closely and successfully together to promote their common interests in a natural and viable regional grouping. These countries happen to be those cast by the theorists in the role of the dominoes. Not one of them will give any thanks for being cast in such a role. Each of them will work in its own way to accommodate itself to the new political realities in South East Asia. Each recognises that it is primarily its own internal strength and resilience which will safeguard it against external threats. Each recognises that the prime guarantee of national integrity and security lies in developing the forms of Government best suited to itself and ensuring that Government is in tune with national needs and popular aspirations.

There is a further cause for confidence. On the Pacific side of the Asian region, Malaysia, Singapore, New Zealand, Australia, Fiji, Western Samoa and Tonga, and on the Indian Ocean side, India, Sri Lanka and Bangladesh, are all members of the Commonwealth of Nations. I have been meeting their leaders in Jamaica this week. In this remarkable association of nations not one Head of Government is Communist, yet not one Head of Government was plunged into despair because of the events in Indo-China. In our communique issued on Tuesday the nations of the Commonwealth 34 of them, said this: 'Heads of Government welcomed the end of the prolonged conflict in Indo-China, urged countries in a position to do so to contribute to international assistance for the urgent tasks of rehabilitation and reconstruction and looked forward to the new Governments of the region playing their full part in the Community of Nations'. No panic here, no desperation. Yet, as I point out, many nations of the Commonwealth are the very nations who are supposed to be the likely victims of the falling dominoes. The truth is that all of us have great problems of one kind or another yet each of us is basically confident of surmounting those problems in our own way. Nor was there throughout our meeting in Jamaica any disposition to knock the United States, to recriminate against her or to suggest that the United States will not be a good ally or a trustworthy friend. Indeed, with the war in Vietnam over, many nations—and Australia is one—will have even greater confidence in America as an ally, for we know that American resolve, American capacity, American resources will no longer be weakened or dissipated in a fruitless cause.

President Ford was entirely justified in remarking two weeks ago, that because the United States' policy had not succeeded everywhere it should not be assumed it had succeeded nowhere. The policy failed in Indo-China because it was foredoomed to failure. The policy succeeded in Japan and in Europe because it had the necessary ingredients of success a realistic appreciation of America's own interests of the people of Japan and Western Europe. It failed in Indo-China because the policy there was based neither on America's true interests nor on anything that was possible or relevant as far as the interests or aspirations of the peoples of Indo-China were concerned. But the great aims of American policy can now continue undiminished and undeterred, free of the impediments and distractions and distortions of Indo-China.

The great thrust of that policy rests upon the detente with the Soviet Union and with associating China in a wider detente. Nothing that has happened in Indo-China would warrant the United States being deflected from that great goal. For the essential meaning of detente is simply the prevention of world war, or world nuclear war. It is precisely because this is the highest risk that mankind has ever faced—the destruction of civilisation itself—that this is the highest goal a nation could ever set for itself.

I view with concern and contempt efforts made by some in countries like Australia and the United States to downgrade or denigrate the efforts being made towards detente. No one asserts that the present partial detente really solves the great question of preserving world peace. But to go back now, to retreat from the Agreements and undertakings already reached, however slight, however tentative, is to retreat towards ultimate disaster. I do not assert that detente as it now exists is complete. But I do assert that it must be made complete if any of us are to survive. We can begin by ensuring that regions of the world still largely untouched by great power rivalry continue to remain free of it. In that connection, Australia has lent her voice to the maintenance of a zone of peace in the Indian Ocean. All of us who support such proposals, all of us who support detente, know that the difficulties in the way of achieving detente are daunting indeed. But certainly, upon our success or failure turns the future of mankind. And it is because of this that the United States remains the true leader of the world and, as much as she used to be, 'the last, best hope of the world'. For it is to the United States that the West chiefly looks for meaningful leadership in that direction. If detente is to succeed, it will continue to require American initiatives, American courage, American leadership.

For many years to come, people like us, Americans, Australians, politicians, journalists, will be examining in arguments, in articles, in speeches, in books what happened in Indo-China. This is as it should be. For so great a disaster, so great a mistake, such great suffering, cannot be easily dismissed or even forgotten. We shall all have to live with it for the rest of our lives. Yet even so, we have to go on to the future. In the two years since I last spoke to you America has undergone a vast domestic, as well as a vast international, catharsis. With those profound traumas behind you, with their bitterness and misery being purged away, what better time to profit by experience and build on the true strengths of American democracy and American idealism? Here is an opportunity not just for America but for all of us to end our long preoccupation with military alignments in Asia, our ideological confrontations, our cold war hangups, and open a new chapter in Western co-operation. Let the deeper issues of poverty, overpopulation and maldistribution of the world's wealth assume their proper importance in our hearts and minds. These are the real problems of Asia. These are the real problems of the world. These, I trust, will be the real concerns of the United States. With your great tradition of moral leadership, your unexampled generosity, your vision, your energy, your sheer zest for accomplishment, you will find new inspiration in this task a task in which Australia will be a ready and a willing partner.

Michael Kirby–The Australian Community and Anti-heroes

LALOR COMMUNITY RELATIONS ADDRESS
Playhouse, Civic Square, Canberra, Wednesday, 3 December 1980
Born 1939, Chairman of Australian Law Reform Commission 1975-84, Justice of High Court of Australia 1996-2009: In a deft welding of subject matter and occasion, The Hon Michael Kirby AC CMG assessed some events in Australia's history to illustrate how the law needs to respond to change in the community. Characteristically, he here drew on historical examples in compelling language, to create a platform for new perspectives which might stimulate action.

Foreign observers and newcomers to Australia must find some of our objects of national pride and celebration curious, to say the least.

We commemorate the modern history of Australia, in the knowledge that it began very largely by accident and as a direct outgrowth of Britain's loss of the penal colonies in America, following the American revolution. Our colonial history started with nothing more elevated than the establishment of a prison colony. The rough early settlers showed little tolerance and less respect for the Indigenous people of the continent, who had lived for thousands of years in harmony with its special environment.

The Eureka Stockade in 1854 is celebrated today, 3 December. Yet this is a tale of a group of gold diggers who defied the legitimate authority of government. They broke the law. They refused to pay taxes. They hoisted a rebel flag over a stockade. They resisted, with arms, a body of the Queen's troops sent by a lawful government. They were defeated in the assault. In fact it was all over in a matter of minutes. Three soldiers and more than 30 diggers were killed. The leaders of the rising were tried for treason, though even in this there was an element of fiasco as each accused was acquitted.

In the very month of the Stockade, there was born the archetypal Australian anti-hero, Ned Kelly. The century of his execution has just been celebrated. It has inspired a great outpouring of writing.[689] The most extravagant prose has been used in praise of a group of bush rangers who (in the eye of the law at least) were desperadoes: guilty of the murder of three policemen and other innocent civilians. Yet Ned Kelly is celebrated today and the judge who tried him is burnt in effigy in Melbourne streets.[690] I have even read the suggestion that Ned be made a saint; the proponent was prepared to settle for what was apparently thought the next best thing: a posthumous knighthood!

Critics of the Kelly legend say that Kelly had to be invented because there are so few genuine Australian heroes. Royal Commissions of Inquiry might denounce Kelly as 'cruel, wanton and inhuman'. But, on the other hand, Professor Manning Clark sees the admiration of Kelly as an Australian quest for 'the life of the free, the fearless and the bold'. Historian Clive Turnbull says that, in Kelly, there are to be found 'those qualities which are deemed the most desirable in the Australian conception of manhood–courage, resolution, independence, loyalty, chivalry, sympathy with the poor and ill-used'.[691]

Many commentators have said that but for the chance of time, the Kelly Gang would have been at Gallipoli, showing the courage in the field of war which is still the chief object of our military pride. Yet Gallipoli must seem to outsiders a strange battle for a country to commemorate. Ten years ago, I stood at Anzac Cove not far from Golibolu in Turkey. I looked down to where the Australian and New Zealand soldiers stormed the impossible cliffs and fought bravely, but unsuccessfully, against the valiant Turkish defenders. One can see from that battlefield where Xerxes crossed the Hellespont, leading his troops across the Dardenelles from Persia to the conquest of Greece. We celebrate Anzac because it was the first great battle, after our country was united in Federation, in which the spirit of its soldiers was tested. But 60 years before, at Eureka, on this day–led by Peter Lalor–an earlier test had demonstrated, within Australia, important and enduring features of the Australian people.

Stung by Kellymania, a recent correspondent to *The Age*[692] declared that he was thoroughly bored with the 'wild and woolly' Ned Kelly legend. He lamented the lack of real interest in Peter Lalor, the hero of Eureka who 'fought only when violence was thrust upon him' and who knew quite well that he could die by the gun or the gallows but he was prepared to do so. Australians, it was suggested, would have far preferred Lalor if he had only died in battle or at the end of a judicially-ordained noose. 'They often seem to prefer a dead "hero" to a live thinker', said the writer.

Of more recent leaders, Mr Whitlam has been equally pessimistic:

> Our chief men and our chief efforts have been singularly associated with failure and frustration. …There is a deep poignancy in the fate of a remarkably long list of our chief figures from the very beginning: Phillip embittered and exhausted; Bligh disgraced; Macquarie despised here and discredited at home; Macarthur mad; Wentworth rejecting the meaning of his own achievements; Parkes bankrupt; Fisher forgotten; Bruce living in self-

chosen exile; Scullen heartbroken; Lyons dying in the midst of relentless intrigue against him; Curtin driven to desperation... and Theodore suddenly struck powerless at the very time when his power and ability were at their peak and most needed.[693]

That passage was written in 1971. The past decade may have even reinforced Mr Whitlam's sentiments. Significantly, the 'Whitlam industry' is now said to be on the way to overtaking even the Ned Kelly industry. At least 12 books have been written on the former Prime Minister since his fall in 1975. Our fascination with these subjects extends even into our own time.[694]

So here we have it. A country began as a prison, over long contemptuous of people here thousands of years before, celebrating a pathetically unsuccessful and short-lived revolt, idolising a 'desperado', annually commemorating a failed military enterprise and dealing out a generally poor hand to many of its leaders: all to the tune of 'Waltzing Matilda:' a stirring song which itself condemns lawful authority. Do we have here a contra-suggestible nation of anti-heroes? Is it all as simple as this?

The Facts of Eureka

Some would doubtless think it strange, even 126 years after the event, for a judge to take part in a celebration of the Eureka Stockade and the leadership of Peter Lalor. Certainly the Governor of Victoria at the time, Sir Charles Hotham, would have found it quite inappropriate. When he wrote to London, to report the unhappy events of the Stockade, he put forward most eloquently the view that legitimate government must always uphold and enforce even unpopular laws. This is what Hotham wrote:

> So long as a law, however obnoxious and unpopular it may be, remains in force, obedience must be rendered, or government is at an end. Concessions made to demonstrations of physical force bring their speedy retribution; the laws which regulate the gold fields are as I found them and until they are legitimately repealed or modified, it is my duty to maintain them.[695]

The dispute which broke out in the gold fields has been blamed by some upon the dishonesty of the colonial judiciary and by others on the indifference of the unelected colonial administration.

So far as the judiciary is concerned, it is said that a magistrate named Dewes wrongly, and to the outrage of the gold diggers, acquitted the owner of the Eureka Hotel of the charge of murdering a popular miner named Scobie. The community denounced the magistrate Dewes. It accused him of having a financial interest in the Eureka Hotel which led him dishonestly to protect his friend the publican. The discontent of the community at the injustice of the magistrate's action led, on 19 October 1854, to a large assembly burning the

Eureka Hotel to the ground. Later, Mr Dewes was removed from office and his conduct criticised as:

> ...tending to subvert public confidence in the integrity and impartiality of the Bench.[696]

The hotel proprietor was also charged and convicted of the manslaughter of Scobie, the digger. In a sense, the law responded to the community's demand that its procedures should be impartial and just and that guilty men should be brought to trial and punished.

The unrest which arose out of the Scobie murder on 6 October lasted to the Stockade itself. The flames of the Eureka Hotel were easily rekindled at the Stockade. The gold diggers were inflamed by an attempt of the Governor to enforce a licence fee resented as unjust, unequal and unfairly imposed.

The injustice of the fee was that it fell equally on the miners, whether or not they discovered gold. The inequality of the fee was that it fell heavily on miners whilst the landed squatters paid little or no tax. It was unfairly imposed because English liberties had been founded on the constitutional principle that there should be no taxation without Parliamentary representation. Within living memory, the American Revolution had been fought, at least in part, for this principle. Yet at the time of Eureka the principle was not observed in Victoria. Sir Robert Menzies, paying tribute to the motivation of the gold diggers' resisting the Governor's force of arms said:

> The Eureka Revolution was an earnest attempt at democratic government[697]... so far as the Eureka revolt indicated any general movement at all, it was a fierce desire to achieve true Parliamentary government and true popular control of public finance.[698]

From the Labor side of politics, it has been said that the Eureka Stockade marked the beginnings of trade unionism in Australia.[699] Dr H.V. Evatt, pointed to the fact that though English and Irish diggers took the lead, participants in the Stockade came from many countries 'united in defence of the Southern Cross'.[700] He declared that the Stockade:

> was of crucial importance in the making of Australian democracy.[701]

When Labor and Liberal politicians agree that this was an event important for Australia's national identity, democratic aspirations and resistance to unfair authority, we can safely assume that Eureka is a national and in no way a class, sectional or partisan event.

Eureka, Lalor and Law Reform

Why have I been chosen to make this address in 1980? As you have heard, I am the Chairman of the Australian Law Reform Commission. That Commission is a permanent body established by the Australian Federal Parliament for the orderly review, modernisation and simplification of the federal laws of our country. Nowadays, the pent-up frustration with unjust laws and unfair administration of those laws need not lead to a stockade, gunfire and death. Soon after the Eureka Stockade, and doubtless hastened by concerns that it should ever have come to this, Victoria adopted a system of elected Parliaments which was the first step here on the road to the modern representative democracy. One of the advantages of having lawmakers who are periodically accountable to the ordinary people through the ballot box is that laws are more likely to be made which are sensitive to the community's modern sense of fairness. Thus it was not long after an elected Parliament assembled that a different system of taxation was introduced, reforming the unjust licence fee on the gold diggers which had led to the Stockade.

Rules which courts enforce in our country are made, for the most part, by Parliament or by judges themselves. Sometimes, they get out of step with society's sense of right and wrong. Some of our criminal laws may fall into this class. Certainly, some of the earlier attitudes to women, to Aborigines, to the poor and to others may be seen today as discrimination. Attitudes to personal morality and to the role of the family appear to be changing. Law reform exists to help lawmakers cope with these difficult problems, so that they will not be swept under the carpet and met with delay and indifference as happened when the gold diggers objected to the licence fee.

Henry Lawson, commenting on those who died at Eureka, referred specifically to the fact that one of the causes for which they died was reform of bad, outdated laws:

> But not in vain the diggers died. Their comrades may rejoice;
>
> For o'er the tyranny is heard the people's voice;
>
> It says: '*Reform your rotten law,* the diggers' wrongs make right;
>
> Or else with them, our brothers now, we'll gather in the fight.[702]

The Law and Better Community Relations

One of the chief forces leading to the need for law reform today is the influx into the Australian community of so many people from a unique variety of linguistic and legal cultures. Absorption by osmosis of the common law of England, unreasonable for Old Australians, is especially unfair in the case of newcomers. For a newcomer arriving from a non-English speaking culture there is a distinct risk of legal culture shock. The provision of interpreter and translation services in courts, important though it is, is inadequate to overcome the problems of a new legal culture. Especially as more migrants come from the Middle East and Asia, the needs of adjustment are much more sophisticated. Literal translation of what is happening is merely the first step in communication. A range of measures is required to ensure that migrants understand at least the rudiments of the Australian legal system and that those involved, whether judges, police, lawyers, court clerks, social workers and others, are made sensitive by their training to the cultural characteristics and differences of a very large minority of the population of this country.

There is a great deal of evidence that the experience and expectations of migrants concerning police and legal procedures make it difficult for them to understand the way we typically do things in Australia. For example, Australian courts have adopted the adversary system of a trial. In most countries of the non-English speaking world, a different system of court trial exists under which the judge or magistrate is in charge of a judicial inquiry. Under this system, the defendant can rely on the judge to protect and even advance his interests. Under our system the judicial officer is, to a very large extent, a neutral umpire. We use juries in serious cases. In most of the countries from which we now draw our immigrants, jury trial does not exist. The Law Reform Commission's latest task on the reform of the laws of evidence in Federal Courts requires us to examine these and other issues relevant to the ethnic communities.

Quite apart from institutional differences it must be frankly acknowledged that the difficulties are not all on the one side. Cultural stereo-types about various migrant groups undoubtedly exist in the minds of many Australians, including educated Australians. The behaviour of those who work in the legal system can be distorted by such stereo-types.

It cannot be said too often that, even with the inadequate data we have on the incidence of crime in Australia, it appears quite clear that migrants do not breach the criminal law more frequently than non-migrants. Compared to people born in Australia, surveys that have been undertaken point to the fact that people born overseas tend to be much more law abiding. Proportionately, they are under-represented in our prisons. This fact is of particular interest since migrants, as a whole, come from a slightly lower socio-economic status group than the average Australian born. Crime indices tend to be higher in lower socio-economic groups, other things being equal. Yet news reporting frequently lays emphasis upon the ethnic background of an offender. Specific attention is called to his or her ethnic origin, distorting the reality which more balanced examination of the data will disclose.

Migrants and Police

Migrant contacts with the police can pose difficulties for both. In the post-war years, police in Australia had to cope with many and rapid changes in Australian society. They were confronted, often for the first time, with members of the public whose lifestyles and values were at variance with the traditional Anglo-Celtic concepts or who were unfamiliar with the procedures accepted as routine in this country. A breakdown in understanding between police and the migrant population was not unusual. For instance, a particular difficulty in police/migrant relations is the unfamiliarity of many migrants with some Australian police procedures. By way of example, fingerprinting in Italy is used only for the most serious crimes. In Australia, it is a more routine practice. For an Italian, the experience of fingerprinting can be quite traumatic. Likewise bail is most unusual in European legal systems. Many migrants have mistaken the payment of bail for payment of a fine and have been surprised by subsequent arrest for non-appearance at court.

Suggestions to overcome some of these difficulties have included the specific recruitment into police forces of more migrants, providing police with an opportunity to learn other languages, in-service training of police officers and production of information in various languages to help migrants understand their rights. The Australian Law Reform Commission suggested important safeguards in the criminal investigation process, designed to equalise the position of non-English speaking persons being interrogated by Federal police. The Federal Government adopted these recommendations in the Criminal Investigation Bill 1977.[703] However, the Bill lapsed and has not yet been re-introduced.

Migrants and the Courts

A study undertaken at the Central Court of Petty Sessions in Sydney has indicated that all migrant groups, except the Greeks, were represented in court substantially less frequently than Australian born accused in the same interval.[704] A clear association has been shown to exist between having legal representation and the outcome of criminal proceedings. A person who is represented has six and a half times better chance of securing an outright decision in his favour than an unrepresented accused. A person who is not represented appears to have a three times greater likelihood of being sent to prison than one who is represented. The New South Wales Anti-Discrimination Board has drawn attention to the importance of representation in proceedings under the Mental Health Act. Under that Act, a hearing before a magistrate determines whether or not a person involuntarily committed to a psychiatric centre, will be held for treatment and if so for how long. If further treatment is considered, the magistrate decides if the patient is to be released or detained. In the case of non-English speaking patients it is often difficult for doctors to secure a history and make a diagnosis, because of the problems of communication. Yet in practical terms, a person's liberty can depend upon his ability to communicate in such circumstances.

The Operation of the System

Sometimes without intending it, our legal system can operate unfairly upon persons from a different cultural background. In the criminal trial especially, the impression which the accused may make on a magistrate, judge or members of the jury may be critical. Yet people from different cultural backgrounds and with different accepted modes of behaviour may act in a way that seems quite alien for the simple reason that it *is* alien. Witnesses may appear excited. The fair administration of justice requires that migrants' cultural and linguistic backgrounds should be taken into account in assessing their conduct and their later evidence in court. But without regular contact with migrants and familiarity with their ways how is this fairness to be achieved?

In criminal cases, legal punishment, especially of confinement, can have an aggravated affect if the sentence is imposed on a person not able to communicate adequately in English. To be removed from an environment which is culturally familiar and from those with whom one can communicate, and imprisoned in an Australian gaol can add a special, exquisite punishment which the non-migrant prisoner may not suffer. Furthermore, the migrant removed from his or her family may leave close relatives alone, isolated, resulting in profound punitive effects that fall unequally upon innocent parties: wives, children and the old. This is not, of course, to say that migrants must be exempt from punishment for wrongdoing. It is simply to call to attention the way in which the criminal justice system, particularly, operates unevenly in its punishments in a country with a large migrant population.

Quite apart from procedural matters, there are areas of the substantive criminal law which may need to be changed to reflect our new society. One instance relates to the defence of provocation to a charge of murder. Should the standard of provocation be an objective or a subjective one? This issue was dealt with in a working paper by the Victorian Law Reform Commissioner *'Provocation as a Defence to Murder'*. The Commissioner said:

> In this State, where there is a considerable cultural mix and where it has been asserted, for example, that Melbourne has the largest Greek population of any city outside Athens, it would seem an insoluble problem to pin-point the qualities or characteristics of the ordinary man when considering such a man's (or woman's) ability or propensity to lose his (or her) self-control.

What may provoke an Italian or a Frenchman or Vietnamese beyond endurance may not be the same as what will provoke an Englishman. The time is fast approaching, if it has not already arrived, when it is quite unsafe in Australia to judge the 'ordinary man' by the characteristics of the 'ordinary Englishman'. Such an approach is perfectly valid in a society of Englishmen. It was acceptable in a community of transported, antipodean Englishmen. It may be doubted, however, whether it is still the fair standard for an Australian society whose cultural composition has so radically changed.

In fact, the process of adjustment to new national circumstances has already begun in the law. In *Glavonjic v. Foster*[705] Mr Justice Gobbo had to deal with the case of a motor accident victim, with a very limited command of English, who refused to undergo surgical treatment. The question arose as to whether his refusal was reasonable. He said he had little faith in the likely success of the operation. In judging what was reasonable the court applied the test: *what would a reasonable man in the position of the plaintiff have done*. Applying that test, it held that the plaintiff's refusal was reasonable:

> That is not to say that one simply applies a subjective test and considers whether the plaintiff thought it was reasonable for him to refuse surgery. It is, however, appropriate to adopt the test that asks whether the reasonable man in the circumstances as they existed to the plaintiff and subject to the various factors such as the difficulty of understanding and the plaintiff's medical history and condition that affected the plaintiff, would have refused treatment. In my opinion, applying the broader test, I am of the view that the defendants have not discharged the onus which is upon them.[706]

Migrant Women

Other migrant groups, perfectly law abiding, suffer special problems. Many migrants, in coming to this country, lose the support of an extended family. Women may be subject not only to the inequalities and discrimination suffered by women in many societies, including Australia. Their status as women in their own societies may conflict significantly with the status and roles expected of them in this country. A recent newspaper report revealed that many New South Wales Government funded women's refuges in Sydney are catering increasingly for women migrants. Half of the Marrickville Women's Refuge, for example, is said to comprise migrant women.

The family and employment disadvantages of women often forces them into a cocoon of their own language and culture, causing crises when they are exposed to ours. In cases of domestic violence, police in our culture (unlike others) may generally be reluctant to intrude. Yet where they do intervene it is not a criticism of the police to say that they may be more likely to accept what is said by a man able to communicate in English than by a woman who has little or no ability to speak the language. The frustration and injustice caused by this predicament is not difficult to imagine. The distress experienced by women in illegal migrant situations, where there is a family breakdown, violence or abuse is even more acute. These women are a silent group who through fear and sometimes through ignorance are unable to go to recognised authorities for protection and guidance. They are susceptible to blackmail, including from amongst their own number. It is for that reason that amnesties may be specially desirable to remove the causes of such injustice.

Migrant women may be particularly disadvantaged in understanding the Family Law Act of this country. It embodies principles which are often quite at variance with the law and customs of their country of origin. For example, in custody matters, migrant women may often assume that their husband or his family would be more likely to be granted custody of the children, as is frequently the case in other cultures. Ignorance about our legal system compounded by an inability to communicate and an ignorance of where to start is all too often the tale of the migrant in Australia with legal problems. The fear which many people have about the law and its institutions is magnified by assumptions brought from other countries and an inability, by communication, to remove misapprehensions.

The Legal Profession

In addition to all these problems, misunderstandings frequently arise between lawyers and migrants. A number of studies have indicated that migrants are more likely than native born Australians to think that lawyers are dishonest, that they are mainly interested in making money and that they tend to take the side of authority rather than their client. In many cases, there is a serious communication breakdown between a migrant and his legal advisor. One confusing aspect of the legal profession in most parts of Australia is the divided profession: solicitors and barristers. This division is simply not known in most countries from which non-English speaking migrants are drawn. In the case of migrants, the trust and understanding that may be built up over a long period of time with a solicitor must suddenly, and in their view unaccountably, be transferred to a barrister, whom they see briefly before the case, in circumstances generally of great stress and confusion.

Many studies have shown that lawyers in Australia continue to be drawn predominantly from families with high education and income backgrounds. A study of the legal profession in Victoria revealed what a small proportion of migrants make their way into the legal profession. The Bench in Australia, whether the magistracy or the judiciary is still overwhelmingly Anglo-Celtic, the last Anglo-Celtic bastion of our country. One is faced with the situation that an important profession in society, integral to the orderly running of society, does not reflect the composition and diversity of society. I can see no ready solution to this problem. But it must be kept steadily in mind for it is unhealthy for a profession so important to the just ordering of Australia to be so little affected by the radical cultural changes that are felt everywhere else. At the very least, it behoves lawyers and courts to be alert to the changes in the general Australian population and the need to review our laws and procedures to take account of those changes.

Conclusion

A large number of those who led the Eureka revolt, and not a few who died, were not English. Of course, a number were Scottish and many were Irish. But there was also a sizeable number of non Britishers. In the actual Eureka command, 'foreigners' certainly predominated. Though the Irish took a leading part, there were two Germans, including Frederick Vern, who it was that first moved that the diggers burn their licences.[707] They were joined by an American and a Canadian.[708]

Since these early days, the role in Australian life of people from countries other than the British Isles has increased apace. The Commissioner for Community Relations (Mr Grassby) has helped to bring home to us all the remarkable changes in the makeup of our country. No country other than Israel has such a high proportion of ethnic minorities. Our legal system should be sensitive to these changes. Its substantive rules, its procedures and its personnel should come to reflect, by orderly processes of reform and renewal, the changes which have taken place. Whilst clinging to the virtues of the legal system we have inherited, we should show Lalor's resolution to reform the law to meet the requirements of our new, diverse, more interesting and multi-cultural community.

Robert J. Hawke–National Economic Summit

ADDRESS AT HOUSE OF REPRESENTATIVES
Canberra, Monday, 11 April 1983
1929-2019, President of Australian Council of Trade Unions 1969-83, Prime Minister 1983-91: This welcoming address to the National Economic Summit Conference by The Hon Bob Hawke AC GCL reads as formal prose and the ideas are presented in an orderly fashion. Throughout a long public career, Hawke inclined to such language. This contrasted with his popular image as an 'ocker', which, if true at all, derived from a combination of his casual behaviour suggesting 'mateship', a nasal delivery, and other well-publicised nonverbal aspects, including standing his ground in verbal conflicts, especially with media interviewers.

On behalf of the Australian government, I have the greatest pleasure in welcoming all participants and observers to this historic National Economic Summit Conference.

And I make that welcome not only on behalf of the government of Australia, but on behalf of the people of Australia.

For in a very real sense, we meet here today as the representatives of the Australian people, in a time of Australia's gravest economic crisis in fifty years.

So it is entirely fitting that this conference should assemble in the House of Representatives in the national capital.

It is true that we have not been directly elected for the purpose of this conference.

But the conference itself springs from the very clear instruction of the Australian people, given in the national elections, just over one month ago.

I do not think there can be the slightest doubt that the proposal for this national economic conference, including its composition, has been clearly endorsed by the Australian people.

And in that sense–going to the very heart of the Australian democratic tradition–we meet here by the express will of the people of Australia.

So we meet not only as the representatives of our respective governments and organisations, but as the representatives of the Australian people.

And whatever our responsibilities and obligations to any particular group or interest or oganisation, I trust that all of us, throughout this conference, will keep to the forefront of our concerns, our wider responsibilities to the people of Australia.

They have imposed a high trust upon us. We must try our very best not to let them down.

From the outset I should emphasise that this conference has a double purpose—the purposes are both of a specific kind and of a symbolic kind.

The specific purposes of this conference may be better understood by reference to its origins. Emphatically, this was not a proposal drummed up for the purposes of the recent election campaign.

The call for it had come from many representative sections of the community. I myself had long been its advocate and in an address to the Australian Institute of Political Science Summer School on 30 January this year—a date, you will note, on which certain events were, to say the least, still unforeseen—I had this to say:

> We will convene a national summit conference with representatives from the employers, the ACTU and the State governments. This will not be some half-day superficial point-scoring exercise but a completely honest attempt to expose all of us, together, to the realities of what is happening in the domestic and international economic scene and the problems, dangers, opportunities and challenges of what is involved in those developments.
>
> As a logical extension of that process of knowledge acquisition and sharing there would then be in that context an attempt to analyse the reciprocal implications of movements in wages, profits, patterns of work and industrial reconstruction. This conference would clearly occupy several days and provision would be made for an early follow-up if the parties considered it desirable to have further discussions after the opportunity to digest and analyse the breadth of information and views presented to them.

I think it will be acknowledged that the concept and procedures which I then outlined on 30 January 1983, have been followed faithfully in the arrangements for this conference.

The results we seek—and these must be regarded as only a minimum measure of our success—should be:

First, a heightened appreciation of the need to work constructively together to meet the great challenges now confronting our country;

and second, an increased likelihood of all participants tailoring their expectations and claims upon the community's resources to the capacities of the economy, and the urgent need for a reduction in unemployment and a restoration of growth to an economy now in deep recession.

In pursuit of our specific undertaking to make this an information-sharing occasion, we have already provided a range of material for the use of all participants at this conference.

In addition, further background papers will be made available during the conference.

You will already be aware that a Steering Committee for the Summit has been established to assist in the conduct of the conference.

Its members are myself, the Premier of New South Wales, Mr Wran, the Premier of Queensland, Mr Bjelke-Petersen, Messrs Dolan, Fitzgibbon and Kelty of the ACTU, and Mr Hughes, President of CAI, Mr Bridgland, President of AIDA, and Mr John Utz (Wormald International Ltd).

You have before you the proposed Agenda for our conference.

But of course, the flow of the Agenda will be determined by the conference itself. I wholeheartedly accept that this conference should enjoy the freedom which the Parliament of this nation itself asserts—and that is the principle that this conference is master of its own destinies.

Those are among the specific purposes and procedures of this conference.

But as I have said, it also has a symbolic purpose and value.

This conference itself is part of the process of bringing Australia together.

Behind the concept of the conference lies my long-held belief—a belief I am convinced is now shared by the overwhelming majority of the Australian people—that Australia can no longer afford to go down the path of confrontation and fragmentation which has embittered and disfigured so many aspects of the national life, for much of the past decade.

It is not only a question of the need for the national reconciliation in this current economic crisis.

It goes far beyond that. It is a question of the shape of the future of Australia, as we approach the end of the twentieth century.

The twenty-first century is only seventeen years away—and that same year, indeed the very same day, the first of January 2001, will see Australia enter its second century as a united Commonwealth.

And I deeply believe that this conference has a part to play, not only in the urgent and immediate task of achieving national economic recovery—and an important part—in establishing what sort of Australia our children will inherit for the rest of the century and beyond.

So, in a double sense, this is an historic conference—historic not only in the sense that nothing of this scale and scope has been attempted before, but as an event of genuine and seminal importance in the life and history of Australia.

Let me say very firmly, that when I speak of the consensus on Australia's economic and social problems which I hope will emerge from this conference, I am not settling—and none of us should be prepared to settle—for the lowest common denominator, the barest minimum of agreement on an approach to a solution of the current crisis.

If a genuine consensus is to emerge, it must mean understanding on the part of all sections of the Australian community, of the constraints they will be called upon to accept and the contribution they will be called upon to make to the process of national reconciliation, national recovery and national reconstruction.

It will mean a recognition and acceptance of restraint by all sections of the community. It must mean a recognition—a sense of realism of what can be achieved in the near future.

We must all understand that there are no miracle cures, no overnight solutions.

It calls for a sustained, concerted national effort. This conference is only a beginning.

> Specifically, the tasks this conference should set itself are:
>
> to secure broad agreement on the role of an incomes and prices policy, in our efforts to promote employment and to achieve recovery and growth; and to ensure that the benefits of recovery are not lost in another round of the wages-prices spiral;
>
> to devise machinery for achieving the necessary restraint, including methods of wage fixation, influencing non-wage incomes, and price surveillance;
>
> to secure a better and wider understanding of the broad economic framework, within which we have to operate;
>
> to seek broad agreement on the relationship between successful prices and incomes policy and the implementation of policies on industrial relations, job creation and training, taxation, social security, health, education, and the other major community services;
>
> to examine the competitiveness and efficiency of the Australian economy;
>
> and finally, to reach agreement on arrangements and machinery to monitor and continue the work of this conference, especially in regard to continuing the process of consultation and co-operation between government, business and unions, initiated by this conference itself.

And of course, I must repeat what I made very clear during the recent election campaign.

This conference and its outcome can in no way be a substitute for effective government policies. The governments of Australia, and in particular, the national government, cannot escape and do not wish to escape their primary and fundamental responsibility for the economic and social policies of this nation. But effective policy can not be made in a vacuum. Decisions that are going to achieve our great national objectives can not be made in isolation from economic and social realities.

And the purpose of this conference is to expose us all, including those with direct responsibility for government decision-making, to those realities—the realities of the current situation and the realities of what must be done if there is to be a resolution of Australia's present crisis.

I shall not pre-empt the Treasurer, who will later address you on the economic position and outlook.

But, while Mr Keating will outline the serious and complex nature of the problems, there can be no doubt that they are encapsulated in the question of unemployment, and the need for a restoration of sustained economic growth which avoids a new bout of destructive inflation. The first problem is how to arrest the explosion of unemployment level and then move towards its steady reduction, with the ultimate goal of genuine full employment as fundamental national economic policy—the bipartisan goal adopted for the first three decades of the post-war era.

It is easy enough to quote all the grim statistics which show that we face the worst economic crisis since the Great Depression itself. But behind the statistics lies an even grimmer human reality.

The raw statistics do not show what unemployment means in terms of the loss of human dignity and self-respect, what it means in terms of the break-up of families and the social alienation of one-third of the best and brightest generation we have ever produced, what it means in terms of the defeat of human hope and the crushing of the human spirit.

The statistics do not show the special difficulties faced by particular groups—the particular burdens placed on young people, on women in the workforce, on single parents, on migrants, on aborigines. There are identifiable groups in this community experiencing unemployment at levels as high as, or even higher than, any ever experienced in the worst years of the Great Depression itself.

For example, total unemployment in 1932—the worst year—reached 29 percent. Unemployment in the 15 to 19 age group is already at least as high as that.

It is true that today we have a social security network far in advance of any that existed 50 years ago.

But while the material deprivation of unemployment may not be now so severe, yet, in another sense, unemployment in the 1980s imposes a burden more crushing than in the 1930s.

And the reason for that is that the expectations to which the people are entitled, are now so much higher—and so they should be.

This is particularly true for the younger generation which is bearing the heaviest brunt of the present recession.

And let us never forget—because it is a measure of our personal responsibility—that it is our generation which taught the new generation to hold those expectations, and that sense of entitlement of what this rich, advanced nation of ours should offer them.

We cannot escape our personal responsibility.

This conference gives us all an unprecedented opportunity to fulfil at least a small part of that responsibility, individually and collectively, in both the personal sense and the national sense.

When we look around the world today, we can see that those comparable countries—comparable in their political, economic and industrial systems, comparable in their standards of living, comparable in their national aspirations—which have had most success in surmounting the present international economic crisis, are those where governments, business and unions and the community as a whole, have agreed on common goals and objectives and have co-operated together for their achievement.

We have to remember at all times that Australia, in common with the rest of the industrialised world, is passing through one of the most dramatic periods of social, economic and technological changes in recorded human history. We have to be prepared for social and economic responses as innovative and radical as the technological achievements which are creating this profound revolution in human affairs, in lifestyles, in work patterns and opportunities. We cannot put the clock back.

This leads me to the very heart of what I believe we must be about in this conference and the time ahead. So often in our affairs the emphasis has been put upon the competing struggle between wage and salary earners and business, and residually, welfare recipients.

I believe we must come to put the emphasis upon the fact that they all have a common goal and therefore a common interest. They all seek the same thing—the maintenance, and through time, an improvement, of their standards of living. The indispensable condition for the achievement of this common legitimate goal is real economic growth—an increase in the per capita output of goods and services.

The attitudes, assumptions and expectations of those participants in the economic and social processes have been fashioned by the environment in which they operated. For a generation and a half that environment was characterised by the conditions of full employment, low inflation and steady economic growth. Such an environment was able, with relative ease, to accommodate the uncoordinated—indeed, adversary-type—pursuit of competing claims. While this process certainly did not provide optimal real growth, the growth that did occur sustained the process.

For a range of reasons applying not only to our own country but operating in varying degree throughout the world, those conditions no longer characterise our economy–indeed the opposite conditions of high unemployment, high inflation and recessed, even negative, growth are now the predominant characteristics.

In all aspects of human behaviour there is always a time-lag in the perceptions of change in the relevant environment. This has been true of us here in Australia in the way we have conducted our economic and social affairs. The attitudes, assumptions and expectations which reflected a former environment are no longer adequate to meet the changed circumstances which characterise our more recent and present condition.

Yet the common goal–the goal of maintaining and increasing standards–remains legitimate. The very essence of our mutual task now is to work together to recreate those conditions in which the achievement of that legitimate, common, goal is possible.

We can restore growth and we can significantly reduce inflation. The task of restoring full employment as we knew it will be harder. But we can, if we work together with this sense of common purpose, also make real progress towards that goal. To move again towards balance in the field of employment, we must of course make decisions calculated to produce more jobs. We must also, I believe, as a concerned society together examine the other side of the equation–the demand for jobs–to see whether we may be able to provide fulfilment in life for some of our people alongside the conventional production system.

It is of the greatest importance that we should make the right economic decisions. But that is not enough. There is no single "correct" decision that can of itself solve our present economic and social problems–any more than a single "wrong" decision was responsible for the present crisis. While I am confident that this conference will help significantly to create the framework for better decision-making and a better economic performance in this nation, that is only a beginning. It will not be enough for any of us to say at the end of this conference: "So much for that–the rest is up to the government". Both the immediate problems to which we are addressing ourselves and these more far-reaching challenges to the whole social, economic and industrial fabric of the nation, require much more than that. They call for a deep and continuing commitment by governments and the community alike. They call for the application of those qualities of innovation, initiative, independence, tolerance–and need I say, mateship–the qualities which we like to think are distinctively Australian.

It is not without significance that Australia's unemployment has now reached the level to which it had risen at the outbreak of the Second World War, which itself prevented the onset of another Depression. That is one measure of the magnitude of the task before us.

During the recent campaign, I frequently drew the parallel between the supreme crisis of the early 1940s and the present crisis.

Of course, the two are very different in nature and scale. Survival itself was at stake in 1942. But in one sense, the present crisis is more complex and at least as challenging to our resourcefulness as a people. Then, the challenge was clear, identifiable and external. Today, the chief challenge comes from within.

But now as then—every bit as much as in 1942—the essential requirement for victory remains the same—the united effort of a united people working together to achieve agreed goals and common objectives.

More than forty years ago, one of the very greatest of all Australians stood in this place in this historic chamber to give this message to the people of Australia. On that occasion, 16 December 1941, John Curtin said:

> Our Australian mode of life, our conditions, our seasons, all that go to make up the natural conditions of living, make us better equipped (for the purpose of meeting this crisis) than are the peoples of many other countries... the qualitative capacity of our population compensates in large measure for the shortage of our numbers... I, like each of you, have seen this country at work, engaged in pleasure, and experiencing adversity; I have seen it face good times and evil times, but I have never known a time in which the inherent quality of Australia has to be used so unstintingly as at this hour.

My fellow Australians, I do not pretend to compare the scale of the crisis through which John Curtin steered this nation to triumph with our task today.

But I do believe that the essential elements which John Curtin defined as the key to victory are as relevant in 1983 as they were in 1941.

And by far the most important of all is the quality of our people. I do not believe for one moment that the essential quality of our people has in any way declined since 1941. On the contrary, it has been enriched and strengthened by the contribution of the millions of our fellow citizens drawn from nearly every country and race around the world.

If we at this conference dedicate ourselves to provide leadership to this great people, I have absolute confidence that they will respond with a united effort and a renewed determination to beat this crisis and to build an even better future for this great nation, Australia.

Sallyanne Atkinson–Expo '88 Welcome Speech

EXPO '88 OPENING CEREMONY
World Expo '88, South Brisbane, Saturday, 30 April 1988
Born 1942, The Right Honourable Lord Mayor of Brisbane 1985-91: In two terms as Lord Mayor of the largest city council in Australia, Sallyanne Atkinson AO led initiatives that made significant changes to the City. Among other accomplishments, she encouraged residents to adjust their way of life, for enjoyment of the river, outdoor dining, and facilities for the arts. In this opening address for the World Expo event that helped catalyse some of these changes, at one of the sites later redeveloped in this new Brisbane, she illuminated the character of the City and its people, and invited all to celebrate the excitement that was to come.

I am very proud this morning to be Lord Mayor of Brisbane.

Expo 88 is something like a coming of age celebration for our City. We are honoured and delighted that Your Majesty and Your Royal Highness are the guests of honour at our party.

Today is the opening of a six month event to which we have invited the rest of the world. Today we formally and officially become an international city.

Your Majesty and Your Royal Highness have been part of the growing-up process. When you first came here more than 30 years ago we were still a city finding its feet.

Back in 1954, we felt we were living in a large country town, friendly and relaxed. City Hall was our tallest building, the railway tracks (and the train) still held up traffic as they crossed the road at the 'Gabba, and Southerners called Brisbane a cultural desert.

Now, you can hardly see the clock tower on City Hall for the tall buildings that surround it; Queen Street, where the trams used to run, is now a sophisticated pedestrian mall; and the Cultural Centre on the Riverbank is the nation's best.

But we are still friendly and relaxed, and we want you to know how welcome you are now and how very much part of our life as a city.

You were here for that other grand growing-up event, the Commonwealth Games, when the rest of Australia came to understand that Brisbane is a "can-do" city with abundant natural resources, the best of which are its people. That was our transition period, our adolescence.

Now as the capital of Australia's fastest growing state on the edge of the Pacific Rim, the fastest growing region in the world, we feel not only proud of our past, but confident of the future.

Expo is our opportunity to show off to the world, to invite other nations to witness, share and enjoy the exciting and dynamic city that is Brisbane.

But most of all it is an opportunity for the people of Brisbane to say to Your Majesty and to Your Royal Highness, that we are glad that you have been with us along the way, and that you are most especially welcome today.

We hope you enjoy our party.

Paul Keating–Redfern Park Speech

AUSTRALIAN LAUNCH OF THE INTERNATIONAL YEAR
FOR THE WORLD'S INDIGENOUS PEOPLE
Redfern Park, Sydney, Thursday, 10 December 1992
Born 1944, Prime Minister 1991-6: The Hon Paul Keating presented this landmark speech inviting reconciliation as a clear statement from the head of government, anticipating continuing changes to Australian laws to improve rights for First Nations. With decades now passed since Keating's call for tangible reconciliation, the speech has endured as a powerful statement that respects the self-determination, values, and rights of First Nations.

Ladies and gentlemen,

I am very pleased to be here today at the launch of Australia's celebration of the 1993 International Year of the World's Indigenous People.

It will be a year of great significance for Australia.

It comes at a time when we have committed ourselves to succeeding in the test which so far we have always failed.

Because, in truth, we cannot confidently say that we have succeeded as we would like to have succeeded if we have not managed to extend opportunity and care, dignity and hope to the indigenous people of Australia–the Aboriginal and Torres Strait Island people.

This is a fundamental test of our social goals and our national will: our ability to say to ourselves and the rest of the world that Australia is a first-rate social democracy, that we are what we should be–truly the land of the fair go and the better chance.

There is no more basic test of how seriously we mean these things.

It is a test of our self-knowledge.

Of how well we know the land we live in. How well we know our history.

How well we recognise the fact that, complex as our contemporary identity is, it cannot be separated from Aboriginal Australia.

How well we know what Aboriginal Australians know about Australia.

Redfern is a good place to contemplate these things.

Just a mile or two from the place where the first European settlers landed, in too many ways it tells us that their failure to bring much more than devastation and demoralisation to Aboriginal Australia continues to be our failure.

More I think than most Australians recognise, the plight of Aboriginal Australians affects us all.

In Redfern it might be tempting to think that the reality Aboriginal Australians face is somehow contained here, and that the rest of us are insulated from it.

But of course, while all the dilemmas may exist here, they are far from contained.

We know the same dilemmas and more are faced all over Australia.

That is perhaps the point of this Year of the World's Indigenous People: to bring the dispossessed out of the shadows, to recognise that they are part of us, and that we cannot give indigenous Australians up without giving up many of our own most deeply held values, much of our own identity—and our own humanity.

Nowhere in the world, I would venture, is the message more stark than it is in Australia.

We simply cannot sweep injustice aside. Even if our own conscience allowed us to, I am sure, that in due course, the world and the people of our region would not.

There should be no mistake about this—our success in resolving these issues will have a significant bearing on our standing in the world.

However intractable the problems seem, we cannot resign ourselves to failure—any more than we can hide behind the contemporary version of Social Darwinism which says that to reach back for the poor and dispossessed is to risk being dragged down.

That seems to me not only morally indefensible, but bad history.

We non-Aboriginal Australians should perhaps remind ourselves that Australia once reached out for us.

Didn't Australia provide opportunity and care for the dispossessed Irish? The poor of Britain? The refugees from war and famine and persecution in the countries of Europe and Asia?

Isn't it reasonable to say that if we can build a prosperous and remarkably harmonious multicultural society in Australia, surely we can find just solutions to the problems which beset the first Australians—the people to whom the most injustice has been done.

And, as I say, the starting point might be to recognise that the problem starts with us non-Aboriginal Australians.

It begins, I think, with that act of recognition.

Recognition that it was we who did the dispossessing.

We took the traditional lands and smashed the traditional way of life.

We brought the diseases. The alcohol.

We committed the murders.

We took the children from their mothers.

We practised discrimination and exclusion.

It was our ignorance and our prejudice.

And our failure to imagine these things being done to us.

With some noble exceptions, we failed to make the most basic human response and enter into their hearts and minds.

We failed to ask–how would I feel if this were done to me? As a consequence, we failed to see that what we were doing degraded all of us.

If we needed a reminder of this, we received it this year.

The Report of the Royal Commission into Aboriginal Deaths in Custody showed with devastating clarity that the past lives on in inequality, racism and injustice.

In the prejudice and ignorance of non-Aboriginal Australians, and in the demoralisation and desperation, the fractured identity, of so many Aborigines and Torres Strait Islanders.

For all this, I do not believe that the Report should fill us with guilt.

Down the years, there has been no shortage of guilt, but it has not produced the responses we need.

Guilt is not a very constructive emotion.

I think what we need to do is open our hearts a bit.

All of us.

Perhaps when we recognise what we have in common we will see the things which must be done–the practical things.

There is something of this in the creation of the Council for Aboriginal Reconciliation.

The Council's mission is to forge a new partnership built on justice and equity and an appreciation of the heritage of Australia's indigenous people.

In the abstract those terms are meaningless.

We have to give meaning to "justice" and "equity"–and, as I have said several times this year, we will only give them meaning when we commit ourselves to achieving concrete results.

If we improve the living conditions in one town, they will improve in another. And another.

If we raise the standard of health by twenty per cent one year, it will be raised more the next.

If we open one door others will follow.

When we see improvement, when we see more dignity, more confidence, more happiness–we will know we are going to win.

We need these practical building blocks of change.

The Mabo Judgement should be seen as one of these.

By doing away with the bizarre conceit that this continent had no owners prior to the settlement of Europeans, Mabo establishes a fundamental truth and lays the basis for justice.

It will be much easier to work from that basis than has ever been the case in the past.

For that reason alone we should ignore the isolated outbreaks of hysteria and hostility of the past few months.

Mabo is an historic decision—we can make it an historic turning point, the basis of a new relationship between indigenous and non-Aboriginal Australians.

The message should be that there is nothing to fear or to lose in the recognition of historical truth, or the extension of social justice, or the deepening of Australian social democracy to include indigenous Australians.

There is everything to gain.

Even the unhappy past speaks for this.

Where Aboriginal Australians have been included in the life of Australia they have made remarkable contributions.

Economic contributions, particularly in the pastoral and agricultural industry. They are there in the frontier and exploration history of Australia.

They are there in the wars.

In sport to an extraordinary degree.

In literature and art and music.

In all these things they have shaped our knowledge of this continent and of ourselves. They have shaped our identity.

They are there in the Australian legend.

We should never forget—they have helped build this nation.

And if we have a sense of justice, as well as common sense, we will forge a new partnership.

As I said, it might help us if we non-Aboriginal Australians imagined ourselves dispossessed of land we had lived on for fifty thousand years—and then imagined ourselves told that it had never been ours.

Imagine if ours was the oldest culture in the world and we were told that it was worthless.

Imagine if we had resisted this settlement, suffered and died in the defence of our land, and then were told in history books that we had given up without a fight.

Imagine if non-Aboriginal Australians had served their country in peace and war and were then ignored in history books.

Imagine if our feats on sporting fields had inspired admiration and patriotism and yet did nothing to diminish prejudice.

Imagine if our spiritual life was denied and ridiculed.

Imagine if we had suffered the injustice and then were blamed for it.

It seems to me that if we can imagine the injustice we can imagine its opposite.

And we can have justice.

I say that for two reasons:

I say it because I believe that the great things about Australian social democracy reflect a fundamental belief in justice.

And I say it because in so many other areas we have proved our capacity over the years to go on extending the realms of participation, opportunity and care.

Just as Australians living in the relatively narrow and insular Australia of the 1960s imagined a culturally diverse, worldly and open Australia, and in a generation turned the idea into reality, so we can turn the goals of reconciliation into reality.

There are very good signs that the process has begun.

The creation of the Reconciliation Council is evidence itself.

The establishment of the ATSIC–the Aboriginal and Torres Strait Islander Commission–is also evidence.

The Council is the product of imagination and good will.

ATSIC emerges from the vision of indigenous self-determination and self-management.

The vision has already become the reality of almost 800 elected Aboriginal Regional Councillors and Commissioners determining priorities and developing their own programmes.

All over Australia, Aboriginal and Torres Strait Islander communities are taking charge of their own lives.

And assistance with the problems which chronically beset them is at last being made available in ways developed by the communities themselves.

If these things offer hope, so does the fact that this generation of Australians is better informed about Aboriginal culture and achievement, and about the injustice that has been done, than any generation before.

We are beginning to more generally appreciate the depth and the diversity of Aboriginal and Torres Strait Islander cultures.

From their music and art and dance we are beginning to recognise how much richer our national life and identity will be for the participation of Aboriginals and Torres Strait Islanders.

We are beginning to learn what the indigenous people have known for many thousands of years–how to live with our physical environment.

Ever so gradually we are learning how to see Australia through Aboriginal eyes, beginning to recognise the wisdom contained in their epic story.

I think we are beginning to see how much we owe the indigenous Australians and how much we have lost by living so apart.

I said we non-indigenous Australians should try to imagine the Aboriginal view.

It can't be too hard. Someone imagined this event today, and it is now a marvellous reality and a great reason for hope.

There is one thing today we cannot imagine.

We cannot imagine that the descendants of people whose genius and resilience maintained a culture here through fifty thousand years or more, through cataclysmic changes to the climate and environment, and who then survived two centuries of dispossession and abuse, will be denied their place in the modern Australian nation.

We cannot imagine that.

We cannot imagine that we will fail.

And with the spirit that is here today I am confident that we won't. I am confident that we will succeed in this decade.

Thank you.

John Howard–Gun Rally

ADDRESS ON GUN LAWS AFTER PORT ARTHUR
Sale, Victoria, Friday, 10 May 1996
Born 1939, Prime Minister 1996-2007: The Hon John Howard OM AC moved with speed to comprehensively transform gun ownership when Australians were shocked by the Port Arthur massacre, in which 35 people died. His success was to secure the cooperative effort of governments and law enforcement in all Australian states. In this speech to opponents of the gun reform, with language characteristically plain-spoken, Howard made repeated acknowledgement of the loss to be experienced by gun owners, while firmly advancing new laws for gun control that recognised how democratic government operates for the good of all.

Well thank you very much Peter McGauran, to my other Parliamentary colleagues, to my fellow Australians.

Last night I saw on national television Mr Ted Drane, the National President of the shooters' organisations in Australia–And he said something with which I totally agree. He said that he and his fellow shooters were not criminals, they were Australians. And I want to start my address to you today by saying at no stage in the weeks that have gone by since the decision taken by the Federal Government and the Police Ministers in that decision, at no stage have I sought to describe or categorise the attitude of people who enjoy shooting or people who are shooters as being in anyway criminal or un-Australian. I have not used language which has thought to label or smear you or other tens of thousands of law abiding citizens.

I acknowledge and I have acknowledged in the very beginning and I do so again today, that the decisions that have been taken by all the Governments in Australia, decisions that were confirmed last Friday at the Premiers' Conference meeting, they are decisions that will inconvenience, they will influence the activities of people who hitherto have engaged in law-abiding pursuits. And at no stage is it the basis of the decision taken by the Federal Government and at no stage is it part of my own personal attitude that in any way any of you or any people who have been involved in what are, up until now, the lawful possession of firearms, in no way have you people been involved in criminal behaviour at no stage. And that is not the basis of the decision. But the basis of the decision ladies and gentlemen is that we believe that it is in the national interest that there be a dramatic reduction in the number of automatic and semi-automatic weapons in the Australian community.

In taking that decision I recognise and my colleagues recognise that many people who previously have been carrying on a lawful pursuit are going to be inconvenienced. I know that, I regret that, I apologise for that but that is the basis of our decision. And it has been taken, ladies and gentlemen because we believe not just because of those tragic events at Port Arthur, they were the culmination of a long series of events in this country which have demonstrated as has been demonstrated in other parts of the world, that there is a clear link between the volume of powerful weapons in the community and the extent to which they are used in an indiscriminate manner

If you look at these statistics out of countries such as the United States, if you compare them with statistics in other parts of the world there is a clear and irrefutable link. And in taking the decisions that we have taken we are mindful that they will impact unevenly on sections of the community.

I am mindful that people who have never owned a weapon, have never had any desire to own a weapon are not going to be affected in the way in which people such as you are being affected. I know that, I regret that and that is a matter of concern and apology to me but it cannot alter the responsibility of a national Government to take a decision that it believes serves the greater good of the entire Australian community. And that my fellow Australians is the basis of the decision that we have taken. We have not sought in taking this decision to brand any of you people as being anti-social. We have not sought in taking this decision to brand people who enjoy shooting as being engaged in any kind of criminal activity and you will find nothing that I have said and you will find nothing that I will say in the future that will in any way take that attitude.

But there come occasions for any Government to take decisions which can only be effectively implemented in the interests of the overall national good if they involve some disproportionate inconvenience and some disproportionate deprivation for one section of the community. I'm sorry about that but there is no other way that we can achieve the objectives. And it is always, my friends it is always the responsibility of a national Government to weigh up the gains and to set them against the losses. And the gains to the Australian community of there being fewer weapons of great destruction in the community are, in my view and in the view of all governments throughout Australia very, very significant indeed and that is why we have taken the decision.

Now I don't pretend for a moment ladies and gentlemen that the decision that we have taken is going to guarantee that in the future there won't be other mass murders. I don't pretend that for a moment. What I do argue to you my friends is that it will significantly reduce the likelihood of those occurring in the future. I wouldn't be so foolish as to say that it is going to completely eliminate them. And I know that in the wake of what happened at Port Arthur I know ladies and gentlemen in the wake of what happened at Port Arthur that people have argued that one of the great weaknesses in the present system and one of the causes of mass murder is that we have an approach to mental health laws that are too permissive.

I certainly agree with that and one of things that I said after the decisions had been taken in relation to automatic and semi-automatic weapons was that we are going to investigate whether the practice of governments throughout Australia over the last years in pushing too many people too soon out of mental health institutions unsupervised into the community, whether in fact those practices ought to change. And that is one of the things that we are going to examine.

And I've also expressed the personal view that is shared by many people throughout Australia that one of the causes of the inculcation of violence in our community is the mind-numbing, repetitive violence that is seen on some of our television screens. And I think that along with the approach to mental health issues, they are other issues that must be seriously examined by society.

I don't pretend that it is simply a matter of imposing a stricter regime regarding the possession of automatic or semi-automatic weapons. But that is an element of turning around the culture in this country and that is the reason why the Government has taken the decision that it has taken.

And I've come here today ladies and gentlemen as I will go to other rural areas of Australia and other provincial areas of Australia to explain directly to people who I know are unhappy with the Government's decision, to go to explain directly to those people the general basis of that decision, to remind you that the effect of the Government's decision is not to take all weapons out of the community.

The effect of the Government's decision has been very, very carefully designed to ensure that, for example, the legitimate use of farmers, of weapons, the entitlement of farmers if they can demonstrate a need to the possession of the low-powered semiautomatic weapons will be retained and the whole purpose of the firearm regulations that have been devised by all the Governments of Australia is to ensure that we achieve our overall objectives of a dramatic withdrawal of the number of potential weapons of destruction from the Australian community.

That is our goal, that is the objective and it is a responsible objective. But in the process we have sought to make reasonable provisions in areas such as primary production. We have also, as you know, decided to introduce an effective, fair compensation scheme for weapons based upon the value of weapons as at March 1996. The goal of the compensation scheme which will be fully met by the Federal Government out of the proceeds of one-oft; special increase in the Medicare levy, which is predicted to raise something like 500 million dollars and if there is any surplus, that surplus will be returned through the health insurance levy system so that there will be no money kept out of that other than the money that is used for the compensation scheme.

But ladies and gentlemen the intention is to pay fair compensation for weapons. That is the intention and that is the commitment and there will be a 12 month amnesty during which any of the weapons that are prohibited as a consequence of the decisions taken by the Government can be handed in and proper, fair compensation will be paid. And I give you that undertaking. I acknowledge that we are asking you to give up, we are taking away property you have previously lawfully owned and in those circumstances you are entitled as Australians under the Constitution of this country to have proper compensation based on fair value as at the time of the decision taken by the Government in March of 1996.

I have read during the past few weeks some reactions to the decision taken by the Government. I acknowledge that many of those reactions, although very strong and very vigorous and very determined have been absolutely measured and the sort of reaction that you would expect in a strong, robust, democratic country such as Australia. But I have also heard suggestions, for example, that the whole idea of this is to bring about the complete disarming of the Australian population. I've heard people make suggestions that this is the first step in some kind of march along a road to the deprivation of peoples' individual liberties. I want to say to you ladies and gentlemen that that is a totally unreasonable, it is a totally inaccurate and it is a totally discredited response to the decision that has been taken by the Government. The decision taken by the Government is not part and parcel of some plan to deprive Australians of their liberty. The decision taken by the Government is taken because we are committed to generating a safer Australian community and that is an aspiration. That is an aspiration that hundreds of thousands, indeed millions of Australians support the decision taken.

So ladies and gentlemen, they support it not only in the urban areas of Australia but they support it throughout the rural and provincial areas of Australia as well. I understand why, I understand why many of you feel angry. I understand why many of you are here today to protest against the decision. I fully understand that and I can sympathise with people who have spent a life in a particular sporting pursuit and they find that life is no longer available to them and that is something that I deeply regret and I do deeply regret it but it does not alter the commitment of the Government in the aggregate national good to take decisions which we believe and all governments around Australia believe will bring about a safer Australian community, and that my friends is a proper objective of Government. It is a democratic objective of Government and in taking that decision and implementing that here what we had sought to do my friends is to frame the regulations and to frame the laws in such a way, ladies and gentlemen that people who have legitimate primary industry needs that the retention of weapons that aren't in the automatic or semi-automatic category will be allowed. We are not touching those, we are introducing a regime for registration that will be nation-wide. It's a registration regime that will bring about a significant reduction of weapons, dangerous weapons in the Australian community. And we have based it upon an approach that will give people fair compensation based upon values as at March 1996.

So ladies and gentlemen, I've come here today to explain to you as directly and as simply as I can the basis of the decision, the reason why we have taken it, the reason why, however reluctant you may be to do so to accept that it has been taken in good faith by the Government in the belief that it will add to the overall safety and good of the Australian community.

And that is the greatest and ultimate responsibility of any Government of any Prime Minister of this country, whatever his political stripe, is to take decisions that if he believes or she believes will benefit the overall national good and that is the reason behind this decision.

Ladies and gentlemen I thank you for coming, I thank you for giving me the opportunity, however much many of you will disagree with me, to explain the basis of the Government's decision I would be very happy to answer questions that you might like to ask and I've agreed to meet after the meeting with some representatives of the shooter organisation here in Victoria.

Ladies and gentlemen thank you for coming and I would be very happy to answer any of your questions.

Julia Gillard–Misogyny Speech

RESPONSE TO MOTION OF LEADER OF THE OPPOSITION
House of Representatives, Canberra, Wednesday, 10 October 2012
Born 1961, Prime Minister 2010-13: The Hon Julia Gillard AC here eviscerated, with a debater's precision, a motion of the Leader of the Opposition that had proposed to remove the Speaker of the House over alleged impropriety. By recalling again and again some occasions on which the Leader of the Opposition reportedly demonstrated his own inappropriate behaviour, Gillard turned the tables to represent his motion as peddling hypocrisy. She closed by reasserting what standards free of sexism and hypocrisy she believed Parliament should observe.

Thank you very much Deputy Speaker and I rise to oppose the motion moved by the Leader of the Opposition. And in so doing I say to the Leader of the Opposition I will not be lectured about sexism and misogyny by this man. I will not. And the Government will not be lectured about sexism and misogyny by this man. Not now, not ever.

The Leader of the Opposition says that people who hold sexist views and who are misogynists are not appropriate for high office. Well I hope the Leader of the Opposition has got a piece of paper and he is writing out his resignation. Because if he wants to know what misogyny looks like in modern Australia, he doesn't need a motion in the House of Representatives, he needs a mirror. That's what he needs.

Let's go through the Opposition Leader's repulsive double standards, repulsive double standards when it comes to misogyny and sexism. We are now supposed to take seriously that the Leader of the Opposition is offended by Mr Slipper's text messages, when this is the Leader of the Opposition who has said, and this was when he was a minister under the last government—not when he was a student, not when he was in high school—when he was a minister under the last government.

He has said, and I quote, in a discussion about women being under-represented in institutions of power in Australia, the interviewer was a man called

Stavros. The Leader of the Opposition says 'If it's true, Stavros, that men have more power generally speaking than women, is that a bad thing'?

And then a discussion ensues, and another person being interviewed says 'I want my daughter to have as much opportunity as my son'. To which the Leader of the Opposition says, 'Yeah, I completely agree, but what if men are by physiology or temperament, more adapted to exercise authority or to issue command'?

Then ensues another discussion about women's role in modern society, and the other person participating in the discussion says, 'I think it's very hard to deny that there is an underrepresentation of women', to which the Leader of the Opposition says, 'But now, there's an assumption that this is a bad thing'.

This is the man from whom we're supposed to take lectures about sexism. And then of course it goes on. I was very offended personally when the Leader of the Opposition, as Minister for Health, said, and I quote, 'Abortion is the easy way out'. I was very personally offended by those comments. You said that in March 2004, I suggest you check the records.

I was also very offended on behalf of the women of Australia when in the course of this carbon pricing campaign, the Leader of the Opposition said 'What the housewives of Australia need to understand as they do the ironing…' Thank you for that painting of women's roles in modern Australia.

And then of course, I was offended too by the sexism, by the misogyny of the Leader of the Opposition catcalling across this table at me, as I sit here as Prime Minister, 'If the Prime Minister wants to, politically speaking, make an honest woman of herself…', something that would never have been said to any man sitting in this chair. I was offended when the Leader of the Opposition went outside in the front of Parliament and stood next to a sign that said, 'Ditch the witch'.

I was offended when the Leader of the Opposition stood next to a sign that described me as a man's bitch. I was offended by those things. Misogyny, sexism, every day from this Leader of the Opposition. Every day in every way, across the time the Leader of the Opposition has sat in that chair and I've sat in this chair, that is all we have heard from him.

And now, the Leader of the Opposition wants to be taken seriously, apparently he's woken up after this track record and all of these statements, he's woken up and he's gone, 'Oh dear, there's this thing called sexism, oh my lord, there's this thing called misogyny. Now who's one of them? Oh, the Speaker must be because that suits my political purpose'.

Doesn't turn a hair about any of his past statements, doesn't walk into this Parliament and apologise to the women of Australia. Doesn't walk into this Parliament and apologise to me for the things that have come out of his mouth. But now seeks to use this as a battering ram against someone else.

Well this kind of hypocrisy should not be tolerated, which is why this motion from the Leader of the Opposition should not be taken seriously.

And then second, the Leader of the Opposition is always wonderful about walking into this Parliament and giving me and others a lecture about what they should take responsibility for.

Always wonderful about that—everything that I should take responsibility for, now apparently including the text messages of the Member for Fisher. Always keen to say others should assume responsibility, particularly me.

Well can anybody remind me if the Leader of the Opposition has taken any responsibility for the conduct of the Sydney Young Liberals and the attendance at this event of members of his frontbench?

Has he taken any responsibility for the conduct of members of his political party and members of his frontbench who apparently when the most vile things were being said about my family, raised no voice of objection? No-one walked out of the room; no-one walked up to Mr Jones and said that this was not acceptable.

Instead of course, it was all viewed as good fun until it was run in a Sunday newspaper and then the Leader of the Opposition and others started ducking for cover.

Big on lectures of responsibility, very light on accepting responsibility himself for the vile conduct of members of his political party.

Third, Ms Deputy Speaker, why the Leader of the Opposition should not be taken seriously on this motion.

The Leader of the Opposition and the Deputy Leader of the Opposition have come into this place and have talked about the Member for Fisher. Well, let me remind the Opposition and the Leader of the Opposition particularly about their track record and association with the Member for Fisher.

I remind them that the National Party preselected the Member for Fisher for the 1984 election, that the National Party preselected the Member for Fisher for the 1987 election, that the Liberal Party preselected Mr Slipper for the 1993 election, then the 1996 election, then the 1998 election, then for the 2001 election, then for the 2004 election, then for the 2007 election and then for the 2010 election.

And across many of those pre-selections, Mr Slipper enjoyed the personal support of the Leader of the Opposition. I remind the Leader of the Opposition that on 28 September 2010, following the last election campaign, when Mr Slipper was elected as Deputy Speaker, the Leader of the Opposition at that stage said this, and I quote.

He referred to the Member for Maranoa, who was also elected to a position at the same time, and then went on as follows, 'And the Member for Fisher will serve as a fine complement to the Member for Scullin in the chair. I believe that the Parliament will be well-served by the team which will occupy the chair in this chamber. I congratulate the Member for Fisher, who has been a friend of mine for a very long time, who has served this Parliament in many capacities with distinction'.

The words of the Leader of the Opposition on record, about his personal friendship with Mr Slipper, and on record about his view about Mr Slipper's qualities and attributes to be the Speaker.

No walking away from those words, they were the statement of the Leader of the Opposition then. I remind the Leader of the Opposition, who now comes in here and speaks about Mr Slipper and apparently his inability to work with or talk to Mr Slipper. I remind the Leader of the Opposition he attended Mr Slipper's wedding.

Did he walk up to Mr Slipper in the middle of the service and say he was disgusted to be there? Was that the attitude he took? No, he attended that wedding as a friend.

The Leader of the Opposition, keen to lecture others about what they ought to know or did know about Mr Slipper. Well with respect, I'd say to the Leader of the Opposition after a long personal association, including attending Mr Slipper's wedding, it would be interesting to know whether the Leader of the Opposition was surprised by these text messages.

He's certainly in a position to speak more intimately about Mr Slipper than I am, and many other people in this Parliament, given this long personal association.

Then, of course, the Leader of the Opposition comes into this place and says, and I quote, 'Every day the Prime Minister stands in this Parliament to defend this Speaker will be another day of shame for this Parliament, another day of shame for a government which should already have died of shame'.

Well can I indicate to the Leader of the Opposition, the Government is not dying of shame, my father did not die of shame, what the Leader of the Opposition should be ashamed of is his performance in this Parliament and the sexism he brings with it. Now about the text messages that are on the public record or reported in the—that's a direct quote from the Leader of the Opposition, so I suggest those groaning have a word with him.

Now, on the conduct of Mr Slipper, and on the text messages that are in the public domain, I have seen the press reports of those text messages. I am offended by their content. I am offended by their content because I am always offended by sexism. I am offended by their content because I am always offended by statements that are anti-women.

I am offended by those things in the same way that I have been offended by things that the Leader of the Opposition has said, and no doubt will continue to say in the future. Because if this today was an exhibition of his new feminine side, well I don't think we've got much to look forward to in terms of changed conduct.

I am offended by those text messages. But I also believe, in terms of this Parliament making a decision about the speakership, that this Parliament should recognise that there is a court case in progress. That the judge has reserved his decision, that having waited for a number of months for the legal matters surrounding Mr Slipper to come to a conclusion, that this Parliament should see that conclusion.

I believe that is the appropriate path forward, and that people will then have an opportunity to make up their minds with the fullest information available to them.

But whenever people make up their minds about those questions, what I won't stand for, what I will never stand for is the Leader of the Opposition coming into this place and peddling a double standard. Peddling a standard for Mr Slipper he would not set for himself. Peddling a standard for Mr Slipper he has not set for other members of his frontbench.

Peddling a standard for Mr Slipper that has not been acquitted by the people who have been sent out to say the vilest and most revolting things like his former Shadow Parliamentary Secretary, Senator Bernardi.

I will not ever see the Leader of the Opposition seek to impose his double standard on this Parliament. Sexism should always be unacceptable. We should conduct ourselves as it should always be unacceptable. The Leader of the Opposition says do something; well he could do something himself if he wants to deal with sexism in this Parliament.

He could change his behaviour, he could apologise for all his past statements, he could apologise for standing next to signs describing me as a witch and a bitch, terminology that is now objected to by the frontbench of the Opposition.

He could change a standard himself, if he sought to do so. But we will see none of that from the Leader of the Opposition because on these questions he is incapable of change. Capable of double standards, but incapable of change. His double standards should not rule this Parliament.

Good sense, common sense, proper process is what should rule this Parliament. That's what I believe is the path forward for this Parliament, not the kind of double standards and political game-playing imposed by the Leader of the Opposition now looking at his watch because apparently a woman's spoken too long.

I've had him yell at me to shut up in the past, but I will take the remaining seconds of my speaking time to say to the Leader of the Opposition, I think the best course for him is to reflect on the standards he's exhibited in public life, on the responsibility he should take for his public statements, on his close personal connection with Peter Slipper, on the hypocrisy he has displayed in this House today.

And on that basis, because of the Leader of the Opposition's motivations, this Parliament today should reject this motion and the Leader of the Opposition should think seriously about the role of women in public life and in Australian society, because we are entitled to a better standard than this.

Scott Morrison–Amid the Coronavirus Pandemic

ADDRESS TO THE NATION
Parliament House, Canberra, Thursday, 12 March 2020
Born 1968, Prime Minister 2018-22: In a straightforward and simply spoken address, the prime minister, The Hon Scott Morrison MP talked to Australians via television concerning the coronavirus pandemic. He described the nature of the pandemic, what actions his Government was taking, and what listeners should do. With analysis and clarity in a confusing situation, his language was conversational and personable, to underpin his style as an individual guided by both medical science and good sense.

Good evening Australia.

Tonight I want to talk to you about the global coronavirus, what it means for you and your family and what the Government is doing to see Australia through. This virus began in China and has now reached some 114 countries. More than 124,000 have contracted the virus, including 140 here in Australia. The medical experts tell us that for most Australians in good health, who contract the virus, they will experience a mild illness. That said, this virus is also highly transmissible and for those Australians whose health is more vulnerable, especially the elderly, the risk is more severe.

While this is a global health crisis, there are very real and significant economic impacts. For all of these reasons, we have been taking the Coronavirus very seriously. I want to assure you and your family tonight that while Australia, cannot and is not immune from this virus, we are well prepared and are well equipped to deal with it, and we do have a clear plan to see Australia through. Our plan has three goals.
1. Protect Australians' health
2. Secure Australians' jobs and livelihoods, and
3. Set Australia up to bounce back stronger when the crisis is over.

Firstly, to protect Australians, we were one of the first countries to recognise the seriousness of the coronavirus.

- We quickly established travel bans from the most affected countries, and scaled up screening on our borders.
- We evacuated Australians from virus hotspots and set up quarantine facilities.

And we have funded a $2.4 billion national health response plan to
- set up more than 100 pop up clinics
- and to provide support for aged care
- increase funding to Public hospitals, and
- boost our National Medical Stockpile of essential medicines and masks.

Secondly, to keep Australians in jobs and businesses in business we have today announced a $17.6 billion economic stimulus plan:
- we're subsidising half the wages of 117,000 apprentices in small businesses
- providing one-off $750 payments to more than 6 million Australians to spend in our economy now. Almost two and half million pensioners will receive this support
- there's direct cash support of up to $25,000 for small and medium sized business that employ over seven million Australians, to boost their cash flow
- and we're backing businesses to keep investing by increasing tax incentives to help them buy new equipment now.

And thirdly, once the virus has run its course, we are making sure Australia can bounce back strongly. For the most affected regions and industries, like tourism and Upper North Queensland, there is a special $1 billion fund to support targeted local recovery plans. And as our economy bounces back, which it will, so will our Budget, because we have not loaded up spending off into the future. We can take this action now because we have worked hard to bring the budget back into balance, to maintain our AAA credit rating and work with State Governments to provide a world-class health system.

Now I know, many Australians are anxious about this and we still have a long way to go. But be assured we are taking action and we have a clear plan.

The months ahead will present many challenges, and we will respond to them. We will continue to keep you updated and take decisions based on the best possible medical advice. And if you have questions please visit health.gov.au or talk to your local GP.

We'll get through this together Australia. We all have a role to play. Employers, nurses, doctors, teachers, scientists, friends, family and neighbours. I know we'll all do our bit.

Thank you for listening tonight and good night Australia.

APPENDICES

Appendix 1: Glossary of Terms

Following are brief descriptions or examples of stylistic/grammatical terms in alphabetical order, to help with detailing style in language. For additional clarifications, recommended references are *How Writing Works: A Field Guide to Effective Writing* by Roslyn Petelin (Routledge, 2nd edn, 2022) and *Rhetorical Style: The Uses of Language in Persuasion* by Jeanne Fahnestock (Oxford University Press, 2011).

Action verb: connotes or denotes identifiable action, also see 'Cognitive Verb'
Active voice: see 'Verb function'
Adjective: modifies noun or substantive. Consider: frequency; attributes referred to; restrictive or not; gradable or not; attributive or predicative
    Isolated adjective: as complement or otherwise without modification
Adjunct [A]: see 'Sentence parts'
Adverb: modifies verb, adjective, or other adverb Consider: frequency; semantic functions; nonreferential (*so, very*); any significant use as conjuncts (*therefore, however*) or disjuncts (*certainly, obviously, frankly*, ...alleviate symptoms of strain *temporarily*)
    Adverb modifying adjective: ...must be *completely* new...
    Adverb, nonreferential: *so/very/some/there*
Alliteration: repeated initial, usually consonant sounds in two or more nearby words or syllables, *tittle of truth*
Allusion: indirect reference, including pun, ...*what this Roman ever did for us*
Ambiguity: uncertainty in meaning, ...*if you had a brother would he like cheese?*
Anadiplosis: repetition at the start of a phrase of a word or words at the end of the previous phrase, ...*here's to the future, a future for us all*
Analogy: comparison based on similarity, ...*political carpentry*...
Anaphora: repetition of the same word at the beginning of successive phrases, clauses, or sentences, *with one fire burning in him, and with one unrivalled capacity*...
Antimetabole: repeat of phrase with order of words reversed, *Ask not what your country can do for you, ask what you can do for your country*
Antithesis: a direct opposite or contrast, ...*not the basis of the decision. But the basis of the decision is*...
Aphorism: concise expression of truth or opinion, ...*selfishness is not loveliness*...
Appeals: methods of persuading someone in argument
    Ethos (credibility, based on moral expertise and knowledge), ***Pathos*** (audience's emotions), ***Logos*** (rational proof)
    Ad hominem: directed to person's character or motivations, *You've only ever lived in*...
    Ad populum: directed to presumed group assumptions, ...*many people are saying*...
Article: identifies a specific noun, *a/an/the*
Assonance: repetition of identical or similar vowel sounds

Asyndeton: omission of connectives, *Duty, Honor, Country: Those three hallowed words reverently dictate what you ought to be, what you can be, what you will be*
B-verb ('to be') finite: *is, am, may be, will be, would be, was*
    As auxilliary: *...it must be done...*
Clause: group of words containing subject and predicate and part of a compound or complex sentence. Consider: relative/adverbial/nominal; non-finite (*-ing/-ed*/verbless clauses); compound–defined according to traditional grammar
    Clause structure: Consider: clause elements; unusual orderings; special constructions
Cliché: a trite, stereotyped expression
Complement [C]: see 'Sentence parts'
Conjunction (including coordinating/subordinating conjunction): connector of clauses, such as *when, because, although, which,* or sentences, including adverbs *however, still, thus,* or coordinating phrases/words in the same clause, *and, but, or, neither, as*
Contraction: shortened version of word, syllable, or word group by omission of a letter, often indicated by an apostrophe; characteristic of conversation, *doesn't, she's, Rev., Dr*
Cognitive verb: not connoting or denoting an identifiable action, see Hogben, George L. (1977), 'Linguistic Style and Personality', *Language and Style*, x, 4, Fall, p. 270
Context: questions of context include:
What is the goal of the communication?
What effect is sought?
What are issues to be addressed, side-stepped, or ignored?
What are concerns of readers/listeners and their current understandings?
How are any opponents likely to respond?
What specific points or turns of phrase might be pre-set for inclusion?
Correctio: immediate amendment to redefine meaning
Dash: marks off a parenthetical element, the—em dash and - en dash commonly reflect conversational interpolation
Determiner: defines relation of a noun or pronoun to the speaker, *this, that, these, those*
    Predeterminer: precedes determiner in noun phrase, to express proportion *all, both*
    Intensifier: strengthens or weakens another word, *very, extremely, incredibly, rather, so*
    Demonstrative: manifests or proves, often emotionally or with excess, *this, those, that*
    Possessive and pronoun: indicating possession, *dog's, your, our, her,* see Crystal, David and Davy, Derek (1969), *Investigating English Style,* London: Longman, pp. 40-59
Ellipsis of subject, verb or auxilliary: omission of word or phrase needed to complete syntax but not needed for understanding, as outlined in Onions, C.T. (1971), *Modern English Syntax,* London: Routledge and Kegan Paul, p. 2
Epistrophe: repeated word/phrase at end of several successive clauses or paragraphs
Ethos: see 'Appeals'
Eulogy: speech in praise or tribute, especially to honour someone who has died
Figure of speech (Grammatical and Lexical): formal/structural repetition (*anaphora,* parallelism etc.); mirror-image patterns (*chiasmus*); other rhetorical effects (*antithesis,* reinforcement, climax, anticlimax)

Finite verb: those that may occur as the only verbal form in independent clauses, see Palmer, F.R. (2014), *The English Verb*, 2nd edn, Abingdon: Routledge, p. 12

Function words: provide context and relation of people, items, things, facts, opinions, ideas, etc., including articles, preposition, personal and impersonal pronouns, auxilliary verbs, conjunctions, negations, and nonreferential adverbs

Genre: conventional way in which a complete text is structured to suit both a situation and a communication purpose, including the classical rhetorical genres: *deliberative* (persuasive), *judicial* (arguing for justice) and *epideictic* (ceremonial praise or blame)

Gerund: formed with a verb but acts as a noun, …to stop *pretending*…

Grammar: underlying system of rules of a language

Homophone: similarly pronounced word, different in spelling and meaning, *one/won*

Humour: comic effect, often via pun, ambiguity, allusion, understatement, or parody

Hyperbole: exaggeration used for effect, …*feeds the stuff to Tyrannosaurus Rex, the computer*

Imperative: verb of command, implies control or influence of another

Impersonal pronoun: see 'Pronoun'

Infinite verb ('to…'): base form of a verb, …find it hard *to abandon*

Interpolation: insertion of new or additional material

Interrogatio/n: act of questioning

Intransitive verb: not taking a direct object (*go, look, appear*)

Logos: see 'Appeals'

Metaphor: 'understanding and experiencing one thing in terms of another', Lakoff, George and Mark Johnson, (2003), *Metaphors We Live By*, Chicago: University of Chicago Press, p. 5, …*the land is our mother*

Morpheme: smallest meaningful unit in language, not able to be divided into smaller parts with meaning, such as prefixes, *un-*, and suffixes, *-ism*

Narrative: account in story mode; a position represented in media, press releases, speeches, and interviews, some as metaphors *nation-building* or *the opportunity society*

Negation: contradiction or denial of something

Neologism: creation of new word or new senses, *Kellymania, Gortonism*, or *Bourbons*

Non-present tense: 'past' and 'present' taken as the two tenses, see Palmer, pp. 37–44

Noun: names person, place, thing, quality, or action. Consider: abstract/concrete; types of abstract nouns; proper nouns/names; collective nouns

> ***Non-qualified noun:*** those not immediately preceded by an adjective, determiner, article, or other modifier, except for preposition and verb; …for *policemen* were not… or …agree to be *outcasts, eccentrics*…
>
> ***Proper noun:*** names of people, organisations, countries, and so on, with each combination, where they occur as more than one element, counted as a unit; *Germaine Greer, Vietnam, Prime Minister's Office*
>
> ***Non-proper noun:*** all other nouns, *co-operatives, women*
>
> ***Noun phrase:*** group of two or more words headed by a noun. Consider: simple/complex; listings; coordination; apposition; function in a sentence

Ocker: slang for stereotypical Australian, characterising comradeship or conviviality or, pejoratively, boorish or uncultivated behaviour

Oxymoron: incongruous or contradictory terms combined, *deafening silence*

Pair: two grammatical items matched or associated. Consider: noun+modifier+; noun+noun; adjective+adjective; verb+verb

Paradox: apparently contradictory statement used to emphasise what may still be true, *festival of the oppressed* and *all animals are equal, but some are more equal than others*

Parallelism: equivalent syntactic constructions in corresponding clauses and phrases, to improve coherence, consistency, or emphasis

Parison: corresponding structure in a series of phrases, clauses, or sentences, *Reaction is not revolution. It is not a sign of revolution when...*

Participle: verb form functioning independently as an adjective
    past: ...*a guided tour*
    present: Going to war...

Passive voice: see 'Verb function'

Pathos: see 'Appeals'

Peroratio/n: final part of a speech recapitulating and reinforcing a case

Persona: role shared in the 'voice' of a speaker

Phonological scheme: pattern of rhyme, alliteration, assonance etc.; rhythmical pattern; vowel or consonant cluster etc.

Phrase types: prepositional; adverbial; adjectival
    Verb phrase: includes a verb and one or more helping verbs, ...*can smell* the pizza... or ...*will have been working* here for three years...

Polemic: aggressive attack on or refutation of the opinions or principles of another

Polyptoton: repeating different inferences of the same word or its derivative, ...*when the oppressed choose to oppress the oppressors...*

Polysyndeton: use of coordinating conjunctions in succession for effect, ...*but work he did not and vote he did not*

Praeteritio: call attention by disregarding a matter, *I won't trouble you with all the sacrifices...*

Predicator [P]: see 'Sentence parts'

Preposition: connecting word before a noun, pronoun or noun phrase to introduce an object, includes post-verbal particle, ...must live *up* to or ...much less *of* it...

Pronoun: substitute for noun or noun phrase, designating person or thing previously noted or understood
    Impersonal pronoun: standing for a non-living thing, commonly *it*
    Personal pronoun: comprising a set that shows contrasts of person, gender, number, and case: first-person *I/my, me, myself/we, us, our*; second-person *you/your/yours*; third-person *he, she/his, hers/ him, her/ they, them, whom*

Proper nouns/Non-proper nouns: see 'Nouns'

Repetitio/n: re-expression of same word, phrase, or idea

Rhetorical question: no answer is expected, ...*Work–isn't that a beautiful word?...*

Register: conventional ways in which a complete text is structured to suit a situation

Semantics: study of meaning in language

Sentence: end of sentence taken by punctuation (period, question mark, and so on) and by the end to sense of a member; also counted as a sentence were occasions where semi-colon, colon, or dash coincided with the end of a meaningful grammatical unit
    Sentence types: declarative; questions; imperative/commands; exclamations; fragment

Sentence parts: **S=Subject**, noun or pronoun naming a person, place, or thing, usually before the predicator; **P=Predicator**, verbal element adding time, aspect, and voice; **C=Complement**, noun, pronoun, or nominal required to complete the meaning; **A=Adjunct**, word, phrase, or clause, normally adverbial, integrated in the sentence structure but can be omitted without causing the sentence to be ungrammatical

Sentence complexity: simple/complex; length; ratio of dependent/independent clauses; variation via coordination/subordination/parataxis-juxtaposition of clauses

Sententia: a proverb, aphorism, or other statement of perceived wisdom

Simile: comparison or likening of two things having resemblance, often introduced by 'like' or 'as', ...*like a dream*... or ...*as* mad *as a hatter*...

Slang: casual or informal language, of coinages or figures of speech, used in place of standard terms, often for colourful or startling effect, ...*have no truck with that*...

Solecism: deviation from language norm, includes impropriety or breach of polite usage

Subject [S]: see 'Sentence parts'

Symbol: word, phrase, or figure of speech that represents something by association, resemblance, or convention, *democracy* or *justice*

Syntax: rules governing relational pattern of words, phrases, and clauses

Trope: figure of speech using words in nonliteral ways, including metaphor and obvious departures from linguistic code, such as neologisms, lexical collocations, semantic or syntactic or phonological or graphological deviations

Understatement: restrained expression, ...*I am the descendant of a singular group of elderly gentlemen...I refer to the Judges of England*...

Verb function: expresses existence, action, or occurrence; carrying meaning; referring to states or actions (cognitive or action); transitive or intransitive; linking; factive (assigning presupposed fact) or non-factive; finite/infinite; auxilliary; tense (especially present/past); positive/negative; active/passive); participles with verbal function

Active voice: subject of verb performs the action

Passive voice: recipient of verb's action becomes subject of sentence, ...their children *could be encouraged*... See Palmer, pp. 77-93

Vocabulary: the words of a language: simple/complex (mono-/bi-/poly-syllabic words); formal/colloquial (cliché, expletive/'four-letter word'/invective, slang); descriptive/evaluative; general/specific

Special vocabulary: use of symbol, slogan, jargon, and political slang (see pp. 63-6)

Word classes: articles; function words; prepositions; conjunctions; pronouns (first-person pronouns, *I, my/me/myself, we/us/our*; other personal pronouns, *you/your, he/she, they/them*); impersonal pronouns, (*it, its*); determiners; auxiliaries; interjections

In general: consider conjunctions; negations; other special effects of grammar recurring or absent (interpolations; ellipsis of subject/verb; pairs)

Walker T. Gibson's 'Style Machine' features (in Appendix 2.2): classified according to the scheme described in Gibson, Walker T. (1966), *Tough, Sweet and Stuffy*, Bloomington: University of Indiana Press, pp. 115-34.

For a ***stylistic checklist***, see Leech, Geoffrey and Mick Short (2007), *Style in Fiction, A Linguistic Introduction to English Fictional Prose*, 2nd edn, Harlow: Pearson Longman, pp. 61-4

Appendix 2: Tables of Counted Language Features

For counting of language features reported in Appendix Two, asterisked (*) items are available in Chapter 18, with references for others listed by author in Source Notes.

2.1: Comparison of Ten Speakers: Passages counted
The introductory 600-words to speeches of
Griffith, Samuel W. (1891), *The Political Geography of Australia*
*Lawson, Louisa (1891b), *Womanhood Suffrage*
*Curtin, John (1942), *Speech to America*
*Menzies, Robert Gordon (1969), *Eulogy for Churchill*
*Whitlam, E. Gough (1975), *Partnership in the Pacific after Vietnam*
Walker, Kath [Oodgeroo Noonuccal] (1970b), *How Well Off are Aborigines in Modern-day Australia?*
Hawke, Robert J. (1975), *In Memoriam, Albert Monk-Panegyric*
*Gilbert, Kevin (1974), *The Needs of First Nations*
Greer, Germaine (1971), *Address to The National Press Club, Washington DC*
*Kirby, Michael D. (1980a), *The Australian Community and Anti-heroes.*

2.2: Comparison of Greer, Millett, Orwell, and Segal: Passages counted
The 5,980-word final chapter of Greer, Germaine (1970), *The Female Eunuch*, final chapter 'Revolution', as well as 600-word samples of
Millett, Kate (1970), *Sexual Politics*, pp. 232-3, from 'Thus sociology examines...' to '... - writers, who, after...'
Orwell, George (1981), "Politics and the English Language," *A Collection of Essays*, pp. 169-71, from '...worst thing one can do...' to end
Segal, Ronald (1967), *The Race War*, pp. 445-6, from '...in a commitment by...' to end.

The total of the texts counted was 13,780 words, comprising the 600-word samples of speeches, the final chapter of *The Female Eunuch* of 5,980 words, and the samples of Millet, Orwell, and Segal. For consistency, the working glossary and examples listed in Appendix One were adhered to, with all features recounted to minimise errors. Use of the counted features was limited to broad ranking or trends and comparisons with qualitative insights.

2.1: Comparison of Ten Speakers: Griffith, Lawson, Curtin, Menzies, Whitlam, Oodgeroo, Hawke, Gilbert, Greer, Kirby

Stylistic Analysis: Language Features	Griffith	Lawson	Curtin	Menzies	Whitlam	Oodgeroo	Hawke	Gilbert	Greer	Kirby	Total Number	Average in 600 words	Average in 100 words
Metaphor: well-used	2	4	7	6	1	1	2	5	4	3	35	3.5	0.58
fresh	1	11	5	1	1	1	1	5	2	4	32	3.2	0.53
Cliché	0	4	2	2	1	0	0	3	3	0	15	1.5	0.25
Slang/colloquialism	0	1	1	0	2	1	1	11	2	0	11	1.1	0.18
TOTAL nouns	119	150	145	127	123	139	144	129	124	159	1359	135.9	22.6
Proper noun/name	12	10	40	17	26	20	38	30	18	41	252	25.2	4.2
TOTAL verb functions	68	88	67	81	72	75	60	98	77	65	751	75.1	12.51
Action verb	27	58	40	27	13	37	11	50	24	36	323	32.3	5.38
Cognitive verb	41	30	27	54	59	38	49	48	53	29	428	42.8	7.1
Infinite verb ('to…')	6	19	5	11	9	8	8	18	9	4	97	9.7	1.6
TOTAL B ('to be') verbs	27	25	22	33	24	23	14	21	29	22	240	24	4
B verb, finite	18	9	12	24	18	14	10	7	24	9	145	14.5	2.4
B verb as auxilliary	7	15	10	6	5	9	4	10	4	12	82	8.2	1.36
Present tense verb	47	56	31	34	30	15	17	59	51	15	355	35.5	5.9
Other tense verb	21	32	36	47	42	60	43	39	26	50	396	39.6	6.6
Negative verb	3	3	5	4	7	3	0	11	4	1	41	4.1	0.68
Passive voice	4	7	0	4	3	9	2	7	5	15	56	5.6	.9
Imperative verb	0	2	1	0	0	0	0	0	0	0	3	.3	.05
Auxilliary verb	23	39	34	26	34	22	8	41	20	30	277	27.7	4.6
Sentences	14	23	32	25	27	30	23	29	20	33	256	25.6	4.2
Word Avg. in sentence	42	26	18	24	22	20	26	20	30	18	246	24.6	-
Clause (relative / subordinate)	33	20	19	20	25	19	18	31	30	22	237	23.7	3.9
Compound clause	9	15	11	18	3	10	5	10	10	3	94	9.4	1.56
TOTAL Function words	271	245	263	261	267	248	217	257	273	239	-	254.1	42.35

[Appendix 2.1 continued]

Stylistic Analysis: Language Features	Speakers										Totals		
	Griffith	Lawson	Curtin	Menzies	Whitlam	Oodgeroo	Hawke	Gilbert	Greer	Kirby	Total Number	Average in 600 words	Average in 100 words
1st person pronoun:													
I	16	0	11	12	10	7	1	1	22	3	83	8.3	1.38
my, me, myself	10	0	5	5	1	5	1	0	5	0	32	3.2	0.53
we, us, our	2	12	11	11	10	26	2	5	3	5	87	8.7	1.45
2nd person pronoun	4	5	11	12	4	2	0	15	10	0	63	6.3	1.05
3rd person pronoun	4	15	7	14	6	5	28	20	4	9	112	11.2	1.86
Impersonal pronoun	3	6	8	4	8	3	0	1	8	4	45	4.5	0.75
Article	64	53	56	33	57	58	67	55	56	65	564	56.4	9.4
Preposition	88	62	78	76	76	77	77	56	75	85	750	75	12.5
Conjunction	49	49	35	60	47	39	29	51	64	36	459	45.9	7.6
Nonreferential adverb	5	1	2	4	7	1	4	1	2	1	28	2.8	0.46
Interpolation	20	10	14	13	8	6	13	17	8	7	116	11.6	1.9
Ellipsis: subject	4	6	6	9	1	6	4	7	3	1	47	4.7	0.78
verb	0	0	0	1	0	0	1	0	0	0	2	0.2	0.03
TOTAL pairs	42	40	38	49	39	59	58	44	37	60	466	46.6	7.76
Pair: noun+noun	2	1	2	1	1	8	1	4	0	7	27	2.7	0.45
Pair: adj.+noun/+	36	33	32	35	30	43	47	28	28	43	355	35.5	5.9
Pair: noun+modifier/+	1	1	1	0	0	3	2	0	0	1	9	0.9	0.15
Pair: adj.+adj.	1	3	3	5	1	2	6	2	5	5	33	3.3	0.55
Pair: verb+verb	2	2	0	8	7	3	2	10	4	4	42	4.2	0.7
Anaphora	1	1	7	9	6	1	3	6	2	1	37	3.7	0.61
Parallelism (excluding anaphora)	0	3	4	4	2	3	3	6	1	2	28	2.8	0.46
Alliteration	0	1	0	1	1	0	0	0	0	0	3	0.3	0.05
Neologism	1	1	0	0	1	1	1	2	3	1	11	1.1	0.18

2.2: Comparison of Greer, Millett, Orwell, and Segal

	Counts averaged to standard of 100 words	Greer	Millett	Orwell	Segal
1	Proportion (%) of monosyllables	65%	60%	71%	70%
2	Proportion (%) of polysyllables	15%	23%	12%	15%
3	1st and 2nd person pronouns	0.7	0.2	3.3	1.3
4	Neuter noun subjects	2.6	2.0	1.0	1.3
5	Personal noun subjects	1.4	1.0	0	0
6	% finite verbs	10%	8%	12%	5%
7	% finite B ('to be') verbs	25%	22%	9%	17%
8	% passive voice verbs	9%	2%	0.3%	0.3%
9	% true adjectives	4%	7%	6%	5%
10	Adjectives modified by adverbs	0.6	1.0	0.16	0.16
11	% noun adjuncts	0.8%	1%	1%	1.5%
12	Average word length of included clauses	9	9	8	8
13	% of passage in such clauses	48%	31%	59%	39.3%
14	Words separating subject and verb	7.5	11.3	3.8	10.6
15	'the'	5.7	5.3	4	6
16	Contractions and fragments	0.2	1.3	2.5	2.5
17	Parentheses, italics, dashes, question marks, exclamation points	0.2	1.16	2.84	2.16

SOURCE NOTES

1: How to Use This Book

1. Pendley, Ethel C. (1899), *Dot and the Kangaroo*, London: Thomas Burleigh
2. [see Chapter 18] Whitlam, E. Gough (1975a), *Partnership in the Pacific after Vietnam: Address to the National Press Club Luncheon*, Washington D.C., 8 May, p. 1
3. Collins, Philip (2017a), *When They Go Low, We Go High*, London: 4th Estate, p. 213; Collins, Philip (2017b), 'The Art of Political Speech', Leith, Sam (interviewer), *The Spectator–podcast*, 25 October
4. Deakin, Alfred (1887), 'Opening Address', *Proceedings of the Colonial Conference 1887*, Colonial Conference, London, England, pp. 24-5
5. Griffith, Samuel Walker (1891), *The Political Geography of Australia*, in *Proceedings of the Royal Geographical Society of Australia–Queensland Branch*, 6, pp. 68-81
6. [see Chapter 18] Forrest, John (1912), *Trans-Australia Railway*, Ceremony at Port Augusta to Turn the First Sod of the Trans-Australia Railway from Port Augusta to Kalgoorlie, *Barrier Miner (Broken Hill, NSW)*, 17 September, p. 3
7. [see Chapter 18] Melba, Nellie (1924), *Goodbye*, Melbourne, His Majesty's Theatre, 13 October
8. [see Chapter 18] Curtin, John (1942), *Speech to America*, 14 March, Canberra: Australian Government, Department of the Prime Minister and Cabinet
9. McLeod, Marian B. (1978), 'R.G. Menzies as Parliamentary Speaker', *Australian Scan: Journal of Human Communication*, 4, p. 1
10. Heath, Evelyn (1977), 'Representative Speeches of Gough Whitlam', *Australian Scan: Journal of Human Communication*, 3, p. 24
11. Greer, Germaine (1971), *Address to The National Press Club*, Washington DC, 18 May
12. [see Chapter 18] Lawson, Louisa (1891b), *Womanhood Suffrage*–'A Meeting of the League. Speeches by Women', at Y.M.C.A. Hall, Sydney, *The Daily Telegraph*, Sydney NSW, 13 June, p. 10
13. Walker, Kath [Oodgeroo Noonuccal] (1970a), *My People*, Milton, Qld: Jacaranda, (i) (1968), *Integration and Queensland Society*, A paper delivered at the Abschol seminar on Aboriginal conditions, May, pp. 42-4; (ii) (1970b), *How Well Off are Aborigines in Modern-day Australia?* Speech at Pius XII Seminary, Banyo, 21 March, pp. 88-92; and (iii) (1988), *Acceptance Speech*, in *Kunapipi*, 16(1), 1994
14. [See Chapter 18] Gilbert, Kevin (1974), *The Needs of First Nations*, first published as a lecture on 'Needs of the Aboriginal Community', in Tatz, Colin and McConnochie,

Keith R. (Eds.) (1975), *Black Viewpoints: The Aboriginal Experience*, Sydney: Australia and New Zealand Book
15. [see Chapter 18] Keating, Paul (1992), *Redfern Park Speech*, Australian Launch of the International Year for the World's Indigenous People, Redfern, Redfern Park, 10 December
16. Rudd, Kevin (2008), *The Apology* to Australia's Indigenous Peoples–Parliament of Australia, *Commonwealth of Australia Parliamentary Debates–House of Representatives*, 13 February 2008, Canberra: Hansard, Parliament of Australia, pp. 167-71
17. [see Chapter 18] Atkinson, Sallyanne (1988), *Expo '88 Opening Ceremony Speech of The Rt Hon Lord Mayor of Brisbane*, South Brisbane, World Expo '88, 30 April
18. [see Chapter 18] Howard, John (1996c), *Gun Rally–Sale, Victoria*, Canberra: Department of the Prime Minister and Cabinet, Australian Government, 16 June
19. [see Chapter 18] Gillard, Julia (2012), *Misogyny Speech*, 'Motion-in-Reply', in *Commonwealth of Australia Parliamentary Debates–House of Representatives Official Hansard*, No. 15, 43rd Parliament, 1st Session, 7th Period, 9 October 2012, Canberra: Hansard, Parliament of Australia, pp. 11581-5
20. Pearson, Noel (2014), *Noel Pearson Remembers Gough Whitlam*, 4 November, at Sydney Town Hall, https://www.youtube.com/watch?v=JsXmYHiuJ8s
21. A usefully comprehensive tabulation of the motivating process applied to various types of audience is available in the Internet version of: McGee, John A. (1929), *Persuasive Speaking*, New York: Scribner's, pp. 268-9 [Appendix C] https://archive.org/details/persuasivespeaki00mcge, Accessed 1 September 2021
22. Kane, John (2014), 'What's at Stake in Australian Political Rhetoric?' in Uhr, John and Ryan Walter (Eds), *Studying Australian Political Rhetoric*, Canberra: Australian National University Press, p. 4
23. Rolfe, Mark (2004), 'The Rhetorical Prime Minister', 19(1) Review Article, pp. 158-64, *researchgate.net*; see James Curran (2004), *The Power of Speech: Australian Prime Ministers Defining the National Image*, Melbourne: Melbourne University Press
24. Grube, Dennis C. (2012), 'A Very Public Search for Public Value: "Rhetorical Secretaries" in Westminster Jurisdictions', *Public Administration*, 90 (2), pp. 445-65
25. Grube, Dennis C. (2019), *Megaphone Bureaucracy: Speaking Truth to Power in the Age of the New Normal*, Princeton, NJ: Princeton University Press
26. Corcoran, Paul (1994), 'Presidential Concession Speeches: The Rhetoric of Defeat', *Political Communication*, 11 (2), pp. 109-31
27. Corcoran, Paul (1998) 'The Rhetoric of Triumph and Defeat: Australian Federal Elections, 1940–1993', *Australian Journal of Communication*, 25(1), pp. 69-86. *Critics of NT Plan Question PM's Motives* (2007) Radio Program, ABC Radio National: World Today, 22 March
28. Finlayson, Alan (2004), 'Political Science, Political Ideas and Rhetoric', *Economy and Society*, 33(4), doi.org/10.1080/0308514042000285279
29. Finlayson, Alan (2007), 'From Beliefs to Arguments: Interpretive Methodology and Rhetorical Political Analysis', *The British Journal of Politics and International Relations*, 9(4), pp. 545-63
30. Finlayson, Alan (2015), 'Becoming a Democratic Audience', in Shirin Rai and Janelle Reinelt (Ed.), *The Grammar of Politics and Performance*, London: Palgrave, pp. 93-105

31. Atkins, Judi; Finlayson A.; Martin, J.; Turnbull, N. (Eds.) (2013), *Rhetoric in British Politics and Society*, Basingstoke: Palgrave Macmillan, doi.org/10.1057/9781137325532_13
32. Bennister, Mark (2012), *Prime Ministers in Power: Political Leadership in Britain and Australia*, Basingstoke: Palgrave Macmillan
33. Charteris-Black (2011)
34. Charteris-Black, Jonathan (2014), *Analysing Political Speeches: Rhetoric, Discourse and Metaphor*, Basingstoke: Palgrave Macmillan
35. Kane, John and Haig Patapan (2010), 'The Artless Art: Leadership and the Limits of Democratic Rhetoric', *Australian Journal of Political Science*, 45(3), 10.1080/10361146.2010.499162
36. Martin, J. (2014), *Politics and Rhetoric: A Critical Introduction*, London: Routledge
37. Martin, J. (2015), 'Situating Speech: A Rhetorical Approach to Political Strategy', *Political Studies*, 63(1), pp. 25-42
38. Rolfe, Mark (2016), *The Reinvention of Populist Rhetoric in The Digital Age: Insiders and Outsiders in Democratic Politics*, Basingstoke: Palgrave Macmillan
39. Uhr and Walter
40. Uhr, John (2015), *Prudential Public Leadership: Promoting Ethics in Public Policy and Administration*, 10.1057/9781137506498
41. Young, S. (2007a), 'Political and Parliamentary Speech in Australia', *Parliamentary Affairs* 60, pp. 234-52
42. Young, S. (Ed.) (2007b), *Government Communication in Australia*, Port Melbourne: Cambridge University Press
43. Dryzek, J.S. (2010), 'Rhetoric in Democracy: A Systemic Appreciation', *Political Theory*, 38(3), pp. 319-39
44. Fairclough, Norman (2013), 'Critical Discourse Analysis and Critical Policy Studies', *Critical Policy Studies*, 7(2), pp. 177-97
45. Tulis, J.K. (1987), *The Rhetorical Presidency*, Princeton: Princeton University Press
46. Tulis, J.K. (2007), 'The Rhetorical Presidency in Retrospect', *Critical Review: A Journal of Politics and Society*, 19(2–3), pp. 481-500
47. Medhurst, M.J. (Ed.) (1996a) *Beyond the Rhetorical Presidency*, College Station, TX: A&M University Press
48. Medhurst, M.J. (1996b), 'A Tale of Two Constructs: The Rhetorical Presidency versus Presidential Rhetoric', in Medhurst, M.J. (Ed.) *Beyond the Rhetorical Presidency*, College Station: Texas A&M University Press, pp. xi–xxv
49. Ellis, R.J. (Ed.) (1998), *Speaking to the People: The Rhetorical Presidency in Historical Perspective*, Amherst: University of Massachusetts Press
50. Stuckey, M.E. (2010), 'Rethinking the Rhetorical Presidency and Presidential Rhetoric', *The Review of Communication*, 10(1), pp. 38-52
51. Friedman, J. and S. Friedman (2012), *Rethinking the Rhetorical Presidency*, Abingdon: Routledge
52. Swanson, David L. (1972), 'The New Politics Meets the Old Rhetoric: New Directions in Campaign Communication Research', *Quarterly Journal of Speech*, 58, p. 39

53. Nimmo, Dan (1970), *The Political Persuaders: Techniques of Modern Election Campaigns*, Englewood Cliffs, NJ: Prentice-Hall, p. 16
54. _____ (1970), 'Electronic Politics: The Image Game', *Time*, 21 September, p. 48
55. Hearn, Mark and Ian Tregenza (2014), '"The Maximum of Good Citizenship": Citizenship and Nation Building in Alfred Deakin's Post-Federation Speeches', in Uhr and Walter, pp. 177-94
56. Anthologies of Australian speeches include: Warhaft, Sally (Ed.) (2014), *Well May We Say: The Speeches that Made Australia*, Melbourne: Text Publishing; Fullilove, Michael (Ed.) (2014), *Men and Women of Australia: Our Greatest Modern Speeches*, Ringwood Vic: Penguin; Robson, Pamela (Ed.) (2009), *Great Australian Speeches: Landmark Speeches that Defined and Shaped Our Nation*, Millers Point, NSW: Murdoch Books; Cathcart, Michael and Kate Darian-Smith (Eds.) (2004), *Stirring Australian Speeches*, Melbourne: Melbourne University Press; Kemp, Rod and Marion Stanton (Eds.) (2004), *Speaking for Australia: Parliamentary Speeches that Shaped the Nation*, Crows Nest, NSW: Allen and Unwin; McLeod, A.L. (Ed.) (1969), *Australia Speaks: An Anthology of Australian Speeches*, Sydney: Wentworth
57. Freudenberg, Graham (1978), Seminar on Advanced Speech Writing at Queensland Institute of Technology (now Queensland University of Technology), Brisbane; see article (1978), 'Special Rapport', *The Courier-Mail*, 6 May
58. Collins (2017b)
59. Scalmer, Sean (2017), *On the Stump: Campaign Oratory and Democracy in the United States, Britain, and Australia*, Philadelphia: Temple University, pp. 97-120
60. Greer, Germaine (1981), communication with author, 2 April
61. Wannan, Bill (1973), *With Malice Aforethought: Australian Insults, Invective, Ridicule and Abuse*, Melbourne: Lansdowne, p. 43 and p. 47
62. Petelin, Roslyn (2020), *How Writing Works: A Field Guide to Effective Writing*, London: Routledge
63. Flower, Linda (1993), *Problem-solving Strategies for Writing*, 4th edn, Fort Worth: Harcourt Brace Jovanovich
64. RHETORIC: Cooper, L. (1960), *The Rhetoric of Aristotle: An Expanded Translation with Supplementary Examples for Students of Composition and Public Speaking*, Englewood Cliffs, NJ: Prentice-Hall; Norlin, George (1928), *Isocrates*, London: W. Heinemann; Bacon, Francis (1952) *Advancement of Learning*, Great Books, Vol. 30, Chicago: Encyclopedia Britannica [1st published 1605]; Booth, Wayne C. (1961), *The Rhetoric of Fiction*, Chicago: University of Chicago Press; Hochmuth, Marie (1962), 'Kenneth Burke and the "New Rhetoric"', *Quarterly Journal of Speech*, 48, pp. 133-44; Brandt, W.J. (1970), *The Rhetoric of Argumentation*, Indianapolis: Bobbs-Merrill; Forsyth, Mark (2014), *The Elements of Eloquence: Secrets of the Perfect Turn of Phrase*, New York: Berkley
STYLISTICS: Ohmann, Richard (1964), 'Generative Grammars and the Concept of Literary Style', *Word*, xx, December, pp. 423-39; Crystal, David and Derek Davy (1969), *Investigating English Style*, London: Longman; Turner, G.W. (1973), *Stylistics*, Harmondsworth, UK: Penguin; Fahnestock, Jeanne (2011), *Rhetorical Style: The Uses of Language in Persuasion*, New York: Oxford University Press; Burke, Michael (Ed.) (2014), *The Routledge Handbook of Stylistics*, New York: Routledge; for a readily accessible summary of the aims and value of stylistics, see 'What is stylistics?' on

Aunty Muriel's Blog, 7 September 2017 auntymuriel.com/2017/09/07/what-is-stylistics/, Accessed 24 January 2021
LINGUISTICS: Fowler, Roger (1980), 'Linguistic Criticism', *UEA Papers in Linguistics 11,* January, University of East Anglia, Norwich, UK, pp. 1-26; Kress, Gunther and Robert Hodge (1979), *Language as Ideology,* London: Routledge and Kegan Paul

65. Cockcroft, Robert and Susan Cockcroft, with Craig Hamilton and Laura Hidalgo Downing, (2014), *Persuading People: An Introduction to Rhetoric,* 3rd edn, Basingstroke: Palgrave Macmillan, pp. 5-6
66. Brandt, pp. 281-4
67. [see Chapter 18] Morrison, Scott (2019), *Address to the Nation amid the Coronavirus Pandemic,* Prime Minister of Australia, Parliament House, Canberra, 12 March
68. Pannam, Clifford L. (1963), 'The Radical Chief Justice', *Australian Law Journal,* 37(9), p. 275
69. [see Chapter 18] Menzies, Robert Gordon (1965), *Eulogy for Churchill/Speech by the Prime Minister, The Rt Hon Sir Robert Menzies, KT, CH, QC, MM, from the Crypt of St Paul's Cathedral, London over BBC Television on the Occasion of the Funeral of the Late Sir Winston Churchill,* Canberra: Australian Government, Department of the Prime Minister and Cabinet
70. Woolley, Samuel C. and Philip N. Howard (Eds.) (2019), *Computational Propaganda: Political Parties, Politicians and Social Manipulation on Social Media,* New York, NY: Oxford University Press; Henderson, Gae Lyn and Braun, M.J. (2016), *Propaganda and Rhetoric in Democracy,* Carbondale, Il: Southern Illinois University Press

2: Language for Persuasion

71. Menzies, Robert (1948), 'Politics as an Art', *The New York Times Magazine,* 28 November
72. Lalor, Peter (1854), 'Eureka Oath', 1 December
73. Collins (2017a), p. 3
74. Robson, p. 103
75. Melba
76. Whitlam, E. Gough (1975b), 'Dismissal Speech on the Steps of Parliament House', Parliament House, Canberra: Department of the Prime Minister and Cabinet, Australian Government, 11 November
77. Whitlam, E. Gough (1976), in Wells, Deane, (1976), *The Wit of Whitlam,* Collingwood: Outback, p. 92-3
78. [see Chapter 18] Griffith, Samuel W. (1895), 'The Certainty of Australian Federation', Gay, W. and Sampson, M.E. (Eds.), *The Commonwealth and the Empire: Special Contributions and Communications on the Subject of Australasian Federation from Leading Colonial and Imperial Writers and Statesmen,* Melbourne: George Robertson, 6 ff.
79. Forrest
80. Lyons, Enid (1943), 'Governor-General's Speech, Address-in-Reply' on Social Welfare, 29 September, in *Commonwealth Parliamentary Debates–Representatives,* Seventeenth Parliament, First Session-First Period, p. 182; also, audio recorded after delivery for radio, *Australian Screen: An NFSA Website*

81. Ryan, Susan (1992), 'Fishes on Bicycles', 23 March, Address to Department of the Senate, Papers on Parliament No. 17, September 1992, *Trust the Women, Women in the Federal Parliament*, Published and Printed by the Department of the Senate, Parliament House, Canberra, p. 27
82. Carnegie, Roderick (1975), *Euthanasia by the Independent Australian*, Address to the Solicitors' Luncheon, 4 June, Wentworth Hotel, Sydney, The Law Society of New South Wales, *Quadrant,* July
83. Howard, John (2002), *Address to Memorial Service*, Australian Consulate, Bali, 17 October
84. Prowse, Linden J. (1975), *Guest of Honour,* 31 August, ABC Radio (Australia)
85. Manne, Robert (2001), *Neither Column in This Moral Ledger Will Cancel the Other Out,* 'My Country–A Personal Journey': the Alfred Deakin Lectures, Capitol Theatre, Melbourne, in Warhaft (2004), p. 58
86. Burnet, Macfarlane (1968), 'The Ethics of a Biologist', *Biology and the Appreciation of Life*, Melbourne: Sun Books, p. 51
87. Cron, Lisa (2021), 'Tell Don't Show? What Brain Imaging Reveals about Readers', *LitHub,* 17 March
88. Atkinson, Max (1984), *Our Master's Voices: The Language and Body Language of Politics*, London: Routledge
89. Hogben, George L. (1977), 'Linguistic Style and Personality', *Language and Style,* x, 4, Fall, p. 270
90. _____ (1880), 'Trial, Conviction, and Sentence of Ned Kelly', *Border Watch* (Mount Gambier, SA: 1861-1954), 3 November, p. 4
91. _____ (1880), 'Trial, Conviction, and Sentence of Ned Kelly', p. 4
92. Whitlam, E. Gough (1975a), p. 5
93. Atkinson, Sallyanne (1988)
94. Atkinson, Sallyanne (2016), *No Job for a Woman*, St. Lucia, Qld: University of Queensland Press, p. 144 [Kindle version]; Atkinson, Sallyanne (2021), 'Where I Belong–Sallyanne Atkinson AO', Love, Wendy (interviewer), *Museum of Brisbane,* podcast, 19 July
95. Atkinson, Sallyanne (1988)
96. Atkinson, Sallyanne (2021), communication with author, 17 October
97. Verdonk, Peter (2002), *Stylistics,* Oxford: Oxford University Press, pp. 5-6
98. Fahnestock (2011), p. 8
99. Simpson, Paul (2004), *Stylistics: A Resource Book for Students,* London: Routledge, p. 5
100. Leech, Geoffrey and Mick Short (2007), *Style in Fiction, A Linguistic Introduction to English Fictional Prose,* 2nd edn, Harlow: Pearson Longman, pp. 61-4
101. van Leeuwen, Maarten (2014), 'Systematic Stylistic Analysis, The Use of a Linguistic Checklist', in Kaal, Bertie, Isa Maks and Annemarie van Elfrinkhof (Eds.), *From Text to Political Positions, Text Analysis across Disciplines,* Amsterdam: John Benjamins, pp. 225-44 [For further discussion on the value and use of checklists, see van Haaften, Ton (2019), 'Argumentative Strategies and Stylistic Devices', *Informal Logic,* 39(4), pp. 309-12]
102. McIntyre, Dan (2010), 'The Year's Work in Stylistics 2010', *Language and Literature: International Journal of Stylistics,* 19(4), pp. 396-411; Lugea, Jane (2018), 'The Year's

Work in Stylistics 2017', *Language and Literature: International Journal of Stylistics*, 10 December, Simon Statham, and Rocio Montoro (2019), 'The Year's Work in Stylistics 2018', *Language and Literature: International Journal of Stylistics*, 4 December; Biber, D. and S. Conrad (2009), *Register, Genre and Style*, Cambridge: Cambridge University Press; and, Jeffries L. and D. McIntyre (2010), *Stylistics*, Cambridge: Cambridge University Press;

103. Stockwell, Peter (2000), '(Sur)real Stylistics: From Text to Contextualising', in Bex, Tony, Peter Stockwell, Michael Burke (Eds.), *Contextualised Stylistics: In Honour of Peter Verdonk*, Amsterdam: Rodopi, p. 19

104. Stockwell, Peter (2006), '31 Language and Literature: Stylistics', *Neuro Humanities Studies*, 1/10/06, p. 755 neurohumanitiestudies.eu>archivio>stylistics, Lugea: Statham and Montoro

105. Kress, Gunther (1980), 'Ideological Unity of Discourse: The Concept of "Textual Congruence"', *Australian Scan: Journal of Human Communication*, 9 & 10, p. 72 [An earlier version of this paper was delivered at the 50th ANZAAS Congress, *Science for a Sustainable Society: Linguistics*, The University of Adelaide, May 1980]

106. Kress (1980), pp. 71-7

107. van Dijk, Teun A., (2018), 'Critical Discourse Analysis', in Tannen, Deborah, Heidi E. Hamilton, and Deborah Schiffrin (Eds.), *The Handbook of Discourse Analysis*, 2nd edn, Chichester: Wiley Blackwell, pp. 466-85

108. Charteris-Black, Jonathan (2011), *Politicians and Rhetoric: The Persuasive Power of Metaphor*, 2nd edn, Basingstoke: Palgrave Macmillan, p. 5

109. Hamilton, Craig (2009), 'Jonathan Charteris-Black, *Politicians and Rhetoric. The Persuasive Power of Metaphor*', *Lexis* [Online], Book reviews journals.openedition.org/lexis/1691 Accessed 9 July 2020

110. Ross, Donald (1981), 'Skimming the Surface: Improvements in the Quality of Syntactic Descriptions for Stylistics', *International Journal of Applied Linguistics*, 52(1), January, pp. 55-73

111. Milic, Louis Tonko (1967), *A Quantitative Approach to the Style of Jonathan Swift*, The Hague: Mouton; Ross, Donald (1977), 'The Use of Word-class Distribution Data for Stylistics: Keats' Sonnets and Chicken Soup', *Poetics*, 6(2), September, pp. 169-95

112. Ellegard, Alvar (1962), *A Statistical Method for Determining Authorship*, Goteborg: Acta Universitas Gothoburgensis; Lake, David J. (1975), *The Canon of Thomas Middleton Plays: Internal Evidence for the Major Problems of Authorship*, London: Cambridge University Press

113. Morton, A. Q. (1978), *Literary Detection: How to Prove Authorship and Fraud in Literature and Documents*, n.p.: Bowker; and Morton, A.Q. and M. Levison (1966), 'Some Indications of Authorship in Greek Prose', in Leed, Jacob (Ed.), *The Computer and Literary Style*, Kent, OH: Kent State University Press, pp. 141-79

114. Enkvist, Nils Erik (1973), *Linguistic Stylistics*, Berlin: Mouton, p. 17; Enkvist, Nils Erik (1964), 'On Defining Style', in Enkvist, Nils Erik, John Spencer, and Michael J. Gregory, (Eds.), *Linguistics and Style*, Oxford: Oxford University Press, pp. 1-56

115. Ross, Donald (1981), pp. 55-73

116. Lakoff, George and Mark Johnson, (2003), *Metaphors We Live By*, Chicago: University of Chicago Press, p. 5

117. Lakoff and Johnson, p. 4
118. Csábi, Szilvia (2014), 'Metaphor and Stylistics', in Burke, Michael (Ed.) (2014), p. 218
119. Csábi, Szilvia, pp. 206-21
120. O'Shea, Robert (2013), '"Speaking to You on the Birthday of the Nation:" Vice-Regal Rhetoric on Australian Identity', *Crossroads: An Interdisciplinary Journal for the Study of History, Philosophy, Religion and Classics*, VI(II), pp. 39-48
121. Gizzi-Stewart, Brooke (2016), 'New Visions and Vintage Values: Shifting Discourses of Australian National Identity in 21st Century Prime Ministerial Rhetoric', *Communication, Politics and Culture*, 49(1), pp. 62-85
122. Gizzi-Stewart, p. 69-79
123. Lawson (1891b), p. 10
124. Griffith (1895)
125. Hawke, Robert J. (1975), *In Memoriam, Albert Monk-Panegyric*, Melbourne: The Australian Council of Trade Unions
126. Oodgeroo Noonuccal [Walker, Kath] (1988)
127. Forrest
128. Gilbert
129. [see Chapter 18] Kirby, Michael D. (1980a), *The Australian Community and Anti-heroes*, Lalor Community Relations Address, Playhouse, Civic Square, Canberra, 3 December, Website Speech No. 206, pp. 1-14
130. Burnet, pp. 51-63
131. Lyons, p. 182
132. McLennan, Ian (1969), *Focus on Australia's Industrial Horizon*, Sydney: Australian Finance Conference
133. Hughes, William M. (1907), *Compulsory Military Training*, Address at Caxton Hall, 24 April, Westminster
134. Carnegie
135. Curtin (1942)
136. Menzies, Robert G. (1939a), *The Place of a University in the Modern Community–An Address*, at the Tenth Annual Commencement of Canberra University, 26 April, Melbourne: Melbourne University Press
137. Whitlam, E. Gough (1971), 'Motion of Want of Confidence in the Government', 15 March, in *Commonwealth Parliamentary Debates–Representatives*, 16 February 1971 to 2 April 1971, 20 Eliz II, Vol. H of R71, p. 828
138. Whitlam, E. Gough (1975a), p. 2
139. Cowen, Zelman (1970), '*The University–Struggling for Balance*', Orientation Keynote Address to Students, 25 February, at The University of Queensland, St. Lucia, Qld
140. Greer (1971)
141. Oliphant, Mark (1970), *Burgmann College Opening Address*, Burgmann College, Canberra
142. Prowse
143. I am grateful to former colleague Bruce Molloy for this insight.
144. Curran (2004), James Curran, and Stephen Ward (2004), *The Unknown Nation: Australia after Empire*, Carlton: Melbourne University Press; O'Shea, pp. 39-48

145. Robson, p. 142
146. Miller, Rodney G. (1980), 'Developing Oral Communication in a Pluralistic Society', in Crocker, W. J. (Ed.), *Developing Oral Communication Competence*, Armidale: The University of New England, p. 85
147. Halloran, S.M. (1975), 'On the End of Rhetoric: Classical and Modern', *College English*, 36(6), February, p. 621
148. Stenhouse, L. (1967), *Culture and Education*, London: Nelson, in Ipswich State High School English Curriculum Guide, Ipswich, Australia

3: Democratic Talk of John Curtin and Sir Robert Menzies

149. After an aphorism from a United States postage stamp. The original: 'A Public that Reads: A Root of Democracy' indicated the continued concern for literacy as an integral part of the democratic process.
150. Curtin (1942)
151. Menzies, Robert G. (1955a), *Address to the National Press Club Luncheon*, 16 March, Washington DC
152. Whitlam, E. Gough (1975a), p. 1
153. Groombridge, Brian (1972), *Television and the People: A Programme for Democratic Participation*, Harmondsworth: Penguin, p. 61
154. Cooper, p. 8
155. Gabis, Stanley T. (1978), 'Political Secrecy and Cultural Conflict: A Plea for Formalism', *Administration and Society*, 10(2), August, p. 146
156. _____ (1942), *The Mail*, Adelaide, S.A., 14 March, p. 1
157. Curtin (1942)
158. Ricks, Thomas E. (2017), *Churchill and Orwell, the Fight for Freedom*, New York: Penguin, p. 149
159. Curtin (1942)
160. Curtin (1942)
161. Miller, Rodney G. (1976a), 'Image Making and Australian Political Rhetoric', *Inter Connections*, 1(1), December, p. 21; see Mount, Ferdinand (1972), *The Theatre of Politics*, London: Weidenfield and Nicholson, p. 9
162. Furphy, Samuel (Ed.) (2015), *The Seven Dwarfs and the Age of the Mandarins: Australian Government Administration in the Post-war Reconstruction Era*, Canberra: Australian National University Press, p. 189
163. Menzies, Robert G. (1961b), *A Talk to the Nation, Federal Election*, 20 November, p.1

4: Polemic and Propaganda

164. Lawson (1891b), p. 10
165. _____ (2020), 'Polemic'. *Merriam-Webster.com Dictionary* Merriam-Webster, *merriam-webster.com/dictionary/polemic* Accessed 11 June 2020
166. Hughes, W.M. (1929), *Speeches of the 1929 Election Campaign*, Audio cassette, The University of Queensland Audio-visual Library
167. Kruger, Arthur N. (1975), 'The Nature of Controversial Statements', *Philosophy and Rhetoric*, 8(3), p. 138

168. Kruger, p. 139; also see Marlin (2013a), p. 120, for a variety of ways in which opinion polls 'can and do mislead'.
169. Dascal, Marcelo (2017), 'Types of Polemics and Types of Polemical Moves', in Cmerjrkova, Svetla, Jana Hoffmanova, Olga Mullerova, Olga M. Llerov (Eds.), *Dialoganalyse VI/1: Referate der 6. Argbeitstagung, Prag 1996,* Berlin/Boston: Walter de Gruyter GmbH, pp. 15-33
170. Lloyd, G.E.R. (1966), *Polarity and Analogy: Two Types of Argumentation in Early Greek Thought,* Cambridge: Cambridge University Press, p. 24
171. Lee, H.D.P. (1955), *Plato, The Republic,* Harmondsworth: Penguin, p. 300
172. Jeffries, L. (2010), *Opposition in Discourse: The Construction of Oppositional Meaning,* London: Continuum
173. Duncan, Hugh Dalziel (1971), 'The Need for Clarification in Social Models of Rhetoric', in Bitzer, Lloyd F. and Edwin Black (Eds.), *The Prospect of Rhetoric,* Englewood Cliffs, NJ: Prentice-Hall, p. 150
174. Andersen, Robin and Jonathan Gray (Eds.) (2008), *Battleground the Media, Volume 2 (O-Z),* Westport, CT: Greenwood, p. 477; Zada, John (2021), *Veils of Distortion: How the News Media Warps Our Minds,* Toronto: Terra Incognita
175. Halloran, p. 621
176. Norlin, George (1928), *Isocrates,* London: W. Heinemann, pp. ix-xlvii
177. United Nations (1948), *Universal Declaration of Human Rights,* Article 3
178. Rhodes, James M. (2010), *Democracy, Language and Rhetoric,* Fifth Annual Tanner Symposium, 22 January, Cedar City: Southern Utah University voegelinview.com/democracy-language-rhetoric/
179. Dascal, p. 29
180. Dascal, p. 21-2
181. McGee, pp. 268-9
182. Carnegie
183. Carnegie
184. Tatz, Colin and Keith R. McConnochie (Eds.) (2001), 'Confronting Australian Genocide', in *Aboriginal History, Vol 25* Canberra: Australian National University Press, p. 24
185. Gilbert
186. McGee, pp. 268-9
187. Gilbert
188. Greer (1971)
189. McGee, pp. 268-9
190. Cowen
191. Cowen
192. Lyons, p. 183
193. Lyons, p. 186
194. McLennan
195. Lawson (1891b), p. 10
196. Prowse
197. Dascal, p. 21
198. Hawke (1975)

199. Griffith (1895)
200. Dascal, pp. 24-8
201. Dascal, p. 27-8
202. Dascal, p. 25
203. Griffith (1895)
204. Gilbert
205. Burnet, p. 52
206. Dascal, p. 25
207. Lawson (1891b), p. 10
208. Lyons, p. 182
209. Ryan, Thomas Joseph (T.J.) (1917), 'I Would Not Allow a Man to Publish Any Lies'–Opposition to Conscription, *Government Gazette Extraordinary*, Brisbane: Government Printer [Speeches and pamphlets blocked via *Hansard 37*], in Robson, Pamela (Ed.) (2009), *Great Australian Speeches: Landmark Speeches that Defined and Shaped Our Nation*, Millers Point, NSW: Murdoch Books, p. 87
210. Wannan, pp. 54-5
211. Dascal, p. 24
212. Dascal, p. 25
213. Hughes (1907); Hughes, William M. (1909), 'The Federal Crisis, Another Heated Debate. Bitter Attacks on Mr Deakin "An Apology to Judas,"' *The Advertiser*, Adelaide, South Australia, Saturday, 29 May, p. 11
214. Greer (1971)
215. Gilbert
216. Dascal, p. 25
217. Whitlam, Nicholas and John Stubbs (1974), *Nest of Traitors*, Milton, Qld: Jacaranda, p. 100 [In 1954 the Petrov Affair that dominated news headlines concerned the defection of a Russian KGB agent, fueling fears of communist espionage.]
218. Curtin, John (1940a), *National Unity: Where Labor Stands, 9 August 1940*, Carlton, Vic.: Industrial Print
219. Baur, E. Jackson (1962), 'Opinion Change in a Public Controversy', *Public Opinion Quarterly*, 26, Summer, p. 222
220. Curtin, John (1937), *Labor's Message to the People of Australia–Policy Speech, 20 September 1937*, Sydney: Labor Daily, p. 3
221. Curtin (1937), pp. 5-6
222. Curtin (1937), p. 28
223. Curtin (1937), p. 14
224. Curtin (1937), p. 26
225. _____ (1940), *The Mercury*, 21 August
226. _____ (1937), *The Mercury*, 21 September
227. Robinson, Ray (1978), *The Wit of Sir Robert Menzies*, Collingwood, Vic: Outback, p. 57
228. Wells, Deane, p. 43
229. Wells, Deane, p. 84
230. Ratcliffe, Susan (2010), *Oxford Dictionary of Quotations by Subject*, Oxford: Oxford University Press, p. 253

231. Wannan, p. 51
232. Daly, Fred (1975), 'Whitlam Labour Rally, public remarks', Brisbane, 14 November, in *Speeches of the 1975 Election – Brisbane Rally*, Audiocassette, The University of Queensland Audio-visual Library
233. Farquharson, John (2007), 'Killen, Sir Denis James (1925-2007)', *Obituaries Australia*, oa.anu.edu.au/obituary/killen-sir-denis-james-562, Accessed 17 June 2020
234. Gregory, Denis (2015), *It's All About Australia Mate*, Gosford, NSW: Exisle, p. 24
235. _____ (2005), 'Don't You Worry about That', *The Sydney Morning Herald*, 25 April
236. Ellul, Jacques (1965), *Propaganda: The Formation of Men's Attitudes*, New York: Vintage, p. xvii
237. Duncan, p. 141
238. Robinson, Peter (1976), 'The Media and Australian Politics', in Major, G. (Ed.) *Mass Media in Australia*, Sydney: Hodder and Stoughton, pp. 8-9
239. Rydon, Joan (1963), 'The Electorate', in Wilkes, J. (Ed.), *Forces in Australian Politics*, Sydney: Angus and Robertson, p. 17
240. Miller, Rodney G. (2020), 'It's Time for Plain Talk', *Word to the wise* blogpost, 25 June

5: Rhetorical Humour

241. Reid, George H. (1917), *My Reminiscences*, London: Cassell, p. 29
242. Hirst, John (2016), *Australian History in 7 Questions*, Carlton, Vic: Black, p. 139; citing Murray, Les A. (1999), 'If You Are Tired of This Old Theme…,' *The Quality of Sprawl*, Sydney: Duffy and Snellgrove, pp. 26-8
243. Wannan, p. 35
244. Menzies, Robert G. (1963a), *The Battle for Freedom–Jefferson Oration*, 4 July, Monticello, Charlottesville, Virginia
245. Hawke, Robert J. (1974), *Address to Australasian Society of Accountants: The Economic Implications of Future Labour Relations*, March
246. Whitlam, E. Gough (1972), 'Reply to: "Electoral Ministerial Statement"', 10 October, in Commonwealth Parliamentary Debates–Representatives, No. 41, 1972, Twenty-Seventh Parliament, Second Session-Sixth Period, pp. 2295-6
247. Heath, p. 26
248. Whitlam, E. Gough (1971), p. 828
249. Greer (1971)
250. Bryant, Jennings with Paul Comiskey, and Dolf Zillmann (1979), 'Teachers' Humor in the College Classroom', *Communication Education*, 28(2), p. 116, citing Freud, Sigmund (1960), *Jokes and Their Relation to the Unconscious*, New York: Norton, and (1928), 'Humour', *International Journal of Psychoanalysis*, 9, pp. 1-6
251. Bryant, Comiskey, and Zillmann, p. 116
252. Raskin, Victor (1985), *Semantic Mechanisms of Humor*, Dordrecht: D. Reidel; Attardo, Salvatore and Victor Raskin (1991), 'Script Theory Revis(it)ed: Joke Similarity and Joke Representation Model', *Humor*, 4(3-4), pp. 293-347, theory of humour to explain verbal jokes widely adapted for efforts to propose universal theories of humour; Phillips-Anderson, Michael Andrew (2007), *A Theory of Rhetorical Humor in American Political Discourse*, PhD Thesis, College Park, MD: University of Maryland, pp. 3-48;

253. Nash, Walter (1985), *The Language of Humour: Style and Technique in Comic Discourse*, New York: Longman, pp. 5-7
254. Bergson, Henri (1969), 'The Comic in General: The Comic Element in Forms and Movements', in Eastman, A.M. et. al., *The Norton Reader: An Anthology of Expository Prose*, New York: Norton, pp. 717-8
255. Bergson, p. 718
256. Leacock, Stephen (1969), 'Humor as I See It', in Eastman, A.M. et. al., *The Norton Reader: An Anthology of Expository Prose*, New York: Norton, p. 725
257. Phillips-Anderson, pp. 41-2
258. Phillips-Anderson, p. 192
259. Wannan, p. 40
260. Wells, Deane, p. 32
261. Menzies, Robert G. (1960c), *Speech at the All Nations Club*, 25 November, pp. 3-4
262. Menzies, Robert G. (1959b), *Press Conference by the Prime Minister of Australia The Rt Hon R.G. Menzies*, 6 December, Medan Merdeka Barat 15, Djakarta, p. 2
263. Menzies, Robert G. (1959a), *Press Conference Given by the Prime Minister, Rt Hon R.G. Menzies CH QC MP*, 14 October, Canberra: Commonwealth of Australia, p.1
264. Wells, Deane, p. 22
265. Deakin, Alfred (1904), 'Mr Deakin on the Situation—Coalition Necessary', *The Australasian*, 6 February, p. 35
266. Tannen, Deborah (1984), *Conversational Style: Analyzing Talk among Friends*, Norwood, NJ: Ablex, p. 130 and p. 132
267. Jefferson, Gail (1985), 'An Exercise in the Transcription and Analysis of Laughter', in van Dijk, Teun (Ed.), *Handbook of Discourse Analysis 3*, London: Academic, pp. 25-34
268. Rolfe, Mark (2010), 'The Pleasures of Political Humour in Australian Democracy', *Journal of Australian Studies*, 34(3), p. 364
269. Rolfe (2010), p. 372
270. Inglis, K.S. (1996), 'Parliamentary Speech', *Papers on Parliament No. 28*, Canberra: Parliament of Australia, Lecture in the Department of the Senate Occasional Lecture Series at Parliament House on 23 February
271. Kirby (1980a), p. 2
272. Kirby (2021b), communication with author, 26 September
273. Kirby, Michael D. (1981a), *The Australian Media Peace Prize*, Sydney, 20 October and (1980b), Australia into the Eighties: The Challenge of Change, Canberra, 25 January, Website Speech No. 280, p. 1
274. Crystal and Davy, pp. 78-9
275. Rolfe, Mark (2019), 'Is This a Dag Which I See before Me? John Clarke and the Politics in His Political Humour', *Comedy Studies*, 10(1), pp. 1-18
276. Frewin, Leslie (1973), *Immortal Jester: A Treasury of the Great Good Humour of Sir Winston Churchill 1874-1965*, London: Frewin, p. 107

6: Political Words and Gough Whitlam

277. Whitlam (1971), p. 832

278. Pedersen, Elena Gagiu (2015), 'Semantics of the symbol: main theories about the symbols and themes of symbols in Alexandru Macedonski's poetry', *Procedia–Social and Behavioral Sciences*, 180, pp. 586-92. The 6th International Conference Edu World 2014 'Education Facing Contemporary World Issues', 7-9 November 2014
279. Young, S. (2006), 'Australian Election Slogans, 1949-2004', *Australian Journal of Communication,* 33(1), pp. 1-19; see also, Brooks, Erik J. (2017), *Slogans We Can Believe In: An Examination of What Makes for an Effective Presidential Campaign Slogan*, MA Thesis, Charlotte, NC: University of North Carolina
280. _____ (2020), 'Slogan'. *Merriam-Webster.com Dictionary* Merriam-Webster, merriam-webster.com/dictionary/slogan, Accessed 21 May 2020
281. Young (2006), pp. 15 ff
282. Whitlam (1971), pp. 827-32
283. Brereton, D. and J. Walter (1979), 'Question Time Performance and Leadership Style: A Study of Whitlam and Fraser', *Australian Political Studies,* August, pp. 301-16
284. _____ (2005), 'Key symbol'. *Dictionary of Military and Associated Terms,* US Department of Defense. Accessed 21 May 2020 thefreedictionary.com/key+symbol
285. Lasswell, Harold D. and Nathan Leites (1949), *Language of Politics: Studies in Quantitative Semantics,* New York: G.W. Stewart, p. 13
286. Williams, Raymond (1985), *Keywords: A Vocabulary of Culture and Society,* Revised edn, New York: Oxford University Press, p. 93
287. Lasswell, p. 13
288. Plato, *The Republic,* Book IV, pp. 426-435, gutenberg.org/files/1497/1497-h/1497-h.htm#link2H_4_0007
289. _____ (2020), 'Jargon'. *Merriam-Webster.com Dictionary* Merriam-Webster, merriam-webster.com/dictionary/jargon, Accessed 21 May 2020
290. Munro, André (2016), 'Ministerial responsibility', *Encyclopedia Britannica*, www.britannica.com/topic/ministerial-responsibility.%20Accessed%20May%2021, Accessed 20 May 2020
291. Crisp, L. F. (1961), *Australian National Government,* London: Oxford University Press, p. 320
292. Lewis, C.S. (1960), *Studies in Words,* 1st edn, Cambridge: Cambridge University Press, p. 7
293. Crystal, David (2008a), *A Dictionary of Linguistics and Phonetics,* 6th edn, Oxford: Blackwell, p. 491
294. Williams, p. 174
295. Crystal and Davy, p. 71
296. Whitlam (1971), p. 827
297. Whitlam (1971), p. 827
298. Whitlam (1971), p. 828
299. Whitlam (1971), p. 827
300. Whitlam (1971), pp. 827-8
301. Whitlam (1971), p. 828
302. Onions, C.T. (1972), *Shorter Oxford English Dictionary: On Historical Principles,* 3rd edn, Oxford, UK: Clarendon, p. 209
303. Whitlam, E. Gough (1980), communication with author, 15 September

304. Lake, D.J. (1971), *Style and Meaning*, St. Lucia, Qld: University of Queensland Press Research Papers
305. Flint, E. H. (1970), 'Comparison of Spoken and Written English: Towards an Integrated Method of Linguistic Description', in Ransom, W.S. (Ed.), *English Transported*, Canberra: Australian National University Press, p. 169
306. Flint, pp. 161-87
307. Whitlam (1971), p. 832
308. A detailed analysis showed this paragraph consisted of:
    1. Six sentences or thirteen breath groups according to the following morpheme count:
    i (34) *ii* (24,21,17) *iii* (15) *iv* (12) *v* (14,23,8) *vi* (26, 9, 7, 9); and
    2. The following sentence structures [with sentence elements represented by S=subject, P=Predicator, C=Complement, and A=Adjunct]:
    SPA / SPC / SPC / SPC / SPC / ASPC

7: Choices for Public Talk

309. Kinney, Thomas (2016) 'Book of Quotations on Rhetoric', *Kairos: A Journal of Rhetoric, Technology, and Pedagogy* [pdf: pp. 2-3]
310. Lerner, Jennifer, Ye Li, Piercarlo Valdesolo, and Karim S. Kassam (2015), 'Emotion and Decision Making', *The Annual Review of Psychology*, 13 September, pp. 33.1-25, doi: 10.1146/annurev-psych-010213-115043
311. [Items asterisked* available in Chapter 18]
(i) Griffith (1891), *The Political Geography of Australia*
(ii) *Lawson (1891b), *Womanhood Suffrage*
(iii) *Curtin (1942), *Speech to America*
(iv) *Menzies (1965), *Eulogy for Churchill*
(v) *Whitlam (1975), *Partnership in the Pacific after Vietnam*
(vi) Walker [Oodgeroo Noonuccal] (1970b), *How Well Off are Aborigines in Modern-day Australia?*
(vii) Hawke (1975), *In Memoriam, Albert Monk-Panegyric*
(viii) *Gilbert (1974), *The Needs of First Nations*
(ix) Greer (1971), *Address to The National Press Club*, Washington DC
(x) *Kirby (1980a), *The Australian Community and Anti-heroes*
312. Hogben, pp. 271-4, with features selected from this study as well as additions from Evelyn Heath's table comparing Churchill, Menzies, Fraser, Burns, and Whitlam, in Heath, Evelyn (unpublished), 'Representative Speeches of Gough Whitlam: The Complete Study'
313. Miller, Carolyn R. and Ashley R. Kelly (Eds.) (2017), *Emerging Genres in New Media Environments*, Basingstoke: Palgrave Macmillan
314. Lakoff and Johnson, p. 5
315. Dascal, p. 21-2
316. Hawke (1974); again in his 1977 'Address to the Farm Writers' and Broadcasters' Society', n.d., n.p., Sheraton Motor Inn, cited by McGregor, Craig (2004), 'Inside Bob Hawke', in Ricketson, Matthew (Ed.), *The Best Australian Profiles*, Melbourne: Black, p. 31; and, in his 1997 *Speech on the Occasion of the Signing of the Memorandum of*

Understanding between the Hon R.J.L. Hawke AC and the University of South Australia to Establish the Bob Hawke Prime Ministerial Centre, 9 December
317. Menzies (1965), p. 2
318. Hamilton, Craig (2013), '"The Rhetoric of Text" Reconsidered in Fiction and Autobiography', *Études de stylistique anglaise [Online]*, Online since 19 February 2019, journals.openedition.org/esa/1433; doi.org/10.4000/esa.1433, Accessed 19 September 2020
319. Flesch, Rudolph (1962), *The Art of Plain Talk*, New York: Collier Macmillan, p. 56
320. Petelin, Roslyn (1985), 'Technical Writing: A Crack in the Paradigm', *Australian Journal of Communication*, 7, p. 14
321. Miller, Rodney G. (1977), 'The Quiet Rhetoric of Sir Samuel Walker Griffith', *Australian Scan: Journal of Human Communication*, 3, p. 62
322. Milic, Louis Tonko (1966), 'Unconscious Ordering in the Prose of Swift', in Leed, J. (Ed.), *The Computer and Literary Style*, Kent, OH: Kent State University Press, pp. 79-106
323. Crystal, David (2006), *Language and the Internet*, 2nd edn, Cambridge: Cambridge University Press
324. Crystal and Davy, p. 113
325. Crystal and Davy, p. 152
326. Whitlam (1975a), p. 5
327. Hamilton (2013)
328. Flint, pp. 161-87
329. Heath, p. 31
330. See for example, Kirby (1981a)
331. Miller, Rodney G. (1976a), p. 23
332. Steffens, Niklas K. and S. Alexander Haslam (2013), 'Power through "Us": Leaders' Use of We-Referencing Language Predicts Election Victory', *Plos One*, October, https://journals.plos.org/plosone/article?id=10.1371/journal.pone.0077952, Accessed 6 February 2021
333. Kirby, Michael D. (1980c) 16 May and (2021a) 21 September, communications with author
334. Crystal and Davy, p. 5
335. Kirby, Michael D. (1981b), communication with author, 16 July
336. Freudenberg, Graham (1978), communication with author, 6 June
337. Whitlam (1975a), p. 5
338. Crystal and Davy, p. 226
339. Hogben, p. 270
340. Hogben, p. 277
341. Hogben, p. 277
342. Crystal and Davy, p. 112
343. Hogben, p. 276
344. Pullum, Geoffrey K (2010), 'Fear and Loathing of the English Passive', *Language and Communication*, 102, Vol. 26, No. 2, June, pp. 34-44
345. Milic (1967), p. 199
346. Kress and Hodge, p. 106

347. Wells, Rulon, pp. 213-20
348. Kress and Hodge, p. 31
349. Kress and Hodge, p. 31
350. Nominals consist of nouns, pronouns, adjectives, prepositions (other than post-verbal prepositions), particles and other parts of speech that attach to nouns (such as noun phrases). Likewise, verbals include verbs, adverbs, post-verbal prepositions and other parts of speech that attach to verbs, including verbal nouns.
351. Crystal and Davy, p. 44
352. Whitlam (1975a), p. 5
353. Curtin (1942)
354. Whitlam (1975a), p. 5
355. Penman, Robyn (1980), 'Interpersonal Communication: Competence and Coordination', *Australian Scan: Journal of Human Communication*, 9 & 10, p. 31
356. Beausang, Chris (2020), 'A Brief History of the Theory and Practice of Computational Literary Criticism (1963-2020)', *magazén*, 1:2, pp. 181-202, doi: 10.30687/mag/2724-3923/2020/02/002; Milic (1966); Enkvist (1964)
357. Jordan, Kayla N.; Sterling, Joanna; Pennebaker, James W.; and Boyd, Ryan L. (2019), 'Examining long-term trends in politics and culture through language of political leaders and cultural institutions', in Pinker, Stephen (Ed.), *Proceedings National Academy of Sciences*, February 26, 2019, 116 (9), pp. 3476-81
358. McGee, pp. 268-9

8: The Quiet Rhetoric of Sir Samuel Walker Griffith

359. Bernays, C.A. (1919), *Queensland Politics during Sixty Years (1859-1919)*, Brisbane: Government Printer, p. 200
360. One example of media exploitation of this view was as late as 1975, 'Are Queenslanders So Different?' *Monday Conference*, No. 166, 17 November, ABC Television (Australia)
361. _____ (1891), *The Bulletin*, 3 October, p. 6
362. _____ (1893), *The Bulletin*, 22 April, p. 5
363. _____ (2020), 'kanaka', *Merriam-Webster Dictionary*, merriam-webster.com/dictionary/kanaka, Accessed 8 August 2020. Used as a generic name for South Sea Islanders transported to Queensland in the nineteenth and early twentieth centuries.
364. _____ (1891), *The Bulletin*, 4 June, p. 6
365. _____ (1892), *Brisbane Courier* [abridged from the *Ipswich Advocate*], 9 March
366. Snyder, Louis L. (1955), *The Age of Reason*, Princeton: Van Nostrand, pp. 87-8
367. Griffith (1919), p. 6
368. Griffith, Samuel Walker (n.d.), Sir Samuel Walker Griffith: Newscuttings, Sydney: MSS Mitchell Library, p. 103
369. Griffith, Samuel Walker (1897), *Notes on the Draft Federal Constitution Framed by the Adelaide Convention*, Brisbane: E. Gregory Government Printer
370. McGee, pp. 268-9
371. [see Chapter 18] Griffith (1895)

372. Griffith, Samuel Walker (1889), 'The Distribution of Wealth', *Centennial Magazine 1888-1889*, 1, pp. 833-42
373. Griffith (1889), p. 1
374. Griffith, Samuel Walker (1892a), 'Sir Samuel Walker Griffith's Manifesto', *Brisbane Courier*, 13 February
375. Griffith, Samuel Walker (1919), 'The Social Problem: a Fundamental Error, The Solution', *The Daily Mail*, 1 November, p. 6
376. Griffith (1889), p. 833-4
377. Griffith (1891), pp. 68-81
378. Griffith (1891), p. 69
379. Griffith (1891), p. 80
380 Griffith (1895)
381. Griffith (1895)
382. Griffith (1895)
383. Griffith, Samuel Walker (1893), 'The Coloured Labour Question in Australia', *Antipodean*, pp. 13-7
384. Griffith, (1892a)
385. Griffith (1892a)
386. Griffith, Samuel Walker (n.d.), 'Letters to Lady Musgrave', Papers of Sir Anthony and Lady Musgrave', Microfilm, Brisbane: Oxley Memorial Library
387. Griffith (n.d.), 'Letters to Lady Musgrave'
388. Griffith (1919), p. 6
389. Pannam, Clifford L. (1963), 'The Radical Chief Justice', *Australian Law Journal*, 37(9), p. 275
390. Derry, John W. (1967), *The Radical Tradition–Tom Paine to Lloyd George*, London: Macmillan, p. xi
391. Griffith (1919)
392. Graham, A. Douglas (1939), *The Life of the Right Honourable Sir Samuel Walker Griffith, G.C.M.G., P.C.*, Sydney: Law Book, p. 91
393. Griffith, Samuel Walker (before November 1889), *Wealth and Want*, Brisbane: Black, Reid & Co, Printers
394. Griffith, Samuel Walker (n.d.), 'A Plea for the Study of the Unconscious Vital Processes in the Life of Communities', *Australian Association for the Advancement of Science 6*, pp. 659-67
395. Griffith, Samuel Walker (1892b), 'Manifesto to the Electors of North Brisbane, 1888, in Adams, F. (Ed.), *The Australians*, n.p., pp. 281-94
396. Griffith, Samuel Walker (n.d.), Sir Samuel Walker Griffith: Letters to His Wife, Sydney: MSS Mitchell and Dixson Libraries, p. 29. I am grateful to the late Roger Joyce for his reference to this letter.

9: Louisa Lawson on Womanhood Suffrage

397. Motto adopted for the Womanhood Suffrage League; cited in O'Connor, Gertrude (1920), 'Womanhood Suffrage League, the Development of the Movement', *Louisa Lawson, Her Life and Work*, Part II, Volume 190: Angus and Robertson Manuscript by Gertrude O'Connor, Mitchell Library of New South Wales, Microfilm CY 1216,

p. 13 [Note: The author of this biography, Gertrude O'Connor, was a daughter of Louisa Lawson.]
398. Lawson, Louisa [Dora Falconer] (1888), 'About Ourselves', *The Dawn*, 1(1), 15 May, pp. 3-4
399. Russell, Penny (2004), 'A Woman of the Future? Feminism and Conservatism in Colonial New South Wales', *Women's History Review*, 13(1), p. 79
400. _____ (2020), 'Lawson, Louisa (1848–1920)', *Obituaries Australia, National Centre of Biography*, The Australian National University, oa.anu.edu.au/obituary/lawson-louisa-7121/text35156, Accessed 22 September 2020
401. Lawson, Louisa [Dora Falconer] (1889), 'Our Anniversary', *The Dawn*, 2(1), 1 May, p. 3
402. Lawson (1891a), in O'Connor, p. 14
403. Lawson (1889)
404. [see Chapter 18] Lawson (1891b), p. 10
405. Lawson (1891b)
406. McGee, pp. 268-9
407. Lawson (1891b)
408. Lawson (1891b)
409. Lawson (1891b)
410. Summers, Anne (2016), *Dammed Whores and God's Police*, Sydney: NewSouth Publishing, p. 12
411. Lawson (1891b)
412. Lawson (1891b)
413. Lawson (1891b)
414. Lawson (1891b)
415. Lawson (1891b)
416. Lawson (1891b)
417. Lawson (1891b)
418. Lawson (1891b)
419. Lawson (1891b)
420. Lawson (1891b)

10: Alfred Deakin's Language Strategy

421. Deakin, Alfred (1898), These Are Times to Try Men's Souls, Address at the Annual Conference of the Australian Natives' Association (ANA), Bendigo, cited in _____ (1913), 'Alfred Deakin. An Appreciation', *The Advance Australia*, 18(1), 1 January, p. 4; also cited in Headon, David (2018), *Alfred Deakin (1856-1919): Australia's Second Prime Minister*, Canberra: Australian Parliamentary Library, p. 96: 'This historic speech is reproduced as Appendix II, in *A. Deakin, The federal story—the inner history of the federal cause 1880–1900*, La Nauze, J.A. (Ed.), (1963), Parkville, Vic: Melbourne University Press, pp. 177-9. Deakin's son-in-law, Herbert Brookes, in collaboration with his wife, Ivy, Deakin's daughter, edited a first edition of The federal story in 1944'
422. Headon, David (2018), *Alfred Deakin (1856-1919): Australia's Second Prime Minister*, Canberra: Australian Parliamentary Library, p. iii

423. McGee, pp. 268-9
424. La Nauze, John Alfred (1965), *Alfred Deakin: A Biography*, Melbourne: Melbourne University Press, pp. 245-6
425. Brett, Judith (2017), *The Enigmatic Mr Deakin*, Melbourne: Text Publishing, p. v
426. Warhaft (2004), p. 11
427. Deakin (1887), p. 24
428. Deakin (1887), p. 25
429. Deakin (1887), p. 25
430. Griffith, Samuel Walker (1887), 'Opening Address', *Proceedings of the Colonial Conference 1887, Colonial Conference*, London, England, p. 25
431. Headon, p. 54
432. Coleman, William (2018), 'Six Problems in the Biography of Alfred Deakin', *Agenda*, 25(1), pp. 79-91
433. Headon, p. 49
434. Brett, Judith (2019), 'Alfred Deakin and Federation', in *Upholding the Australian Constitution*, Vol. 31, Melbourne: The Samuel Griffith Society, August, p. 129
435. Hearn and Tregenza, p. 182
436. Headon, p. 54
437. Headon, p. 54
438. Deakin, Alfred (1897), 'The Determination of the Large Colonies to Resist', Alfred Deakin to Sir Samuel Griffith, 21 May 1897, Griffith Papers, ADD. 452, Dixson Library, Sydney, in Bennett, Scott Cecil (1969), *Annotated documents on the making of the Commonwealth of Australia*, M.A. Thesis, Canberra: The Australian National University, p. 235
439. Deakin (1898), in Warhaft, Sally (Ed.) (2004), *Well May We Say: The Speeches That Made Australia*, Melbourne: Black,
440. Deakin (1898), p. 12
441. _____ (1913), 'Alfred Deakin. An Appreciation', p. 4
442. Deakin (1898), in Warhaft (2004), p. 13
443. Deakin (1898), in Warhaft (2004), p.14
444. Deakin (1898), in Warhaft (2004), p.14
445. Deakin, Alfred (1899), 'Address at Melbourne Town Hall', *The Argus*, 27 July
446. Deakin, Alfred (1903), *Federal Campaign Policy Speech*, 29 October 1903, at Ballarat
447. Hamilton (2013)
448. Hamilton (2013)
449. Deakin (1903)
450. Hearn and Tregenza, p. 179 and p. 182
451. Deakin (1903)
452. Deakin (1903)
453. Deakin (1903)
454. Deakin (1903)
455. Deakin (1903)
456. Deakin (1903)
457. _____ (2020), '1906 Australian Federal Election', *Wikipedia*, Accessed 12 September 2020

458. Deakin, Alfred (1906), *Policy Speech: Protectionist Party*, 17 October 1906, at Ballarat
459. Deakin (1906)
460. Deakin (1906)
461. Deakin (1906)
462. Deakin (1906)
463. Deakin (1906)
464. _____ (2020), 'kanaka', *Merriam-Webster Dictionary*
465. Deakin (1906)
466. Deakin (1906)
467. Deakin (1906)

11: Sir Robert Menzies's Measured Style

468. Menzies (1965), p. 1
469. Murphy, James C. (2020), '"The time has come to say something of the forgotten class": How Menzies Transformed Australian Political Debate', *The Conversation*, June 17
470. Menzies, Robert G. (1942), *The Forgotten People*, 22 May Liberals.net, www.liberals.net/theforgottenpeople.htm, Accessed 27 May 2020
471. McCabe, Katherine (2013), 'From Town Hall to Global Village: The Transformation of Australian Political Speech', *Australian Journal of Communication*, 40(3), p. 140; see also, Gorman, L. (1998), 'Menzies and Television: A Medium He "Endured"', *Media International Australia*, 87, pp. 49-67
472. Wannan, p. 51
473. Menzies (1961b), p. 3
474. Menzies (1961b), p. 1
475. Menzies, Robert G. (1964), *Address to National Press Club Luncheon*, Canberra: National Archive
476. Halloran, p. 621
477. Miller, (1976a), p. 24
478. Menzies (1965), p. 1
479. Miller, (1976a), p. 21
480. _____ (2020), 'Robert Menzies', *Australia's Prime Ministers*, Canberra: National Archives of Australia
481. Copeland, L. and Lamm, L.W. (Eds.) (1972), *The World's Great Speeches*, New York: Dover, pp. 3-8
482. McGee, pp. 268-9
483. Menzies (1965), p. 1
484. Menzies (1965), pp.1-2
485. Menzies (1965), p. 2
486. Copeland and Lamm, p. 446
487. Menzies (1965), p. 2
488. Menzies (1965), p. 2
489. Menzies (1965), p. 2
490. Menzies (1965), p. 1
491. Flint, pp. 161-87

492. Menzies (1948)
493. _____ (1953), *Queen Elizabeth's Coronation Book*, Melbourne: Colourgravure
494. Governor-General of Australia, uploaded (2010), 'Queen in Canberra', *YouTube*, 19 November
495. Robson, p. 142

12: Action Calls of Kevin Gilbert and Oodgeroo Noonuccal

496. [see Chapter 18] Gilbert
497. Gilbert
498. Gilbert
499. Australian Law Reform Commission (2010), 'Changing Policies towards Aboriginal People', *Aboriginal Societies: The Experience of Contact*, Report 31, 18 August
500. Walker, Kath [Oodgeroo Noonuccal] (1970b), p. 92
501. Brennan, Elliott (2013), 'On This Day: Indigenous People Get Citizenship', *Australian Geographic*, November 7
502. Robinson, S. (1994), 'The Aboriginal Embassy: An Account of the Protests of 1972', *Aboriginal History*, 18 (1/2), pp. 49-63
503. _____ (2021), The Whitlam Institute, https://www.whitlam.org/whitlam-legacy-aboriginal-and-torres-strait-islander-peoples, Accessed 14 February 2021
504. Walker (1970b), p. 88
505. Walker (1970b), pp. 88-9
506. Shoemaker, Adam (2004), *Black Words, White Page: Aboriginal Literature* 1929-1988, Canberra: ANU Press, p. 186
507. Walker, Kath [Oodgeroo Noonuccal] (1970a), *My People*, Milton, Qld: Jacaranda, (i) (1968), *Integration and Queensland Society*, A paper delivered at the Abschol seminar on Aboriginal conditions', May, pp. 42-4; (ii) (1970b), *How Well Off are Aborigines in Modern-day Australia?* Speech at Pius XII Seminary, Banyo, 21 March, pp. 88-92; and (iii) (1988), 'Acceptance Speech', in *Kunapipi*, 16(1), 1994
508. Gilbert
509. Headon, David (1994), 'A Response to Gordon Briscoe', *Aboriginal History*, 18(1/2), p. 40
510. Headon (1994), p. 40
511. Briscoe, Gordon (1994), 'The Struggle for Grace: An Appreciation of Kevin John Gilbert', *Aboriginal History*, 18(1/2), p. 28
512. _____ (2009), 'Abstract', *The Cherry Pickers, drama-Three acts*, Author: Kevin Gilbert, First known date: 1968, austlit.edu.au/austlit/page/C115619, Accessed 25 June 2020
513. Gilbert
514. Gilbert
515. Gilbert
516. McGee, pp. 268-9
517. Dascal, pp. 15-33
518. Connors, Libby (1995), 'My People, Our Past', *LiNQ*, (22)2, p. 129
519. Walker (1968), pp. 42-4
520. Walker (1970b), pp. 88-92

521. Oodgeroo (1988)
522. Walker (1968), p. 42
523. Walker (1968), p. 42
524. Walker (1970b), p. 88
525. Walker (1970b), p. 89
526. Oodgeroo (1988)
527. Oodgeroo (1988)
528. Walker (1968), pp. 42-4
529. Walker (1970b), pp. 89-90
530. Oodgeroo (1988)
531. Oodgeroo (1988)
532. Dascal, pp. 15-33
533. Gilbert
534. Gilbert
535. Gilbert
536. Gilbert
537. Tollefson, Michael M. (2017), 'Rhetoric, Aristotle's Pathos 3', in Allen, Mike (Ed.) (2017), *The SAGE Encyclopedia of Communication Research Methods,* Thousand Oaks, CA: Sage, p. 1483
538. Gilbert
539. Gilbert
540. Gilbert
541. Gilbert
542. Tatz, Colin (2011), *Genocide in Australia: By Accident or Design?, Indigenous Human Rights and History: occasional papers,* 1(1), Melbourne: Monash University, p. 83

13: 'Revolution' Rhetoric of Germaine Greer

543. Gillard, p. 11583
544. Greer, Germaine (1970), *The Female Eunuch,* London: Paladin
545. Nelson, Camilla (2020), 'Friday Essay: The Female Eunuch at 50, Germaine Greer's Fearless, Feminist Masterpiece', *The Conversation,* 8 October
546. PhyllisauFeu (2014), Comment on 26 January, 5.33 #2, 'What Germaine Greer and The Female Eunuch Mean to Me', *The Guardian,* 25 January, www.theguardian.com/books/2014/jan/26/germaine-greer-female-eunuch-feminists-influence
547. PhyllisauFeu
548. Greer, Germaine (2008), *The Female Eunuch,* New York: Harper Collins, p. 28
549. Booth
550. Quirk, Randolph (1972), *The English Language and Images of Matter,* London: Oxford University Press, p. 106
551. Greer (1971)
552. Partridge, Eric (1949), *A Dictionary of Slang and Unconventional English,* London: Routledge and Kegan Paul, p. 198
553. Partridge, Eric (1970), Slang Today and Yesterday, London: Routledge and Kegan Paul, p. 325 [citing Matthews, B., 'The Function of Slang']

554. Partridge (1949), p. 198
555. Greer (1970), pp. 315-31
556. Brandt, W.J., pp. 281-4; and B. Vickers (1970), *Classical Rhetoric in English Poetry*, London: St. Martins', pp. 125-50, for definitions of these devices with Vickers's definition accepted when differences occur
557. Greer (1970), p. 315
558. Thompson, W.N. (1967), *Quantitative Research in Public Address and Communication*, New York: Random House, p. 63
559. Brandt, p. 167
560. Lower-case *italic* Roman numeral [e.g. '*i*'] refers to sentence number in paragraph.
561. Onions, C.T. (1971), *Modern English Syntax*, London: Routledge and Kegan Paul, p. 2
562. Quirk, p. 103
563. Twaddell, W.F. (1968), *The English Verb Auxiliaries*, Providence, RI: Brown University Press, p. 16
564. Upper-case Roman numeral [e.g., 'I'] refers to paragraph number and the lower-case *italic* Roman numeral [e.g., '*i*'] refers to sentence number in paragraph.
565. Greer (1970), p. 316
566. Brown, H. (1966), *Prose Styles – Five Primary Types*, Minneapolis, MN: University of Minnesota Press, p. 20
567. Dixon, P. (1971), *Rhetoric*, London: Methuen, p. 36
568. Segal, Ronald (1967), *The Race War*, Harmondsworth, Pelican, p. 446
569. Millett, Kate (1970), *Sexual Politics*, Garden City, NY: Doubleday
570. Orwell (1981), 'Politics and the English Language', *A Collection of Essays*, Orlando, FL: Harvest, pp. 156-71
571. Orwell (1981), p. 170
572. I acknowledge the late David Lake, Reader in English at The University of Queensland, for this comment.
573. Wells, Rulon (1960), 'Nominal and Verbal Style', in Sebeok, T.A. (Ed.), *Style in Language*, Cambridge, MA: MIT Press, pp. 213-20
574. Andreasen, Nancy J. C. and Bruce Pfohl (1976), 'Linguistic Analysis of Speech in Affective Disorders', Arch Gen Psychiatry, 33(11), *JAMA Psychiatry*, American Medical Association, November, pp. 1361-7
575. Milic (1967), p. 199
576. Milic (1967), p. 195
577. Wells, Rulon, pp. 213-20
578. Milic (1966), pp. 79-106
579. Gibson, Walker T. (1966), *Tough, Sweet and Stuffy*, Bloomington: University of Indiana Press
580. Gibson, pp. 134-6
581. Bormann, Ernest G. et al, (1978), 'Power, Authority, and Sex: Male Response to Female Leadership', *Communication Monographs*, 45(2), June, pp. 119-55
582. Johnson, Carole S. and Inga K. Kelly (1975), '"He" and "She": Changing Language to Fit a Changing World', *Educational Leadership*, 32(8), May, p. 530

14: Winning on Television—Bob Hawke

583. Hawke, Robert J. (1983a), *Australian Labor Party Federal Election Policy Speech 1983*, delivered at Sydney Opera House, 16 February, Kingston, ACT: Australian Labor Party
584. Mills, Stephen and Rodney Smith (2020), 'Leaders' Debates in Australian Elections', Juárez-Gámiz, Julio, Christina Holtz-Bacha, Alan Schroeder (Eds.), *Routledge International Handbook on Electoral Debates*, New York: Routledge, pp. 281-2
585. Pateman, Trevor (1974), *Television and the February 1974 General Election*, London: British Film Institute, p. 6
586. Gizzi-Stewart, Brooke (2018), *The Language of Strategy: A Study in Australian Prime Ministerial Rhetoric and Campaign Speechmaking, 1983-2013*, PhD Thesis, Newcastle, NSW: The University of Newcastle, p. 122
587. Gizzi-Stewart (2018), p. 124
588. Fraser, Malcolm (1983), *Liberal Party Federal Election Policy Speech 1983*, delivered at Melbourne on 15 February, Barton, ACT: Liberal Party of Australia
589. Menzies (1961b), p. 1
590. Hawke (1983)
591. _____ (2020) 'Bob Hawke formally launched his election policy speech on Ash Wednesday', 16 February 1983 australianpolitics.com/1983/02/16/bob-hawke-alp-federal-election-policy-speech.html Accessed 20 June 2020
592. Cooper, L. (1960), *The Rhetoric of Aristotle: An Expanded Translation with Supplementary Examples for Students of Composition and Public Speaking*, Englewood Cliffs, NJ: Prentice-Hall
593. Corcoran, Paul (1980), *Rhetoric and Political Language*, St. Lucia, Qld: University of Queensland Press
594. Cushman, Donald P. and John M. Penhallurick (1984), 'Political Images in the Hawke-Fraser Campaign', Smith III, Ted J., Graeme Osborne, and Robyn Penman (Eds.), *Communication and Government: Issues Policies and Trends*, p. 35
595. Cushman and Penhallurick, p. 26
596. Cushman and Penhallurick, p. 24
597. Wiemann, John M. and Philip Backlund (1980), 'Current Theory and Research in Communicative Competence', *Review of Educational Research*, 50(1), pp.185-99
598. Wiemann and Backlund, p. 190
599. Hawke, Robert J. (1983b), *Speech at Labor Day Dinner*, by The Hon R.J. Hawke, AC MP, Prime Minister, Melbourne, The Labor Day Dinner, 12 March, p. 1
600. [see Chapter 18] Hawke, Robert J. (1983c), *Address by the Prime Minister, Hon R.J. Hawke AC MP, to the National Economic Summit Conference*, House of Representatives, Canberra, 11 April, p. 9
601. Gizzi-Stewart (2018), p. 139
602. Gorman, L., pp. 49-67
603. McCabe, p. 140

15: Reform Advocacy of Michael Kirby

604. Kirby (1980a), p. 31

605. Kirby, Michael D. (2020), *The Hon Michael Kirby AC CMG—Speeches Website*, www.michaelkirby.com.au/speeches, Accessed 16 September 2020
606. Kirby, Michael D. (2016a), *Academic and Institutional Law Reform in Australia: Past, Passing and To Come*, 15 April, Canberra, Website Speech No. 2845, p. 30
607. Kirby (2016a), p. 36
608. Kirby, Michael D. (2020), 'Welcome message', Website
609. Dascal, p. 23
610. Kirby, Michael D. (2010), *The Internalisation of Domestic Law and Its Consequences, Public Conversation between The Hon Justice Antonin Scalia, Associate Justice of the Supreme Court of the United States of America and The Hon Michael Kirby, Justice of the High Court of Australia, 1996-2009*, 9 February, Website Speech No. 2441, pp. 1-21
611. Kirby (2010), p. 21
612. Kirby, Michael D. (1980b), *Australia into the Eighties: The Challenge of Change*, Canberra Australia Day Council, National Press Club, 25 January, Website Speech, No. 138, p.1
613. Kirby (1980b), p. 2
614. Kirby, Michael D. (1980d), *Interview with Mr John Laws, Sydney Radio Station 2UE*, 31 January, Website Speech, No. 139A, p. 1
615. Kirby, Michael D. (1992), *Dinner to Celebrate the 80th Birthday of The Hon Sir Asher Joel, KBE, AO*, May, Sydney: Parliament of New South Wales, Website Speech, No. 946, p. 2
616. Kirby, Michael D. (2012a), 'Eleanor Roosevelt Drives By', Grodin, Michael; Tarantola, Daniel; Annas, George; and Gruskin, Sophia (Eds.), *Health and Human Rights*, Website Speech, No. 2609, p. 10
617. Kirby, Michael D. (2015), *Whatever Would Miss Telfer Think of a Queer Collective*, Website Speech No. 2764, p. 1
618. Kirby (2015), p. 2
619. Kirby, Michael D. (2014), *Neville Wran—The Enigma, State Funeral of The Hon Neville Kenneth Wran, AC, CNZM, QC*, 1 May, Sydney, Website Speech, No. 2710, pp. 8-9
620. Kirby, Michael D. (2016b), *Memorial Occasion for the Late Judy Cassab AO, CBE: Conversations with Judy & A Stringbag of Adjectives*, 11 February, Sydney Domain, Website Speech No. 2818, p. 1
621. Kirby (2016b), pp. 1-6
622. Kirby (1980a), pp. 16-31
623. Leech and Short, p. 76
624. Kirby (1980a), p. 16
625. Kirby (1980a), pp. 18-19
626. Hamilton (2013)
627. Kirby (1980a), p. 16
628. Kirby (1980a), p. 16
629. Kirby (1980a), p. 16
630. Kirby (1980a), p. 17
631. Kirby (1980a), p. 17
632. Kirby (1980a), p. 16
633. Kirby (1980a), p. 21

634. Kirby (1980a), p. 22
635. Kirby (1980a), p. 29
636. Kirby (1980a), p. 31
637. Kirby, Michael D. (2012b), *Human Rights Protection in Australia–A Riposte to Chief Justice Keane, Austin Asche Lecture 2012*, 27 August, Darwin: Charles Darwin University, Website Speech, No. 2622, p. 24

16: Continuing to Speak Out–Paul Keating, John Howard, Kevin Rudd, Julia Gillard, Noel Pearson, and Scott Morrison

638. Morrison
639. Metherell, Lexie (2014), 'Keating Speechwriter Don Watson Says Gough Whitlam's Memorial Shows Thirst for Meaty Speeches', *ABC News*, 14 November
640. Metherell
641. Clark, Andrew (2014), 'The "Old Man" Laid to Rest', *Financial Review*, 6 November
642. Collins (2017b)
643. [see Chapter 18] Keating (1992)
644. Keating (1992)
645. Clark, Tom (2013), 'Paul Keating's Redfern Park Speech and Its Rhetorical Legacy', *Overland*, 213
646. Keating (1992)
647. Howard, John (1996a), 'Tasmania: Tragedy at Port Arthur–Address to Parliament', 30 April, *Commonwealth Parliamentary Debates–Representatives*, No. 206, 38th Parliament, First Session, First Period, p. 23
648. Howard (1996a), p. 23
649. Howard, John (1996b), *Press Conference, Parliament House,* Canberra: Department of the Prime Minister and Cabinet, Australian Government, 10 May
650. [see Chapter 18] Howard (1996c)
651. Clark, Tom (2008), 'The Cup of John Howard's Poetry: A Brief Rhetorispective', *Overland*, 190, p. 28
652. Howard (1996c)
653. Howard (1996c)
654. Howard (1996c)
655. Kane and Patapan, p. 384
656. Rudd
657. Morgan, D.L., Slade, M.D., C.M.A. Morgan (1997), 'Aboriginal Philosophy and Its Impact on Health Care Outcomes', *Australian and New Zealand Journal of Public Health*, 21, p. 598
658. Rudd, p. 167
659. Rudd, p. 173
660. [see Chapter 18] Gillard
661. Clark, Tom (2016), 'Form Versus Content', *Overland*, 225, Summer
662. Gillard, pp. 11581-5
663. Gillard, p. 11584

664. Trimble, Linda (2016), 'Julia Gillard and the Gender Wars', *Politics and Gender*, (12)2, June, pp. 296-316
665. Pearson
666. Pearson
667. Pearson
668. Sharpe, Matthew J. (2018), '"This Old Man": Noel Pearson's Eulogy to Gough Whitlam, Four Years On', www.academia.edu/37702416/_This_Old_Man_Remembering_Noel_Pearson_s_November_2014_Eulogy_to_Gough_Whitlam, Accessed 29 January 2021
669. Pearson
670. Pearson
671. [see Chapter 18] Morrison
672. Morrison
673. McGee, pp. 268-9
674. Petelin, Roslyn (2021), '"Strollout" Has Gathered Pace, Romping Home as the Macquarie Word of the Year. I'd Have Gone for "Vax", if on the List', *The Conversation*, 29 November

17: Conclusion

675. Ellul, p. 250
676. Rolfe, Mark (2014), 'Looking Backwards to the Future: The Evolving Tradition of Ideal Political Rhetoric in Australia', in Uhr and Walter, p. 123, citing Hanson, Russel (1985), *The Democratic Imagination in America: Conversations with our Past*, Princeton: Princeton University Press, pp. 23-4
677. Collins (2017a), p. 337
678. Collins (2017a), p. 78
679. Collins (2017a), p. 78
680. Morrison
681. Biden, Joseph R. (2021), *Inaugural Address, January 20, 2021*, Washington DC: The White House, United States Government
682. Trump, Donald (2020), *Remarks by President Trump at the National Thanksgiving Turkey Pardoning Ceremony*, Washington DC: White House, United States Government, November 24
683. Petelin, Roslyn (2021)
684. Packard, Vance (1957), *The Hidden Persuaders*, London: Longmans Green
685. Crystal, David (2006); and (2008b), *Txtng: The gr8 db8*, Oxford: Oxford University Press
686. Woolley and Howard
687. McGee, pp. 268-9

18: Notable Speeches and Writing

688. _____ (1924), 'Melba's Good-Bye in Opera', *The Argus*, 14 October, p. 11
689. See e.g. N. Brown, Ned Kelly: Australian Son; C.F. Cave, Ned Kelly: Man and Myth; K. Dunstan, Saint Ned; J. Molony, I am Ned Kelly; J. McQuilton, The Kelly

Outbreak 1878-1880. These recent additions to the Kelly Library are reviewed in *The Bulletin,* 11 November 1980, p. 97

690. For the alternative point of view, see R. Ryan, Redmond Barry: A Colonial Life 1813-1880 and Sir Zelman Cowen, 'Redmond Barry Oration – Extract', *Australian Law News,* November 1980, 6; See also Sir Zelman Cowen, *Address to the Annual Dinner of the Chamber of Commerce and Industry,* South Australia, 21 November 1980, mimeo, p. 13
691. Cited in K. Dunstan, Ned!, a condensed version of Saint Ned in *Reader's Digest,* June 1980, 191, p. 238
692. O. Gray, 'Lalor Makes a Better Hero', Letter to *The Age,* 27 October 1980, 12
693. E.G. Whitlam in Young's biography of Theodore, cited in W.F. Broderick, 'Gough Whitlam: His Blessed Dawn and the Tragic Flaw of Omnipotence', *The Age,* 13 November 1980, p. 11
694. Broderick, ibid
695. Sir Charles Hotham, Letter to Sir George Gray, No. 162, 20 December 1954 in G. Blainey, *Eureka Documents,* Melbourne: The Public Record Office, 6, p. 8
696. ibid, No. 148, p. 5
697. R.G. Menzies, *Melbourne Sun,* 17 July 1946, cited in Historical Studies of Australia and New Zealand, Special Eureka Supplement, The University of Melbourne, December 1954, p. 79
698. R.G. Menzies, *Melbourne Sun,* 9 July 1946, cited loc cit
699. W. Forgan-Smith, Report of Speech to Annual Convention of Australian Workers' Union, *Sydney Morning Herald,* 2 February 1938, cited ibid, p. 78
700. H.V. Evatt, *Golden Jubilee Souvenir of the ALP, 1890-1940,* Sydney, 1940, cited ibid, p. 78
701. Evatt, loc cit
702. Henry Lawson, cited in L. Fox, *Eureka and Its Flag,* 1973, p. 14
703. See the Law Reform Commission, Criminal Investigation, 1975. The relevant provisions of the Criminal Investigation Bill 1977 (Cwlth) are clauses 18 (notification of rights in a language in which the accused is fluent); 22 (communication with relatives or friends); 27 (presence of a competent interpreter)
704. Bureau of Crime Statistics and Research (NSW), Pilot Study of Central Court of Petty Sessions, Sydney, 1973, cited in Jakubowicz and Buckley, Migrants and the Law, 1975, p. 25
705. [1979] V.R. 536
706. ibid, 538
707. Fox, p. 5
708. See Special Eureka Supplement, op cit, p. 45

BIBLIOGRAPHY

Primary Sources

Asterisked (*) items available in Chapter 18

_____ (1880), 'Trial, Conviction, and Sentence of Ned Kelly', *Border Watch* (Mount Gambier, SA: 1861-1954), 3 November

_____ (1913), 'Alfred Deakin. An Appreciation', *The Advance Australia*, 18(1), 1 January, pp. 2-4

*Atkinson, Sallyanne (1988), *Expo '88 Opening Ceremony Speech of The Rt Hon Lord Mayor of Brisbane*, South Brisbane, World Expo '88, 30 April

Atkinson, Sallyanne (2021), 'Where I Belong–Sallyanne Atkinson AO', Love, Wendy (interviewer), *Museum of Brisbane*, podcast, 19 July

Atkinson, Sallyanne (2021), communication with author, 17 October

Biden, Joseph R. (2021), *Inaugural Address, January 20, 2021*, Washington, DC: The White House, United States Government, Accessed 21 January 2021, www.whitehouse.gov/briefing-room/speeches-remarks/2021/01/20/inaugural-address-by-president-joseph-r-biden-jr/

Burnet, Macfarlane (1968), 'The Ethics of a Biologist', *Biology and the Appreciation of Life*, Melbourne: Sun Books, pp. 51-63

Carnegie, Roderick (1975), *Euthanasia by the Independent Australian*, Address to the Solicitors' Luncheon, 4 June, Wentworth Hotel, Sydney, The Law Society of New South Wales, in *Quadrant*, July

Cathcart, Michael and Kate Darian-Smith (Eds.) (2004), *Stirring Australian Speeches*, Melbourne: Melbourne University Press

Copeland, L. and L.W. Lamm (Eds.) (1972), *The World's Great Speeches*, New York: Dover

Cowen, Zelman (1970), *The University–Struggling for Balance*, Orientation Keynote Address to Students, 25 February, at The University of Queensland, St. Lucia, Qld

Curtin, John (1937), *Labor's Message to the People of Australia–Policy Speech, 20 September 1937*, Sydney: Labor Daily [Mitchell Library]

Curtin, John (1939), *Australia and the War: Labor's Standpoint*, Sydney: Australian Labor Party [Mitchell Library]

Curtin, John (1940a), *National Unity: Where Labor Stands, 9 August 1940*, Carlton, Vic.: Industrial Print

Curtin, John (1940b), *The Policy of the Labor Party, Federal Elections 1940*, Melbourne: Industrial Printing and Publicity Co. Ltd. [Mitchell Library]

Curtin, John (1941), *Motor Car Agreement: Statement Made to the Press on 27 February 1940 by the Leader of the Opposition*, Sydney [Fisher Pamphlet Library, University of Sydney]

*Curtin, John (1942), *Speech to America*, 14 March, Canberra: Australian Government, Department of the Prime Minister and Cabinet

Curtin, John (1943), *General Elections 1943: Statement of Policy by the Prime Minister*, Canberra: Australian Labor Party [Mitchell Library]

Curtin, John (1945), *Message for Brotherhood Week*, Melbourne: Brotherhood Week Committee [Mitchell Library]

Daly, Fred (1975), 'Whitlam Labour Rally, public remarks', Brisbane, 14 November, in *Speeches of the 1975 Election–Brisbane Rally*, Audio cassette, The University of Queensland Audio Visual Library

Deakin, Alfred (1887), 'Opening Address', *Proceedings of the Colonial Conference 1887*, Colonial Conference, London, England, pp. 24-25, archive.org/details/proceedingsofcol00colo_1/

Deakin, Alfred (1898), *These Are Times to Try Men's Souls*, Address at the Annual Conference of the Australian Natives' Association (ANA), Bendigo; also cited in Headon, David (2018), *Alfred Deakin (1856-1919): Australia's Second Prime Minister*, Canberra: Australian Parliamentary Library, p. 96: 'This historic speech is reproduced as Appendix II, in A. Deakin, *The federal story—the inner history of the federal cause 1880–1900*, J.A. La Nauze, (Ed.), (1963), Parkville, Vic: Melbourne University Press, pp. 177–9. Deakin's son-in-law, Herbert Brookes, in collaboration with his wife, Ivy, Deakin's daughter, edited a first edition of *The federal story* in 1944'

Deakin, Alfred (1899), Address at Melbourne Town Hall, *The Argus*, 27 July

Deakin, Alfred (1903), *Federal Campaign Policy Speech*, 29 October, at Ballarat

Deakin, Alfred (1904), 'Mr Deakin on the Situation–Coalition Necessary', *The Australasian*, 6 February, p. 35

Deakin, Alfred (1906), *Policy Speech: Protectionist Party*, 17 October, at Ballarat

Escolme-Schmidt, Elizabeth and Camilla Sandell (Ed) (1987), *Women of the Year: A Collection of Speeches by Australia's Most Successful Women*, Buderim, Qld: National Council of the Women of the Year Luncheon

*Forrest, John (1912), *Trans-Australia Railway*, Ceremony at Port Augusta to Turn the First Sod of the Trans-Australia Railway from Port Augusta to Kalgoorlie, *Barrier Miner (Broken Hill, NSW)*, Tuesday, 17 September, p. 3

Fraser, Malcolm (1971), *Towards 2000: Challenge to Australia*, The Fifth Deakin Lecture, Melbourne: University of Melbourne

Fraser, Malcolm (1983), *Liberal Party Federal Election Policy Speech 1983*, delivered at Melbourne on 15 February, Barton, ACT: Liberal Party of Australia

Freudenberg, Graham (1978), Seminar on Advanced Speech Writing at Queensland Institute of Technology (now Queensland University of Technology), Brisbane; see article (1978), 'Special Rapport', *The Courier-Mail*, 6 May

Freudenberg, Graham (1978), communication with author, 6 June

Frewin, Leslie (1973), *Immortal Jester: A Treasury of the Great Good Humour of Sir Winston Churchill 1874-1965*, London: Frewin

Fullilove, Michael (Ed.) (2014), *Men and Women of Australia: Our Greatest Modern Speeches*, Ringwood Vic: Penguin

Furse-Roberts, David (Ed.) (2017), *Menzies: The Forgotten Speeches*, Redland Bay, Qld: Jeparit Press/Connor Court

*Gilbert, Kevin (1974), *The Needs of First Nations*, first published as a lecture, in Tatz, Colin (Ed.) assisted by Keith R. McConnochie (1975), *Black Viewpoints: The Aboriginal Experience*, Sydney: Australia and New Zealand Book

*Gillard, Julia (2012), *Motion-in-Reply*–'Misogyny Speech', in *Commonwealth of Australia Parliamentary Debates–House of Representatives Official Hansard*, No. 15, 43rd Parliament, 1st Session, 7th Period, 9 October 2012, Canberra: Hansard, Parliament of Australia, pp. 11581-5, parlinfo.aph.gov.au/parlInfo/; also available at youtube.com/watch?v=fCNuPcf8L00

Greer, Germaine (1970), *The Female Eunuch*, London: Paladin

Greer, Germaine (1971), *Address to The National Press Club*, Washington D.C., 18 May

Greer, Germaine (1981), communication with author, 2 April

Greer, Germaine (2008), *The Female Eunuch*, New York: Harper Collins

Griffith, Samuel Walker (n.d.), 'A Plea for the Study of the Unconscious Vital Processes in the Life of Communities', *Australian Association for the Advancement of Science 6*, pp. 659-67

Griffith, Samuel Walker (n.d.), Sir Samuel Walker Griffith: Letters to His Wife, Sydney: MSS Mitchell Library

Griffith, Samuel Walker (n.d.), Sir Samuel Walker Griffith: Newscuttings, Sydney: MSS Mitchell Library

Griffith, Samuel Walker (n.d.), 'Letters to Lady Musgrave', Papers of Sir Anthony and Lady Musgrave, Microfilm, Brisbane: Oxley Memorial Library

Griffith, Samuel Walker (1887), 'Opening Address', *Proceedings of the Colonial Conference 1887*, Colonial Conference, London, England archive.org/details/proceedingsofcol00colo_1/page/n5/mode/2up

Griffith, Samuel Walker (before November 1889), *Wealth and Want*, Brisbane: Black, Reid & Co, Printers

Griffith, Samuel Walker (1889), 'The Distribution of Wealth', *Centennial Magazine 1888-1889*, 1, pp. 833-42

Griffith, Samuel Walker (1891), *The Political Geography of Australia*, in *Proceedings of the Royal Geographical Society of Australia - Queensland Branch*, 6, pp. 68-81

Griffith, Samuel Walker (1892a), 'Sir Samuel Walker Griffith's Manifesto', *Brisbane Courier*, 13 February

Griffith, Samuel Walker (1892b), 'Manifesto to the Electors of North Brisbane, 1888, in Adams, F. (Ed.), *The Australians*, n.p., pp. 281-94

Griffith, Samuel Walker (1893), 'The Coloured Labour Question in Australia', *Antipodean*, pp. 13-7

*Griffith, Samuel Walker (1895), 'The Certainty of Australian Federation', Gay, W. and M.E. Sampson (Eds.), *The Commonwealth and the Empire: Special Contributions and Communications on the Subject of Australasian Federation from Leading Colonial and Imperial Writers and Statesmen*, Melbourne: George Robertson, 6 ff.

Griffith, Samuel Walker (1897), *Notes on the Draft Federal Constitution Framed by the Adelaide Convention*, Brisbane: E. Gregory Government Printer

Griffith, Samuel Walker (1919), 'The Social Problem: a Fundamental Error, The Solution', *The Daily Mail*, 1 November, p. 6

Hawke, Robert J. (1957), 'The Trade Unions', in Walker, K. R. (Ed.) *Research Needs in Industrial Relations*, Canberra: n.p., pp. 68-80 [Mitchell Library]

Hawke, Robert J. (1974), *Address to Australasian Society of Accountants: The Economic Implications of Future Labour Relations*, March, Sydney, Australasian Society of Accountants Annual Conference

Hawke, Robert J. (1975), *In Memoriam, Albert Monk-Panegyric*, Melbourne: The Australian Council of Trade Unions

Hawke, Robert J. (1977), 'Address to the Farm Writers' and Broadcasters' Society', n.d., n.p., Sheraton Motor Inn, cited by McGregor, Craig (2004), 'Inside Bob Hawke', in Ricketson, Matthew (Ed.), *The Best Australian Profiles*, Melbourne: Black

Hawke, Robert J. (1983a), *Australian Labor Party Federal Election Policy Speech 1983*, delivered at Sydney Opera House, 16 February, Kingston, ACT: Australian Labor Party

Hawke, Robert J. (1983b), *Speech at Labor Day Dinner, by The Hon R.J. Hawke, AC MP, Prime Minister*, Melbourne, The Labor Day Dinner, 12 March, pmtranscripts.pmc.gov.au/sites/default/files/original/00006051.pdf

*Hawke, Robert J. (1983c), *Address by the Prime Minister, Hon R.J. Hawke AC MP, to the National Economic Summit Conference, House of Representatives, Canberra*, 11 April, pmtranscripts.pmc.gov.au/sites/default/files/original/00006083.pdf

Hawke, Robert J. (1983d), *Address by the Prime Minister, Hon R.J. Hawke AC MP, to the National Press Club, Canberra*, 27 June, pmtranscripts.pmc.gov.au/sites/default/files/original/00006141.pdf

Hawke, Robert J. (1997), *Speech on the Occasion of the Signing of the Memorandum of Understanding between the Hon R.J.L. Hawke AC and the University of South Australia to Establish the Bob Hawke Prime Ministerial Centre*, 9 December, https://parlinfo.aph.gov.au/parlInfo/

Howard, John (1996a), 'Tasmania: Tragedy at Port Arthur–Address to Parliament', 30 April, *Commonwealth Parliamentary Debates–Representatives*, No. 206, 38th Parliament, First Session, First Period, pp. 24-5, parlinfo.aph.gov.au/parlInfo/

Howard, John (1996b), *Press Conference, Parliament House*, Parliament House, Canberra: Department of the Prime Minister and Cabinet, Australian Government, 10 May, pmtranscripts.pmc.gov.au/release/transcript-9996

*Howard, John (1996c), *Gun Rally–Sale, Victoria*, Canberra: Department of the Prime Minister and Cabinet, Australian Government, 16 June, pmtranscripts.pmc.gov.au/release/transcript-10030

Howard, John (2002), *Address to Memorial Service*, Australian Consulate, Bali, 17 October, pmtranscripts.pmc.gov.au/release/transcript-12917

Hughes, William M. (1907), *Compulsory Military Training*, Address at Caxton Hall, 24 April, Westminster

Hughes, William M. (1916a), *Australia and the War: Address at a Meeting of the Pilgrims of Great Britain*, London: Jordan Gaskell [Mitchell Library]

Hughes, William M. (1916b), *National Referendum of 1916: Manifesto and Speeches*, Melbourne: National Referendum Council [Mitchell Library]

Hughes, William M. (1917), *Win the War Policy: Prime Minister's Speech*, Sydney: W. Brooks and Co. Ltd. [Mitchell Library]

Hughes, William M. (1922), *National Policy Record: Prime Minister's Policy Speech*, n.p.: National Party of Australia [Mitchell Library]

Hughes, William M. (1925a), *A Policy for Australia: An Address Delivered before the Chamber of Manufactures of New South Wales*, Sydney: Motor Press of Australia [Mitchell Library]

Hughes, William M. (1925b), *Post War Problems*, Sydney: Hemmingway and Robertson Accountancy and Secretarial Educational Society of New South Wales [Mitchell Library]

Hughes, William M. (1929), *Speeches of the 1929 Election Campaign*, Audio Cassette, The University of Queensland Audio-visual Library

Hughes, William M. (1932), *The Ottawa Agreements and Their Bearing on Overseas Trade*, Birmingham, UK: Birmingham Chamber of Commerce [Mitchell Library]

Hughes, William M. (1940), *Communism: Broadcast*, Sydney: Australian Democratic Front [Fisher Pamphlet Library, The University of Sydney and Mitchell Library]

Hughes, William M. (1941a), *Australia Awake!*, Sydney: Australian Democratic Front [Fisher Pamphlet Library, The University of Sydney and Mitchell Library]

Hughes, William M. (1941b), *Two Years of War! Where Australia Stands Today*, Sydney: Australian Democratic Front [Mitchell Library]

Hughes, William M. (1943), *Election Manoeuvres: Broadcast*, Sydney: Association of Business Services [Fisher Pamphlet Library, The University of Sydney]

Hughes, William M. (1944), *Winning the War and the Peace: Think and Act*, n.p. [Mitchell Library]

*Keating, Paul (1992), *Redfern Park Speech*, Australian Launch of the International Year for the World's Indigenous People, Redfern, Redfern Park, 10 December, pmtranscripts.pmc.gov.au/release/transcript-8765; also video: youtube.com/watch?v=x1S4F1euzTw

Kemp, Rod and Stanton, Marion (Eds.) (2004), *Speaking for Australia: Parliamentary Speeches that Shaped the Nation*, Crows Nest, NSW: Allen and Unwin

*Kirby, Michael D. (1980a), *The Australian Community and Anti-heroes*, Lalor Community Relations Address, Playhouse, Civic Square, Canberra, 3 December, Website Speech No. 206, pp. 1-14, www.michaelkirby.com.au/images/stories/speeches/1980s/vol6/1980/206

Kirby, Michael D. (1980b), *Australia into the Eighties: The Challenge of Change*, Canberra Australia Day Council, National Press Club, 25 January, Website Speech, No. 138, pp. 1-5, www.michaelkirby.com.au/images/stories/speeches/1980s/vol5/1980/138

Kirby, Michael D. (1980c), communication with author, 16 May

Kirby, Michael D. (1980d), *Interview with Mr John Laws*, Sydney Radio Station 2UE, 31 January, Website Speech, No. 139A, www.michaelkirby.com.au/images/stories/speeches/1980s/vol5/1980/139A

Kirby, Michael D. (1981a), *The Australian Media Peace Prize*, 20 October, Sydney, Website Speech No. 280, pp. 1-3, www.michaelkirby.com.au/images/stories/speeches/1980s/vol8/1981/280

Kirby, Michael D. (1981b), communication with author, 16 July

Kirby, Michael D. (1992), *Dinner to Celebrate the 80th Birthday of The Hon Sir Asher Joel, KBE, AO,* May, Sydney: Parliament of New South Wales, Website Speech, No. 946, pp. 1-8, www.michaelkirby.com.au/images/stories/speeches/1990s/vol27/946

Kirby, Michael D. (2010), *The Internalisation of Domestic Law and Its Consequences, Public Conversation between The Hon Justice Antonin Scalia, Associate Justice of the Supreme Court of the United States of America and The Hon Michael Kirby, Justice of the High Court of Australia, 1996-2009,* 9 February, Website Speech No. 2441, pp. 1-21, www.michaelkirby.com.au/images/stories/speeches/2000s/2010_Speeches/2441

Kirby, Michael D. (2012a), 'Eleanor Roosevelt Drives By', Grodin, Michael; Tarantola, Daniel; Annas, George; and Gruskin, Sophia (Eds.), *Health and Human Rights*, Website Speech, No. 2609, pp. 1-10, www.michaelkirby.com.au/images/stories/speeches/2000s/2012/2609

Kirby, Michael D. (2012b), *Human Rights Protection in Australia – A Riposte to Chief Justice Keane, Austin Asche Lecture 2012,* 27 August, Darwin: Charles Darwin University, Website Speech, No. 2622, pp. 1-24, www.michaelkirby.com.au/images/stories/speeches/2000s/2012/2622

Kirby, Michael D. (2014), *Neville Wran–The Enigma*, State Funeral of The Hon Neville Kenneth Wran, AC, CNZM, QC, 1 May, Sydney, Website Speech, No. 2710, pp. 1-9, www.michaelkirby.com.au/images/stories/speeches/2014/2710

Kirby, Michael D. (2015), *Whatever Would Miss Telfer Think of a Queer Collective*, Website Speech No. 2764, pp. 1-5, www.michaelkirby.com.au/images/stories/speeches/2015/2764

Kirby, Michael D. (2016a), *Academic and Institutional Law Reform in Australia: Past, Passing and To Come,* 15 April, Canberra, Website Speech No. 2845, pp. 1-36, www.michaelkirby.com.au/sites/default/files/speeches/2845

Kirby, Michael D. (2016b), *Memorial Occasion for the Late Judy Cassab AO, CBE: Conversations with Judy & A Stringbag of Adjectives,* 11 February, Sydney Domain, Website Speech No. 2818, pp. 1-6, www.michaelkirby.com.au/sites/default/files/speeches/2818

Kirby, Michael D. (2020), *The Hon Michael Kirby AC CMB - Speeches*, Website www.michaelkirby.com.au/speeches Accessed 3 September 2021

Kirby, Michael D. (2021a), communication with author, 21 September

Kirby, Michael D. (2021b), communication with author, 26 September

Lawson, Louisa [Dora Falconer] (1888), 'About Ourselves', *The Dawn*, 1(1), 15 May, pp. 3-4

Lawson, Louisa [Dora Falconer] (1889), 'Our Anniversary', *The Dawn*, 2(1), 1 May, p. 3

Lawson, Louisa (1891a), 'Womanhood Suffrage League', in O'Connor, Gertrude (1920), *Louisa Lawson, Her Life and Work,* Volume 190: Angus and Robertson Manuscript by Gertrude O'Connor, Mitchell Library of New South Wales, Microfilm CY 1216, archival.sl.nsw.gov.au/Details/archive/110581158

*Lawson, Louisa (1891b), *Womanhood Suffrage*–'A Meeting of the League. Speeches by Women', at Y.M.C.A. Hall, Sydney, *The Daily Telegraph (Sydney, NSW: 1883-1930)*, 13 June, p. 10

Lyons, Enid (1943), 'Governor-General's Speech, Address-in-Reply' on Social Welfare, 29 September, in *Commonwealth Parliamentary Debates–Representatives*, Seventeenth Parliament, First Session-First Period, pp. 182-6, 828https://parlinfo.aph.gov.au/; also available, audio recorded delivery later on radio, *Australian Screen: An NFSA Website*, aso.gov.au/titles/radio/dame-enid-lyons-maiden-speech/clip1/

Manne, Robert (2001), *Neither Column in This Moral Ledger Will Cancel the Other Out*, 'My Country–A Personal Journey': the Alfred Deakin Lectures, Capitol Theatre, Melbourne, in Warhaft (2004), pp. 58-72

McLennan, Ian (1969), *Focus on Australia's Industrial Horizon*, Sydney: Australian Finance Conference

McLeod, A.L. (Ed.) (1969), *Australia Speaks: An Anthology of Australian Speeches*, Sydney: Wentworth

Melba, Nellie (1924), *Goodbye*, Melbourne, His Majesty's Theatre, 13 October

Menzies, Robert G. (1932), *Growth of the Constitution*, n.p.: Bienerhassett's Community Education Society of Australasia [Mitchell Library]

Menzies, Robert G. (1933), *Distribution of the Industrial and Trade and Commerce Powers*, n.p.: Australian Institute of Political Science [Mitchell Library]

Menzies, Robert G. (1935), *International Situation in 1935*, Melbourne: Australian Institute of International Affairs [Mitchell Library]

Menzies, Robert G. (1939a), *The Place of a University in the Modern Community–An Address*, Delivered at the Tenth Annual Commencement of Canberra University, Melbourne: Melbourne University Press

Menzies, Robert G. (1939b), *Broadcast to the People of Australia: Declaration of War, 3 September*, n.p. [Mitchell Library]

Menzies, Robert G. (1939c), *Australia's Place in the Empire*, London: Royal Institute of International Affairs [Fisher Pamphlet Library, The University of Sydney]

Menzies, Robert G. (1939d), *War Objectives: Address by the Prime Minister*, Melbourne: Government Printer [Fisher Pamphlet Library, The University of Sydney]

Menzies, Robert G. (1940a), *Prime Minister on War Programme: Address Delivered to Business Men of Sydney*, Assembly Hall, Sydney, 7 June, Canberra: Commonwealth Government Printer [Mitchell Library]

Menzies, Robert G. (1940b), *General Election 1940 Policy Speech Delivered at Camberwell Town Hall on 2 September 1940*, Melbourne: The Craftsman Press Ltd. [Mitchell Library]

Menzies, Robert G. (1941a), *Address by Robert G. Menzies at Town Hall, Sydney*, Sydney: W.F. Smith [Mitchell Library]

Menzies, Robert G. (1940b), *To the People of Britain at War, 1941*, London: Longmans Green and Co. [Fisher Pamphlet Library, The University of Sydney]

Menzies, Robert G. (1940c), *Unlimited War Effort, a National Prospectus*, Canberra: Government Printer [Mitchell Library]

Menzies, Robert G. (undated), *Huge Defence Programme Expansion 1939-40: Statement by the Prime Minister*, Melbourne: Government Printer [Mitchell Library]

Menzies, Robert G. (1942a), *The Australian Economy during the War: Joseph Fisher Lecture in Commerce*, Adelaide: The University of Adelaide [Fisher Pamphlet Library, The University of Sydney and Mitchell Library]

Menzies, Robert G. (1942b), *The Forgotten People: A Broadcast Address*, Melbourne: Robertson and Mullens [Fisher Pamphlet Library, The University of Sydney]

Menzies, Robert G. (1945), *Speech Delivered at the First Annual Convention of the Liberal Party of Australia, Held in Sydney on 17 October, 1945*, n.p. [Mitchell Library]

Menzies, Robert (1948), 'Politics as an Art', *The New York Times Magazine*, 28 November

Menzies, Robert G. (1949a), *Joint Opposition Policy, 1949: Policy Speech of Leader of the Opposition Delivered at Canterbury Victoria on 19 November, 1949*, Sydney: Liberal Party of Australia [Mitchell Library]

Menzies, Robert G. (1949b), *For a Liberal Australia: Essence of the Policy Speech, 1949*, Sydney: Liberal Party of Australia [Mitchell Library]

Menzies, Robert G. (1951a), *Joint Government Policy, 1951*, Canberra: Liberal Party of Australia [Mitchell Library]

Menzies, Robert G. (1951b), *The Answer is Yes: The Prime Minister States the Case against Communism's Fifth Column*, Kooyong, Vic: n.p. [Fisher Pamphlet Library, The University of Sydney]

Menzies, Robert G. (1953), *Senate Campaign: Opening Speech by the Prime Minister at the Brisbane City Hall on 14 April, 1953*, Sydney: Liberal Party of Australia [Mitchell Library]

Menzies, Robert G. (1954), *The First William Queale Memorial Lecture–Democracy and Management*, Adelaide: Australian Institute of Management [Fisher Pamphlet Library, The University of Sydney and Mitchell Library] http://www.emersonkent.com/speeches/democracy_and_management.htm

Menzies, Robert G. (1955a), *Address to the National Press Club Luncheon*, 16 March, Washington DC

Menzies, Robert G. (1955b), *Federal Election 1955: Policy Speech of the Prime Minister Delivered in Canterbury Memorial Hall on 15 November, 1955*, Canberra: Liberal Party of Australia [Mitchell Library]

Menzies, Robert G. (1957), *Australian Universities: Ministerial Statement in Connexion with Report of Committee on Australian Universities*, Canberra: Government Printer [The University of New South Wales Library]

Menzies, Robert G. (1958), *Federal Election 1958: Joint Policy Speech*, Canberra: Liberal Party of Australia [Mitchell Library]

Menzies, Robert G. (1959a), 'Press Conference Given by the Prime Minister, Rt Hon R.G. Menzies CH QC MP', 14 October, Canberra: Commonwealth of Australia, pmtranscripts.pmc.gov.au/sites/default/files/original/00000117_0.pdf

Menzies, Robert G. (1959b), 'Press Conference by the Prime Minister of Australia The Rt Hon R.G. Menzies', 6 December, Medan Merdeka Barat 15, Djakarta https://pmtranscripts.pmc.gov.au/sites/default/files/original/00000142.pdf

Menzies, Robert G. (1960a), *The Changing Commonwealth*, London: Cambridge University Press [Fisher Pamphlet Library, The University of Sydney]

Menzies, Robert G. (1960b), *Text of Television Interview with R.G. Menzies, Recorded by Channel ATN at UN Headquarters N.Y. on 13 October 1960*, Canberra: n.p. [Mitchell Library]
Menzies, Robert G. (1960c), *Speech at the All Nations Club*, 25 November, pmtranscripts.pmc.gov.au/sites/default/files/original/00000248.pdf
Menzies, Robert G. (1960d), *The Challenge to Federation*, Melbourne: Melbourne University Press [Mitchell Library]
Menzies, Robert G. (1961a), *Federal Election 1961: Policy Speech of the Prime Minister Delivered in the Kew City Hall, Melbourne on 15 November 1961*, Canberra: Liberal Party of Australia [Mitchell Library]
Menzies, Robert G. (1961b), *A Talk to the Nation, Federal Election*, 20 November, pp.1-4, pmtranscripts.pmc.gov.au/sites/default/files/original/00000401.pdf
Menzies, Robert G. (1961c), *The Challenge to Australian Education*, Melbourne: Australian College of Education [Fisher Pamphlet Library, The University of Sydney and Mitchell Library]
Menzies, Robert G. (1963a), *The Battle for Freedom–Jefferson Oration*, 4 July, Monticello, Charlottesville, Virginia, pmtranscripts.pmc.gov.au/release/transcript-764
Menzies, Robert G. (1963b), *Federal Election 1963: Policy Speech*, Canberra: Liberal Party of Australia [Mitchell Library]
Menzies, Robert G. (1964a), *The Universities–Some Queries*, Sydney: The University of New South Wales [Fisher Pamphlet Library, The University of Sydney and Mitchell Library]
Menzies, Robert G. (1964b), *The Interdependence of Political and Industrial Leadership in the Modern State*, London: British Institute of Management [The University of New South Wales Library and Mitchell Library]
*Menzies, Robert Gordon (1965), *Eulogy for Churchill/Speech by the Prime Minister, The Rt Hon Sir Robert Menzies, KT, CH, QC, MM, from the Crypt of St Paul's Cathedral, London over BBC Television on the Occasion of the Funeral of the Late Sir Winston Churchill*, Canberra: Australian Government, Department of the Prime Minister and Cabinet, pmtranscripts.pmc.gov.au/sites/default/files/original/00001049.pdf
Menzies, Robert G. (1967a), *Central Power in the Australian Commonwealth: An Examination of the Growth of Commonwealth Power in the Australian Federation*, London: Cassell
Menzies, Robert G. (1967b), *The English Speaking Peoples in a Changing World*, Enstone, Oxfordshire: Ditchley Foundation [Mitchell Library]
Menzies, Robert G. (1968), *The Postgraduate Student*, n.p.: Institute of Radio and Electronics Engineers [Mitchell Library]
Millett, Kate (1970), *Sexual Politics*, Garden City, NY: Doubleday
*Morrison, Scott (2020), *Address to the Nation amid the Coronavirus Pandemic*, Prime Minister of Australia, Parliament House, Canberra, 12 March, www.pm.gov.au/media/address-nation, Accessed 15 January 2021
Oliphant, Mark (1970), *Burgmann College Opening Address*, Burgmann College, Canberra
[Oodgeroo Noonuccal] Walker, Kath (1968), *Integration and Queensland Society*, A paper delivered at the Abschol seminar on Aboriginal conditions, May, in Walker, Kath (1970a), *My People*, Milton, Qld: Jacaranda, pp. 42-4
[Oodgeroo Noonuccal] Walker, Kath (1970a), *My People*, Milton, Qld: Jacaranda

[Oodgeroo Noonuccal] Walker, Kath (1970b), *How Well Off are Aborigines in Modern-day Australia?* Speech at Pius XII Seminary, Banyo, 21 March, in Walker, Kath [Oodgeroo Noonuccal] (1970a), *My People,* Milton, Qld: Jacaranda, pp. 88-92

Oodgeroo Noonuccal (1988), *Acceptance Speech,* in *Kunapipi,* 16(1), ro.uow.edu.au/kunapipi/vol16/iss1/5

Pearson, Noel (2014), *Noel Pearson Remembers Gough Whitlam,* 4 November, at Sydney Town Hall, https://www.youtube.com/watch?v=JsXmYHiuJ8s

Prowse, Linden J. (1975), *Guest of Honour,* 31 August, ABC Radio (Australia)

Reid, George H. (1917), *My Reminiscences,* London: Cassell, https://nla.gov.au/nla.obj-2575806/

Robson, Pamela (Ed.) (2009), *Great Australian Speeches: Landmark Speeches that Defined and Shaped Our Nation,* Millers Point, NSW: Murdoch Books

Robinson, Ray (1978), *The Wit of Sir Robert Menzies,* Collingwood, Vic: Outback

Rudd, Kevin (2008), 'Apology to Australia's Indigenous Peoples–Parliament of Australia', in *Commonwealth of Australia Parliamentary Debates–House of Representatives,* 13 February 2008, Canberra: Hansard, Parliament of Australia, pp. 167-71; also at: parlinfo.aph.gov.au/parlInfo/

Russell, Penny (2004), 'A Woman of the Future? Feminism and Conservatism in Colonial New South Wales', *Women's History Review,* 13(1), pp. 69-90, tandfonline.com/doi/pdf/10.1080/09612020400200383

Ryan, Susan (1992), 'Fishes on Bicycles', 23 March, Address to Department of the Senate, Papers on Parliament No. 17, September 1992, *Trust the Women, Women in the Federal Parliament,* Published and Printed by the Department of the Senate, Parliament House, Canberra, pp. 27-44, www.aph.gov.au/binaries/senate/pubs/pops/pop17/pop17.pdf, Accessed 31 January 2021

Ryan, Thomas Joseph (T.J.) (1917), 'I Would Not Allow a Man to Publish Any Lies'– Opposition to Conscription, *Government Gazette Extraordinary,* Brisbane: Government Printer [Speeches and pamphlets blocked via *Hansard 37*], in Robson, Pamela (Ed.) (2009), *Great Australian Speeches: Landmark Speeches that Defined and Shaped Our Nation,* Millers Point, NSW: Murdoch Books, pp. 84-8

Segal, Ronald (1967), *The Race War,* Harmondsworth: Pelican

Summers, Anne (1985), *Status of Women and their Role in Australian Society,* at National Press Club, Canberra, 1 August, https://nla.gov.au/nla.obj-222482769/listen

Trump, Donald (2020), *Remarks by President Trump at the National Thanksgiving Turkey Pardoning Ceremony,* Washington DC: White House, United States Government, November 24, Accessed 11 December 2020, rev.com/blog/transcripts/donald-trump-pardons-thanksgiving-turkey-transcript-november-24

Walker, Kath [see Oodgeroo Noonuccal]

Wannan, Bill (1973), *With Malice Aforethought: Australian Insults, Invective, Ridicule and Abuse,* Melbourne: Lansdowne

Wahlquist, Calla (2016), 'Notable Speeches by Indigenous Australians: "We Refuse to Be Pushed into the Background"', *The Guardian,* Jan 25

Warhaft, Sally (Ed.) (2004), *Well May We Say: The Speeches That Made Australia,* 1st edn, Melbourne: Black

Warhaft, Sally (Ed.) (2014), *Well May We Say: The Speeches that Made Australia*, 2nd edn, Melbourne: Text Publishing

Wells, Deane (1976), *The Wit of Whitlam*, Collingwood: Outback

Whitlam, E. Gough (1957), *The Constitution Versus Labor*, Melbourne: Carlton A.L.P. Club, Melbourne University [Fisher Pamphlet Library, The University of Sydney and Mitchell Library]

Whitlam, E. Gough (1963), *Australian Foreign Policy, 1963*, Melbourne: Australian Institute of International Affairs [Mitchell Library]

Whitlam, E. Gough (1965), *Labor and the Constitution: Three Papers*, Melbourne: Victorian Fabian Society [Fisher Pamphlet Library, The University of Sydney and Mitchell Library]

Whitlam, E. Gough (1966), *Australia–Base or Bridge?* Sydney: Sydney University Fabian Society [Fisher Pamphlet Library, The University of Sydney and Mitchell Library]

Whitlam, E. Gough (1967), *The Role of the Specialist in Journalism*, Canberra: Summer School of Professional Journalism [Fisher Pamphlet Library, The University of Sydney]

Whitlam, E. Gough (1968a), *Beyond Vietnam: Australian Regional Responsibility*, Melbourne: Victorian Fabian Society [Fisher Pamphlet Library, The University of Sydney and Mitchell Library]

Whitlam, E. Gough (1968b), *Address to the Annual Conference of the New South Wales Branch of Australian Labor Party, 8 June 1968*, Sydney: Australian Labor Party [Mitchell Library]

Whitlam, E. Gough (1968c), *Labor's Role Today: Lecture at University of Queensland, 28 August 1968*, St. Lucia, Qld: The University of Queensland [Mitchell Library]

Whitlam, E. Gough (1969), *An Urban Nation*, Melbourne: Victorian Fabian Society [Fisher Pamphlet Library, The University of Sydney and Mitchell Library]

Whitlam, E. Gough (1971), 'Motion of Want of Confidence in the Government'. 15 March, in *Commonwealth Parliamentary Debates–Representatives*, 16 February, 1971 to 2 April, 1971, 20 Eliz II, Vol. H of R71, pp. 827-32, parlinfo.aph.gov.au/parlInfo/

Whitlam, E. Gough (1972), 'Reply to: Electoral Ministerial Statement', 10 October, in *Commonwealth Parliamentary Debates - Representatives*, No. 41, 1972, Twenty-Seventh Parliament, Second Session-Sixth Period, pp. 2295-6, parlinfo.aph.gov.au/parlInfo/

Whitlam, E. Gough (1972), *It's Time!: Policy Speech of the Australian Labor Party Delivered at Blacktown Civic Centre, 13 November 1972*, Canberra: Australian Labor Party [Mitchell Library]

Whitlam, E. Gough (1973a), *Australian Foreign Policy: New Directions, New Definitions*, Brisbane: Australian Institute of International Affairs [Fisher Pamphlet Library, The University of Sydney]

Whitlam, E. Gough (1973b), 'Human Rights Day: Speech by Prime Minister E.G. Whitlam for the UN Association, 10 December 1973', in *Australian Foreign Affairs Record*, December, pp. 866-71

Whitlam, E. Gough (1974a), *Australia and South East Asia: Principal Speeches Made by the Prime Minister, The Hon. E.G. Whitlam during his Visit to South East Asia, 28 January to 13 February 1974*, Canberra: Department of Foreign Affairs [Mitchell Library]

Whitlam, E. Gough (1974b), *Labor Policy Speech, 1974*, Canberra: Australian Labor Party [Mitchell Library]

*Whitlam, E. Gough (1975a), *Partnership in the Pacific after Vietnam: Address to the National Press Club*, Washington DC, 8 May, Canberra: Australian Government, Department of the Prime Minister and Cabinet, Available at pmtranscripts.pmc.gov.au/sites/default/files/original/00003731.pdf

Whitlam, E. Gough (1975b), *Dismissal Speech on the Steps of Parliament House*, Parliament House, Canberra: Department of the Prime Minister and Cabinet, Australian Government, 11 November, pmtranscripts.pmc.gov.au/release/transcript

Whitlam, E. Gough (1980), communication with author, 15 September

Secondary Sources

_____ (1891), *The Bulletin*, 4 June

_____ (1891), *The Bulletin*, 3 October

_____ (1892), *Brisbane Courier* [abridged from the *Ipswich Advocate*], 9 March

_____ (1893), *The Bulletin*, 22 April

_____ (1937), *The Mercury*, 21 September

_____ (1940), *The Mercury*, 21 August

_____ (1953), *Queen Elizabeth's Coronation Book*, Melbourne: Colourgravure

_____ (1970), 'Electronic Politics: The Image Game', *Time*, 21 September, p. 48

_____ (1975), 'Are Queenslanders So Different?' *Monday Conference*, No. 166, 17 November, ABC Television (Australia)

_____ (2005), *Dictionary of Military and Associated Terms*, US Department of Defense, Accessed 21 May 2020 thefreedictionary.com/

_____ (2005), 'Don't you worry about that', *The Sydney Morning Herald*, 25 April, smh.com.au/national/dont-you-worry-about-that-20050425-gdl6zb.html, Accessed 17 June 2020

_____ (2009), 'Abstract', *The Cherry Pickers*, drama-Three acts, Author: Kevin Gilbert, First known date: 1968, austlit.edu.au/austlit/page/C115619, Accessed 25 June 2020

_____ (2020), '1906 Australian Federal Election', Wikipedia, Accessed 12 September 2020

_____ (2020) 'Bob Hawke formally launched his election policy speech on Ash Wednesday', 16 February 1983 *australianpolitics.com*/1983/02/16/bob-hawke-alp-federal-election-policy-speech.html, Accessed 20 June 2020

_____ (2020), 'Lawson, Louisa (1848–1920)', *Obituaries Australia*, National Centre of Biography, The Australian National University, oa.anu.edu.au/obituary/lawson-louisa-7121/text35156, Accessed 22 September 2020

_____ (2020), *Merriam-Webster Dictionary* merriam-webster.com/dictionary/

_____ (2020), 'Robert Menzies', *Australia's Prime Ministers*, Canberra: National Archives of Australia primeministers.naa.gov.au, Accessed 6 June 2020

_____ (2021), *The Whitlam Institute*, https://www.whitlam.org/whitlam-legacy-aboriginal-and-torres-strait-islander-peoples, Accessed 14 February 2021

Abrams, M. (1964), 'Opinion Polls and Party Propaganda', *Public Opinion Quarterly*, 28, Spring, pp. 13-9

Andersen, Robin and Jonathan Gray (Eds.) (2008), *Battleground the Media, Volume 2 (O-Z)*, Westport, CT: Greenwood

Atkins, Judi, Alan Finlayson, James Martin, Nick Turnbull (Eds.) (2013), *Rhetoric in British Politics and Society*, Basingstoke: Palgrave Macmillan, doi.org/10.1057/9781137325532_13

Atkinson, Max (1984), *Our Master's Voices: The Language and Body Language of Politics*, London: Routledge

Atkinson, Sallyanne (2016), *No Job for a Woman*, St. Lucia, Qld: University of Queensland Press

Attardo, Salvatore and Victor Raskin (1991), 'Script Theory Revis(it)ed: Joke Similarity and Joke Representation Model', *Humor*, 4(3-4), pp. 293-347

Attardo, Salvatore (2015), 'Humour and Laughter', in Tannen, Deborah, Heidi E. Hamilton, and Deborah Schiffrin, (Eds.), *The Handbook of Discourse Analysis, Vol II*, 2nd edn, Chichester: Wiley Blackwell, pp. 168-88

Bacon, Francis (1952), *Advancement of Learning*, Great Books, Vol. 30, Chicago: Encyclopedia Britannica [1st published (1605), *Of the Proficience and Advancement of Learning, Divine and Human*, https://ia600304.us.archive.org/18/items/proficienceanda00bacogoog/proficienceanda00bacogoog.pdf]

Baur, E. Jackson (1962), 'Opinion Change in a Public Controversy', *Public Opinion Quarterly*, 26, Summer, pp. 212-26

Beausang, Chris (2020), 'A Brief History of the Theory and Practice of Computational Literary Criticism (1963-2020)', *magazen*, 1:2, pp. 181-202, doi: 10.30687/mag/2724-3923/2020/02/002

Bennister, Mark (2012), *Prime Ministers in Power: Political Leadership in Britain and Australia*, Basingstoke: Palgrave Macmillan, 10.1057/9780230378445

Bergson, Henri (1969), 'The Comic in General: The Comic Element in Forms and Movements', in Eastman, A.M. et. al., *The Norton Reader: An Anthology of Expository Prose*, New York: Norton, pp. 716-25

Biber, D. and S. Conrad (2009), *Register, Genre and Style*, Cambridge: Cambridge University Press

Blyden, Jackson and Louis D. Rubin Jr (1974), *Black Poetry in America*, Baton Rouge: Louisiana State University Press

Booth, Wayne C. (1961), *The Rhetoric of Fiction*, Chicago: University of Chicago Press

Bormann, Ernest G. et al, (1978), 'Power, Authority, and Sex: Male Response to Female Leadership', *Communication Monographs*, 45(2), June, pp. 119-55

Brandt, W.J. (1970), *The Rhetoric of Argumentation*, Indianapolis: Bobbs-Merrill

Brennan, Elliott (2013), 'On This Day: Indigenous People Get Citizenship', *Australian Geographic*, November 7, https://www.australiangeographic.com.au/blogs/on-this-day/2013/11/on-this-day-indigenous-people-get-citizenship/, Accessed 14 February 2021

Brereton, D. and J. Walter (1979), 'Question Time Performance and Leadership Style: A Study of Whitlam and Fraser', *Australian Political Studies*, August, pp. 301-16

Brett, Judith (2017), *The Enigmatic Mr Deakin*, Melbourne: Text Publishing

Brett, Judith (2019), 'Alfred Deakin and Federation', in *Upholding the Australian Constitution, Vol. 31*, Melbourne: The Samuel Griffith Society, August, pp. 119-31

Briscoe, Gordon (1994), 'The Struggle for Grace: An Appreciation of Kevin John Gilbert', *Aboriginal History*, 18(1/2), pp. 13-31, jstor.org/stable/24046083?seq=1

Broder, David S. (1964), 'Great Speeches Aren't Necessarily Good Politics', *New York Times Magazine*, 29 March, p. 7

Brooks, Erik J. (2017), *Slogans We Can Believe In: An Examination of What Makes for an Effective Presidential Campaign Slogan*, MA Thesis, Charlotte, NC: University of North Carolina

Brown, H. (1966), *Prose Styles–Five Primary Types*, Minneapolis, MN: University of Minnesota Press

Bryant, Jennings, with Paul Comiskey and Dolf Zillmann (1979), 'Teachers' Humor in the College Classroom', *Communication Education*, 28(2), citing Freud, Sigmund (1960), *Jokes and Their Relation to the Unconscious*, New York: Norton, and (1928), 'Humour', *International Journal of Psychoanalysis*, 9, pp. 1-6

Burke, Michael (Ed.) (2014), *The Routledge Handbook of Stylistics*, New York: Routledge

Cahill, Rowan (2017), 'A Forgotten Address', *Overland*, 15 June, https://overland.org.au/2017/06/a-forgotten-address/

Cameron, David Bruce (1999), *An Historical Assessment of Economic Development, Manufacturing and the Political Economy of Queensland, 1900 to 1930*, PhD Thesis, St. Lucia, Qld: The University of Queensland

Carter, Ronald and Walter Nash (1990), *Seeing Through Language: A Guide to Styles of English Writing*, Oxford: Blackwell

Charteris-Black, Jonathan (2011), *Politicians and Rhetoric: The Persuasive Power of Metaphor*, 2nd edn, Basingstoke: Palgrave Macmillan

Charteris-Black, Jonathan (2014), *Analysing Political Speeches: Rhetoric, Discourse and Metaphor*, Basingstoke: Palgrave Macmillan

Chovanec, Jan and Isabel Ermida (Eds.) (2012), *Language and Humour in the Media*, Newcastle upon Tyne: Cambridge Scholars, cambridgescholars.com/download/sample/59339

Clark, Andrew (2014), 'The "Old Man" Laid to Rest', *Financial Review*, 6 November, afr.com/politics/federal/the-old-man-laid-to-rest-20141106-11hjts

Clark, Tom (2008), 'The Cup of John Howard's Poetry: A Brief Rhetorispective', *Overland*, 190, pp. 23-9, core.ac.uk/download/pdf/10826573.pdf

Clark, Tom (2012), *Stay on Message: Poetry and Truthfulness in Political Speech*, Melbourne: Australian Scholarly Publishing

Clark, Tom (2013), 'Paul Keating's Redfern Park Speech and Its Rhetorical Legacy', *Overland*, 213, Summer, overland.org.au/previous-issues/issue-213/feature-tom-clarke/

Clark, Tom, Michael Meaney, and Lisi Lianeste (2014), 'Comedy, Creativity, and Culture', *International Journal of Literary Humanities*, 11(4), pp. 1-15

Clark, Tom (2014), 'A Closer Look at Noel Pearson's Eulogy for Gough Whitlam', *The Conversation*, 6 November, theconversation.com/a-closer-look-at-noel-pearsons-eulogy-for-gough-whitlam-33932

Clark, Tom (2016), 'Form Versus Content', *Overland*, 225, Summer, overland.org.au/previous-issues/issue-225/feature-tom-clark/

Clark, Tom (2019), *Talking Up a Legacy: Australian Prime Ministers and the Speeches We Remember*, Crawley, WA: University of West Australia Publishing

Coatney, Caryn (2013), 'John Curtin's Forgotten Media Legacy: The Impact of a Wartime Prime Minister on News Management Techniques, 1941-45', *Labour History*, 105, November, pp. 63-78

Cockcroft, Robert and Susan Cockcroft, with Craig Hamilton, and Laura Hidalgo Downing (2014), *Persuading People: An Introduction to Rhetoric*, 3rd edn, Basingstroke: Palgrave Macmillan

Coleman, William (2018), 'Six Problems in the Biography of Alfred Deakin', *Agenda*, 25(1), pp. 79-91, press-files.anu.edu.au/downloads/press/n4280/pdf/05_coleman.pdf

Collins, Philip (2017a), *When They Go Low, We Go High*, London: 4th Estate

Collins, Philip (2017b), 'The Art of Political Speech', Leith, Sam (interviewer), *The Spectator–podcast*, 25 October

Connors, Libby (1995), 'My People, Our Past', *LiNQ*, (22)2, pp. 127-31

Cooper, L. (1960), *The Rhetoric of Aristotle: An Expanded Translation with Supplementary Examples for Students of Composition and Public Speaking*, Englewood Cliffs, NJ: Prentice-Hall

Corcoran, Paul (1977), 'The Obsolescence of Political Language', *Australian Scan: Journal of Human Communication*, 3, pp. 47-57

Corcoran, Paul (1980), *Rhetoric and Political Language*, St. Lucia, Qld: University of Queensland Press

Corcoran, Paul (1994), 'Presidential Concession Speeches: The Rhetoric of Defeat', *Political Communication*, 11 (2), pp. 109-31, 10.1080/10584609.1994.9963019

Corcoran, Paul (1998) 'The Rhetoric of Triumph and Defeat: Australian Federal Elections, 1940–1993', *Australian Journal of Communication*, 25(1), pp. 69-86. 'Critics of NT Plan Question PM's Motives', (2007) *Radio Program, ABC Radio National: World Today*, 22 March, parlinfo.aph.gov.au/parlInfo/search/

Crisp, L. F. (1961), *Australian National Government*, London: Oxford University Press

Cron, Lisa (2021), 'Tell Don't Show? What Brain Imaging Reveals About Readers', *LitHub,* 17 March

Crook, D. P. (1958), *Aspects of Brisbane Society in the Eighteen-Eighties*, BA (Hons) Thesis, St. Lucia, Qld: The University of Queensland

Crystal, David and Derek Davy (1969), *Investigating English Style*, London: Longman

Crystal, David (2006), *Language and the Internet*, 2nd edn, Cambridge: Cambridge University Press

Crystal, David (2008a), *A Dictionary of Linguistics and Phonetics*, 6th edn, Oxford: Blackwell

Crystal, David (2008b), *Txtng: The gr8 db8*, Oxford: Oxford University Press

Csábi, Szilvia (2014), 'Metaphor and Stylistics', in Burke, Michael (Ed.), *The Routledge Handbook of Stylistics*, New York, Routledge, pp. 206-21

Curran, James and Ward, Stephen, (2004), *The Unknown Nation: Australia after Empire*, Carlton: Melbourne University Press

Curran, James (2004), *The Power of Speech: Australian Prime Ministers Defining the National Image*, Melbourne: Melbourne University Press

Cushman, Donald P. and John M. Penhallurick (1984), 'Political Images in the Hawke-Fraser Campaign', in Smith III, Ted J., Graeme Osborne, and Robyn Penman (Eds.), *Communication and Government: Issues Policies and Trends*, Bruce, ACT: Canberra CAE, pp. 77-112

Dalvean, Michael (2017), 'Changes in the Style and Content of Australian Election Campaign Speeches from 1901 to 2016', *ICAME Journal*, 41, 10.1515/icame-2017-0001

Dascal, Marcelo (2017), 'Types of Polemics and Types of Polemical Moves', in Cmerjrkova, Svetla, Jana Hoffmanova, Olga Mullerova, Olga M. Llerov (Eds), *Dialoganalyse VI/1: Referate der 6. Argbeitstagung, Prag 1996*, Berlin/Boston: Walter de Gruyter GmbH, pp. 15-33

Derry, John W. (1967), *The Radical Tradition–Tom Paine to Lloyd George*, London: Macmillan

Dickinson, Paul (2009), *A Systemic Linguistic Analysis of Two Prime Ministerial Speeches*, March, birmingham.ac.uk/Documents/college-artslaw/cels/essays/functional/dickinsonFG.pdf

Dixon, P. (1971), *Rhetoric*, London: Methuen

Dryzek, J.S. (2010), 'Rhetoric in Democracy: A Systemic Appreciation', *Political Theory*, 38(3), pp. 319-39, doi.org/10.1177/0090591709359596

Duncan, Hugh Dalziel (1971), 'The Need for Clarification in Social Models of Rhetoric', in Bitzer, Lloyd F. and Black, Edwin (Eds.), *The Prospect of Rhetoric*, Englewood Cliffs, NJ: Prentice-Hall, pp. 140-50

Elfstrom, G. (2011), 'The Rhetoric of Democracy', in Nikolaev, A.G. (Ed.), *Ethical Issues in International Communication*, London: Palgrave Macmillan doi.org/10.1057/9780230306844_4

Ellegard, Alvar (1962), *A Statistical Method for Determining Authorship*, Goteborg: Acta Universitas Gothoburgensis

Ellis, R.J. (Ed.) (1998), *Speaking to the People: The Rhetorical Presidency in Historical Perspective*, Amherst: University of Massachusetts Press

Ellul, Jacques (1965), *Propaganda: The Formation of Men's Attitudes*, New York: Knopf

Enkvist, Nils Erik (1964), 'On Defining Style', in Enkvist, Nils Erik; Spencer, John; and Gregory, Michael J. (Eds.), *Linguistics and Style*, Oxford: Oxford University Press, pp. 1-56

Enkvist, Nils Erik (1973), *Linguistic Stylistics*, Berlin: Mouton

Fahnestock, Jeanne (2011), *Rhetorical Style: The Uses of Language in Persuasion*, New York: Oxford University Press

Fahnestock, Jeanne (2021) 'Analyzing Rhetorical Style: Toward Better Methods', in Boogaart R., Jansen H., van Leeuwen M. (Eds.), *The Language of Argumentation. Argumentation Library, vol 36*, Springer, Cham. https://doi.org/10.1007/978-3-030-52907-9_5, Accessed 4 February 2021

Fairclough, Norman (2013), 'Critical Discourse Analysis and Critical Policy Studies', *Critical Policy Studies*, 7(2), pp. 177-97, doi.org/10.1080/19460171.2013.798239

Farquharson, John (2007), 'Killen, Sir Denis James (1925-2007)', *Obituaries Australia*, oa.anu.edu.au/obituary/killen-sir-denis-james-562 Accessed 17 June 2020

Finlayson, Alan (2004), 'Political Science, Political Ideas and Rhetoric', *Economy and Society*, 33(4), doi.org/10.1080/0308514042000285279

Finlayson, Alan (2007), 'From Beliefs to Arguments: Interpretive Methodology and Rhetorical Political Analysis', *The British Journal of Politics and International Relations*, 9(4), pp. 545-63, doi.org/10.1111/j.1467-856x.2007.00269.x

Finlayson, Alan (2015), 'Becoming a Democratic Audience', in Rai, Shirin M. and Janelle Reinelt (Ed.) (2015), *The Grammar of Politics and Performance*, London: Palgrave, pp. 93-105

Flesch, Rudolph (1962), *The Art of Plain Talk*, New York: Collier Macmillan

Flint, E. H. (1970), 'Comparison of Spoken and Written English: Towards an Integrated Method of Linguistic Description', in Ransom, W.S. (Ed.), *English Transported*, Canberra: Australian National University Press, pp. 161-87

Flower, Linda (1993), *Problem-solving Strategies for Writing*, 4th edn, Fort Worth: Harcourt Brace Jovanovich

Forsyth, Mark (2014), *The Elements of Eloquence: Secrets of the Perfect Turn of Phrase*, New York: Berkley

Fowler, Roger (1980), 'Linguistic Criticism', *UEA Papers in Linguistics 11*, January, University of East Anglia, Norwich, UK, pp. 1-26

Freeman, James B. (1997), 'What Types of Statements Are There? A Philosophical Look at Stasis Theory', *OSSA Conference Archive*, 36, University of Windsor, scholar.uwindsor.ca/ossaarchive/OSSA2/papersandcommentaries/36

Friedman, J. and S. Friedman (2012), *Rethinking the Rhetorical Presidency*, Abingdon: Routledge

Furphy, Samuel (Ed.) (2015), *The Seven Dwarfs and the Age of the Mandarins: Australian Government Administration in the Post-war Reconstruction Era*, Canberra: Australian National University Press

Gabis, Stanley T. (1978), 'Political Secrecy and Cultural Conflict: A Plea for Formalism', *Administration and Society*, 10(2), August

Gibson, Walker T. (1966), *Tough, Sweet and Stuffy*, Bloomington: University of Indiana Press

Gizzi-Stewart, Brooke (2012), *The Mechanisms of Persuasive Language: An Analysis of Australian Federal Election Campaign Speeches*, BA (Hons) Thesis, Newcastle, NSW: The University of Newcastle

Gizzi-Stewart, Brooke (2016), 'New Visions and Vintage Values: Shifting Discourses of Australian National Identity in 21st Century Prime Ministerial Rhetoric', *Communication, Politics and Culture*, 49(1), pp. 62-85

Gizzi-Stewart, Brooke (2018), *The Language of Strategy: A Study in Australian Prime Ministerial Rhetoric and Campaign Speechmaking*, 1983-2013, PhD Thesis, Newcastle, NSW: The University of Newcastle

Gorman, L. (1998), 'Menzies and Television: A Medium He 'Endured'', *Media International Australia*, 87, pp. 49-67

Graham, A. Douglas (1939), *The Life of the Right Honourable Sir Samuel Walker Griffith, G.C.M.G., P.C.*, Sydney: Law Book

Gregory, Denis (2015), *It's All About Australia Mate*, Gosford, NSW: Exisle

Groombridge, Brian (1972), *Television and the People: A Programme for Democratic Participation*, Harmondsworth: Penguin

Grube, Dennis C. (2012), 'A Very Public Search for Public Value: "Rhetorical Secretaries" in Westminster Jurisdictions', *Public Administration*, 90 (2), pp. 445-65

Grube, Dennis C. (2013), *Prime Ministers and Rhetorical Governance*, Basingstoke: Palgrave Macmillan

Grube, Dennis C. (2019), *Megaphone Bureaucracy: Speaking Truth to Power in the Age of the New Normal*, Princeton, NJ: Princeton University Press

Halloran, S.M. (1975), 'On the End of Rhetoric: Classical and Modern', *College English*, 36(6), February, pp. 621-31

Hamilton, Craig (2009), 'Jonathan Charteris-Black, Politicians and Rhetoric. The Persuasive Power of Metaphor', *Lexis* [Online], Book reviews journals.openedition.org/lexis/1691 Accessed 4 July 2020

Hamilton, Craig (2013), '"The Rhetoric of Text" Reconsidered in Fiction and Autobiography', *Études de stylistique anglaise*, Online since 19 February 2019, journals.openedition.org/esa/1433; DOI: doi.org/10.4000/esa.1433, Accessed 19 September 2020

Hanson, Russel (1985), *The Democratic Imagination in America: Conversations with our Past*, Princeton: Princeton University Press

Headon, David (1994), 'A Response to Gordon Briscoe', *Aboriginal History*, 18(1/2), pp. 39-44, https://www.jstor.org/stable/24046085?refreqid=excelsior%3Ae707b407793e25c0030f0ac891ec3c85&seq=1

Headon, David (2018), *Alfred Deakin (1856-1919): Australia's Second Prime Minister*, Canberra: Australian Parliamentary Library

Heath, Evelyn (1977), 'Representative Speeches of Gough Whitlam', *Australian Scan: Journal of Human Communication*, 3, pp. 23-34

Heath, Evelyn (unpublished), 'Representative Speeches of Gough Whitlam: The Complete Study'

Henderson, Gae Lyn and Braun, M.J. (2016), *Propaganda and Rhetoric in Democracy*, Carbondale, Il: Southern Illinois University Press

Herman, Edward S. and Noam Chomsky (1988), *Manufacturing Consent: The Political Economy of the Mass Media*, New York: Pantheon

Higgie, Rebecca Louise (2013), *Speaking Truth: The Play of Politics and Australian Satire*, PhD Thesis, Bentley, WA: Curtin University

Hirst, John (2016), *Australian History in 7 Questions*, Carlton, Vic: Black

Hochmuth, Marie (1962), 'Kenneth Burke and the "New Rhetoric"', *Quarterly Journal of Speech*, 48, pp. 133-44

Hogben, George L. (1977), 'Linguistic Style and Personality', *Language and Style*, x, 4, Fall, pp. 270-84

Honar, William H. (1969), 'The Men Behind Nixon's Speeches', *New York Times Magazine*, January 19, p. 20

Hutchins, Robert M. (1952), 'A Letter to the Reader', *The Great Conversation: The Substance of a Liberal Education*, Chicago: William Benton, pp. 74-82

Inglis, K.S. (1993), *Men and Women of Australia: Speech Making as History*, Canberra: Australian Defence Force Academy in association with Barry Andrews Memorial Trust and The University of New South Wales

Inglis, K.S. (1996), *Parliamentary Speech*, Papers on Parliament No. 28, Canberra: Parliament of Australia, Lecture in the Department of the Senate Occasional Lecture Series at Parliament House on 23 February

Inglis, Ken (2007), 'Speechmaking in Australian History', *the Allan Martin Lecture*, Canberra: The Australian National University

Jefferson, Gail, (1985), 'An Exercise in the Transcription and Analysis of Laughter', in van Dijk, Teun (Ed.), *Handbook of Discourse Analysis 3*, London: Academic, pp. 25-34

Jeffries, L. (2010), *Opposition in Discourse: The Construction of Oppositional Meaning*, London: Continuum

Jeffries, L. and D. McIntyre (2010), *Stylistics*, Cambridge: Cambridge University Press

Johnson, Carole S. and Inga K. Kelly (1975), '"He" and "She": Changing Language to Fit a Changing World', *Educational Leadership*, 32(8), May, p. 325

Jordan, Kayla N.; Sterling, Joanna; Pennebaker, James W.; and Boyd, Ryan L. (2019), 'Examining long-term trends in politics and culture through language of political leaders and cultural institutions', in Pinker, Stephen (Ed.), *Proceedings National Academy of Sciences*, February 26, 2019, 116 (9) 3476-81; first published February 11, 2019, doi.org/10.1073/pnas.1811987116

Kaal, Bertie, Isa Maks, and Annemarie van Elfrinkhof (Eds.) (2014), *From Text to Political Positions, Text analysis across disciplines*, Amsterdam: John Benjamins

Kane, John and Haig Patapan (2010), 'The Artless Art: Leadership and the Limits of Democratic Rhetoric', *Australian Journal of Political Science*, 45(3), 10.1080/10361146.2010.499162

Kinney, Thomas (2016) 'Book of Quotations on Rhetoric', *Kairos: A Journal of Rhetoric, Technology, and Pedagogy*, pp. 1-121, kairos.technorhetoric.net/stasis/2016/kinney/Rhetorical_Definitions.pdf

Koren, Varda Furman (2016), 'Paradoxes of Political Conflicts. Case Study: The Eclipse of the Belgium First Prime Minister (Belgium 1830)', in Scarafile, Giovanni and Leah Gruenpeter Gold (Eds.), *Paradoxes of Conflicts*, Switzerland: Springer, pp. 13-28

Kress, Gunther and Robert Hodge (1979), *Language as Ideology*, London: Routledge and Kegan Paul

Kress, Gunther (1980), 'Ideological Unity of Discourse: The Concept of 'Textual Congruence'", *Australian Scan: Journal of Human Communication*, 9 & 10, pp. 71-7

Kress-Rose, Nicolle (1974), 'The Analysis of the Speech Event in Stylistic Study', *Style*, 8(1), Winter, pp. 46-55

Kruger, Arthur N. (1975), 'The Nature of Controversial Statements', *Philosophy and Rhetoric*, 8(3), Summer, pp. 137-58

Lake, D.J. (1971), *Style and Meaning*, St. Lucia, Qld: University of Queensland Press Research Papers

Lake, David J. (1975), *The Canon of Thomas Middleton Plays: Internal Evidence for the Major Problems of Authorship*, London: Cambridge University Press

Lakoff, George, and Mark Johnson (2003), *Metaphors We Live By*, Chicago: University of Chicago Press

La Nauze, John Alfred (1965), *Alfred Deakin: A Biography*, Melbourne: Melbourne University Press

Lasswell, Harold D., Nathan Leits, and Associates (1949), *Language of Politics: Studies in Quantitative Semantics*, New York: G.W. Stewart

Leacock, Stephen (1969), 'Humor As I See It', in Eastman, A.M. et. al., *The Norton Reader: An Anthology of Expository Prose*, New York: Norton, pp. 725-31

Leech, Geoffrey and Mick Short (2007), *Style in Fiction, A Linguistic Introduction to English Fictional Prose*, 2nd edn, Harlow: Pearson Longman

Leed, Jacob (Ed.) (1978), *The Computer and Literary Style*, Kent, OH: Kent State University Press

Lerner, Daniel (Ed.) (1972), on 'Effective Propaganda: Conditions and Evaluation', in *Propaganda in War and Crisis*, New York: Arno

Lerner, Jennifer, Ye Li, Piercarlo Valdesolo, and Karim S. Kassam (2015), 'Emotion and Decision Making', *The Annual Review of Psychology*, 13 September, pp. 33.1-25, doi: 10.1146/annurev-psych-010213-115043

Lewis, C.S. (1960), *Studies in Words*, 1st edn, Cambridge: Cambridge University Press

Lugea, Jane (2018), 'The Year's Work in Stylistics 2017', *Language and Literature: International Journal of Stylistics*, 10 December, journals.sagepub.com/doi/full/10.1177/0963947018799777, Accessed 4 January 2021

MacLean, Eleanor O'Donnell (1981), *Between the Lines: How to Detect Bias and Propaganda in the News and Everyday Life*, Montreal: Black Rose Books

Maks, Isa and Annemarie van Elfrinkhof (Eds.) (2014), *From Text to Political Positions, Text Analysis across Disciplines*, Amsterdam: John Benjamins

Marlin, Randal (2013a), *Propaganda and the Ethics of Persuasion*, 2nd edn, Peterborough, Canada: Broadview

Marlin, Randal (2013b), 'Jacques Ellul's Contribution to Propaganda Studies', in Auerbach, Jonathan and Castronovo, Russ (Eds.), *The Oxford Handbook of Propaganda Studies*, doi: 10.1093/oxfordhb/9780199764419.013.009

Marlin, Randal (2021), 'Dynamic Tension for Pandemic Times', *Current Drift*, 10 May, IJES Elul Society, https://ellul.org/current-drift/dynamic-tension-for-pandemic-times/

Martin, J. (2014), *Politics and Rhetoric: A Critical Introduction*, London: Routledge

Martin, J. (2015), 'Situating Speech: A Rhetorical Approach to Political Strategy', *Political Studies*, 63(1), pp. 25-42

McCabe, Katherine (2013), 'From Town Hall to Global Village: The Transformation of Australian Political Speech', *Australian Journal of Communication*, 40(3), pp. 139-49

McGee, John A. (1929), *Persuasive Speaking*, New York: Scribner's
https://archive.org/details/persuasivespeaki00mcge, Accessed 1 September 2021

McGregor, Craig (2004), 'Inside Bob Hawke', in Ricketson, Matthew (Ed.), *The Best Australian Profiles*, Melbourne: Black, pp. 22-46

McIntyre, Dan (2010), 'The Year's Work in Stylistics 2010', *Language and Literature: International Journal of Stylistics*, 19(4), pp. 396-411, core.ac.uk/reader/194627982, Accessed 4 January 2021

McLeod, Marian B. (1978), 'R.G. Menzies as Parliamentary Speaker', *Australian Scan: Journal of Human Communication*, 4, pp. 1-12

McLeod, Marian B. (2007), *Commonwealth Public Address: Essays in Criticism*, New Delhi: Sterling

Medhurst, M.J. (Ed.) (1996a), *Beyond the Rhetorical Presidency*, College Station, TX: A&M University Press

Medhurst, M.J. (1996b), 'A Tale of Two Constructs: The Rhetorical Presidency versus Presidential Rhetoric', in Medhurst, M.J. (Ed.) *Beyond the Rhetorical Presidency*, College Station: Texas A&M University Press, pp. xi–xxv

Metherell, Lexie (2014), 'Keating Speechwriter Don Watson Says Gough Whitlam's Memorial Shows Thirst for Meaty Speeches', *ABC News*, 14 November, abc.net.au/news/2014-11-14/speechwriter-says-australians-want-substantial-speeches/5891074?nw=0

Milic, Louis Tonko (1966), 'Unconscious Ordering in the Prose of Swift', in Leed, J. (Ed.), *The Computer and Literary Style*, Kent, OH: Kent State University Press, pp. 79-106

Milic, Louis Tonko (1967), *A Quantitative Approach to the Style of Jonathan Swift*, The Hague: Mouton

Miller, Carolyn R. and Ashley R. Kelly (Eds.) (2017), *Emerging Genres in New Media Environments*, Basingstoke: Palgrave Macmillan, DOI.1007/978-3-319-40295-6

Miller, Rodney G. (1976a), 'Image Making and Australian Political Rhetoric', *Inter Connections*, 1(1), December, pp. 20-5

Miller, Rodney G. (1976b), 'Polemic and Propaganda in Australian Election Campaigns', *Proceedings Conference on Interpersonal and Mass Communication*, Sydney, NSW: New South Wales Institute of Technology, pp. 195-212

Miller, Rodney G. (1977), 'The Quiet Rhetoric of Sir Samuel Walker Griffith', *Australian Scan: Journal of Human Communication*, 3, pp. 59-65

Miller, Rodney G. (1980), 'Developing Oral Communication in a Pluralistic Society', in Crocker, W. J. (Ed.), *Developing Oral Communication Competence*, Armidale: The University of New England, pp. 85-91

Miller, Rodney G. (1981), 'Rhetoric of Democracy: Communication and the Politics of Information', in Ward, W.T. and Bryden, M.M. (Eds.), *Public Information: Your Right to Know*, St. Lucia, Qld: The Royal Society of Queensland, pp. 15-20

Miller, Rodney G. (1983), 'Language Styles for Public Communication: Research into Practice', in Smith, T.J. (Ed.), *Communication in Australia*, Australian Communication Association Conference on Communication in Australia, Warrnambool, Vic: Warrnambool Institute Press, pp. 123-8

Miller, Rodney G. (2020), 'It's Time for Plain Talk', *Word to the wise* blogpost, 25 June

Mills, Stephen and Rodney Smith (2020), 'Leaders' Debates in Australian Elections', Juárez-Gámiz, Julio; Holtz-Bacha, Christina; Schroeder, Alan (Eds.), *Routledge International Handbook on Electoral Debates*, New York: Routledge, pp. 276-86

Morgan, D.L., M.D. Slade, C.M.A. Morgan (1997), 'Aboriginal Philosophy and Its Impact on Health Care Outcomes, *Australian and New Zealand Journal of Public Health*, 21, pp. 597-601

Morton, A. Q. (1978), *Literary Detection: How to Prove Authorship and Fraud in Literature and Documents*, n.p.: Bowker

Morton, A.Q. and M. Levison (1966), 'Some Indications of Authorship in Greek Prose', in Leed, Jacob (Ed.), *The Computer and Literary Style*, Kent, OH: Kent State University Press, pp. 141-79

Munro, André (2016), 'Ministerial responsibility', *Encyclopedia Britannica*, britannica.com/topic/ministerial-responsibility, Accessed 21 May 2020

Murphy, James C. (2020), '"The time has come to say something of the forgotten class": How Menzies Transformed Australian Political Debate', *The Conversation*, June 17, theconversation.com/the-time-has-come-to-say-something-of-the-forgotten-class-how-menzies-transformed-australian-political-debate-131383, Accessed 24 January 2021

Murray, Les A. (1999), 'If You Are Tired of This Old Theme…,' *The Quality of Sprawl*, Sydney: Duffy and Snellgrove, pp. 26-8

Nash, Walter (1985), *The Language of Humour: Style and Technique in Comic Discourse*, New York: Longman

Nelson, Camilla (2020), 'Friday Essay: The Female Eunuch at 50, Germaine Greer's Fearless, Feminist Masterpiece', *The Conversation*, 8 October, theconversation.com/friday-essay-the-female-eunuch-at-50-germaine-greers-fearless-feminist-masterpiece-147437

Nimmo, Dan (1970), *The Political Persuaders: Techniques of Modern Election Campaigns*, Englewood Cliffs, NJ: Prentice-Hall

Norlin, George (1928), *Isocrates*, London: W. Heinemann

O'Connor, Gertrude (1920), *Louisa Lawson, Her Life and Work*, Volume 190: Angus and Robertson Manuscript by Gertrude O'Connor, Mitchell Library of New South Wales, Microfilm CY 1216, archival.sl.nsw.gov.au/Details/archive/110581158

Ohmann, Richard (1964), 'Generative Grammars and the Concept of Literary Style', *Word*, xx, December, pp. 423-39

Onions, C.T. (1971), *Modern English Syntax*, London: Routledge and Kegan Paul

Onions, C.T. (1972), *Shorter Oxford English Dictionary: On Historical Principles*, 3rd edn, Oxford: Clarendon

Orwell, George (1954), 'Principles of Newspeak', *Nineteen Eighty-Four*, Harmondsworth: Penguin, pp. 241-51 [1st published 1949]

Orwell, George (1981), 'Politics and the English Language', *A Collection of Essays*, Orlando, FL: Harvest, pp. 156-71 [1st published 1946]

O'Shea, Robert (2013), '"Speaking to You on the Birthday of the Nation": Vice-Regal Rhetoric on Australian Identity', *Crossroads: An Interdisciplinary Journal for the Study of History, Philosophy, Religion and Classics*, VI(II), pp. 39-48

Packard, Vance (1957), *The Hidden Persuaders*, London: Longmans Green

Palmer, F.R. (2014), *The English Verb*, 2nd edn, Abingdon: Routledge

Pannam, Clifford L. (1963), 'The Radical Chief Justice', *Australian Law Journal*, 37(9), pp. 275-88

Partridge, Eric (1949), *A Dictionary of Slang and Unconventional English*, London: Routledge and Kegan Paul

Partridge, Eric (1970), *Slang Today and Yesterday*, London: Routledge and Kegan Paul, [citing Matthews, B., 'The Function of Slang']

Pateman, Trevor (1974), *Television and the February 1974 General Election*, London: British Film Institute

Pedersen, Elena Gagiu (2015), 'Semantics of the symbol: main theories about the symbols and themes of symbols in Alexandru Macedonski's poetry', *Procedia – Social and Behavioral Sciences*, 180, pp. 586-92. The 6th International Conference Edu World 2014 'Education Facing Contemporary World Issues', 7-9 November 2014, sciencedirect.com

Pedro, Joan (2011), 'The Propaganda Model in the Early 21st Century', *International Journal of Communication* 5, pp. 1865-1905 1932-6/20111865

Penman, Robyn (1980), 'Interpersonal Communication: Competence and Coordination', *Australian Scan: Journal of Human Communication*, 9 & 10, pp. 31-3

Petelin, Roslyn (1985), 'Technical Writing: A Crack in the Paradigm', *Australian Journal of Communication*, 7, pp. 13-7

Petelin, Roslyn (2014), *UQx Write101x English Grammar and Style-Video*, St. Lucia, Qld: The University of Queensland, Website, https://www.youtube.com/channel/UC8qZTqvQsFomCo6xFNX7GZg, Accessed 11 February 2021

Petelin, Roslyn (2020), *How Writing Works: A Field Guide to Effective Writing*, 1st edn, London: Routledge

Petelin, Roslyn (2021), '"Strollout" Has Gathered Pace, Romping Home as the Macquarie Word of the Year. I'd Have Gone for "Vax", if on the List', *The Conversation*, 29 November, theconversation.com/strollout-has-gathered-pace-romping-home-as-the-macquarie-word-of-the-year-id-have-gone-for-vax-if-on-the-list-172759, Accessed 9 December 2021

Petelin, Roslyn (2022), *How Writing Works: A Field Guide to Effective Writing*, 2nd edn, New York: Routledge

Phillips-Anderson, Michael Andrew (2007), *A Theory of Rhetorical Humor in American Political Discourse*, PhD Thesis, College Park, MD: University of Maryland, drum.lib.umd.edu/bitstream/handle/1903/7739/umi-umd-5020.pdf;jsessionid=87622F0EEA4047C4C2104AD520817070?sequence=1

PhyllisauFeu (2014), Comment on 26 January, 5.33 #2, 'What Germaine Greer and The Female Eunuch Mean to Me', *The Guardian*, 25 January, www.theguardian.com/books/2014/jan/26/germaine-greer-female-eunuch-feminists-influence

Plato, *The Republic, Book IV*, pp. 426-435, gutenberg.org/files/1497/1497-h/1497-h.htm#link2H_4_0007

Pullum, Geoffrey K (2010), 'Fear and Loathing of the English Passive', *Language and Communication*, 102, Vol. 26, No. 2, June, pp. 34-44

Quirk, Randolph (1972), *The English Language and Images of Matter*, London: Oxford University Press

Rai, Shirin M. and Janelle Reinelt (Eds.) (2015), *The Grammar of Politics and Performance*, London: Palgrave

Raskin, Victor (1985), *Semantic Mechanisms of Humor*, Dordrect: D. Reidel

Raskin, Victor (Ed.) (2009), *The Primer of Humor Research (Humor Research, 8)*, Berlin: Mouton de Gruyter

Ratcliffe, Susan (2010), *Oxford Dictionary of Quotations by Subject*, Oxford: Oxford University Press, google.com/books/edition/_/eWycAQAAQBAJ?hl=en&gbpv=0

Rhodes, James M. (2010), *Democracy, Language and Rhetoric*, Fifth Annual Tanner Symposium, 22 January, Cedar City: Southern Utah University, voegelinview.com/democracy-language-rhetoric/, Accessed 20 June 2020

Ricks, Thomas E. (2017), *Churchill and Orwell, the Fight for Freedom*, New York: Penguin

Robinson, Peter (1976), 'The Media and Australian Politics', in Major, G. (Ed.) *Mass Media in Australia*, Sydney: Hodder and Stoughton

Robinson, S. (1994), 'The Aboriginal Embassy: An Account of the Protests of 1972', *Aboriginal History*, 18 (1/2), pp. 49-63

Rolfe, Mark (2004), 'The Rhetorical Prime Minister', 19(1) Review Article, pp. 158-64 *researchgate.net*

Rolfe, Mark (2010), 'The Pleasures of Political Humour in Australian Democracy', *Journal of Australian Studies*, 34(3), pp. 363-76, *researchgate.net*

Rolfe, Mark (2014), 'Looking Backwards to the Future: The Evolving Tradition of Ideal Political Rhetoric in Australia', in Uhr, John and Ryan Walter (Eds.) (2014), *Studying Australian Political Rhetoric*, Canberra: Australian National University Press, pp. 121-42

Rolfe, Mark (2016), *The Reinvention of Populist Rhetoric in The Digital Age: Insiders and Outsiders in Democratic Politics*, Basingstoke: Palgrave Macmillan, 10.1007/978-981-10-2161-9

Rolfe, Mark (2017), 'The Populist Elements of Australian Political Satire and the Debt to the Americans and the Augustans', in Milner Davis, Jessica (Ed.), *Satire and Politics*, Basingstoke: Palgrave Macmillan, pp. 37-71

Rolfe, Mark (2019), 'Is This a Dag Which I See before Me? John Clarke and the Politics in His Political Humour', *Comedy Studies*, 10(1), pp. 1-18, www.researchgate.net/publication/332193682_Is_this_a_Dagg_which_I_see_befo re_me_John_Clarke_and_the_politics_in_his_political_humour

Ross, Donald (1977), 'The Use of Word-class Distribution Data for Stylistics: Keats' Sonnets and Chicken Soup', *Poetics*, 6(2), September, pp. 169-95

Ross, Donald (1981), 'Skimming the Surface: Improvements in the Quality of Syntactic Descriptions for Stylistics', *International Journal of Applied Linguistics*, 52(1), January, pp. 55-73

Rydon, Joan (1963), 'The Electorate', in Wilkes, J. (Ed.), *Forces in Australian Politics*, Sydney: Angus and Robertson, pp. 167-204

Sayers, Dorothy L. (1948), *The Lost Tools of Learning: Paper Read at a Vacation Course in Education, Oxford, 1947,* London: Methuen

Scalmer, Sean (2017), *On the Stump: Campaign Oratory and Democracy in the United States, Britain, and Australia*, Philadelphia: Temple University

Sharpe, Matthew J. (2018), '"This Old Man": Noel Pearson's Eulogy to Gough Whitlam, Four Years On', *www.academia.edu*/37702416/_This_Old_Man_Remembering_Noel_Pearson_s_No vember_2014_Eulogy_to_Gough_Whitlam, Accessed 29 January 2021

Shoemaker, Adam (2004), *Black Words, White Page: Aboriginal Literature 1929-1988*, Canberra: Australian National University Press

Simpson, Paul (2004), *Stylistics: A Resource Book for Students*, London: Routledge
Smith, William R. (1969), *The Rhetoric of American Politics: A Study of Documents*, Westport, CT: Greenwood
Snyder, Louis L. (1955), *The Age of Reason*, Princeton: Van Nostrand, pp. 87-8
Sproule, J. Michael (1980), *Argument: Language and Its Influence*, New York: McGraw-Hill
Sproule, J. Michael (1989), *Propaganda: Five American Schools of Thought*, Singapore: The Biennial Convention of the World Communication Association, 2-10 August files.eric.ed.gov/fulltext/ED312689.pdf
Statham, Simon and Rocio Montoro (2019), 'The Year's Work in Stylistics 2018', *Language and Literature: International Journal of Stylistics*, 4 December, journals.sagepub.com/doi/10.1177/0963947019887565, Accessed 4 January 2021
Steffens, Niklas K. and S. Alexander Haslam (2013), 'Power through "Us": Leaders' Use of We-Referencing Language Predicts Election Victory', *Plos One*, October, https://journals.plos.org/plosone/article?id=10.1371/journal.pone.0077952, Accessed 6 February 2021
Steinfatt, Thomas M. (1979), 'Evaluating Approaches to Propaganda Analysis', *ETC: A Review of General Semantics*, 36(2), Summer, pp. 157-80
Stockwell, Peter (2000), '(Sur)real Stylistics: From Text to Contextualising', in Bex, Tony, Peter Stockwell, Michael Burke (Eds.), *Contextualised Stylistics: In Honour of Peter Verdonk*, Amsterdam: Rodopi, pp. 15-38
Stockwell, Peter (2006), '31 Language and Literature: Stylistics', *Neuro Humanities Studies*, 1/10/06, pp. 742-57 neurohumanitiestudies.eu>archivio>stylistics
Stuckey, M.E. (2010), 'Rethinking the Rhetorical Presidency and Presidential Rhetoric', *The Review of Communication*, 10(1), pp. 38-52
Summers, Anne (2016), *Dammed Whores and God's Police*, Sydney: NewSouth Publishing
Swanson, David L. (1972), 'The New Politics Meets the Old Rhetoric: New Directions in Campaign Communication Research', *Quarterly Journal of Speech*, 58, pp. 31-40
Siracusa, Joseph M. (1987), *Sallyanne: Portrait of a Lord Mayor*, Milton, Qld: Jacaranda
Tannen, Deborah (1984), *Conversational Style: Analyzing Talk among Friends*, Norwood, NJ: Ablex
Tannen, Deborah, Heidi E. Hamilton, and Deborah Schiffrin (Eds.) (2018), *The Handbook of Discourse Analysis*, 2nd edn, Chichester: Wiley Blackwell
Tatz, Colin and Keith R. McConnochie (Eds.) (1975), *Black Viewpoints: The Aboriginal Experience*, Sydney: Australia and New Zealand Book
Tatz, Colin (2001), 'Confronting Australian Genocide', in *Aboriginal History*, Vol 25, Canberra: Australian National University Press, pp. 16-36, press-files.anu.edu.au/downloads/press/p72971/pdf/book.pdf
Tatz, Colin (2011), *Genocide in Australia: By Accident or Design?*, Indigenous Human Rights and History: occasional papers, 1(1), Melbourne: Monash University, www.monash.edu/__data/assets/pdf_file/0020/141554/tatz-essay.pdf
Thompson, W.N. (1967), *Quantitative Research in Public Address and Communication*, New York: Random House
Tollefson, Michael M. (2017), 'Rhetoric, Aristotle's Pathos 3', in Allen, Mike (Ed.) (2017), *The SAGE Encyclopedia of Communication Research Methods*, Thousand Oaks, CA: Sage, pp. 1482-83

Trimble, Linda (2016), 'Julia Gillard and the Gender Wars', *Politics and Gender*, (12)2, June, pp. 296-316, cambridge.org/core/journals/politics-and-gender/
Tulis, J.K. (1987), *The Rhetorical Presidency*, Princeton: Princeton University Press
Tulis, J.K. (2007), 'The Rhetorical Presidency in Retrospect', *Critical Review: A Journal of Politics and Society*, 19(2–3), pp. 481-500
Turner, G.W. (1973), *Stylistics*, Harmondsworth: Penguin
Twaddell, W.F. (1968), *The English Verb Auxiliaries*, Providence, RI: Brown University
Uhr, John and Ryan Walter (Eds.) (2014), *Studying Australian Political Rhetoric*, Canberra: Australian National University Press
United Nations (1948), *Universal Declaration of Human Rights*, Article 3
van Dijk, Teun A. (2018), 'Critical Discourse Analysis', Tannen, Deborah, Heidi E. Hamilton, and Deborah Schiffrin (Eds.), *The Handbook of Discourse Analysis*, 2nd edn, Chichester: Wiley Blackwell, pp. 466-85
van Haaften, Ton (2019), 'Argumentative Strategies and Stylistic Devices', *Informal Logic*, 39(4), pp. 301-28
van Leeuwen, Maarten (2014), 'Systematic stylistic analysis, The use of a linguistic checklist', Kaal, Bertie, Isa Maks, and Annemarie van Elfrinkhof (Eds.), *From Text to Political Positions, Text analysis across disciplines*, Amsterdam: John Benjamins, pp. 225-44
Verdonk, Peter (2002), *Stylistics*, Oxford: Oxford University Press
Vickers, B. (1970), *Classical Rhetoric in English Poetry*, London: St. Martins'
Wallace, Christine (1997), *Germaine Greer: Untamed Shrew*, Sydney: Pan Macmillan
Walter, James (1981), 'Language and Habits of Thought: Biographical Notes on E.G. Whitlam', *Biography*, (4)1, pp. 14-44
Wells, Rulon (1960), 'Nominal and Verbal Style', in Sebeok, T. A. (Ed.), *Style in Language*, Cambridge, MA: MIT Press, pp. 213-20
Whitlam, Nicholas and John Stubbs (1974), *Nest of Traitors*, Milton, Qld: Jacaranda
Wiemann, John M. and Philip Backlund (1980), 'Current Theory and Research in Communicative Competence', *Review of Educational Research*, 50(1), pp.185-99
Williams, Raymond (1985), *Keywords: A Vocabulary of Culture and Society*, Revised edn, New York: Oxford University Press
Woolley, Samuel C. and Philip N. Howard (2019), *Computational Propaganda: Political Parties, Politicians and Political Manipulation on Social Media*, New York: Oxford University Press
Younane, Stephanie (2007), '"Men and Women of Australia": Political Rhetoric in Australian Political Science and Communication', Melbourne: Australasian Political Studies Association Conference, Monash University, September
Young, S. (2006), 'Australian Electoral Slogans, 1949-2004: Where Political Marketing Meets Political Rhetoric', *Australian Journal of Communication*, 33(1), pp. 1-19
Young, S. (2007a), 'Political and Parliamentary Speech in Australia', *Parliamentary Affairs* 60, pp. 234-52
Young, S. (Ed.) (2007b), *Government Communication in Australia*, Port Melbourne: Cambridge University Press
Zada, John (2021), *Veils of Distortion: How the News Media Warps Our Minds*, Toronto: Terra Incognita

PERMISSION ACKNOWLEDGEMENTS

I acknowledge permission to publish speeches in whole or in part provided by: former prime ministers, The Hon Julia Gillard AC for *Motion-in-Reply*–'Misogyny Speech', The Hon John Howard OM AC for *Speech to Gun Rally–Sale, Victoria* and the excerpt of *Address to Memorial Service*, The Hon P.J. Keating for *Redfern Park Speech: Australian Launch of the International Year for the World's Indigenous People*, Redfern Park, Sydney, 10 December 1992–Reproduced with permission of The Hon P. J. Keating, and The Hon Kevin Rudd AC for *Apology to Australia's Indigenous Peoples*; Sallyanne Atkinson AO for *Expo '88 Opening Ceremony Speech of The Rt Hon Lord Mayor of Brisbane;* the Australian Labor Party for an excerpt from the *Australian Labor Party Federal Election Policy Speech 1983* of Robert J. Hawke MP; the Commonwealth of Australia for prime ministerial transcripts of The Rt Hon John Curtin *Speech to America*, The Rt Hon Sir Robert Menzies KT AK CH QC FAA FRS *Speech on the Occasion of the Funeral of the Late Sir Winston Churchill*, an excerpt of *Talk to the Nation, November 1961* and other speech excerpts, The Hon Gough Whitlam AC QC *Partnership in the Pacific after Vietnam: National Press Club, Washington DC* and *Dismissal Speech on the Steps of Parliament House*, The Hon Bob Hawke AC GCL *Address by the Prime Minister, Hon R.J. Hawke AC MP, to the National Economic Summit Conference* and the excerpt of *Speech at Labor Day Dinner, by The Hon R.J. Hawke, AC MP, Prime Minister*, The Hon Paul Keating *Redfern Park Speech*, The Hon John Howard OM AC *Speech to Gun Rally–Sale, Victoria* and the excerpt of *Address to Memorial Service*, and The Hon Scott Morrison MP *Address to the Nation amid the Coronavirus Pandemic*, Licensed from the Commonwealth of Australia under a Creative Commons Attribution 4.0 International Licence. The Commonwealth of Australia does not necessarily endorse the content of this publication; Eleanor Gilbert for *The Needs of First Nations* by Kevin Gilbert; The Hon Michael Kirby AC CMG for *The Australian Community and Anti-heroes* and excerpts of his speeches and writing; the Liberal Party of Australia for an excerpt from the *Liberal Party Federal Election Policy Speech 1983* of The Right Hon Malcolm Fraser AC CH GCL PC; and the Parliament of Australia for speeches in whole or in part of The Hon Dame Enid Lyons AD

GBE *Governor-General's Speech, Address-in-Reply*, E. Gough Whitlam QC *Motion of Want of Confidence in the Government*, The Hon John Howard OM AC *Tasmania: Tragedy at Port Arthur*, The Hon Kevin Rudd AC *Apology to Australia's Indigenous Peoples*, and The Hon Julia Gillard AC *Motion-in-Reply*–'Misogyny Speech', Licensed from the Commonwealth of Australia under a Creative Commons Attribution-NonCommercial-NoDerivs 3.0 Australia Licence with the requirement to adhere to the non-commercial requirement waived. I also acknowledge the courtesy of the Mitchell Library, within the State Library of New South Wales for the speech published in 1891 by Louisa Lawson *Womanhood Suffrage*, the article in 1895 by Sir Samuel Walker Griffith GCMG PC KC 'The Certainty of Australian Federation', and the speech in 1912 by The Right Hon Sir John Forrest GCMG *Trans-Australia Railway, Ceremony at Port Augusta to Turn the First Sod of the Trans-Australia Railway from Port Augusta to Kalgoorlie*. I have made every effort to locate sources and copyright holders of original work material, but if there are errors or omissions, I will be pleased to add appropriate credit in any later edition.

ABOUT THE AUTHOR

Rodney G. Miller founded and edited the *Australian Journal of Communication*, while teaching communication, speech, and writing at Queensland University of Technology (QUT) in Brisbane, Australia for over a decade. With early publication in *The Australian* newspaper, his thoughts on communication are published by The State University of New York Press, other universities, and The Royal Society of Queensland.

He has since led the advancement of innovative education for universities in the United States and internationally, consulted on communication, served as adjunct faculty at Indiana University's center on philanthropy, and chaired or served on governing boards of educational, professional, and community organisations.

INDEX

A

Abbott, Tony, 202-3
Aboriginal Embassy, 140, 239
Aboriginal and Torres Straight Island people (see First Nations)
ACTU (Australian Council of Trade Unions), 258, 259
Adams, Phillip, 62
adjectives, 159, 161, 164, 165
  as speech topic, 185
  pairs, 82, 187
adjunct, 70
advertising, 6, 39, 87, 211
alliteration, 23, 90, 91, 93, 105
  Lawson, 114
  Deakin, 122
allusion, 23, 76, 79, 110
  to democracy, 30
  historical/literary, 16, 56, 70-1
  for humour, 46, 58, 205
America, 5, 24, 27, 56, 186, 188, 219
  McMahon polemic, 45
  Curtin speech to, 20, 29-34, 226-9
  democracy, 2, 20, 29-30
  language of president, 210-1
  Whitlam speech, 20, 30, 79, 59, 88-9, 240-5
  women's petition in, 45, 219
American Revolution, 186, 188
anadiplosis, 161
analogy, 20, 23, 46, 76, 143, 167
  Greer, 158
  Griffith, 106
  Hawke, 176
  Kirby, 182
  Whitlam, 20
anaphora, 20, 23, 90, 93, 210
  Curtin, 90-1
  Deakin, 126
  Gilbert, 81, 90, 149
  Gillard, 202
  Greer, 157, 161
  Howard, 196, 197
  Keating, 194
  Kirby, 81, 187, 188, 190

  Lawson, 114, 115
  Menzies, 81, 90, 135
  Morrison, 206, 207
  Oodgeroo, 146
  Rudd, 199-200
  Whitlam, 20, 81, 83, 90
Anglo-Celtic reference, 27, 130, 136
  Kirby, 252, 255
  Menzies, 27, 58, 130
anti-hero, 25, 82, 185-6, 187-8, 246-56
antimetabole, 157
Anti-Socialist Party, 123, 124
antithesis, 23, 39, 143
  Hawke, 43
  Howard, 197
  Kirby, 187
  Menzies, 36, 135
  Rudd, 199
Anzac, 30, 31, 188, 228, 247
argument, 10, 52, 58, 161
  Carnegie, 17, 41
  Curtin, 49
  Gilbert, 44, 146, 147, 149
  Gillard, 204
  Greer, 151, 153, 156, 160
  Griffith, 25, 97-102, 104-6
  Hughes, 26, 46
  Menzies, 130
  out of opposites, 38-9
  polemical, 43-4, 46-7, 77
  Reid, 58
  Whitlam, 68, 72, 245
apartheid, 237
Aristotle, 148, 171
  democracy, 30
  on polemic, 40
article, 82, 92, 163
Asean nations, 243
assimilation, policy of, 140, 145, 235
Atkinson, Sallyanne, 3, 11, 20-2, 38, 73, 80, 265-6
audience, 3, 5, 8-10, 27, 52, 73-9, 83-7, 92-3, 95-6, 98-9, 105, 110-1, 116, 121, 129, 131-2, 138-9, 144, 152-4, 157, 167-8

355

attention of, 16-8, 22, 131-2, 139-40, 142, 146, 151-3, 155-7, 162, 174
and communication, 22, 27-8, 168
emotions, 4, 12, 17, 41, 92-3, 95-8, 101, 112, 118, 121-2, 127, 132, 141, 144, 147, 161-3, 167, 169, 182, 189, 195-6, 200, 201, 202
focus, 23, 92, 122, 182
and humour, 55-6, 57-9, 61, 78, 93, 127-8, 182
and jargon, 69
of media, 39, 54, 167-8, 169, 177
and polemic, 38, 41, 44, 46, 53
relationship, 15-7, 69-71, 77, 83-4, 85-90, 129-30, 177-9, 209-11
segments of, 4, 28, 31, 42, 92, 110-1, 116, 144, 152, 170, 212
Australian Labor Party (ALP), 4, 35, 47-9, 50, 64, 166, 169, 174-5
Australian Law Reform Commission, 89, 139, 182, 185, 246, 250, 251, 252
Australian Natives' Association
Deakin's address to, 59, 120-1
authenticity, 5, 18, 34, 50, 62, 207
authority of speaker, 98, 103, 112, 132, 174, 183-4, 209

B

Bali, 17
Ballarat, Victoria, 14, 121, 122, 123
Barry, Sir Redmond, 19
'bastards', 25, 41, 141, 233-4
Battle
of Britain, 134, 227
of the Atlantic, 227
BBC, 30, 131, 230
Bendigo, 120
Bergson, Henri, 58
Bernhardt, Sarah, 15
Biden, Joseph R., 210, 211
Bjelke-Petersen, Sir Joh, 51-2, 92, 259
blitz, 227
Bonner, Helen, 52
Botany Bay, 182
Bourbons, 26, 56, 65, 69-71
Bourne, Senator Vicki, 60

Boyer Lecture, 17
Britain, 1, 2, 8, 24, 30, 31, 59, 227, 268
colonial settlement, 27, 29, 186, 246
and Commonwealth, 27, 132, 134
Deakin, 117-8
and Menzies, 27, 127, 130, 136-7
and monarchy, 27, 130, 136-7
as motherland, 2
transported, 27, 130, 136-7
British Empire, 46, 118, 216
British Labour Party, 63
Burke and Wills, 26
Burnet, Sir Macfarlane, 11, 17, 25, 44

C

cabinet, 65, 67, 118
Camus, Albert, 2
Capitol, 1, 91, 229
Carnegie, Sir Roderick, 11, 17, 26, 41
Cassab, Judy, 185
catharsis, 20, 53, 201, 245
CDA (critical discourse analysis), 5, 23
censorship, 45-6
Charles, HRH The Prince of Wales, 176
Chiang Kai-Shek, Generalissimo, 241
choice, rhetorical/stylistic, 4, 8, 9-11, 14, 44, 56, 73-6, 79, 92-3, 136, 157
analysis of, 22-4, 26, 34, 79, 84, 92
types of, 17-8, 206-7, 212
vocabulary, 114, 141, 159, 187, 195, 204, 207
Christian, 104
Churchill, Sir Winston, 12, 62, 65, 130-5, 158, 230-2
Cicero, 157
Clarke, John, 62
clauses, 74, 89, 93, 121, 149, 154, 157-8, 160, 163-5, 187, 210
in complex sentences, 114, 149
compound, 21, 78, 80-1, 93, 154, 164-5, 204, 210
embedding, 80, 93, 105, 158
relative/subordinate, 80
cliché, 81, 85, 93, 193, 210
in use, 26, 71, 106, 120, 129, 157, 200

climax, 84, 212
  Gilbert, 147
  Gillard, 203-4
  Griffith, 100
  Lawson, 112, 113
  Menzies, 133
  Whitlam, 70, 72
coalition, 95, 56, 66-7, 116
Cold War, 20, 47, 85, 245
colloquialism, 76, 85, 87, 93, 120
  Gilbert, 149
  Greer, 13, 154, 155, 159-60
  Griffith, 105, 106
  Morrison, 207
Colonial Conference (1887), 117-8
colonisation, 139, 147, 182, 186, 238, 246
communication competence, 6, 26, 34, 55, 166-8, 176, 210
  digital, 6, 8-9, 12, 127, 211-12
  nonverbal, 167-8, 171-5, 177-8
communication goals, 6, 8, 10, 116, 123, 136, 175, 177
complement, 70
conclusion, 18, 44, 212
  Curtin, 49
  Deakin, 121, 126
  Gilbert, 139, 146
  Gillard, 204
  Greer, 157, 161, 162
  Griffith, 96, 97, 99-100, 102
  Howard, 197, 198
  Kirby, 183, 189, 190
  Lawson, 113, 115
  Menzies, 133
  Morrison, 206-7
  Pearson, 205
  Rudd, 201
  Whitlam, 72
conjunction, 92, 130
conscription, 26, 45-6, 131, 220-1
conservative, 37, 41, 60, 63, 94, 129, 163
  Griffith, 98
  Menzies, 134

Constitution, 30, 35, 96, 116, 120, 181, 214, 240, 249, 276
  and dismissal, 51, 168, 188
controversy, 37-43, 77, 93, 193
  Curtin, 47-8, 49
  Gilbert, 147, 149
  Greer, 46, 153, 157, 163
  Griffith, 95
  Kirby, 181, 186
  Lawson, 37-8
  Menzies, 47-8
  sidelining of, 34, 43
conversation, similarity to, 8, 70, 74, 80-91, 93, 194, 196, 207, 210
  Atkinson, 21
  Curtin on radio, 8, 32, 34
  Deakin, 124, 126
  Gilbert, 146, 148-9
  Gillard, 203
  Greer, 83, 153-7, 160, 163-5
  Griffith, 95, 98, 105
  Menzies, 36, 81, 127-8, 130, 133-4, 135
  Morrison, 207, 290
  Oodgeroo, 149
  Rudd, 198
  Whitlam, 70
correction, 30, 146, 156, 157
Country Party, 56
court, 18-9, 40, 123, 149, 156, 193
  Gillard, 288
  Griffith, 95, 214
  Kirby, 11, 180, 246, 246-56
Cowen, Sir Zelman, 11, 26, 42, 77
Crystal, David, 66, 83, 88, 212
Cuba, 242
culture, multicultural, 1, 4, 17, 27, 28, 130, 136, 185-6
  and Britain, 1, 26, 130, 136
  and First Nations, 27-8, 139-40, 145-6, 236-7, 270, 271, 272
  law reforms, 189-90
  policy, 4, 27, 139-40, 146, 201
Curtin, John, 2, 11, 30-4, 36, 74, 176, 248, 264

357

action verbs, 87
anaphora, 90
cliché, 85
clauses, 80, 81
see democracy
ellipsis, 83
imperative verb, 88
interpolations, 82, 91
introduction, 32
metaphor, 24, 25, 76
negative verbs, 88
pairs, 82
parallelism, 33, 90, 91
polemic, 47-50, 77
pronouns, personal, 91-2
proper nouns, 84, 93
sentences, 33, 79, 90
slang, 32
speech, 29, 76-7, 84-7, 91, 226-9
verbs and nouns, 87-90

D

Daly, Fred, 11, 38, 51
Dante, 105
Darlinghurst Gaol, 111, 218
The Dawn, 108-9, 217
Deakin, Alfred, 2, 4, 6, 11, 38, 46, 116-26
  humour, 50, 59, 117, 126
  parallelism, 118
  speech, 46, 55, 59
debate, 29, 36, 38-9, 40, 42, 52, 63, 64, 152, 172, 192, 195, 208
  art of, 160, 202, 278
  television, 12, 166-7, 177-8
de la Perouse, Captain, 182
demagogue, 52, 208
democracy, 1-2, 14, 17, 28, 52, 60, 92, 135, 166, 178, 198, 227, 237, 240-5
  aspirations for, 54, 188-90, 208-9
  Curtin, 29-34, 226-9
  and freedom, 67, 76
  parliamentary, 35-6, 65, 68, 71-2
  and polemic, 40, 53-4
  representative, 11, 39, 71, 130
  and rhetor/ic, 14, 39, 40

  in speeches, 41, 198, 227, 237, 240-5, 249-50, 267, 270-1, 276-7
  as symbol, 5, 29-31, 64-5, 66
  Westminster, 65, 130
  Whitlam, 20, 67-72, 240
Democrat, 60, 69
Depression (1930), 50, 261, 264
de-tribalisation, 142
Diana, HRH The Princess of Wales, 176
digger, 27, 187-9, 246, 248-50, 256
discrimination
  First Nation, 147-9, 193, 205, 235, 238-9, 250, 267-8
  migrant, 254
dispossession, 27, 193, 268, 272
dopamine, 212
Dunkirk, 227

E

economy, 94, 97, 176
  impacts on, 170-1, 173, 285
  summit conference on, 176, 257-64
education, 2, 10, 27, 143, 217, 255
  and First Nations, 3, 85, 138, 143, 147, 234
  in management, 25, 43
  and women's suffrage, 45, 219
effigy, 95, 187, 247
election, 2, 6, 12, 27, 39, 64, 66-8, 72, 84, 127, 172, 176-7, 198, 286
  broadcast, 12, 35, 166-7, 178-9
  campaign, 37, 47, 171
  humour in, 50-1, 56, 59
  and polemic, 47-8
  speech, 76, 121-3, 123-6, 169, 170, 260-1, 280
  slogans, 63-4
  and voting rights, 53, 108, 126, 140
Elizabeth II, HRH The Queen
  and HRH The Duke of Edinburgh, 3, 21, 265-6
  Menzies's Welcome of, 28, 137
Elkin, Professor, 145
ellipsis, 82-3, 93, 157, 163, 164-5, 194, 209

Ellul, Jacques, 211
embedding, of clauses, 80, 93
   Greer, 158
emotions, 36, 73-4, 97, 141, 157, 161-5, 160, 164-5, 167-8, 195, 198, 207, 210, 217
   affinity in, 32
   appeal to, 10, 15-6, 25-6, 74, 92-3, 121, 122, 127, 144, 162, 169, 195
   accumulation of, 110, 132, 134, 147, 189, 200-1
   of audience, 12, 15, 72, 96-8, 101, 127, 132, 196, 201-2
   as evidence, 110, 132, 182
   and humour, 58, 60
   and polemic, 38, 47, 49
   and slang, 69, 86, 93, 155-6
   in slogans, 63, 86, 93
   cited in speech, 241, 269, 276
   stability of, 89, 163, 165
emphasis, 21, 23, 26, 31-5, 39, 68-70
   see alliteration, anaphora, parallelism
   through metaphor, 26, 33, 76
   of stance, 32, 34, 35, 42
   of topic, 74, 88, 100, 135, 258
ethos, 10, 74, 89, 171, 184, 207
   Greer, 155
   Melba, 15
   Menzies, 131, 136
   of nation, 29, 45
eulogy, 3, 11, 12, 10, 184
   for Churchill, 127-35, 230-2
   for Monk, 43, 74, 79
   for Whitlam, 193, 204-5
Eureka Stockade, 27, 185, 187, 188-9, 246-50
Evatt, H.V., 33, 227, 228, 249
exaggeration, 41, 46, 117, 167
   absence of, 111, 206
Expo '88, 3, 20-2, 73, 265-6

F

Falconer, Dora, 108
'fatherland', 97, 214
features, of language, 10, 11, 18, 22-4, 26, 70, 72, 141, 144, 159, 162-4, 168
   see conversation and colloquialism
   foregrounded, 22, 35, 206
   stylistic, 22-4, 81, 130
   subordinated, 22, 93, 101-3, 105, 114
Federation, 2, 4, 27, 188, 222-3, 247
   conventions, 97, 126
   Deakin, 116, 119-21
   Griffith, 16, 25, 43-4, 96-7, 98-9, 119, 214-6
figures, rhetorical, 10, 153, 157, 159
First Fleet, 27, 139, 182, 201
First Nations, 27-8, 130, 138-50, 147, 186, 205, 233-9, 267-8
   Aboriginal and Torres Strait Islander Commission (ATSIC), 271
   apology to, 3, 198-200, 201
   see genocide
   identity of, 41-2, 46-7, 139, 140, 143, 149, 200
   land rights, 12, 25, 138, 140, 143-6, 148-9, 268-9
   reconciliation, 194, 267, 269, 271
   Redfern Park Speech, 267-72
   right to vote, 3, 44, 130
flag, 34, 121, 169, 183, 184, 229
   Australian, 34, 122, 173-4
   Old Glory, 34, 229
   rebel/Southern Cross, 14, 188
Ford, Thomas, 137
formality, 70, 93, 104, 130, 146, 155
Forrest, Sir John, 2, 11, 16, 25, 221-4
Fraser, Malcolm, 12, 16, 68, 168-75
fraud, 24, 54
freedom, 14, 29, 34, 161, 2
   Carnegie, 41
   Curtin, 32, 34, 36, 226, 229
   and democracy, 1, 30, 40, 67, 76, 209
   Forrest, 223
   Gilbert, 142
   Greer, 152, 153
   Hawke, 259
   of individual, 52, 54, 208
   of information, 53
   Menzies, 36, 132, 134-5, 230-2
   of speech, 4

as symbol, 64
Free Trade Party, 123-4
Freudenberg, Graham, 7, 85
Frost, David, 59
function words, 86, 92, 93, 210
    conversational effect, 136, 148, 163

G

'Gabba, 21, 265
Gallipoli, 27, 188, 228, 247
gay, 184
genocide, 143, 147, 237
genre, 10, 76, 91, 92
    deliberative, 41, 121-4, 141, 186, 201
    hybrid, 10, 76
    epideictic, 133, 144, 184, 198, 204
    judicial, 204
Gilbert, Kevin, 3, 11, 12, 74, 138-50, 200
    action verbs, 87
    anaphora, 81, 90, 146
    cliché, 85
    clauses, 80-1, 90, 149
    genre, 141
    informality, 148
    interpolations, 81, 91, 143
    metaphor, 25, 76-7
    negative verbs, 88
    neologisms, 87
    pairs, 82
    parallelism, 44, 146, 148-9
    passive voice, 89
    polemic, 41, 44, 47
    pronouns, personal, 84
    sentences, 80-1, 90, 145, 148-9
    slang, 77, 85
    speech, 233-9
    tense of verbs, 87, 88
    verbs and nouns, 47, 87-90
Gillard, Julia, 3, 38, 151, 201-4, 278-83
Gladesville Asylum, 111, 218
Glavonjic v Foster, 254
Gobbo, Mr Justice, 254
God, 16, 112, 115, 121, 133, 134, 139, 185, 217-8, 231, 236, 239
god, 98, 143
god-heroes, 143, 236
Gorton, John, 66, 67-8, 69, 71
Gortonism, 65, 67-8, 69
Governor-General, 11, 16, 221
grammar, 23, 26, 80
Greer, Germaine, 9, 11, 12, 38, 45, 74
    action verbs, 87
    anaphora, 90, 157, 161
    argument, 153, 156, 160
    audience, 42, 152-4, 157
    cliché, 85
    clauses, 80, 157-8, 160, 163-5
    ellipsis, 83, 157, 163, 164-5
    expletives, 85-6, 152, 155-6
    The Female Eunuch, 57, 151-65
    humour, 26, 57, 78
    infinite verbs, 163
    interpolations, 82
    metaphor, 26
    negative verbs, 88
    neologisms, 87
    pairs, 82
    parallelism, 160
    see polyptoton
    polemic, 42
    pronouns, 84, 152, 155, 158, 162-3
    proper nouns, 85
    pun, 26, 57
    as rhetor, 156-7, 160-2, 165
    sentences, 154-5, 157-9, 161, 163
    slang, 85-6, 155-6
    speech, 26, 42, 46, 73
    structure and rhythm, 160, 161
    tense of verbs, 88
    verbs and nouns, 87-90, 158, 163, 164
Griffith, Sir Samuel, 2, 4, 11, 16, 74, 83, 94-107, 119
    anaphora, 105
    authority, 103
    clauses, 85, 90
    cognitive verbs, 88
    ellipsis, 83
    formality, 103-4
    interpolations, 81, 91

introduction, 16
metaphor, 25
neologisms, 105
pairs, 82
parallelism, 98
polemic, 43, 44
pronouns, personal, 84
proper nouns, 85
rhythm, 105-6
sentences, 79, 80, 97-8, 101-2, 105-6
speech, 16, 118, 214-6
subordination, 101-3
tense of verbs, 88
verbs and nouns, 87-90, 99, 102
guns, control of, 3, 194-8, 273-7
gunya, 141

H
handout, 142, 143, 233, 234, 235
Hawke, Bob, 4, 11, 12, 25, 74, 166-79
   anaphora, 90
   B (to be) verbs, 88
   communication competence, 167-8
   ellipsis, 83
   humour, 56, 78
   interpolations, 81-2, 91
   metaphor, 25
   pairs, 82
   parallelism, 91
   polemic, 43
   pronouns, personal, 84
   proper nouns, 85
   pun, 78
   sentences, 79
   slang, 85
   speech, 170, 176-7, 257-64
   verbs and nouns, 87-90
Hitler, Adolf, 65
Hogan, Paul, 62
ad hominem, 35, 44, 46, 52, 119, 210
Honourable, 46, 66, 68-9, 124
Hotham, Sir Charles, 248
Howard, John, 3, 5, 11, 17, 29, 82
   Gun Rally Speech, 194-8, 273-7
Hughes, William 'Billy', 9, 10, 38, 46, 77
   metaphor, 24, 25

polemic, 37, 77
humour, 12, 51, 55-62, 78, 93, 209, 231
   parliamentary, 56, 60
   causes of, 57-8
   Bjelke-Petersen, 52
   Daly, 51
   Deakin, 59, 117
   effects of, 56-7, 58-9
   Hawke, 56
   Killen, 51
   Kirby, 61, 182, 186
   Menzies, 51, 58, 78, 127-8
   Oodgeroo, 141
   and polemic, 37, 42, 50, 52
   types, 57-8
   Whitlam, 50, 56-7, 58, 59,
hyperbole, 23, 38, 58, 114

I
ideas, 8, 9, 10-1, 18, 49, 75, 78, 80-1, 92-3, 104, 105-6, 118, 209, 210
   in contrast, 39, 135, 145, 148, 181-2
   and humour, 55, 60, 78
   in metaphor, 25-6
   organisation of, 18, 80-1, 105-6, 130, 154, 157, 181-2, 211
indigenous peoples (see First Nations)
Inferno (by Dante), 106
'Indo-China', 240-5
indoctrination, 25, 138, 142, 233
inflation, 17, 26, 168, 261, 262, 263
informality, 41, 76, 83, 85-6, 88, 93, 209
   Gillard, 204
   Greer, 153
   Menzies, 133, 136
   Morrison, 207
   Whitlam, 70-1
integration, policy of, 140, 141, 201
interjector, 28, 50, 51, 56, 58, 59, 126, 127-8, 136
Internet, 82, 212
interpolation, 34, 74, 79, 81-2, 83, 91, 93, 163, 210
   Gilbert, 143, 145, 148
   Gillard, 204
   Greer, 155, 160

Kirby, 182
Menzies, 130, 136
Oodgeroo, 145
interrogatio/n, 148, 161
introduction, 16-8, 138, 156-7
Isocrates, 10, 40, 73, 209, 211

J

'Jacky', 87, 149, 233
jargon, 12, 65, 66, 86, 93, 210
Deakin, 125
Whitlam, 65-7, 86
Jefferson Oration, 55
Joel, Sir Asher, 183
Judas, 46, 95
Jupiter, 110, 217
justice, 1, 36, 40, 43, 54, 92, 209-10
appeal to, 10, 30, 64, 76, 81, 229
for First Nations, 148, 237, 238, 239, 268-71
and law, 102, 180, 186, 189, 190, 253
for women, 110, 114, 115, 153, 217, 219-20

K

kanaka, 95, 125
karate, 159-60
Keating, Paul, 3, 50, 77, 82, 192, 261
Redfern Park Speech, 193-4, 267-72
Kelly, Ned, 19-20, 28, 61, 77, 82, 85, 187-8, 246-8
Kerr, Sir John, 16,
Killen, Sir James, 11, 38, 51
Kingsford-Smith, 228
Kirby, Michael, 4, 11, 12, 25, 74, 85, 87, 187-8
anaphora, 187, 188, 190
avoidance of slang, 85
clauses, 81, 90
ellipsis, 83
genre, 184
and humour, 60-2, 78, 182-3
interpolations, 81-2, 182
metaphor, 60, 185
neologisms, 87
on nonverbal features, 61
pairs, 82

parallelism, 90, 187
parody, 184
passive voice, 89, 187
polemic, 77, 181, 186
proper nouns, 84-5
pronouns, personal, 84
sentences, 79-80, 81, 187, 188
speech, 61, 246-56
verbs and nouns, 87-90

L

labourers, coloured (see kanaka)
larrikin, 27, 174
law
natural, 43, 97, 99-100, 103
rule of, 30, 35
logos, 10, 74
Lalor, Peter, 14, 28, 180, 185-6, 190, 246-8, 250, 256
language, figurative, 30, 66, 76, 93, 114, 153, 159
Laws, John, 182
Lawson, Henry, 109, 189, 250
Lawson, Louisa, 3, 10, 37, 74, 108-15
action verbs, 87-8, 112, 114
alliteration, 91, 114
anaphora, 114, 115
cliché, 85
clauses, 80
debate, 38
genre, 10
imperative verb, 88
infinite verbs, 87-8
interpolations, 82
metaphor, 25, 77, 110, 111, 114
neologisms, 87
parallelism, 90, 114-5
passive voice, 89
polemic, 43, 45-6, 77, 110
proper nouns, 84
sentences, 114
speech, 37, 215-8
tense of verbs, 87-8
verbs and nouns, 87-90
Leacock, Stephen, 58
Liberalism, 67

Liberal-Country Party Coalition, 56, 67
Liberal Party of Australia, 12, 168, 169-70, 174, 175, 177, 189, 249, 286
  Whitlam on, 50, 56, 66-70, 71
Liberal Protectionist Party, 123-4, 126
liberty, 26, 34, 36, 40, 66, 197, 220-3, 223, 228, 229, 253, 276
Lincoln, Abraham, 91, 229
linguistics, 10, 23-4, 155, 212
lists, 74, 79, 81, 82, 83, 93
literacy, rhetorical, 6, 12, 211
Lyons, Dame Enid, 11, 16, 25, 42, 45-6, 60, 77
Lyons, Joseph, 48, 50, 248

M

Mabo, 149, 193, 270
MacArthur, Douglas General, 33, 227
Macquarie University, 144-6, 183
McLennan, Sir Ian, 11, 25, 43
McMahon, Sir William, 45-6, 67-8, 236
Mark Antony, 68, 71, 205
Marquess of Queensberry, 159-60
mateship, 28, 29, 141, 257, 263
mayor, lord, 3, 11, 20-1, 58, 265
media, 6, 8, 26, 27, 30, 39, 42, 49-51, 69, 87, 138, 140, 191, 204, 208
  broadcast, 29, 35, 71, 127, 128, 131
  controversy, 38-9, 46, 53-4, 57, 193
  digital, 6, 8, 127, 211-12
  peace prize, 61
  social, 6, 8, 17, 211-12
  television, 8, 12, 35, 54, 59, 127-8, 136, 166-79
meiosis, 58, 182
Melba, Dame Nellie, 11, 15, 74, 225
Menzies, Sir Robert, 3, 11, 14, 74, 89, 127-37-8, 135, 140, 169, 178, 249
  anaphora, 81, 90, 135
  see Anglo-Celtic
  see antithesis
  broadcast, 35, 128
  cliché, 85, 129
  clauses, 80-1, 90
  on communism, 47
  on Curtin, 50
  on democracy, 29-30, 35-6
  dialogue, 35-6,
  ellipsis, 83
  informality, 136
  'The Forgotten People', 127
  genre, 10, 133
  see humour
  interpolations, 81-2, 91, 136
  metaphor, 25, 26, 77, 133-4
  and monarchy, 27, 35, 134
  organisation approach, 78, 129-33
  pairs, 82
  parallelism, 129-30, 134
  polemic, 38, 47, 50-1, 77
  see polysyndeton
  pronouns, personal, 84
  sentences, 78, 80, 81, 130, 136
  slang, 85
  speech, 28, 35, 73, 230-2
  verbs and nouns, 82-3, 87-90
metaphor, 23, 24-6, 39, 66, 77, 93, 210
  Burnet, 25
  Carnegie, 25
  Cowen, 26
  Curtin, 25, 33
  Deakin, 116, 119, 125
  Gilbert, 25, 142
  Gillard, 204
  Greer, 26
  Griffith, 25, 100
  Hughes, 25, 26
  Kirby, 25, 60-1, 184, 185
  Lawson, 25, 79, 110-1, 114
  Lyons, Dame Enid, 25, 60
  McLennan, 25
  Menzies, 25, 26, 35
  Oodgeroo, 25
  Prowse, 26, 43
  Rudd, 199, 200, 201
  Whitlam, 26
migrants, 27-8, 138, 189, 238, 251-5, 261
misogyny, 201, 203, 278-83
mission, 143, 145, 147, 234, 236, 237-8
missionaries, 236

monarchy, 28, 35, 130, 136-7
Monk, Albert, 25, 43
monologue, 73, 124
Montesquieu, 30
Monty Python, 205
Morrison, Scott, 3, 11, 192, 210-1
   anaphora, 206, 207
   genre, 207
   parallelism, 206
   pronouns, personal, 207
   sentences, 206-7
   speech, 206-7, 290-1
   verbs and nouns, 206
mother, 25, 49, 109, 111, 112, 141, 142, 146, 185, 193, 199, 216-7, 269
mother country, 120, 126, 223
motherland, 2, 16, 45, 136
motion, 201
   in-reply, 45, 202, 203-4, 278-83
   of no confidence, 12, 64, 66-7
Musgrave, Lady, 102

N

Nader, Ralph, 45-6
Nash, Walter, 57-8
narrative, 25, 79, 92, 125-6, 167
   in humour, 58
   Deakin, 119, 122, 125
   Gilbert, 148
   Gillard, 202
   Greer, 157, 159-60
   Howard, 195
   Keating, 193
   Kirby, 187, 188, 190
   Lawson, 110-4
narrator, 144, 145, 146, 149
National Economic Summit Conference, 176, 257-64
National Party, 286
Nazi, 132, 133, 135, 158, 228, 231
neologism, 65, 67, 74, 86, 87, 93, 105, 207, 210
New Zealand, 5, 30, 62, 64, 125-6, 227, 243, 247
Nixon, Richard, 20, 166
non sequitur, 52

Norton, John, 9
noun, 22, 75, 82, 93, 188, 206, 209
   abstract, 75
   concrete, 22, 34, 75, 84, 85, 93, 188, 205, 209
   Greer, 155, 158-9, 163-4
   Griffith, 99
   pairs, 82, 187
   proper, 34, 74, 81, 84-5, 93, 99, 114, 155, 158-9, 188

O

oath, 14, 201
objectivity, analytical, 24
Old Glory, 30, 34, 76, 229
Oliphant, Sir Mark, 11, 26
Oodgeroo Noonuccal, 3, 11, 13, 25, 38, 74, 75, 79, 82, 85, 86, 90, 138-50, 200
   anaphora, 146
   clauses, 80, 149
   ellipsis, 83
   genre, 144
   interpolation, 82
   neologism, 87
   parallelism, 90, 146
   passive voice, 89
   polemic, 77
   pronouns, 84
   proper nouns, 85
   sentences, 80, 145
   verbs and nouns, 87, 88-9, 90
opposition, leader of, 64, 67, 122, 201-4, 278-83
Oration, Jefferson, 55
organisation, 61, 76, 90, 210
   Gilbert, 147
   Gillard, 203-4
   Greer, 160
   Griffith, 105
   Howard, 196-7
   Lawson, 110, 112-3
   Menzies, 78, 129-30, 132-3
Orwell, George, 211
   comparison with, 163-5
outrage, 40, 139, 142, 248
   language of, 9, 39, 52-4, 210-11

oxymoron, 23
P
the Pacific, 2, 20, 26, 30-4, 226-9
pairs, 38, 82, 93, 187
pandemic, coronavirus, 12, 206-7, 210, 290-1
paradox, 157, 161
parallelism, 15, 20, 21, 23, 44, 83, 90-1, 93, 210
   Curtin, 33
   Deakin, 118
   Gilbert, 44, 139, 146, 148-9
   Gillard, 202
   Greer, 160
   Griffith, 98,
   Howard, 197
   Kirby, 90, 187
   Lawson, 111, 114, 115
   Morrison, 206
   Oodgeroo, 90, 145-6
   Menzies, 90, 129, 130, 134-5
   Rudd, 199
   Whitlam, 20, 90-1
parison, 161
Parkes, Sir Henry, 55, 247
Parliament, 17, 30, 60, 140, 190
   Deakin, 59, 123-5
   Forrest, 222
   Gillard, 3, 201-4, 278-83
   Hawke, 259
   Howard, 194-5
   Hughes, 46
   Kirby, 249-50
   Lyons, 16-7, 25, 45
   Menzies, 59, 136
   Rudd, 199-201
   Whitlam, 16, 50, 63-72
parody, 38, 58, 167, 205
pathos, 10, 15, 74, 113, 121
Peacock, Andrew, 12, 167, 177-8
Pearl Harbor, 31, 32, 86, 226, 227
Pearson, Noel, 3, 193, 204-5
Pendley, Ethel C., 1
Perkins, Charles, 140
peroratio, 156, 161

peroration, 121, 123, 126, 156, 161
persona, 18, 155
personality, 4, 10, 18, 19-22, 52, 60, 87, 168, 171
persuasion, 12, 10, 41, 47, 172, 181, 212
   Menzies on, 14
Petrov affair, 47
platypus, 1
polemic, 12, 37-48, 50-4, 77, 153, 163
   effects of, 53-4
   incoherence in, 51-2
   in election, 48-50
   humour and, 50-1
   tactics, 43-7
   types, 40-3
police, 2, 14, 112, 142, 187, 196, 247, 273
   and migrants, 251-4
polyptoton, 157, 160, 161
polysyndeton, 133, 135
ad populum, 35, 46, 52, 119, 198, 210
Port Arthur, 3, 194, 273-5
Port Augusta, 221-2
Port Darwin, 222
praeteritio, 157
predation, 25, 142
predicator, 70, 157, 158
press club, national
   Canberra, 129
   Washington DC, 3, 9, 20, 29-30, 42, 46, 57, 83, 240
prime minister, 5, 11, 12, 25, 29-30, 56
   Barton, 122
   Bruce, 37, 247
   Curtin, 2, 11, 29, 47-50, 226-9
   Deakin, 6, 55, 59, 116-26
   Fisher, 247
   Fraser, 12, 16, 68, 166-76
   Gillard, 3, 11, 201-4, 278-83
   Gorton, 66-9, 71
   Hawke, 4, 11, 166-79, 257-64
   Howard, 3, 5, 11, 17, 29, 82, 194-8, 273-7
   Hughes, 9, 11, 46

Keating, 3, 11, 50, 149, 193-4, 267-72
Lyons, 48, 50, 248
McMahon, 45-6, 67-8, 236
Menzies, 3, 4, 11, 45, 29-30, 47, 50-1, 55, 58-9, 127-37, 140, 169, 178, 230-2, 249
Morrison, 11, 206-7, 210-1, 290-1
Parkes, 247
Reid, 55, 58
Rudd, 3, 11, 149, 198-201
Scullen, 248
Theodore, 248
Whitlam, 2-3, 11, 16, 20, 50, 58-9, 63-72, 188, 204-5, 240-5
Prince Alfred Hospital, 113, 218
prison, 186, 188, 246, 248, 251, 252
prisoner, 18, 52, 191, 253
promise, 48-9, 125, 171, 172, 176, 206, 209, 221-2
pronouns, personal, 83-4, 84
  Curtin, 32, 34
  Deakin, 120, 124
  Gilbert, 148
  Greer, 152, 155, 158, 162-3
  Griffith, 105
  Kelly, 19
  Lawson, 114
  Menzies, 129, 135-6
  Oodgeroo, 145
proof, 38, 43-4, 52, 171
propaganda, 12, 36, 40, 54, 92, 208, 211, 212, 239
propagandist, 38, 47, 52, 54, 208-9
proper civilian authority, 65
province, 66, 100, 214
Prowse, Linden, 11, 17, 26, 43, 77
pseudo-populist, 9, 208, 209-10
Pullum, Geoffrey, 89
pun, 16, 26, 57, 58, 78
Purfleet Mission, 147, 237

Q

Queensland Criminal Code, 214
Queensland University of Technology (QUT), 5, 7

question, rhetorical, 90, 91
  Gilbert, 149
  Greer, 160-2
  Griffith, 91, 106
  Keating, 194
  Kirby, 184
  Lawson, 91, 114
  Oodgeroo, 145
  Pearson, 205
  Prowse, 17
  Segal, 162
  Whitlam, 242

R

race, 28, 86, 119, 146, 162, 228, 235
radical, 12, 98, 102-3, 129, 256, 262
radio, 2, 8, 17, 20, 29-31, 34, 127, 136, 178, 182, 211, 226
reconciliation, 3, 193-4, 241, 259-60, 267, 269, 271
reaction, 37, 56, 156-7, 162, 172, 178, 184, 197-8, 276
rebellion, 156, 157, 190
referendum, 44, 130, 140, 145, 238
reform, 3, 11, 205, 220-4
  law, 4, 79, 89, 103, 139, 180-1, 182-3, 184-7, 189-90, 246-56, 273
  social, 41, 45-6, 60, 153, 184
register, 159
Reid, Sir George, 55, 58, 123-5
repetition, 15, 20-1, 71, 82, 88, 90, 172
  Curtin, 91
  Deakin, 118, 124, 126
  Gilbert, 44, 91, 139, 148-9
  Greer, 157, 161
  Griffith, 91
  Hawke, 91
  Keating, 194
  Menzies, 91, 129, 135
  Oodgeroo, 145
  Whitlam, 91
reporter, 55, 96, 141, 144-6, 178, 209
responsibility, 6, 14, 17, 113, 115, 220, 227, 238
  cabinet, 65, 67
  collective, 65, 66, 67

personal, 41, 45, 54, 203
political, 121, 169, 193, 196, 199, 200-1, 261-2, 267-8, 274, 277, 280, 282
revolution, 66, 69, 89, 241
American, 89, 186, 188, 246, 249
Eureka, 248-50, 256
Greer, 3, 151, 153, 156-7, 161-2
rhetor, 28, 40, 96, 130, 209
rhetoric, 5-6, 10, 18, 25, 60, 62, 171, 192, 209-10
Australian, 9, 14-6, 35, 49, 193-4, 198, 201, 205
choices, 10, 24, 76, 79, 92
in democracy, 14, 29-31, 39, 40-1, 53-4, 64-9, 71-2, 92, 166, 189
features in, 10, 18, 20, 22-4, 81, 90, 115, 205
genre in, 10, 76, 91, 92, 124, 126, 133, 141, 144, 184, 198, 201, 204
literacy in, 12, 16, 165, 211
patterns of, 135, 210
pseudo-populist, 209, 210
strategies, 98, 101, 116, 196, 133, 136, 156-7, 160-2, 208-10
rights, 1, 14, 44, 64, 140-1, 170-1, 198-200, 267
for freedoms, 20, 30, 41, 229
human, 4, 40, 183
Human Rights, Universal Declaration of, 40, 183
individual, 30, 40-1, 52
land, 3, 12, 25, 41, 139, 140, 143-4, 145-50, 193, 233-9
migrant, 28, 189, 251-5
voting, 44, 69, 108, 130, 219
women's, 2, 10, 11, 42, 43, 108-9, 151, 158, 215-8
Roberts, Sir Stephen, 184
Rogers, Will, 62
Roosevelt
Eleanor, 183
Franklin D., 33, 226
Rudd, Kevin, 3, 198-201
Ryan, Senator Susan, 17

Ryan, Thomas Joseph (T.J.), 45-6
S
satire, 38, 62
Scalia, Justice Antonin, 181
Schreiner, Olive, 110, 217
scripture, 114
semantics, 23, 68, 70
sentences, 1, 18, 23, 68, 70-2, 74-5, 83, 117, 133, 156-7, 161, 182
brief, 135, 145, 148, 183, 193
complexity of, 80, 93, 98, 101-2, 105-6, 114-5, 117, 124
compound, 149, 204
fragment, 21, 70, 83, 93, 136, 162, 210
length of, 44, 79-80, 93, 105, 115, 124, 125, 130, 160, 188
simple, 21, 70-1, 106, 157, 187, 206, 209, 210
structure of, 22, 34, 44, 70, 72, 75, 78, 79-80, 81, 105, 115, 129-30, 135, 157, 182, 202
sententia, 157, 16
series, 47, 59, 74, 79, 81, 83, 90, 93, 125, 146, 148, 157, 158, 162, 210
1788, 26, 139, 142, 233
sexism, 3, 26, 60, 151, 201-3, 278-83
sexuality, 153, 156
Shakespeare, William, 4, 68, 71
simile, 23, 79, 110, 157
sincerity, 40, 45, 199, 203, 233, 235
sister, 108, 115, 153, 156, 162, 219-20
slogan, 12, 50, 63-4, 66, 86, 93, 172, 210
socialist, 98, 125
solecism, 156
Southern Cross, 14, 249
southerners, 21, 265
speechwriter, 7, 8, 85, 192, 193, 208
spirit-beings, 143, 236
stance, 10, 18, 19, 20, 57, 161
Curtin, 32, 34
Deakin, 119, 121
Fraser, 169
Gilbert, 141, 142, 144, 146, 149
Gillard, 202

Greer, 42, 153, 159, 165
Griffith, 96
Kirby, 89, 184, 186
Menzies, 35, 131, 135, 136
Oodgeroo, 141, 144, 145-6, 149
Pearson, 205
Rudd, 201
St. John, Edward, 69
St. Paul's Cathedral, 132, 230-2
subordination, 8, 73, 75, 93
   language for, 22, 43
   syntax for, 101-3, 114
Sullivan, Senator Kathy Martin, 60
stolen generations, 199, 200
stratagem, 43, 44, 46
style, 4, 5, 10, 18-20, 22, 24, 60, 93, 185
   Bjelke-Petersen, 51-2, 92
   checklist, 23
   Churchill, 133, 134, 135
   communication, 167, 171-3, 208-9
   conversational, 21, 60, 134
   and credibility, 171
   Curtin, 48
   deliberative, 153
   Fraser, 174
   Greer, 153, 157-8, 163-5
   Hawke, 174, 176
   Keating, 194
   Kirby, 190
   language, 10-2, 22, 171, 192-3
   Morrison, 206-7, 210-1, 290
   of life, 1, 234-5, 237-8, 252, 262, 265
   Menzies, 127-37
   nominal/verbal, 84, 164-5
   nonverbal, 167, 173
   ornate, 51, 91, 98, 103-4, 117, 135
   quantitative approaches to, 24, 164
   Whitlam, 90
'style machine', 164
stylistics, 10-2, 18, 22-4, 211-2
Swift, Jonathan, 80
subject, as sentence element, 70, 82-3, 136, 148, 157, 158
suffrage, womanhood, 10, 11, 25, 43, 108-15, 215-8

suicide, 158
Sydney University, 140, 184
symbol, 33-4, 63-4, 66, 68, 71, 86, 93, 133, 142, 174, 186, 194, 201, 236
   appeal to, 34, 86, 93, 236, 258-9
   democratic, 31, 229
   of woman, 156
syntax, 9, 23-4, 26

T

taboo, 57, 156
tactics, see polemic tactics
talk, public, 5, 9, 12, 47, 73-93, 145, 146, 177, 209, 211, 212
   Curtin, 226
   democratic, 28, 29-36
   Gillard, 278, 282
   and humour, 50, 61
   Kirby, 191
   Menzies, 128, 130, 131, 135, 230-2
   Morrison, 206-7, 290-1
   and polemic, 37-9, 41, 47, 50
television, 8, 12, 54, 59, 193, 196, 211
   and Hawke, 166-79
   and Howard, 196, 273, 275
   and Menzies, 35, 127-8, 131, 136, 178, 230
   and Morrison, 290
Telfer, Margaret, 184
tolerance, 141, 186, 188, 208, 246, 263
topic, 4, 16-8, 58, 88, 89, 93, 192, 212
   Gilbert, 141
   Greer, 57, 151, 154, 162
   Griffith, 103-4, 105
   Howard, 197
   Lawson, 112
   Menzies, 78, 129, 132
   in metaphor, 25, 77
   Oodgeroo, 141
   Orwell, 163
   in polemic, 43, 77
   Whitlam, 72
tourism, 291
Trans-Australia Railway, 16, 2, 123, 221
treason, 95, 187, 246
tropes, 10, 23, 157

Trump, Donald, 210
truth, 1, 5, 36, 40, 54, 96, 208-11
    Curtin, 34
    Deakin, 122
    Gilbert, 41, 147, 148
    Greer, 153
    Griffith, 97, 104
    Keating, 193, 267, 270
    Kirby, 184, 186
    Lawson, 115, 219, 220
    Menzies, 35
    Oodgeroo, 140
    Orwell, 163
    and polemic, 38, 40, 44, 47, 93
    Whitlam, 241, 243
Twitter, 6, 39, 78
Tyrannosaurus Rex, 26

U

understatement, 23, 49, 58
unemployment, 168, 170-1, 235, 258, 261, 263-4
United Australia Party, 48
United States, 2, 3, 27, 29-30, 53, 64, 69, 109, 166
    Curtin, 20, 29, 30-4, 84, 226-9
    Greer, 45, 57
    Howard, 274
    Kirby, 181
    McMahon, 45
    mass media, 26
    Menzies, 27, 29-30, 131, 136
    National Press Club, 20, 29-30, 57
    President, 5, 20, 210
    Rogers, Will, 62
    Whitlam, 20, 30, 69, 83, 240-5

V

Valery, Paul, 182
values, 12, 25, 28, 38, 60, 192, 209, 252
    controversy and, 38, 49
    Curtin, 30, 34, 48, 91
    of democracy, 1, 30, 40, 66, 209-10
    Deakin, 122
    of First Nations, 25, 138-9, 141, 149, 193, 233-4, 267
    Gilbert, 138-9, 141, 148-9, 233-4
    of guns, 275-6, 277
    Keating, 193, 267-72
    Kirby, 185, 186-7, 252
    Lawson, 45
    Lyons, 42
    Menzies, 35, 131-2, 135
    Oodgeroo, 25
    Pearson, 204
verbs, 19, 75, 82, 87-8, 89-90, 92, 93, 162-4, 209, 210
    action, 34, 87, 93, 99, 112, 114
    active voice, 89, 93, 154-5, 209
    auxilliary, 92, 93, 120, 164-5
    cognitive, 87-8, 93, 99
    Deakin, 120, 126
    ellipsis of, 83, 157, 164-5
    factive, 92, 210
    Greer, 154-5, 156, 158, 161, 163-5
    Griffith, 99, 102, 105
    imperative, 88, 93, 183, 194, 210
    infinite, 22, 87, 88, 93, 155, 164, 209
    Keating, 194
    Kirby, 187
    Lalor, 14
    Morrison, 206
    Lawson, 112, 114
    negative, 47, 88, 93
    passive voice, 43, 89, 93, 102, 105, 156, 158, 187
    tense of, 22, 87, 88, 89, 93, 105, 114, 165, 187, 209, 210
Verdonk, Peter, 22
verse, 106, 111, 113, 114, 196
violence, 39, 152, 153, 158-60, 162, 189, 254-5, 275
visualisation, 18, 93, 183, 212
    Carnegie, 17, 26
    Curtin, 31, 33
    Deakin, 125
    Gilbert, 3, 44, 47, 142-4, 233
    Kirby, 183-4
    Lawson, 111, 217
    Oodgeroo, 144
    Pearson, 205
vocabulary, 23, 26, 34, 74-5, 81, 85, 93

Curtin, 34
emotive, 110, 114, 195
informal, 204
formal, 103-4, 154, 155, 156, 187
Gilbert, 149
Gillard, 204
Greer, 159
Griffith, 103-4
Howard, 195
Kirby, 187
Lawson, 114
Morrison, 207
Oodgeroo, 141, 149
political, 12, 63-6, 68, 63-72, 86
tangible, 84, 93, 141, 146, 188, 211
voice, 114, 131, 142, 144, 146, 181, 201, 244, 250, 280
  'Aboriginal', 143, 147, 233
  active, 93, 158, 209
  conservative, 134
  conversational, 8, 165
  'ocker', 4, 257
  official, 102-3, 106
  passive, 43, 89, 93, 102, 105, 156, 158, 187
  personal, 133, 135
  quiet, 96, 101, 103
  speaking, 117, 195, 207, 211
  unforgettable, 131, 230
  women's, 108, 109, 112, 113, 218

W

Walker, Kath (see Oodgeroo Noonuccal)
Waltzing Matilda, 186, 248
war, 17, 39, 61, 64, 135, 144, 158-9, 162, 204, 215, 244, 247, 268, 270
  Cold War, 20, 47, 85, 245
  post-World War II, 127, 252, 261
  Vietnam, 12, 131, 134, 135, 240-5
  World War I, 11, 16, 25, 247
  World War II, 11, 20, 30-4, 49, 130-5, 158-9, 176, 183, 226-9, 230-2, 242, 252, 261, 264

Ward, Eddie, 51
Watson, Chris, 123
Watson, Don, 192
Westminster, 5, 29, 30, 65, 68, 130
Whitlam, Gough, 11, 38, 51, 63-72, 73, 74, 83, 140, 174, 185, 188, 247-8
  analogy, 20
  anaphora, 20, 81, 83, 90
  clauses, 80-1, 90
  on democracy, 2, 30
  dismissal of, 16, 168
  ellipsis, 83
  eulogy for, 3, 193, 204-5
  historical reference, 20, 56-7
  use of humour, 50, 56-7, 58, 59, 78
  and interjectors, 50
  interpolations, 81-3, 91
  metaphor, 26
  narratives, 25
  neologisms, 65, 67
  pairs, 82
  parallelism, 20, 80-1, 83, 90-1
  polemic, 16, 77
  pronouns, personal, 84
  sentence, 67, 68, 70-1, 80-1, 83
  slang, 85
  speech, 4, 20, 73, 240-50
  vocabulary, 12, 63-72
  verbs and nouns, 87-90
Windeyer, Lady, 109
Wiradjuri, 142
wordplay, 57, 78
words, syllables of, 75, 85, 93, 114, 124, 155, 157-9
Wran, Neville, 184, 259

Y

Year of the Indigenous People, 194, 267, 268
YouTube, 6, 7, 8, 78, 198, 204

Z

Zoom, 8

www.ingramcontent.com/pod-product-compliance
Lightning Source LLC
Chambersburg PA
CBHW020900080526
44589CB00011B/374